Premiere® 6.5

Complete Course

Donna L. Baker

FIND YOURS

Wiley Publishing, Inc.

Premiere® 6.5 Complete Course

TR899
B3
2 0034
0 52033514

Published by:

Wiley Publishing, Inc.
111 River Street
Hoboken, NJ 07030
www.wiley.com/compbooks

Published simultaneously in Canada

For general information on our other products and services or to obtain technical support, please contact our Customer Care Department within the U.S. at 800-762-2974, outside the U.S. at 317-572-3993, or fax 317-572-4002.

Library of Congress Control Number: 2002114781

ISBN: 0-7645-1896-8

Manufactured in the United States of America

10 9 8 7 6 5 4 3 2 1

» Credits

Publisher: Barry Pruett

Project Editor: Cricket A. Krengel

Acquisitions Editor: Michael Roney

Editorial Manager: Rev Mengle

Technical Editor: Dennis Short

Copy Editor: Jill Burke

Production Coordinator: Regina Snyder

Layout and Graphics: Beth Brooks, Sean Decker, Joyce Haughey, Kristin McMullan, Shelley Norris, Heather Pope

Quality Control: Laura Albert, John Bitter

Indexer: Sharon Hilgenberg

Proofreader: Vickie Broyles

» Dedication

This book is dedicated to Michael Feerer with thanks.

» Acknowledgments

What a singular pleasure for me to write a dedication to the man who wrote a book that had so much impact on my life.

I learned to use Premiere many years ago in design school. It became one of my passions, due in no small part to Michael Feerer's book, *Premiere with a Passion.*

Although it is a complex program to learn and left me feeling less than passionate at times, Premiere is one of my favorite programs. Michael's book was inspirational as a student; it was interesting, informative, funny, and passionate. I measure my personal writing success on whether I think *my* books would convey the same sense of interest and excitement to my readers. Now I have come full circle, from learning to use Premiere to teaching others to use the program and develop their own passions, both through classes and this book.

I would like to thank Michael Roney, Acquisitions Editor at Wiley for the opportunity to write this book, and my agent Matt Wagner at Waterside Productions for finding me the gig. I would also like to thank the editorial and development team at Wiley. A most special thanks to Cricket Krengel — the editor with the eagle eye and devilish sense of humor. It has been a very great pleasure to work with all of you.

Thanks to my ever-tolerant husband, Terry, whose hair would be gray by now (if he had any!), and my daughter, Erin, for her inspiration. Thanks of course to my pals, Brad and Margaret, for their ongoing encouragement and feedback, and to Deena for the ongoing chats.

Thanks to Adobe for producing such a sweet product.

Finally, my usual thanks to Tom Waits for musically accompanying me on my quest.

» Table of Contents

Introduction

Many people, me among them, often have watched television programs or movies and wondered how things were made. How do they make the superhero fly? Why does a dream sequence look dreamy? My particular area of fascination has been music videos, in which you can find every combination of real and imaginary objects and people in a never-ending visual feast.

One of the big changes in recent years has been digital video. Graphic designers and movie folks are making movies, and so are keen hobbyists. Computers have advanced to support complex graphics and animations, and Premiere has changed to take advantage of the hardware power.

You can learn to use a program like Premiere by trial and error. You can certainly learn to use many of the program's functions and create simple video projects, but you are likely to reach a point at which you wonder if that is all there is to Premiere. The answer is no.

Premiere is a complex piece of software used for creating complex projects. Understanding how to create a project, and then how best to approach its design and construction when using Premiere are key elements of your ongoing success.

These key elements are where this book comes in. It uses a project-based approach to teach you how to use Premiere. You learn how to use the tools that make a superhero fly, but also learn how to use the tools in combination with one another to build a project. You also learn how to plan a project, how to choose specific techniques, and how to choose effects such as transitions.

Each session builds on the previous session. This way, you can see the progressive development of a project and learn to use Premiere in a systematic and practical way. This book is also a structured course that leads you through the project development process, giving you instruction on the intricacies of the program as well as the project design process.

There is something incredibly satisfying about watching a movie you created play on the screen in front of you. As you work through the lessons in this book, you will understand this satisfaction even more. By the end of the course, you will have both a finished product suitable for use in a portfolio and a deeper under-standing of the intricacies of this very rich program. I also hope I will have been able to share the fascination I have with the program.

Is This Book for You?

Yes — if you are a creative professional, a digital artist, a motion graphics designer, a passionate hobbyist, a student, or a teacher of Premiere. The sessions offered in this course were designed with you in mind. An instructor's guide for this book is available from the author at www.donnabaker.ca. The 90-page guide includes tips, answers to the review questions, and supplementary materials.

What's in This Book?

This course is divided into eight parts. To introduce you to the program this book begins with a quick-start tutorial called the Confidence Builder; this is followed by seven sections.

> » "Confidence Builder" is a hands-on introduction that gives you a hint of what you can create in Premiere. At the end of it, you will have made your first movie — complete with sound!

> » **Part I: Course Setup.** This introductory section of the book contains informa-tion about Premiere and this course:

>> » "Premiere Basics" includes an overview of what you can create using Premiere, a discussion of how to install Premiere, set storage preferences, choose a workspace, and a summary of new features.

>> » "Project Overview" includes an explanation of the project that you create as you work through this course.

» **Part II: Getting Started.** This is the first of the tutorials that get you started in Premiere 6.5.

> » Session 1, "Starting the Project," includes tutorials to show you how to start a project in Premiere. You learn how to choose project settings, how to use time codes, and other technical aspects of starting a project. You also learn how to import clips — which is the first step in project development — and how and where to save a project.

> » Session 2, "Assembling the Project," includes tutorials to show you how to use the Storyboard window to organize clips for a project. You learn to use the Automate to Timeline feature. You also learn to assemble a project manually in the Timeline.

» **Part III: Basic Editing.** This section includes information that is the heart of any video project.

> » Session 3, "Working with Clips," shows you techniques to edit the length and content of clips used in your movies. You learn to edit clips in different program locations using different techniques.

> » Session 4, "Editing Clips," is where you learn how to work with and manage clips in the Timeline. You also learn how to edit clips for length and content, and to add markers for controlling different aspects of your project.

> » Session 5, "Using Transitions," shows you how to use the first of several categories of effects. You see how and why to add transitions, and also how to use transitions for specific purposes, like managing the view of other clips.

» **Part IV: Working with Audio.** This part discusses and explains editing and using audio in a Premiere project.

> » Session 6, "Preparing Audio Files," teaches you how to use audio in a movie. You learn how to edit clips and work with them in the Timeline, how to adjust the signal strength, and work with multiple copies of your audio clips.

> » Session 7, "Editing Audio Files," shows you how to use the Audio Mixer, which is a real-time audio editing feature. You also learn to coordinate the audio and video portions of your movie.

» **Part V: Creating and Animating Titles.** Here you learn about using the all-new Adobe Title Designer and how to add animation to your project's elements:

> » Session 8, "Working with Titles," is an exploration of the Adobe Title Designer. From simple text titles to saving styles and using templates, you see many of the Title Designer features in this session.

» Session 9, "Creating Animation," is an introduction to the Motion Settings window. Learn how to create simple animations by changing a clip's position and size.

» Session 10, "Building Complex Animations," is another look at the Motion Settings window. You learn to use animation effects such as rotation and distortion, and how to save and reuse your animation.

» **Part VI: Adding Transparency and Video Effects.** In this section you learn how to use different types of transparency to make your clips blend with one another, and how to use some of Premiere's many video effects.

» Session 11, "Adding Transparency to Clips," introduces you to transparency settings. You learn to use transparency tools on the Timeline and how to work with the customizable settings in the Transparency Settings window.

» Session 12, "Working with Transparency," is a continuation of the previous session. Here you learn how to work with more types of transparency, and how to use images to create transparency.

» Session 13, "Moving from Transparency to Video Effects," is where you learn to work with more complex types of transparency, such as Chroma and Luminance. You learn how to use effects and transparency keys together, and how to reuse effects from clip to clip.

» Session 14, "Working with Keyframes and More Video Effects," teaches you how to control effects in your movie by using keyframes. You also learn to work with multiple effects and how to add a single effect to multiple clips over time.

» **Part VII: Final Edits and Exporting.** This final part is an explanation of how you prepare a project for export. You also learn optional ways to distribute your movie.

» Session 15, "Adding Visual Sparkle and Audio Effects," is a look at some final touches you can add to your project. Here you learn how to use audio effects. You also learn some special techniques for adding impact.

» Session 16, "Exporting the Movie and Archiving the Project," is where you learn about preparing your movie for export. You learn how to do a final review of your project and how to make last-minute adjustments. Finally, you learn how to create a movie to share with an audience and archive your finished project.

Confidence Builder

Television programs, movies, interactive presentations — these types of media share many techniques and processes. One of the most common is the use of logos that identify everything from production companies to sneakers. Now it's your turn. In this tutorial, you make your own personalized logo to tag your video projects.

This logo project uses many of Premiere's tools and techniques so you can get a little taste of what Premiere can really do. You make a simple animated logo with music that runs approximately five seconds. As you work through the book, revisit the logo project occasionally to experiment or add other features.

TOOLS YOU'LL USE
Project window, Timeline, Transitions palette, Video Effects palette, Effect Controls window, Title Designer window, Text tool, Properties palette, Shadow settings, Stroke settings, Color Matte command, fade controls, keyframe controls, Duration dialog, selection tool, scissors tool, Audio clip window

CD-ROM FILES NEEDED
logo.mov
logo_bounce.pmt
SmartSound-Calm Wave.aif
SmartSound-Contact!.aif
SmartSound-Flute build.aif
SmartSound-Kick off!.aif
SmartSound-Power up.aif
SmartSound-Sax tune.aif
SmartSound-Solo out.aif
SmartSound-Watery.aif

TIME REQUIRED
90 minutes

Tutorial
» Building the Basic Project

Before you start, you can preview the finished QuickTime movie, named `logo.mov`. In this tutorial, you assemble clips and start the project.

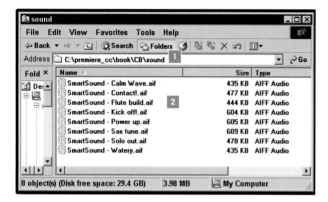

1. **Create a new folder on your hard drive where you want to store your project files.**

2. **Open the Premiere Complete Course CD; open the Confidence Builder folder.**
   Select the set of eight audio files (with the extension `.aif`) and copy them to the new folder on your hard drive.

3. **Open Adobe Premiere.**
   From the desktop, choose Start→Program→Adobe→ Premiere 6.5. The program opens with a Load Project Settings dialog box.

4. **Click Multimedia QuickTime in the Available Presets column, and then click OK.**
   The Multimedia QuickTime settings are general settings that can be used for a variety of projects.

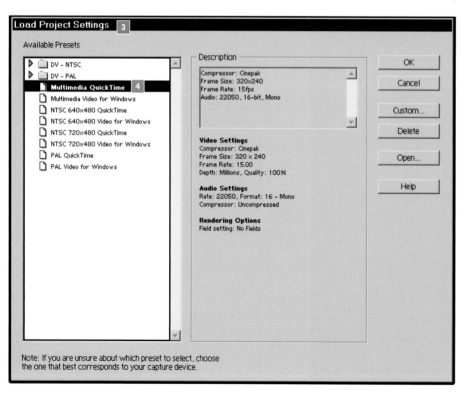

5. **Close extra palettes and windows.**
   Close the palette windows at the right of the screen. Leave the Monitor, Timeline, and Project windows open. You need as much space on the screen as possible to work on your project.

6. **To import sound files, choose File→Import→Files.**
   Browse to the location of the storage folder on your hard drive. Shift + click to select the group of eight SmartSound files. Click OK. The files are brought into the Project window.

7. **Save your project. (Save early, and save often.)**
   Choose File→Save. Browse to the hard drive location where you created the new folder. Save your file as "logo". Premiere adds the .ppj file extension. The file name appears at the top of the Project window.

8. **Click a clip in the Project window.**
   When it displays a controller and audio waveform in the preview area, click the play arrow to preview the clip. It is simpler to listen to the clips from Project window than to drag them to the Timeline for previewing.

9. **When you have listened to the eight clips and decided on the music clip you want to use, delete the other seven clips.**
   Click and drag a clip from the listing in the Project window to the trashcan at the bottom of the window. Delete all but your chosen clip.

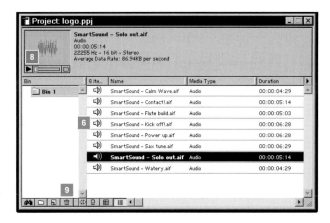

<TIP>
If you have never opened the program before, you first see a display asking you to choose a working space, either Single-Track Editing or A/B Editing. Click A/B Editing.

<TIP>
This is a default workspace layout. You do not have to reset it every time you open the program. From now on, the layout shown when you close the program is what you see the next time you open it.

<NOTE>
The sample project keeps the entire set of clips.

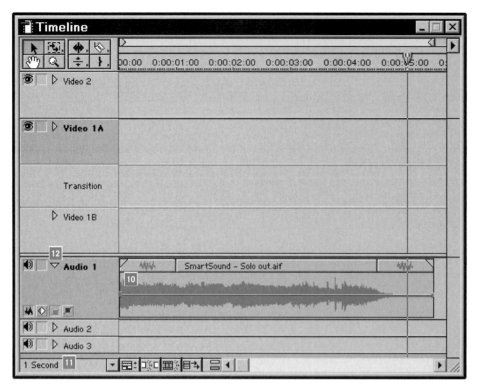

<TIP>

The Timeline window is one of the three windows you should have left open when you started the program. If you closed it by mistake, choose Window→Timeline to reopen it.

10. **Click and drag the audio clip you chose to the Audio 1 track in the Timeline.**

Drop it into position at the far left of the Timeline. The audio clip will start at the 0 second time mark. The example uses the SmartSound-Solo out.aif file. The audio clip is the first element in your project.

11. **Change the zoom control for a better view of the clip and its waveform.**

The navigation zoom controls are at the bottom left of the Timeline. The default zoom is at 2 seconds. Click the 2 Second label to open a dropdown menu. Click 1 Second. You see the tracks in the Timeline expand.

12. **Click the spindown arrow to the left of the Audio 1 name.**

This opens the Audio 1 track to display the audio waveform. The audio waveform extends the full length of the clip. You now have the sound track added to your project.

Tutorial
» Creating Titles for Your Logo

After you've chosen your music and built your basic project, it's time for the visual elements. You need two titles and a background color. Your choice of fonts and colors should reflect the basic sense of the music you chose.

1. **Choose File→New→Title.**
   The Adobe Title Designer window opens.

2. **Click the horizontal text tool and click in the window to start the text process.**
   Type a name for your production company (Diamond Dog Productions in the example). Click out of the text frame or click another tool to end the typing process.

3. **Click the selection tool, and then click the text.**
   Notice the selection handles, which look like small boxes, in the corners around the text. These indicate the text is selected.

<TIP>
If you want to change the text after it is deselected, double-click the text.

4. **Open the Properties panel.**
   Click the arrow to the left of the Properties title to open the panel. Five panels are always displayed — Properties, Fill, Strokes, and Shadow to the right of the design pane, and the Transform panel to the bottom right of the Title Designer window. Each panel has an arrow to the left of its title. Click the arrow to open the panel. Some panels have subpanels within them.

5. **Click anywhere on the bar displaying the font name to open the dropdown list.**
   Find the font you want to use from the list (the example uses Babelfish).

6. **Set the font size to 55.**
   Click the font size and type the new size. The text should take up a significant portion of the screen without crowding.

7. **Change the Aspect to 85.0%.**
   The Aspect refers to the relationship between the text block's width and height. To fit the text used in the example without crowding or sacrificing font size, I reset the aspect to a lower value, which decreases with width of the text in its text block.

8. **Change the Tracking to 1.1.**
   Tracking sets the distance between the letters. Changing the tracking in combination with changing the aspect makes the text fit within the Safe Title Margins. The Safe Title Margins identify the amount of the screen that is distorted if the title is output to television. It also serves as a good guide for placing the title's text.

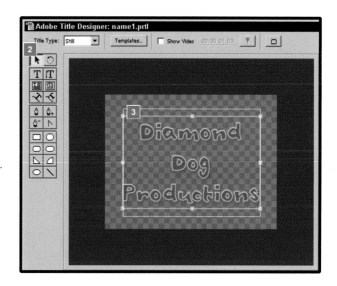

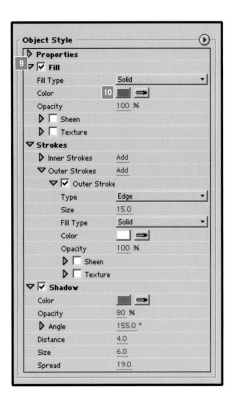

< N O T E >
The default font is a standard serif font. Choose a font that is suggestive of the type of music you are using. The example uses an edgy font that is in keeping with the drum-based music. Fonts can be purchased from a number of foundries, including Adobe. Thousands of fonts, such as Babelfish, are freely available online.

< T I P >
You can also use the hot text feature. Hold the cursor over the value until it changes to a pointing finger, and then click and drag left (to decrease the value) or right (to increase the value.)

9. **Click the checkbox to the left of the Fill heading to activate the panel.**
   Click the arrow to the left of the Fill title to open the panel. The default fill type is Solid, which is already selected.

10. **Click the color swatch to open the Color Picker.**
   The color swatch is used to set a particular color according to its color values, while the eyedropper tool can be used to sample color from any part of the screen.

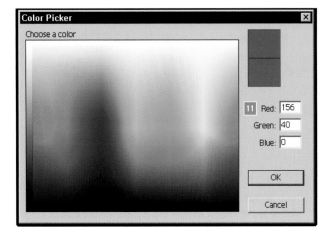

11. **Enter an RGB value of 156/40/0, and click OK.**
   RGB color is the only color model available for defining color in the titles.

12. **Click the arrow to the left of the Strokes heading to open the Strokes panel.**

    You will see two options for Inner and Outer Strokes, which are each sub-panels. Click Add to activate the Outer Strokes panel.

<NOTE>

When you add text to your title, the text options do not include strokes. In order to activate the strokes sub-panels, you have to click Add first to add a stroke to the text. When you open the strokes sub-panel, the stroke is listed (named Inner S or Outer S depending on whether you added an inner stroke or an outer stroke to the text).

13. **Click the arrow to the left of the Outer Strokes heading.**

    A set of options you can use to customize the stroke display.

14. **Use these settings for the outer stroke:**

    » Type Edge (choose from the Type menu; Edge is the default selection).

    » Size 15.0 (click the field to select it and type the value, or move the mouse over the field and drag to display the value when you see a double-arrow icon).

    » Fill Type Solid (choose from the Fill Type menu; Solid is the default selection).

    » Color RGB value 255/255/255 (click the color swatch and enter the values in the Color Picker).

    » Opacity 100% (click the field to select it and type the value, or move the mouse over the field and drag to display the value when you see a double-arrow icon).

15. **Click the checkbox to the left of the Shadow panel heading to activate the panel.**

    Click the arrow to the left of the check box to open the Shadow panel.

16. **Add a shadow using these settings:**

    Click the color swatch and enter an RGB value of 151/73/0 in the Color Picker.
    Opacity 80%
    Angle 155 degrees
    Distance 4.0 pixels
    Size 6.0 pixels
    Spread 19.0 pixels

<NOTE>

For all values except the color, click the field to select it and type the value, or move the mouse over the field and drag to display the value when you see a double-arrow icon.

17. **Right-click the title to display the shortcut menu.**

    Choose Position→Horizontal Center. Right-click the title again, and this time choose Position→Vertical Center. Your title is positioned in the center of the display.

18. **Save the title.**

    The easy way to save a title is to click the Close button at the upper right corner of the Title window. You receive a prompt to save the file. Name it "name1", and click OK. The title is added to the Project window file list. Titles have a .prtl extension (PRemiere TitLe).

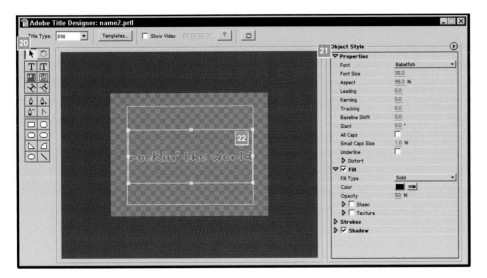

< N O T E >

Pay attention to where you save titles. The program uses its installation location as the default storage location for titles. Save your titles to the same location you are storing the other material for your project. If you 'lose' a title, look in the Program Files section of your hard drive. It's probably there.

19. **Double-click** name1.prtl **in the Project window to open the title in the Title Designer window.**

< T I P >

You can reuse the original file to create the second title.

20. **Click the Selection tool.**
    Select the example text (rockin' the world), and then delete it. Replace it with your catchy slogan.

21. **Click the arrow to the left of the Properties heading to open the Properties panel.**
    Change the following settings:
    Font Size 35.0
    Aspect 95.0%
    Tracking 0.0

22. **Center the title horizontally and vertically.**
    Right-click the title to display the shortcut menu. Choose Position→Horizontal Center. Right-click again, and choose Position→Vertical Center.

23. **Save your title.**

Choose File→Save As and name the title "name2". When you click OK, you can see that the second title is added to your Project window.

< T I P >

You can start the second title from scratch, but you have to select all the options for colors, strokes, and shadow settings again. By following the previous steps, the options are the same as the settings for the first title, which makes for consistent titling and also saves time. Later in the book, you learn how to create and save styles, which is another way to reuse titles.

24. **Add a color matte.**
    Choose File→New→Color Matte. Pick a color from the Color Picker (the example uses an RGB value of 192/205/153). Click OK to open the name dialog box. Type "**bkgd**" and click OK. This is the background color for your video.

< N O T E >

The color matte is added to the project but isn't saved as a separate file.

25. **Save the project.**
    You have now added two title files to your project. In later tutorials you animate the titles for more interest.

< T I P >

To save time when saving your work, use the shortcut keys Ctrl + S (⌘ + S) rather than the menu.

Tutorial
» Adding the Clips to the Timeline

Projects are assembled in the Timeline, and you have already added music to the Timeline. Now it's time to add the visual elements. Before you can add the titles you created, you must add additional video tracks to hold the elements.

1. **The Timeline window should still be open, or choose Window→Timeline.**

2. **Add another track to the Timeline.**
   You need one more track to accommodate the clips for your logo project. To add another track to the Timeline, click the Timeline menu arrow, and then click Add Video Track. The new track is added to your Timeline and named Video 3.

3. **Add the clips to the Timeline.**
   First, click and drag the bkgd clip to the Video 1A track. Next, click and drag your first title, name1.prt1, to Video 2. Last, click and drag the second title, name2.prt1 to Video 3. The length of a clip is shown in timecode at the top of the Timeline window. A five-second clip is shown as 0:00:05:00.

4. **Resize the length of the clips.**
   Click the selection tool in the Timeline, and then click the clip in Video 1A. Move the cursor slowly over the end of the clip at the five-second mark. When the cursor changes to a red bracket, click and drag. The clip's length is resized. As you resize the clip's length, a vertical bar displays showing the edit line location. Continue to slowly drag the cursor until the bkgd clip is the same length as your music clip in Audio 1, and then release the mouse.

5. **Resize the title in Video 2 using the same process that you used in step 4.**

6. **Resize the** name2.pt1 **clip in the Video 3 track to a length of 3:25.**
   Right-click the clip in the Timeline, and then choose Duration. In the Clip Duration window, type the new length to read 0:00:03:25, and then click OK.

7. **Move the Video 3 clip.**
   Click the clip in Video 3 to select it and drag it to the right 10 frames or you can use shortcut keys to move the clip. Alt+.(period) (Option+.) nudges the clip frame by frame to the right. If you nudge too far, use Alt+,(comma) (Option+,) to move it left.Your slogan starts at the same point in the movie as the company name unless it is moved over in the Timeline.

8. **Save your work again.**
   You have a total of three tracks with content and resized titles set up for an animation sequence.

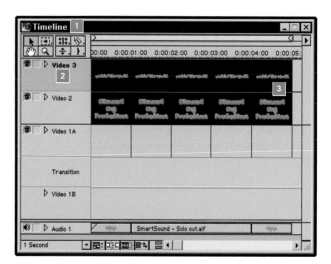

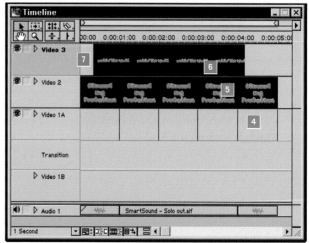

<TIP>
You can use shortcut keys to move a clip. Press Alt + . (period) (Option + .) to nudge the clip frame by frame to the right. If you nudge too far, press Alt + , (comma) (Option + ,) to move the clip left.

Tutorial

» Adding Transitions to Begin and End Your Movie

Transitions are tools that visually switch what you see from one image to another. Use them at both ends of the movie for impact. Transitions are the last step before the basic logo is complete.

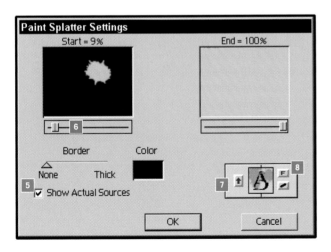

1. **Choose Window→Show Transitions to open the Transitions palette.**
   You can see a number of headings listed. Each represents a transition category.

2. **Click Wipe to open the folder.**
   The set of Wipe transitions available in Premiere display.

3. **Click and drag the Paint Splatter transition to the Transition track in the Timeline.**

4. **Position the transition.**
   Make sure it is to the far left of the Timeline at the beginning of the video.

5. **Double-click the transition in the Timeline to open its dialog box.**
   Click the Show Actual Sources checkbox at the bottom left of the Paint Splatter Settings dialog box to see the actual clips used in your project.

6. **Click and drag the Start slider to 9%.**
   A transition can start and end at any point from 0% to 100%. At 0%, you see the first clip only. At 100% you see only the second clip. At 9%, you see a small paint splatter. When you add fades to the logo in a later tutorial the paint splatter appears to fade into view.

7. **Set the direction of the transition.**
   The transition's motion is simulated in the blue box at the right of the dialog box. Changing settings changes the motion simulation. The arrow to the left of the animation should point upward; you want the transition to change from black to the background color matte you created earlier.

8. **To the right of the blue animation, make sure you see "F" in the top box, and then click OK.**
   This means the transition runs forward. The default direction for a transition is forward (F), but it can also run in reverse (a transition running in reverse displays an R). You can toggle the direction by clicking the F/R button.

9. **Copy the first transition.**

   Click the first transition in the Transition track to select it. Choose Edit→Copy, or use the shortcut Ctrl + C (⌘ + C).

10. **Click the transition track to the right of the first transition to activate the track.**

    Select the blank track to the right of the transition to indicate the location the copy will paste into.

11. **Choose Edit→Paste, or use the shortcut Ctrl + V (⌘ + V).**

    The copy of the transition is pasted into the Transition track to the right of the first transition. Click the copy and drag it right until it lines up with the end of the other clips. That is, if your music and title clips end at 05:00, the second transition should also end at 05:00.

12. **Double-click the second copy of the transition.**

    The Paint Splatter Settings dialog box opens again.

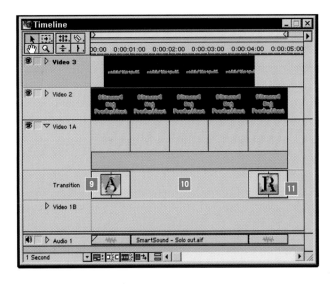

13. **Click the arrow to the left of the blue animation.**

    It toggles to point down. You want the transition to change from the color matte to black (this is the opposite of how the first transition runs).

14. **Change the start and end settings.**

    Click and drag the slider located under the left image until you see "Start = 11%" above the source image. Click and drag the slider located under the right image until you see "End = 70%". Click OK.

< N O T E >

A transition replaces one clip with another over time using one of many methods. In the most traditional sense, you transition from one clip to another. In this case, the transition is from the default background and your color matte. You can add a black matte to the Video 1B track, but because the default for a blank track is black, this isn't necessary.

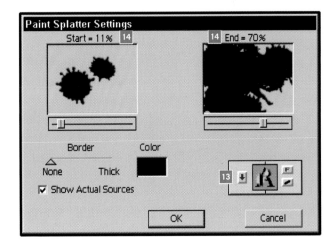

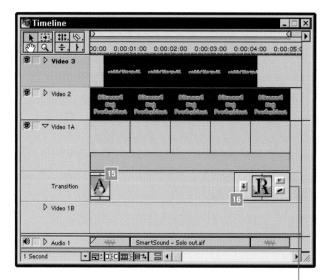

line up this edge

15. **Set the transition lengths.**
    The default length of a transition is 1 second. Shorten the first transition to 15 frames (1/2 second). Right-click the transition, and choose Duration. Set the time as 0:00:00:15, and click OK.

16. **Lengthen the second transition to 0:00:01:12.**
    You do this in the Duration panel, as you did in step 13. Make sure the transition lines up with the end of the other clips.

17. **Save the file.**
    You have completed more modifications and customizations and don't want to lose your work in the event of a computer problem.

18. **Preview the clip for the first time.**
    Press Enter and you see a build progress window.

<NOTE>
The defaults for transitions are to start at 0% and end at 100%. In a longer piece, the defaults are the most attractive and most practical way to use transitions. In this case, time is short, so there isn't an opportunity for a long, elegant transition. Plus, stopping a transition before it ends is a simple way to give an edgy ending to the video.

19. **Watch your clip play in the Monitor window once the preview is built.**
    You can review it again and again (and you will because it is so neat) by clicking Play in the Monitor window or pressing Enter. Your logo is now complete in its basic form. You have added all its components and set an animation sequence including transitions.

<TIP>
If you play a preview and can't see your background layers behind the text (only a title on a white background), don't panic. Think back to how you added the clips to the Timeline. If you moved a clip into the Video 1 track by mistake, and then moved it to the Video 2 track, you have reset the transparency. Right-click the title that has lost its transparency, and then choose Video Options➜ Transparency. When the Transparency Settings dialog box opens, click the Key type dropdown list, and choose White Alpha Matte. Click OK. Now save the file again, and then preview the clip. You're back in business.

Tutorial

» Adding Fade Controls

The next types of effects you add are fade controls. These are used to change the transparency of the title clips. Rather than switching from one title to the next in a single frame, adding fades gradually fades one title out as the other fades in, making for a more professional animation.

1. **Open the controls for the first title track on the Timeline.**
   Click the arrow to the left of the Video 2 label on the Timeline. The Video 2 track expands and displays a pink horizontal bar below the clip on the track. The red horizontal line is the fade control.

2. **Using the selection tool, click the line at the approximate time point in Video 2 where the Video 3 track starts.**
   A red dot, called a fade control point, is added to the line.

3. **Click and drag the red dot at the left endpoint of the line downward.**
   When you can't drag it any further down, release the mouse. This fades in the clip.

4. **Using the selection tool, click the red fade control line at the 0:10 location to add another fade control dot.**

5. **Select the scissors tool from the top right tool set on the Timeline toolbox.**
   The default tool at the top right of the toolbox is a razor tool. Click and hold the razor tool icon until the subpalette opens. Then click the scissors tool to select it.

6. **Move the scissors over the Video 2 fade control line.**
   Click the line with the scissors at the time the Video 3 clip ends, which is at 4:05. The scissors tool adds two points to the fade control next to one another.

7. **Click the selection tool in the toolbox to change back from the scissors.**
   Click and drag the first dot of the pair you just added downward to the bottom of the track and release the mouse.

8. **Using the selection tool, click the fade control line at the 1:10 mark.**
   This adds a dot for the fade controls on the second title track, which is Video 3. Drag the dot at the left endpoint of the line downward to set the fade controls for the second title track.

9. **Save your project again.**
   This is also a good time to do another preview. So far, you have assembled your basic project, and added fade controls to smooth the animation.

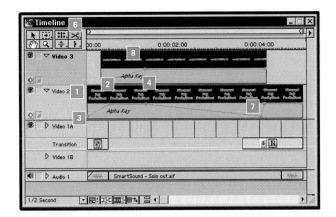

<NOTE>

There are more tools in the Timeline toolbox than the eight you see. Five of the tools have subpalettes containing a number of similar tools. Those tools with subpalettes have small arrows to the bottom right of the icon in the toolbox. To select another tool from the sub-palette, click and hold the tool displayed until the subpalette opens.

<TIP>

You can easily remove fade control points. Click a dot on a track with the selection tool, and then quickly drag it down below the bottom of the track. It snaps back into its original location, and the dot is removed.

<NOTE>

The two title tracks are called super tracks. That is, they are super-imposed over the basic tracks of the video. Adjusting the fade controls changes the visibility of the clips.

Tutorial

» Animating Your Slogan

Your project is coming along, but it needs some sparkle. There are numerous ways to animate an object in Premiere and create a sense of motion. For this project, you animate the slogan to bounce into view. Instead of building the animation from scratch, you use pre-built animation settings.

Motion settings

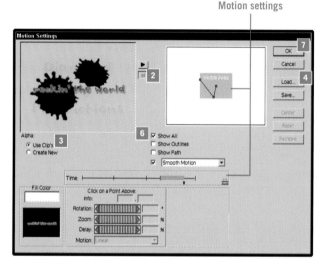

<TIP>

When you have added the motion settings, look at the clip on the Timeline. You see a solid red line running across the title's thumbnail image — this means the clip has applied Motion settings.

1. **Using the selection tool, right-click the** name2.ptl **clip on the Video 3 track.**
   The shortcut menu opens. Choose Video Options➔Motion. The Motion Settings window opens.

2. **After you have seen your slogan move across the preview screen enough times, click the Pause control to the right of the preview area.**
   The default animation path is from left to right.

3. **Check the Alpha setting.**
   Make sure the Use Clip's option is selected for the Alpha setting (located below the preview area). Titles are created with a transparent background, referred to as an alpha channel. If you use the clip's Alpha setting, the text is visible while the background is transparent. If you choose the Create New option, the title's background loses its alpha channel. The text AND a solid background are both visible; your animation shows a solid box moving across the screen rather than just the text.

4. **Click Load.**
   Browse to the storage location of the logo file, find the file named logo_bounce.pmt, and then click Open. The contents of the pre-built animation file are added to your Motion Settings window. The graph below the preview windows and markers in the top right preview area change.

5. **Click the Play arrow to the right of the preview window.**
   The title runs in the Preview window.

6. **Click Show All to see how the animation works with your other tracks.**
   Until this point, only the clip you work with is animated in the Preview window. Show All displays other layers in your project that are visible during the time frame of the clip you are modifying.

7. **When you have seen the animation in all its glory, click OK.**
   The Motion Settings window closes and returns you to the Timeline.

8. **Save the project again.**
   Your logo's slogan is animated.

Tutorial

» Adding Some Flare with Lens Flares

Your logo is almost finished. The last step before you build a finished movie is to add video effects. Lens flares are dramatic effects and add sparkle to the logo. There are different types of lens flares, but they all simulate shining a light on or across the screen. The lens flare you add to your title appears to move. As it moves, it also gets brighter and then fades. The light starts at the left of the text, gets brighter as it moves to the center of the screen, and then fades out as it moves to the right of the text. In this tutorial you work with some advanced features, including keyframes and effect controls.

1. **Add an effect to the Video 2 track.**
   Choose Window→Show Video Effects. The Video Effects palette opens. Premiere offers 75 different effects.

2. **Open the Render effect file and choose Lens Flare.**
   Click and drag the effect to the clip in the Video 2 track. When the effect is over the clip, the clip's appearance is inverted (that is, rather than a black background and dark gold text, the title thumbnail looks as though it has a white background and blue text). Release the mouse.

3. **The Lens Flare Settings dialog box opens on top of the Timeline when the effect is applied to the clip.**
   Click OK to close the dialog box. You are not adding a uniform lens flare to the entire clip. You use keyframes to control the effect. Once you add keyframes (discussed in the next several steps), you adjust the settings in the Lens Flare Settings dialog box.

The edit line is over the first key frame

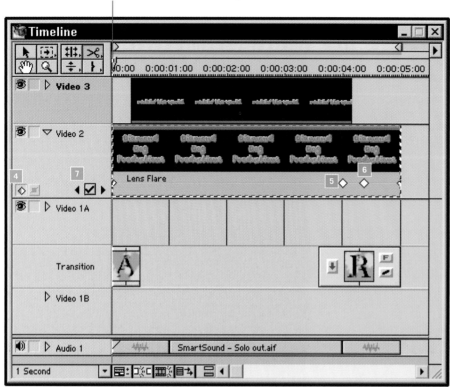

4. **Using the Selection tool, click the shaded diamond at the far left of the Video 2 track on the Timeline.**

   The keyframe line and the Keyframe navigator display. The keyframe line is the pale blue line running for the duration of the clip. The white triangles at either end of the keyframe line are the two default keyframes. The Keyframe navigator is the checkbox straddled by a pair of black triangles to the left of the Timeline.

5. **Add a keyframe at 4:00 seconds.**

   Move the edit line marker to 4:00 seconds. Click the Keyframe navigator checkbox. A black checkmark displays. At the 4:00 second mark on the keyframe line a white diamond displays. This is the new keyframe.

6. **Move the edit line marker to the 4:10 mark and click the Keyframe navigator checkbox again.**

   A black checkmark displays in the Keyframe navigator, and another white diamond appears on the keyframe line.You have a total of four keyframes strung across the keyframe line. In addition to the default keyframes at either end of the keyframe line (that look like white triangles) you have two new keyframes.

7. **Click the left-pointing arrow of the Keyframe navigator.**

   You see how the current-time marker jumps from keyframe to keyframe? Click it until you are at the first keyframe.

< N O T E >

The beginning and ending keyframes are actually diamonds. In their default positions at the ends of the keyframe line, you only see the inner half of the diamonds, hence the triangle appearance. If the end keyframes are moved into the keyframe line, the full diamond is displayed.

< N O T E >

Always use the Keyframe navigator to jump between keyframes. If you drag the edit line manually, you may or may not move to the correct frame. Unless the edit line is at the correct frame, when you try to adjust settings you add new keyframes instead.

8. **Choose Window→Show Effect Controls.**

   The Effect Controls palette lists Motion, Transparency, and any audio or video effects you add to a clip. The Lens Flare effect was added to the clip and is listed in the Effect Controls window. Click Setup to open the Lens Flare Settings dialog box.

   <TIP>

   You use at least two windows when you work with effects. The clip and its keyframes are located on the Timeline, the effects are stored in the Video Effects palette, the effects are controlled in the Effect Controls window, and many effects (such as the Lens Flare) have a separate Setup dialog box. Keep the Timeline and the Effect Controls windows open at all times. Close the Video Effects palette once you have chosen your effects. The setup dialog boxes close when you click OK to apply the custom settings.

This type of
effect is active

This effect has
active keyframes

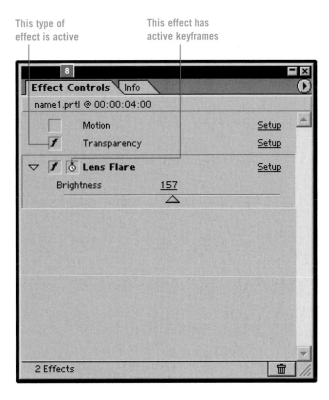

9. **Drag the slider to the far left.**

   This sets the Brightness at 10% (the default is 100%). You want to animate the light getting brighter and then fading over time. A Brightness value of 10% produces a faint light. It is important to start this effect with a dim light. Otherwise, at the peak brightness of the flare, you won't be able to see any of the logo.

10. **Click the 105mm Prime Lens Type at the bottom of the dialog box, move the flare center left, and then click OK to close the Lens Flare Settings dialog box and return to the Effect Controls and Timeline windows.**

    The 105mm Prime light is a broad beam of light and adds general brightness. The other lens types produce a more focused and harsher light effect. The default location for the light is the center of the screen. Click the Flare Center preview window in the desired location to move the flare center crosshairs to the left of the center row of text.

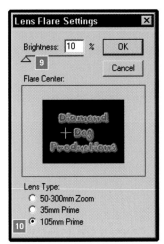

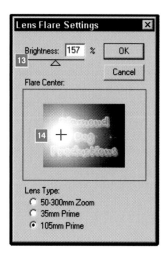

11. **On the Timeline, click the forward black arrow on the Keyframe navigator.**

    This jumps you to the next keyframe, which is at the 04:00 second mark.

12. **In the Effect Controls window, click Setup for the Lens Flare effect to open the Lens Flare Settings dialog box again.**

13. **Set the Brightness to 155-158%.**

    You are customizing settings for the keyframe at the 04:00 second mark, which is the beginning of the actual flare in your logo. A brightness setting in the 155-158% range provides a bright light effect and still allows the text to be visible.

14. **In the Flare Center display, click the display to the left of the center of your text to move the center crosshairs.**

    Make sure the Lens Type is 105mm Prime again. Click OK. The Lens Flare Settings dialog box closes, and you return to the Timeline and Effect Controls windows.

15. **On the Timeline, click the forward black arrow on the Keyframe navigator to jump to the next keyframe, which is at the 04:10 second mark.**

    You set the end of the flare at this keyframe.

16. **In the Effect Controls window, click Setup for the Lens Flare effect to open the Lens Flare Settings dialog box again.**

    The settings created for the last keyframe display in the dialog box. Leave the settings as is, except move the Flare Center. Click the Flare Center preview window to the right of the center of your text to move the center of the light. Click OK. The Lens Flare Settings dialog box closes, and you return to the Timeline and Effect Controls windows.

17. **On the Timeline, click the forward black arrow on the Keyframe navigator to jump to the last keyframe (it appears as a white triangle at the end of the clip).**

    You fade out the light at this keyframe.

18. **In the Effect Controls window, click Setup for the Lens Flare effect to open the Lens Flare Settings dialog box one last time.**

    The settings created for the last keyframe display in the dialog box. Decrease the Brightness control to 10% (the brightness value used at the beginning of the effect). The dialog box settings are the same as those described in steps 9 and 10. Click OK to close the Lens Flare Settings dialog box and return to the Timeline and Effect Controls windows.

19. **Save the file and make another preview.**

    At this point your logo is finished. You have sound, text, motion, and light effects.

Tutorial
» Making Your Movie

All your hard work is about to pay off. It's time to finish up and make your movie.

1. **Make any final adjustments.**
   Your movie may be slightly longer or shorter than five seconds depending on your music selection. The settings listed for fade controls or the length and position of your `name2.ptl` clip may look better if you adjust them slightly.

2. **Choose File→Export Timeline→Movie.**
   The Export Movie dialog box opens. The project settings you chose at the beginning of the project are listed at the bottom left of the dialog box. You use these settings for the exported movie.

3. **In the Export Movie dialog box, name your file, and then click Save.**
   You see an Export dialog box that shows the export progress. A Clip window opens when the export is complete.

4. **Click the Play arrow in the Clip window to run your movie.**

5. **Close Premiere.**
   Your logo is finished. Share your video with everyone you know who has a QuickTime player!

Part I
Course Setup

Premiere Basics

An Overview of Premiere 6.5

Premiere is a workhorse program. It was originally designed as a video editing program, and the program's designers have never lost sight of that goal. The type of work you can accomplish in Premiere has greatly expanded, primarily because you can use many more different types of material in your projects. You can also export a project in so many more different formats.

Premiere was in its infancy back in the "old" days when I was in design school. The only type of export available was to videotape. The broad range of export options available now is one of the program's strengths.

How Do You Use Premiere?

Premiere is an editing program. Therefore, you wouldn't use it to design all parts of a flashy sports program opener. You would use it to assemble, edit, and enhance material from a range of other sources to make the final product.

Some types of source material are best prepared in Premiere, such as video footage. Depending on the extent and complexity of the editing required, you can work with your audio source materials within Premiere or use an external audio editing program.

Other types of material commonly used come from illustration or image editing programs, such as Illustrator or Photoshop. You can format images in an external editor before bringing them into Premiere, or use effects in Premiere for image manipulation, such as color balancing or levels.

A key part of what you commonly see on television program openers and in commercials uses graphical animations, such as animated circles, lines, logos, and so on. The decision to build these animations in Premiere or use another program depends on the complexity. You can build almost any kind of animation you want in Premiere's Motion Settings window. However, the animation process can be laborious and complicated. It's not that you can't do it — you certainly can. The decision is based rather on the amount of time available, and whether you have other software you can use, such as Adobe After Effects. In the major project in this book, you do a fair bit of graphic animation but the complexity is manageable.

Working with Premiere

As I mentioned, Premiere is an editing program. Consider a typical news broadcast. You see the reporter, then the subject of the piece, then the reporter, then the material, and so on. This type of editing is referred to as A/B roll editing. Two rolls of tape run, and you make transitions back and forth from one clip to the other, add titles, adjust the audio tracks so they synchronize, and the piece is assembled.

You start working in Premiere in the same way. The two basic tracks and a transition track are still used. You can also add titles. But that is only the beginning. After the basic movie is assembled, you can add transparencies and superimposed tracks, animation, and effects, split screens, and track mattes — the opportunities are almost endless.

When your movie is completed, you have to decide how you want to distribute your movie. You choose project settings as you start a project, but you can choose different settings for exporting. This feature gives you an enormous amount of freedom.

For example, I have been hired to design media for a furniture manufacturer. The company will likely need a variety of products including consumer or trade show promotions, training video, material for prospective investors, and online materials. Using Premiere, I can design and export all these different types of material.

Let's take this example further. My client prides itself on the quality of their products' construction. How is this information used? If the processes involved are complex or the company does a great deal of staff training, one of the most efficient training methods is creating instructional video. The goal of the video, shot as digital video footage, is to show the employee step-by-step how to perform a particular task. The footage is then digitized for use in Premiere.

Now what? When the video is in Premiere, I then edit it for length and content. I add titles and text and probably use a voiceover to provide some or all of the instruction. The training material can then be output to CD or to video. I can also export individual frames as still images in a number of file formats for print work.

This same video footage can be used over and over. Promotional video is another common use for Premiere. For a consumer show, I would use clips from the training material that show the strength of the product construction along with shots of the finished product lines. An industry trade show could use the same source material, but modified for the audience. These projects can be output from Premiere in whatever formats that the trade show staff requires, probably as CD or video formats.

This manufacturer also has an online sales division, and wants to create new materials to use online. What do the consumers shopping online want to see? I doubt they want to watch wood glue drying, but I am sure that they are interested in seeing how a table's joints are constructed. Again, I can use the same footage but this time, the output is broken into small segments for online use. Depending on requirements, I would create one or several versions of each clip in different file formats. With Premiere, I have the option to output Windows Media, QuickTime, and RealPlayer movies in different bandwidths and as downloadable or streaming media.

All these products are created from the same source material. This ability is the power of Premiere.

New Features in Premiere 6.5

Premiere has changed considerably over the years. Version 6.0 had some interesting new features, including digital video support, a Storyboard function to lay out a project before adding it to the Timeline, enhanced editing capabilities, and an Audio Mixer for real-time audio editing. Numerous changes to effects capabilities, customizable workspaces, project file storage as well as integration with other Adobe programs were also added.

Version 6.5 expands on some of these features and adds more new ones. Premiere is a production tool. Version 6.5 supports more types of digital video hardware than previous versions. Memory management, security, networking, and interface changes for using Premiere 6.5 with Windows XP and Mac OS X operating systems have been made.

Version 6.5 uses a Real-Time Preview for the first time. If you prefer, you can see any effects or titles you add as you preview the project rather than making formal previews.

The Adobe Title Designer is one of the most exciting changes in 6.5. The Title window up to this version hadn't changed much. But wait until you see this! The Title Designer uses many of the features you would expect to find in other Adobe products, such as Photoshop. The new window includes a range of typographical effects and animations. You can also use a Pen tool for drawing. The Title Designer also includes a set of PostScript fonts (over 90) appropriate for video use. Not only that, but the fonts can also be used with other applications.

Version 6.5 adds more After Effects filters. These filters are sophisticated, professional-quality effects; there are now more than 30.

Changes have been made to the audio capabilities of Premiere, based on the operating system that you are using. PC users can now use three DirectX plug-ins for sound engineering. Mac users now have real-time two-track audio processing that uses the SparkLE application.

Regardless of operating system, SmartSound Quicktracks is still part of the program. In Version 6.5, it has been expanded so that you can now create more custom-length tracks for your video projects.

Premiere 6.5 has more export options than any previous version. Regardless of your operating system, you can use the new Adobe MPEG Encoder to create and export movies directly from the Timeline in formats including DVD, Super Video CD, Video CD, and cDVD formats.

New Macintosh Options: For the Mac user, DVD creation is easier. Exported files can be integrated with Apple iDVD and Apple DVD Studio Pro (you must own the Apple products, of course).

New Windows Options: Support for Windows Media formats has been expanded. DVD authoring uses Sonic DVDit! LE, which can support a range of DVD and CD-R equipment and media types.

General Work Tips and Computer Instructions

How to Get Started

The first step begins before you even install Premiere. Many programs put your computer's capabilities to the test, and Premiere is certainly one of them. Make sure that your computer meets the *required* hardware capabilities — and preferably the recommended capabilities. Nothing is as frustrating as waiting and waiting and waiting for your computer to catch up to you. I have long viewed an underpowered computer as an enormous inspiration killer. After all, how do you sustain your enthusiasm and artistic vision when you have to wait to see it? By the time the machine catches up to you, you have forgotten what you wanted to do! However, you don't need to buy the latest and greatest machine. You can do good work with a middle-of-the-road machine.

If you are planning to upgrade your computer to run high-demand programs, such as Premiere, buy RAM. Many people think the bigger their hard drive, the better. That isn't the case. Your emphasis is to process data, not store it. The only exception is video capture. If you are planning to capture your own video, you can't have too much hard drive space.

System Requirements

Your system should meet the requirements as listed here to properly run with Premiere 6.5.

PC System

- » Pentium III 500MHz processor (Pentium 4 or multiprocessor recommended)
- » Windows 98 (Second Edition), ME, XP, 2000 (Service Pack 2)
- » 128MB of RAM (256MB or more recommended)
- » 600MB of available hard drive space for installation
- » 256-color video display adapter
- » CD drive
- » QuickTime 5.0
- » Pentium III 800MHz processor (Pentium 4 dual processors recommended) for Real-Time Preview

Macintosh System

» PowerPC G3 or faster processor (G4 or G4 dual recommended)

» Mac OS 9.2.2 or Mac OS X v.10.1.3

» 64MB of RAM (128MB or more recommended)

» 600MB of available hard drive space for installation

» 256-color video display adapter

» CD drive

» QuickTime 5.0.2

» G4 processor (G4 dual recommended) for Real-Time Preview

Digital Video Capture

You won't need digital video capture capabilities to do the project in this book.

PC System

» Microsoft DirectX certified IEEE 1394 interface

» Dedicated 7200RPM UDMA 66 IDE or SCSI hard drive or disk array

» DirectX compatible video display adapter

Macintosh System

» QuickTime compatible IEEE 1394 (FireWire) interface

» Hard drive or disk array capable of sustaining 5MB/sec

» FireWire 2.7

Third-Party Capture Cards

» For both Mac and PC: Premiere-certified capture card

Tutorial
» Starting the Program for the First Time

The first time you open Premiere, you have to choose from two different workspaces. A workspace refers to a Timeline layout. Choose an option based on your experience and background. If you are coming to Premiere from a traditional video editing background, you may find the Single-Track Editing option more familiar. The A/B Editing option shows the clips and transitions on separate tracks. The projects in this book use the A/B Editing option.

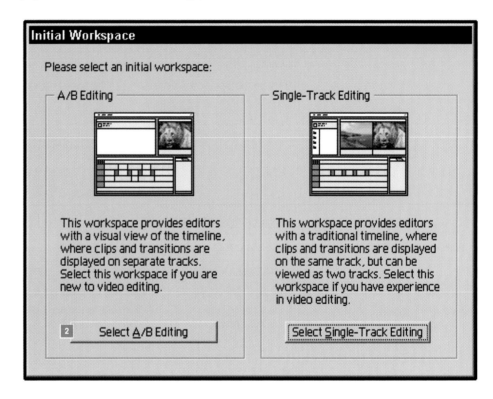

1. **From the Start menu, click Start→Programs→Adobe→ Premiere.**
   The workspace dialog box opens.

2. **Click Select A/B Editing.**

Tutorial

» Customizing Storage Locations

The more memory available to Premiere, the better it can perform. Editing that is done in a project is processed in RAM. If you don't have enough RAM, Premiere uses some hard drive space as a work area, called a *scratch* disk. This work area is used to create temporary files and build previews. Requirements for scratch disk space increase as your project becomes longer and/or more complex.

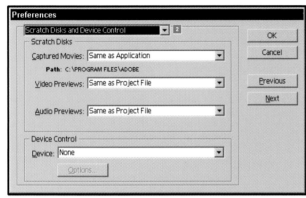

<NOTE>
RAM (Random Access Memory) is a memory type. Processes read and write to this memory to perform the work of the program. This memory is also referred to as volatile memory, because as soon as you shut down your machine, the work is lost.

1. **Open Premiere.**
   The Load Project Settings window opens. Click Cancel to close this window.

2. **Choose Edit→Preferences→Scratch Disks and Device Control.**
   The three scratch disks list their default locations.

<NOTE>
If you have more than one hard drive, install the program on one hard drive, and the storage files on another hard drive.

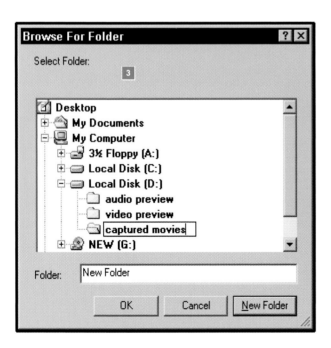

3. **Click the dropdown arrow and click Select Folder.**
   When the Browse for Folder dialog box opens, select the storage folder or create a new one, and click OK.

4. **Click OK to close the dialog box.**

5. **Close and reopen the program to activate the changes.**

<NOTE>
You can see in the example that I allocate a separate drive partition just for Premiere file storage. Most people aren't that fortunate. If you have more than one hard drive partition, set the storage files in the partition with the most available space.

Where Do the Files Go?

When it comes to most types of software, you don't usually have to worry about where the files are stored. Typically, inserting the CD and installing the program is all that you need to do. Premiere needs defined areas for working and storage. You can either let the program define areas by default, or create custom locations.

For a regular installation, Premiere lets you know where different areas are being set up including:

» The program

» Storage for captured video

» Storage for video preview files

» Storage for audio preview files

The program finds what it needs when it needs it. Here's an example. A project lists the video clips you are using. In reality, these clips aren't in your project. They are actually linked from their storage location. While you are working, you create previews that also need storing. Like the clips for your projects, previews are also stored externally to the program and linked.

Change the Low Disk Space Warning Level

You can also have Premiere warn you when your scratch disk is running low on space. This is another prefer-ence. In the General and Still Image preferences, you can change the Low Disk Space Warning Level. I use the default setting.

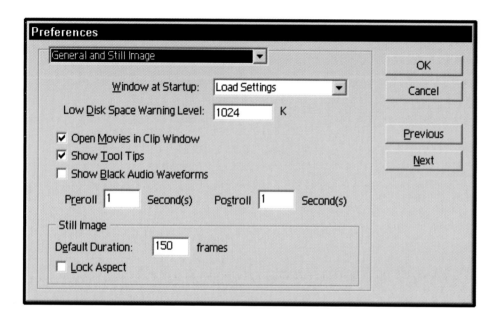

In this chapter I've shown you how to install, configure, and tweak Premiere. Ready to start? Turn the page. Work hard, think harder, and enjoy!

Project Overview

This book is a tutorial-based course in Premiere 6.5 for students, educators, and design professionals. There are two ways you can use this book. For those of you who have been using Premiere, this is a handy reference; use it for learning the new features of Premiere 6.5. Unless you are one of those obsessive types, you probably haven't fully explored each and every part of the program. I recommend you start with the Confidence Builder tutorial, which is an overview of the program.

If you are new to Premiere, welcome to a new world! I recommend you take a different approach to learning Premiere. Carefully work through the Confidence Builder as it covers the highlights of the program as you produce an animated logo. This introductory tutorial, though it touches on many of the program's features, is not elaborate. I suggest an experiment: Build the introductory project in Confidence Builder now, and then work through the book. When you are finished, come back to the introductory project and modify and enhance it. You'll be pleasantly surprised by how much you have learned.

Understanding the Project Story

A video project requires a number of stages. First and foremost is the stage in which you define the purpose of the video. Using this book, you create a video that runs for 1:30 (one and one-half minutes). The video concept is a travel association promoting tropical resort vacations to the harried, overworked office crowd. This travel video could be used as a promotion at a consumer trade show, such as a lifestyle or travel show.

Here's the story. The video opens with different aspects of congested city life: traffic, crowds, more traffic, more crowds. The images and video of city life are accompanied by a heavy drum sound track, as well as common city noises such as telephones, traffic, and vehicle horns. This runs for about 15 seconds. The first part fades to black.

The movie segues to the second section, which opens with the sound of waves crashing against the shore. A lovely tropical beach appears, and then you see a happy, carefree young woman running down a beach. A slightly exotic and active musical score begins.

Sounds good already, doesn't it? Over the next minute, various scenes appear and disappear. Clips of water sports, such as surfing and sailing, are interspersed with clips of tropical resorts. The movie ends with an understated message about how vacations can restore your perspective on life.

Essentially, the project is two separate segments connected by the theme and intent of the video. I intentionally use two sections that are very different — for design reasons and for this book. For design purposes, the two segments of the movie create contrast and emphasize the message. For example, when you picture a tropical vacation, what do you think about? You probably envision sun and fun — a relaxing situation. This is the theme of the second segment of the movie. The first segment of the movie creates a sense of tension by showing the fast pace, noise, and crowds of everyday city life. Think how much more you would wish for a vacation under those hectic circumstances.

I mentioned that the project is designed in two parts for the book as well. When you run the video, you see that the two segments are very different in their look and visual effects. Having this range in material allows you to use more of the program's editing and effects features. This gives you a sense of how the features work in a particular situation.

Developing the Project

Through the process of building this project, you pass through several stages of development. These stages correspond with the sections in this book:

> » **Project creation and assembly of materials.** This includes creating the project and custom project settings and importing and organizing the set of clips used at the start of the project.

» **Basic editing.** This includes organizing and trimming the clips to fit the length of the project, as well as adding transitions between clips.

» **Using audio.** This includes both prepared and self-designed audio. The first section of the video uses sound files from the CD. For the second section, you make your own sound track.

» **Adding other visual elements.** Titles, transparency, animation, and video effects are added.

» **Exporting the movie.** This is the final stage of a project when you distribute the finished movie and show it to others.

Working with the Tutorial Files

The CD contains a folder called Tutorial Files. This folder houses all the material you need for finishing the Complete Course project.

Before you work on the tutorials, copy the files to your computer. Make a folder on your hard drive to store the project folders and files. Open the Tutorial Files folder, which contains some files and folders. The simplest way to use the files is to copy the entire set named SessionX.ptl to your hard drive (where X is the Session number; there are 16 in total). You then copy the folder named Footage and all its contents to your hard drive.

Each session has its own project file. The beginning of each tutorial picks up where the last one leaves off. For example, if you want to start working on Session 4, open the `session4.ptl` file. If you want to see what the project layout looks like at the end of Session 4, open the `session5.ptl` file. More instructions for copying files and folders to your computer are in Appendix A.

Rename the project file when you save it. This way, if you need to start over or make changes, you can start again with the original project file or with your project file from the previous session.

The CD has a set of sample movie files. Sessions 1 to 3 have no movie files as they wouldn't show you anything of value. At that point, you are still assembling clips, so at best the movie would look like a slideshow with blank black spaces. Some sessions have single completed files, while other sessions have two movie files.

Make notes in the margins of the book as you are working through the project. The hallmarks of a good tutorial book are generous slatherings of highlighter, scribbles in the margins, and wrinkles in the pages. Above all, experiment as you learn.

Part II
Getting Started

Session 1

Starting the Project

Session Introduction

Making a movie starts before you open the program. You cannot make a movie until you decide how it should work technically. When you start a new project, you have to pick settings that range from video to audio and everything in between. This session covers the setup phase of a new project. You learn how to choose common settings and how to modify presets for a particular purpose. Discussions introduce you to many of the common project settings and what they mean. You also learn how to find, import, and organize the clips used to make your movie. The tutorials on the Project window and how to organize your clips into bins point out a key ingredient of successful movie-building — organize your source material both for smooth program operation and to remember what you have to work with!

TOOLS YOU'LL USE
Load Project Settings window, Custom Project Settings command, General Project Settings dialog box, Video Project Settings dialog box, Audio Project Settings dialog box, Keyframe and Rendering Project Settings dialog boxes, Save Project command, Import Folder command, Project window, Project menu, Project Window Options dialog box, Project window view buttons, New Bin command, Delete Bin command

CD-ROM FILES NEEDED
Contents of folder premierecc_video

TIME REQUIRED
90 minutes

Tutorial
» Choosing General Project Settings

There are many, many ways to start a project using a wide range of settings. Not only can you choose presets, but you can also create your own custom settings. In this tutorial, you learn how to pick a basic project format.

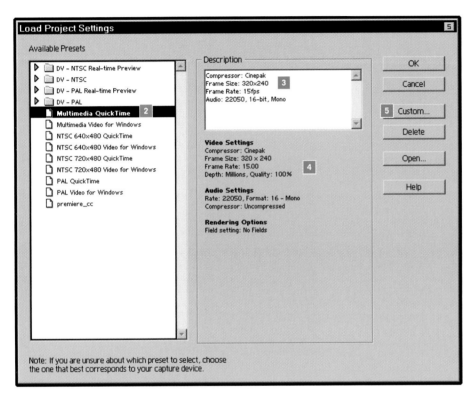

1. **Open the program.**
   Choose Start→Programs→Adobe→Premiere 6.5. The Load Project Settings window opens.

2. **Click Multimedia QuickTime from the Available Presets list in the Load Project Settings window.**
   Premiere includes a collection of presets that you can use to save time when starting a project. You can choose from a range of digital video, television presets, and screen-based presets.

3. **Review the settings in the Description area for the selected option.**
   These are the highlights of the chosen settings. The general description includes information on major settings, such as the frame rate and frame size.

4. **Review the Video, Audio, and Rendering Settings on the dialog box.**
   You can see the description information is included. These groups of settings display options selected by the preset.

5. **Click Custom to open the New Project Settings dialog box.**
   You have chosen general settings that are closest to those you want to work with for your project, the preset Multimedia QuickTime settings. This is simpler and faster than starting from a preset totally unlike the output you are planning (such as a television preset). The New Project Settings dialog box includes the Multimedia QuickTime settings.

Tutorial
» Customizing Project Settings

After you select a project setting format from which to start, you can customize the settings. Custom settings are chosen in a set of five dialog boxes. In this tutorial, you learn how to customize project settings.

1. **Click the drop-down arrow to the right of the Editing Mode and choose QuickTime as the Editing Mode.**
   When the New Project Settings dialog box opens, the General Settings options are displayed. The QuickTime editing mode you select is used as the default editing mode. QuickTime can be used regardless of your operating system.

2. **Click Next to open the Video Settings dialog box.**
   There is a set of five settings panels. Click Next to cycle through the panels.

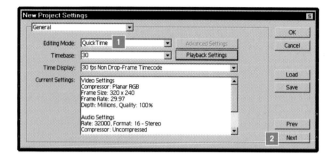

3. **Change the frame size by typing into the fields.**
   Enter 320 in the horizontal (h) field and 240 in the vertical (v) field. Previewing and rendering processes are faster when you use a smaller frame size. This size is also sufficiently large for screen output.

4. **Click the 4:3 Aspect option to select it.**
   The 4:3 Aspect option creates a relationship between the horizontal and vertical sizes of the frame. For every four image pixels displayed horizontally, there are three pixels displayed vertically. This relationship is applied to the footage you use in your movie, and your clips will be adjusted to fit this ratio.

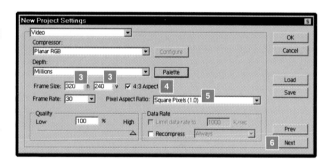

5. **Click the drop-down arrow to the right of Pixel Aspect Ratio and choose Square Pixels (1.0).**
   You are working with screen output, which uses square pixels. You have to use a range of different pixel aspect ratios for use with film, digital video, or high-definition television output (HDTV).

6. **Click Next to open the Audio Settings dialog box.**

7. **Change the default audio preview files settings from 5 to 3.**
   The project uses several audio tracks, and using audio preview files gives you a good sense of how your project is coming along.

8. **Click Next to open the Keyframe and Rendering dialog box.**
   Premiere uses keyframes in two different ways, either as control points for effects, or as part of the output production process. In the project settings dialog box, keyframe options refer to producing output. There are a number of different options for rendering, which is the process of creating finished frames of your movie.

9. **Click the Optimize Stills checkbox to select it.**
   Optimizing stills in the project saves file space. Rather than rendering a still image many times (once for each frame for the length of time it appears on the screen), the image is rendered only once if you choose this option.

10. **Click the Real Time Preview checkbox to select it.**
    This option lets you make previews on the fly as you work. Check the hardware requirements in the appendix to see if your computer is able to support the Real Time Preview option.

11. **Click the drop-down arrow at the right of Fields to choose No Fields from the drop-down menu.**
    Field settings are used for video playback.

12. **Click Save.**

13. **Name the settings premiere_cc.**
    You can add identifying information to the dialog box to distinguish the settings further. You can create any number of custom settings; extra information may help to distinguish your settings more clearly than the name you give to the settings.

14. **Click OK.**
    The dialog box closes.

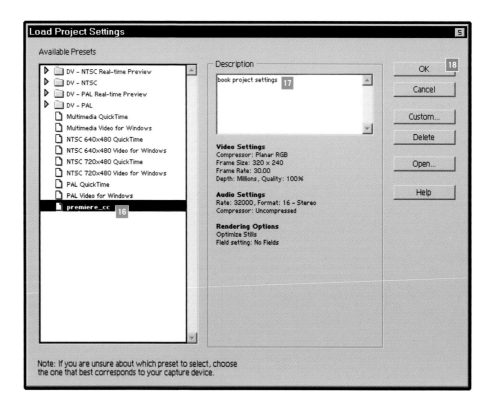

15. **Click Load when you are returned to the New Project Settings dialog box.**

    Under ordinary circumstances, when you are building custom settings you would click OK from the New Project Settings dialog boxes, which applies the settings and starts the program. In this case, I wanted to show you how and where your custom settings are used.

16. **Click premiere_cc from the Presets list.**

    Your custom settings have been added to the Available Presets list.

17. **Read the Description.**

    You see the information that you added in Step 13 (I added book project settings).

18. **Click OK to apply the settings.**

    The dialog box closes, and you are finally at the program interface. Time to get the show underway!

Discussion

Understanding the General Project Settings

It is important for you to understand why you choose specific settings when starting a project. It is also important to understand what they mean. Refer back to the image of the General Settings dialog box for reference.

Editing mode

The editing mode you choose determines what kind of video method is used to playback video from the Timeline. Regardless of operating system, you always have QuickTime available as an option. Windows users also have DV Playback (Digital Video) and Video for Windows editing modes. If you install video capture cards, you may find that they also have editing modes.

Timebase

The timebases are divisions used in the program to identify the position of each edit. There are variations in the time base depending on the type of output you are planning as well as the part of the world your project is used in. For example, if you are working with video output in Europe, you should choose a time base of 25; while in North America, you should choose a time base of 29.97. Use a time base of 24 for motion picture film. If you are designing a project that is most likely to be used for purposes other than broadcast (such as the project in this book), choose a time base of 30.

time divisions

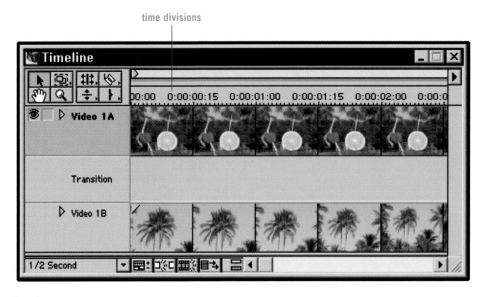

Time Display

In Premiere, time is displayed across the time ruler at the top of the Timeline as well as on the Clip and Monitor windows. You can specify options that coincide with the type of project you are working on. Again, there are specific settings for video and motion-picture film, as well as other display types such as frames or samples. For the type of output you are creating in this project, the default 30 fps (frames per second) Non Drop-Frame timecode is the best choice.

Discussion

Understanding Characteristics of Video and Audio

You view your project as you are working on it and make previews to chart your progress. It is important to test how the movie looks before you export it as a final product. The export process can be very lengthy so you want the project error-free before exporting. For the most predictable results, the project's video settings should match the export video settings you use. You can refer back to the image of the Video Settings dialog box for reference.

Compressors

These are special program components that Premiere will use for building previews. A codec (compressor/decompressor) compresses the video data in your project using a variety of processes, and then decompresses it for playback.

Your choice of codec depends on several things. The editing mode you choose limits the available codecs. That is, if you choose QuickTime as the editing mode, you do not have the same number of codecs that are available when using DV Editing. Choose a codec based on video capture, hardware requirements, or the speed of the codec.

Color Depth

For the most part, a codec or the editing mode you choose controls color depth. Some codecs allow you to create custom palettes. If you are building a project for Web display and are having problems with file size or playback, changing the color depth to an 8-bit (256 color) palette may help. You sacrifice color quality when changing color palettes. For example, look at the following images. The image at the left uses a depth of millions of colors. The same image on the right uses a 256-color palette.

Aspect Ratios

The conventional aspect ratio for television is 4:3. This means that there are 4 units horizontally for every 3 units vertically, as you can see in the following image. This ratio constrains the size of your movie regardless of how you resize it. For example, a size of 400 x 300 pixels uses the same ratio as a size of 800 x 600 pixels.

Pixels also have an aspect. In this project you are using square pixels. Other pixel aspects are available for different formats, such as digital video or widescreen TV. Widescreen TV used in North America, for example, uses a ratio of 1.78:1.

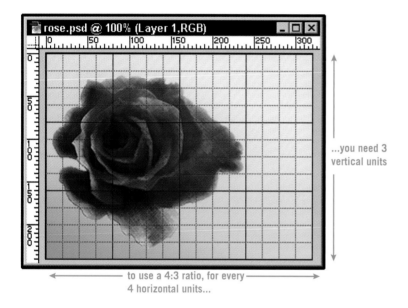

...you need 3 vertical units

to use a 4:3 ratio, for every 4 horizontal units...

Frame Rate

This setting is one of the most important settings in a project. Frame rate is simply the number of frames seen in one second. If the frame rate is high (30), you have the smoothest video playback but also the largest file size. The rule of thumb is to use the same frame rate for working as you plan to use for export. Using a lower frame rate for a very large project saves processing time. Choose an alternate frame rate that equally divides into the planned export frame rate. For example, if your exported project uses a frame rate of 30 fps, you can work with 15 or 10 fps.

Quality

Quality refers to the Timeline display. The higher the quality, the better the image looks, but the larger the amount of storage required. If you find that you are stressing your hard drive's capacity while working on your project, you can readjust this setting. Drag the Quality slider on the Video panel of the Project Settings dialog box left to decrease quality (to a minimum of 1%) or right to increase quality (to a maximum of 100%).

Data Rate

This setting may or may not be available, depending on the codec you choose. Data Rate limits the amount of video data used for previews. You can choose from specific or general settings for data rate. Unless your previews are jerky, you can probably leave this setting at its default. When your previews are hesitant, set this value lower. That means a smaller amount of data is processed at one time, which often produces a smoother preview.

<NOTE>

The smartest way to work with these settings is to use your best judgment and experience. Invariably your project setting won't work exactly the same way from project to project simply because of the amount and types of content.

Setting Audio Options

The best way to use audio in Premiere is to plan it before you start. That is, modify audio externally to the program, or capture it at the settings you want to use for output. If the audio clips are prepared before you use them, you won't need to have them translated through the program settings, which makes for faster previews.

That doesn't mean you can't adjust the settings in the program. Changes in bitrate and format result in varied quality of your preview and output. Audio quality is better at higher sampling rates. Of course, this also results in larger file sizes and slower previews.

Using the highest sample rate and the highest bit depth for all your clips or projects is unnecessary. Motion picture output should use the highest-quality settings possible. On the other hand, Web output can't use all the information, which means that your files are unnecessarily large. Music should use higher-quality settings than voice.

You can refer back to the image of the Audio Settings dialog box to see where the settings are located.

Discussion
Choosing Characteristics for Previews

The Keyframe and Rendering Settings contain a number of options for deciding how your preview is built from a technical perspective. Refer to the Keyframe and Rendering Settings dialog box for reference.

Rendering Options

Your custom project settings include the Optimize Stills option. As you begin working with the project files, you can see that you use still images for varying lengths of time. When stills are optimized, the rendering process is more efficient. Here's an example. If you have a project using a frame rate of 30 fps, and use a still image for two seconds, it requires rendering 60 frames, each $\frac{1}{30}$ of a second long. With optimized stills, a single two-second frame is created. This setting is especially important for projects that use large numbers of still images. The optimized stills concept is shown in the following image. At the top you can see one copy of the image, while along the bottom there are multiple copies. Premiere can render (prepare for output) one copy of the image much more quickly than it can render multiple copies.

1 frame for the duration
of the still image

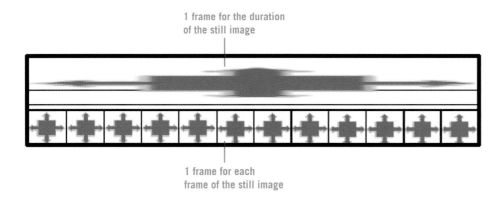

1 frame for each
frame of the still image

You also chose Real Time Preview as part of your custom settings. Therefore, you can preview within the program and instantly see the results, complete with effects.

Keyframe Options

Keyframes for previewing are different than keyframes you may have come across in design programs (including Premiere). When you design with keyframes, you determine a point in time and space and then set another point in time and space using different values. The movement of your layer or object from one point (keyframe) to another produces animation. Compression keyframes are used by many codecs but work differently than animation keyframes. This type deals with frame information. A keyframe defines the content of a frame. The next keyframe defines the content of that frame. The codec works by interpreting information between the two frames. Basically, it tests each keyframe to see what information is the same, such as a background, and then stores only the information that is different, such as the location of a moving object.

Tutorial
» Importing Footage

You should have a good understanding of the Project Settings at this point. So, now the moment you have been waiting for — the program interface is open, and you are finally inside the program. At the end of the last tutorial, you created custom settings for your project and loaded those settings. Once the settings were chosen, the program opens. Learn how to import files into your project in this tutorial.

1. **With the program interface open, click anywhere on the Project window to activate it.**
   The Project window contains a folder labeled Bin 1. A new project always starts with one default bin. Bins work the same ways as folders. You can add, remove, rename, and stack bins within each other.

<NOTE>
If you closed the program at the end of the last tutorial, reopen it. Choose Start→Programs→Adobe→Premiere 6.5. The Load Project Settings window opens. Select your custom settings (created in the last tutorial) from the Available Presets and click OK. Your custom settings load, and the program interface displays.

2. **Choose File→Import→Folder.**
   The Browse for Folder dialog box opens. The directories on your hard drive (and network if available) are listed in a folder hierarchy.

3. **Browse to the location where you stored the files copied from the CD.**
   You should have the files copied to your hard drive. The storage process is discussed in the book's appendix.

4. **Select the folder named premierecc_video and click OK.**
   The folder contains the video and still image clips you use to start the project.

<NOTE>
All the files for this project are contained in one folder, so it is simplest to import the entire folder. You can also import single files. Choose File→Import→File. When the Browse dialog box opens, locate the file you want to import, select it, and click OK on the dialog box. The file is added to your project into whatever bin is selected. You can also import several files the same way (if they are located in the same folder) by using Shift + click to select them.

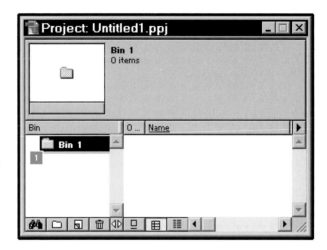

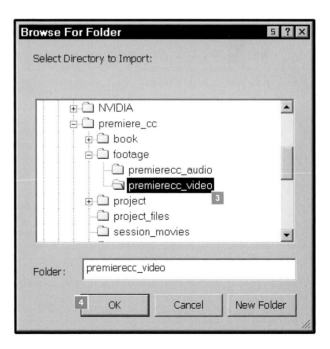

5. **Scroll through the Project window.**

   You can see the collection of video and stills for your project. At this point, you have 35 files. The files are all within the Bin 1 folder.

6. **Choose File→Save.**

   Browse to the location where you stored the copied files. Name the project. Click OK. The new project name displays at the top of the Project window. You now have a project, complete with project settings and content. You use this project file throughout the course.

   <NOTE>

   The title for your project can be descriptive, catchy, or utilitarian. The important thing is to save it in the same location as your source files. This saves time, both yours and your computer's. If you do a lot of Premiere work in the future, collecting everything for one project in one place saves you time searching for files. From the program's perspective, if the project file is in the same location as the source files, it can link to them more quickly, and start, process, and save faster.

Understanding Data Rates

You can see a value called Average Data Rate when you select a clip in the Project window. You can also analyze the clip further. Right-click the clip in the Project window and choose Properties. When the Properties dialog box opens, click Data Rate to display the graph. A graph for a project clip is shown here.

The graph shows you information about each frame of a video file: The white line shows the average data rate, and the red bars show the sample size of each keyframed frame. In a file using different keyframe configurations, a blue bar is also displayed, which shows the sample size of the frames between keyframes.

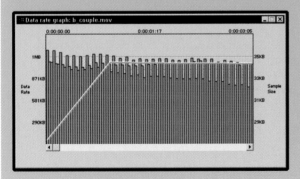

Tutorial
» Working with the Project Window

Now your files are inside the program and the project is saved. In this tutorial, you learn how to customize the layout of the Project window. This window controls the program, and stores a lot of information. You can customize the window depending on the type of project you are working on, as well as how much information you want to look at as you work. You can use thumbnails and information, images only, or data only.

1. **Click the icon view option to view the clips as small image icons.**
   You may prefer to see what each clip looks like rather than trying to identify the clips by name. For video clips, the first frame of the clip displays in the icon view.

2. **Click a clip to select it, and preview the clip in the Project window by clicking the play arrow.**
   When you select a clip, an active preview displays at the top of the Project window. The type of preview depends on the type of clip. For example, video or audio clips have a play controller; still images have no controls.

3. **Click the play slider to jump the preview to a location partway through the clip.**
   It isn't necessary to preview the entire clip. Move the play slider right to the approximate time of a clip segment you plan to use.

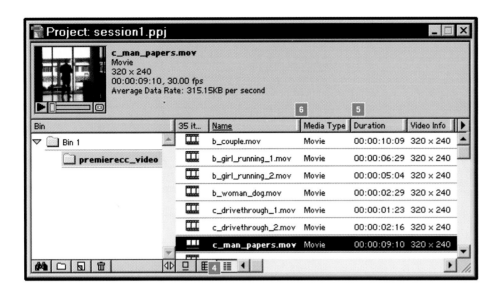

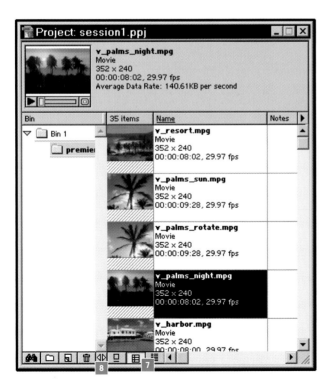

4. **Click the list option to view more information about the clips.**

   Use this option if you need to access information about the clips such as Log Comments or Timecode.

5. **Read data about the clips.**

   Click and drag any of the headings to reorder the information display. You can identify your clips on the basis of their data rather than how they look visually. For example, you can have a number of audio clips with similar names that are easily identified on the basis of their duration. To make the identification process simpler, drag the duration column to follow the name of the clip.

6. **Resize the information columns.**

   Drag the vertical bar on the right of the column headings. Expand and shrink the size of columns to show information as you work with your clips. Expand the columns to read the content, and then shrink them to conserve space on the screen.

7. **Click the thumbnail button to return the Project window to its default view.**

   This layout is convenient for most people. It shows you a thumbnail of the clip, as well as basic information about the clip including the name, type of clip, and frame size (except for audio clips).

8. **To resize the two columns in the Project window, drag the double-arrows at the bottom of the window left or right.**

   Sometimes you want to see the names of the bins clearly, while other times it is more important to view information about the clips. Resizing the columns is an easy way to read information about your project without having to resize the entire Project window.

9. **Click the arrow at the top right of the Project window column headers.**
A menu containing several Project window commands opens. Choose Project Window Options from the list to open the Project Window Options dialog box.

10. **Choose the smallest icon in the Icons list and click OK to close the dialog box.**
There are four sizes of icon to choose from. You are working with a large number of clips. If you choose the small icon, you can see more clips in the Project window at one time without having to resize the window.

11. **Click a clip in the Name column of the Project window.**
Now the clips are resized, you can view more of them at one time in the same-sized Project window.

12. **Read more information on the clip such as duration of the clip and frame rate.**
The same type and quantity of information is displayed regardless of the icon size.

13. **Choose File→Save to save the file again.**
Or, use the Ctrl + S (⌘ + S) shortcut keys. You have set the Project window view to accommodate the large number of clips in your project and learned how to change the view to access different information about your clips.

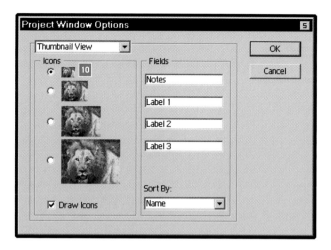

Tutorial
» Organizing the Project Contents into Bins

The last tutorial for this session shows you how to organize your material. It is very important to have control of your project assets. This becomes very obvious when you start working with the files. Video projects can use a great number of files, and anything you can do to enhance your access to the files is a good thing.

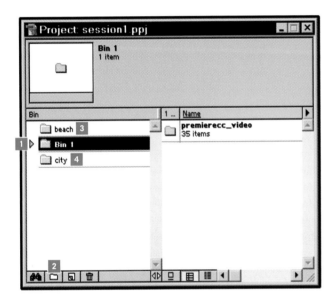

1. **Click the arrow to close Bin 1.**

2. **Click the New Bin button to add a new bin.**
   The Create Bin dialog box opens, displaying a field for you to type a name for the new bin. Bins are given a default numerical name when you create them.

3. **Name the bin beach and click OK.**
   The Create Bin dialog box closes, and the text you typed becomes the bin's name.

4. **Click the New Bin button again, and add another bin named city.**
   The Create Bin dialog box opens again, and this time the default name you see is Bin2. Replace the default by typing in the custom name.

   <TIP>
   Close the Bin1 folder before adding new bins. Otherwise the bins become subfolders of the Bin1.

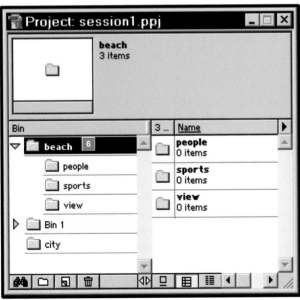

5. **Use the same process to add three more bins.**
   Name the bins people, sports, and view. The set of bins is used to organize some of the content of your project.

6. **Drag each of these new bins to the bin named beach.**
   They become dependent folders of the main bin. The main bin becomes a container for the three sub-bins. Later you will sort the clips into these bins.

7. **Repeat the process once more.**

   This time name the new bins stills and video. Just as you created a set of bins to house the clips for the second segment of
   your movie, you make a set of bins for the clips in the first
   segment of your movie.

8. **Drag each new bin to the bin named city.**

   The two bins become dependent folders of the main bin. The
   city bin is used as a container for the sub-bins.

9. **Click Bin 1 to open it again.**

   Before you can move any of the clips into their bins, you have
   to open the main folder.

10. **Click the premierecc_video bin to open it.**

    This folder contains all the video and still image clips you
    imported into the project in the last tutorial. Opening the bin
    displays its contents in the Project window.

<NOTE>
You add more bins in further sessions to hold title and audio clips.

11. **Move a clip from one bin to another.**

    Click on the clip in the Name column and drag it to the
    appropriate bin in the Bin column. For example, click the
    b_couple.mov file and drag it into the people folder.

12. **Click the bin to see the clip listed.**

    The clip you moved is now listed in the Name column that
    corresponds with the selected bin.

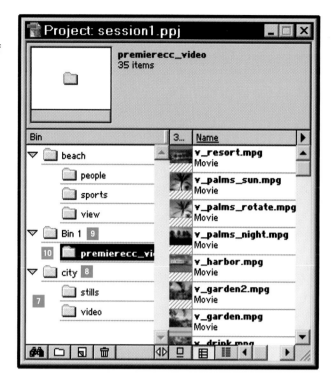

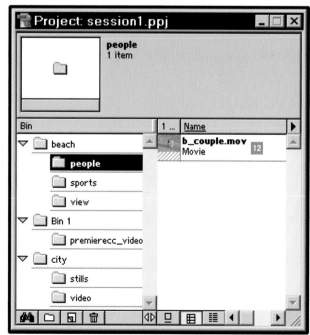

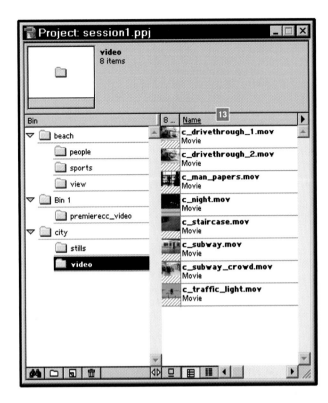

13. **Move the clips into their appropriate bins.**

   Table 1.1 lists the clips and their destination bins. Click each clip in the Name column and drag it to the appropriate bin. When you have completed the process, the premierecc_video bin should be empty. Check the locations of the clips to be sure you moved them to the correct bins.

   < T I P >

   The files are named to correspond with their folder locations, and to provide an abbreviated description of the clip. For example, c_subway_crowd.mov means that the file is intended for use in the city section of the project, shows a crowd of people in a subway, and is a QuickTime movie file.

14. **Select and delete Bin 1.**

   Drag it to the Trashcan, press Delete on the keyboard, right-click the bin and choose Cut from the shortcut menu, or click the trash can icon.

   < N O T E >

   I have used much the same system for organizing files for a number of years. Not only can I keep track of what files are where, but I can also see what I have available for use. The bins do not add to the file size, so you can use as many as you need to keep organized. As you gain experience, you will find a filenaming system that works best for you.

15. **Save the project one more time.**

   At this point, your project contains the first set of video and still image clips you need for upcoming sessions. You have a set of 35 clips sorted into five sub-bins housed within two main bins.

Table 1.1: Project Clip Bins and Contents

Bin	Sub-bin	File
beach	people	b_couple.mov
		b_girl_running_1.mov
		b_girl_running_2.mov
		b_woman_dog.mov
	Sports	s_boards.mpg
		s_boards2.mpg
		s_sail.mpg
		s_surf.mpg
		s_surf_girl.mpg
		s_surf2.mpg
		s_windsurf.mpg
	View	v_beach.mpg
		v_drink.mpg
		v_garden.mpg
		v_garden2.mpg
		v_harbor.mpg
		v_palms_night.mpg
		v_palms_rotate.mpg
		v_palsm_sun.mpg
		v_resort.mpg
city	Stills	city1.jpg
		city2.jpg
		city3.jpg
		city4.jpg
		sign1.jpg
		sign2.jpg
	Video	c_drivethrough_1.mov
		c_drivethrough_2.mov
		c_man_papers.mov
		c_night.mov
		c_staircase.mov
		c_subway.mov
		c_subway_crowd.mov
		c_traffic_light.mov

» Session Review

This session introduced you to working with Premiere. It included lessons on starting a project and using the Load Project Settings window, as well as creating and saving custom settings. Once you were into the program proper, you learned how to import files, how to save a project, how to use and customize the Project window, and how to organize a collection of clips.

Your project is assembled. All the video and still image files are in the project, which has been saved on your hard drive. The project contains 35 files at this point. When you initially brought the files into your project, they were contained in one folder, starting with a couple walking on a beach. You should also have a system of bins in place. The beach bin should contain three sub-bins; the city bin should contain two sub-bins. Footage of similar type should be stored in each bin. For example, the young lady shown in the final figure of this session is the subject of a clip named b_girl_running_2.mov, which is one of four clips in the beach sub-bin named people.

Here are some questions to help you review the information in this session. You can find the answer to each question in the tutorial noted in parentheses.

1. Is it necessary to create settings every time you start a new project? (See "Tutorial: Choosing General Project Settings.")

2. What editing mode can be used regardless of your operating system? (See "Tutorial: Customizing Project Settings.")

3. Is a preview automatically generated for audio in a project? (See "Tutorial: Choosing General Project Settings.")

4. Will a Real Time Preview be used in your project by default? (See "Tutorial: Choosing General Project Settings.")

5. What does timebase refer to? (See "Discussion: Understanding the General Project Settings.")

6. What is a codec? (See "Discussion: Understanding Characteristics of Video and Audio.")

7. What is an aspect ratio? What does it apply to? (See "Discussion: Understanding Characteristics of Video and Audio.")

8. Must the frame rate for building a project be the same as for the finished output? (See "Discussion: Understanding Characteristics of Video and Audio.")

9. What effect does increasing audio sample quality have on file size? (See "Discussion: Understanding Characteristics of Video and Audio.")

10. What is the most space-efficient method of handling still images in a project? (See "Discussion: Choosing Characteristics for Previews.")

11. Can you import files from more than one location into a project? (See "Tutorial: Importing Footage.")

12. Where is the best place to store your project files? (See "Tutorial: Importing Footage.")

13. What is the best way to name your project? (See "Tutorial: Importing Footage.")

14. What is the best way to view clips in the Project window? (See "Tutorial: Working with the Project Window.")

15. Should you always display information about your clips in the same way? (See "Tutorial: Working with the Project Window.")

16. How do you preview a clip in the Project window? (See "Tutorial: Working with the Project Window.")

Session 2

Assembling the Project

Session Introduction

The Timeline is Premiere's main work area — this is where it all happens. Clips are edited, manipulated, and enhanced after they are sited on tracks in the Timeline. In this session you learn two different methods of getting your clips into the Timeline. You learn how to use the Storyboard, which gives you a visual overview of your project (just like storyboards used for other types of visual media and motion graphics design). The Storyboard is more like a staging area though, in that you use it to assemble and organize the clips prior to moving them to the Timeline. You can even preview a collection of clips.

In the opening chapters you chose an initial editing space or editing mode for Premiere, and chose A/B Editing mode. You learn to automatically move clips from the Storyboard to the Timeline. The clips are distributed according to the Editing mode, with each clip alternating positions in Video 1A and Video 1B — the two tracks used for A/B Editing mode.

You also learn to add clips directly from the Project window, and how to move both the time ruler and the clips themselves to precise locations. Also in this session, you learn your first editing method — modifying a clip's speed.

TOOLS YOU'LL USE
General and Still Preferences settings, Project window, Storyboard window, Timeline, Duration setting, Automate to Timeline command, Print to Video command, Info window

CD-ROM FILES NEEDED
Session 1 project file you created or the session1.ptl file from the CD-ROM

TIME REQUIRED
90 minutes

Tutorial
» Revising Program Startup Settings

Every time Premiere starts the Load Project Settings window displays, and you have to close the window before you can get to work. The Startup Settings are part of Premiere's preferences. This tutorial teaches you how to change the way the program opens.

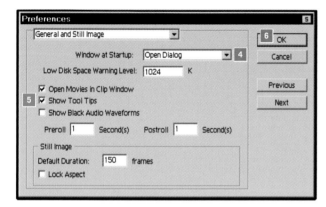

1. **Choose Start→Programs→Adobe→Premiere.**
   Premiere opens, and the Load Project Settings window opens.

2. **Click Cancel in the Load Project Settings window to close it without creating new project settings.**
   You are adjusting the settings first, and then will open your project file.

3. **Choose Edit→Preferences→General and Still Image.**
   The Preferences dialog box opens. The General and Still Image panel displays by default.

4. **Click the dropdown menu for the Window at Startup setting in the General and Still Image panel, and then select Open Dialog.**
   There are four options available in the menu. These include None (no dialog boxes open when you launch Premiere), New Project (the New Project dialog box opens when you launch Premiere), Open Dialog (the Open Project dialog box opens when you launch Premiere), and Load Settings (this is the default option that opens the Load Settings dialog box when you launch Premiere).

5. **Select Show Tool Tips.**
   This option isn't required to reset the startup preference, but because you are here anyway, it's a good idea to choose this setting. When you select this option, you see the names of tools as you hover the cursor over them.

6. **Click OK.**
   The Preferences dialog box closes and you return to the program's interface. The new preferences do not take effect until you have had a project open in the program and saved it. You see a file selection dialog box the next time you open Premiere.

Timebase Notation

Your project uses standard timebase notation at a frame rate of 30. Standard timebase notation uses 00:00:00:00, which indicates hours/minutes/seconds/frames. You can write the entire string, or shorten it to match the length of the clip you are describing. For example, a 2½ second clip can be written as 02:15, and means the clip is 2 seconds and 15 frames long using the project's frame rate of 30. One-half second is 15 frames and is written as 00:15 (0 seconds, 15 frames). It is natural to think one-half second should be written as 00:30, but in timebase notation, this is actually the same thing as writing 01:00, or 1 second. Rest assured, over time the translation becomes second nature!

Tutorial
» Working with a Storyboard

The Storyboard is a program component in which you organize clips in one place before adding them to the project Timeline. This tutorial walks you through how it works.

1. **Choose File➔Open and navigate to the location you stored your project files.**
   You can also choose File➔Open Recent Project and choose your project file from the list.

<NOTE>
If you didn't do the tutorials in Session 1, copy the session1.ptl file from the CD to your hard drive. Open the file and resave it as session2.ptl (or use another filenaming convention).

2. **Resave the project file as** session2.ptl.
   Follow the same naming convention that you used in Session 1. If your file is named session1.ptl, rename it as session2.ptl. The important thing is to distinguish one session project file from another.

3. **Click the video bin to open it.**
   It is nested within the city bin in the Project window. You start the Storyboard using video from this folder.

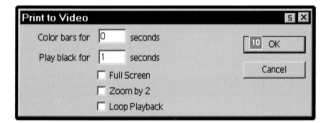

4. **Choose File→New→Storyboard.**
   A blank Storyboard opens. The window is named
   Storyboard:Untitled1.psq.

5. **Click** c_night.mov **and drag it into the Storyboard window.**
   The clip is shown in the Storyboard window. It is numbered, and its duration is also listed below the thumbnail image.

6. **Drag six additional clips from the video bin to the Storyboard window in this order:**
   c_subway_crowd.mov
   c_night.mov
   c_subway.mov
   c_man_papers.mov
   c_drivethrough_1.mov
   c_drivethrough_2.mov
   You have a total of seven clips in the Storyboard now.

7. **Choose File→Save As.**
   Browse to your storage location. Name the file
   project_footage and click OK. The window is renamed
   Storyboard:project_footage.psq. The .psq file format refers to a Storyboard file.

8. **Check the length of the Storyboard at this point.**
   The time display is at the bottom of the Storyboard window, and shows total time at 50:22. The time alters as you work through the next tutorial and change clip properties.

9. **Click Print to Video to preview the Storyboard layout.**
   The Print to Video dialog box opens. There are options for color bars, black screen, video size, and so on. This is one of Premiere's export options. Although it is formally used to print the content of your Timeline directly to videotape, it works very well as a previewing method. Leave the default settings.

10. **Click OK to preview the clips in sequence.**
    The Print to Video command plays the selected clips against a black background. When the sequence is complete, the program reopens. Your Storyboard is now assembled and contains clips from the first segment of the project.

Tutorial
» Setting Clip Durations

Clips have some basic characteristics. A clip has a duration, that is, a length of time that it runs. It also has a speed, which is how fast the clip moves in relation to its default speed of 100%. You adjust the speed of some of the clips in your project for effect.

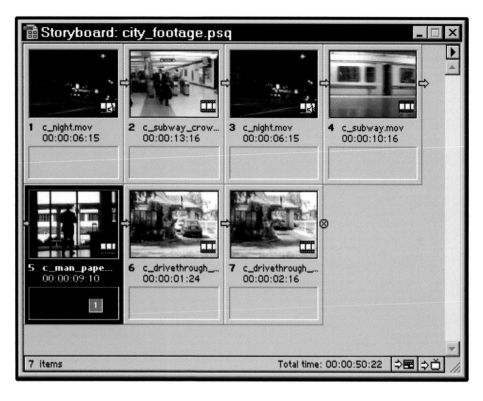

1. **Click** c_man_papers.mov **in the Storyboard window to select it.** Note the duration of the clip, 09:10 (nine seconds and ten frames long). A selected clip is highlighted.

2. **Right-click the clip to open a shortcut menu, and then select Speed.** The Clip Speed dialog box opens, and the New Rate option is selected. The default rate of the clip, 100%, is highlighted in the text field.

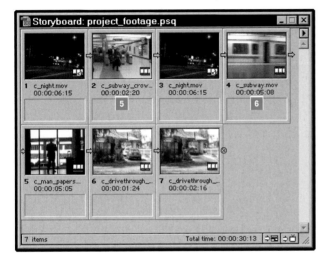

3. **Type** 180 **for the percentage in the New Rate setting box.**
   This means the man in the clip throws the papers into the air at almost twice the speed of the original clip.

4. **Click OK to close the Clip Speed dialog box.**
   You can see the effect of the change in speed. Look at the clip in the Storyboard. The duration for this clip drops from 09:10 to 05:05.

5. **Reset the speed for** c_subway_crowd.mov**.**
   Repeat Steps 2 and 3, typing 500 for the percentage in the New Rate setting box. Click OK to close the Clip Speed dialog box. Check the duration in the Storyboard, which drops from 13:16 to 02:20.

6. **Reset the speed for** c_subway.mov**.**
   Repeat Steps 2 and 3, typing 200 for the percentage in the New Rate setting box. Click OK to close the Clip Speed dialog box. When you check this clip's duration in the Storyboard, you see it drops from 10:16 to 05:08.

7. **Choose File→Save to resave the Storyboard.**
   The Total time notation of the Storyboard changes to reflect the speed changes you have made to the clips. The total length is now 30:13. Leave the Storyboard window open for the next tutorial.

<NOTE>

Speed and duration are inversely proportional. A clip with a duration of two seconds at 100% speed extends to four seconds if you slow the clip down to a speed of 50%. On the other hand, if you increase the speed to 200%, the duration drops to one second. Changes in speed or duration have no effect on the content of the clip, only how long it takes to view it.

Tutorial
» Transferring Clips to the Timeline Automatically

In previous tutorials you assembled and saved a Storyboard, and changed the lengths of certain clips. Now it's time to move the clips to the Timeline. You work with the Storyboard modified and saved in the last tutorial.

1. **At the bottom of the Storyboard window, click the Automate to Timeline button.**
   The Automate to Timeline dialog box opens.

2. **Choose Whole Bin from the Contents dropdown menu.**
   This moves the entire contents of the Storyboard to the Timeline.

3. **Choose Sequentially for the Placement option.**
   Placement refers to the way the clips are added to the Timeline. Sequentially places the clips one after the other on the Timeline. If you want clips to be added at specific locations along the Timeline, you can add markers to the Timeline before starting the automation process.

4. **Choose Beginning for the Insert At location.**
   There are several options for placing the sequence of clips. The clips you added to the Storyboard are used at the beginning of your project. If you have clips added to the Timeline, you can choose to have the Storyboard contents added following the last clip in the Timeline. You can also move the edit line on the Timeline to a specific location and choose the Insert At Edit Line option to add the clips at the edit line.

5. **Type 30 for the Clip Overlap value, and then choose frames as the count type.**
   The count type options are frames and seconds. Your project uses a frame rate of 30 fps (frames per second). This step instructs Premiere to place the clips with an overlap of 30 frames (which is equal to one second).

6. **Click Use Default Transition to deselect it.**
   The Use Default Transition option places transitions between pairs of clips throughout. You add specific transitions in specific locations, so you don't need transitions added by default.

7. **Click OK to close the window and transfer the clips to the Timeline.**
   The clips are distributed in Video 1A and Video 1B tracks with a 30-frame (or one second) overlap. That is, a clip in Video 1B starts 30 frames before the end of the previous clip in Video 1A; the next clip in Video 1A starts 30 frames before the end of the clip in Video 1B and so on.

8. **Save the project and storyboard files.**
   Close the Storyboard window. At this point, your project has seven clips automatically transferred from the Storyboard window to Video 1A and Video 1B. Leave the Timeline open for the next tutorial.

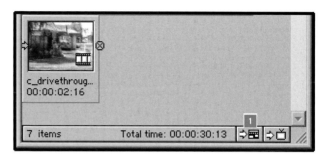

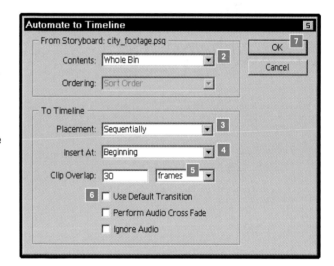

<NOTE>
The size of the clip thumbnails in the Storyboard window are smaller in this image. Click the menu arrow on the Storyboard, choose Storyboard window settings, and then select a different icon size.

<TIP>
You could type 1 for the Clip Overlap value, and then choose seconds as the count type for the same outcome.

Tutorial
» Adjusting Clips in the Timeline

You need to adjust the locations of certain clips once they are added to the Timeline. At this point, you have clips in tracks Video 1A and Video 1B. You can move clips to alternate positions in the same track, or even change tracks. Use the Info window for assistance in placing clips precisely.

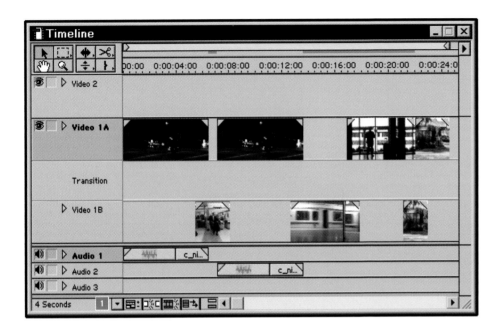

1. **On the Timeline, click the Time Zoom level to open the options list.**
   Choose 4 seconds from the list. Now you can easily see the clips that have been transferred. The Time Zoom level can be set in a range from 1 frame to 8 minutes.

   <TIP>
   Use the Time Zoom control regularly. Along with resizing the Timeline horizontally, this is the one tool that allows you to see what you are doing at the proper magnification and helps preserve your eyesight.

2. **From the main menu selections, click Window→Show Info.**
   The Info window opens. Arrange the Info window and the Timeline on the screen so both are visible. Leave the Info window open as you work through the rest of the steps in this tutorial. If you are unsure of the name of a clip in the Timeline, click to select it, and read its name in the Info window.

   <TIP>
   When you select a clip on the Timeline, the window lists the clip name and other data such as location, duration, and speed.

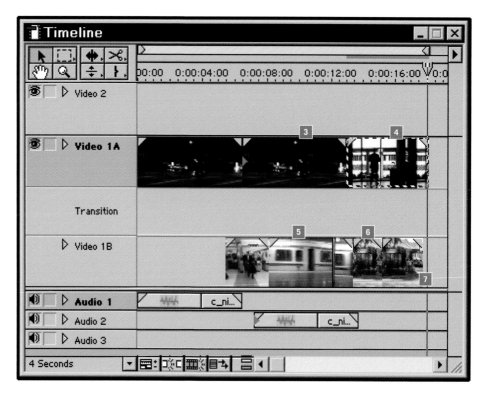

3. **On the Timeline, click the second copy of** c_night.mov.
   Drag it left until it meets the first copy of the clip. At this
   point, you move the clips into their approximate locations. You
   come back to them in the next session to edit their length.

<NOTE>
Look carefully at the second copy of the c_night.mov clip.
Notice a red arrow at the left margin. Now look down to the Audio
2 track. You find an audio clip in this track, also with a red arrow
at the left margin. This means the audio and video clips are
unsynchronized. The audio and video portions of the clip remain
unsynchronized throughout the project.

4. **In Video 1A, click and drag the** c_man_papers.mov **clip left**
   until it meets the other clips (following the two copies of the
   c_night.mov **clips).**

5. **In Video 1B, click and drag the** c_subway.mov **clip left to meet**
   the c_subway_crowd.mov **clip.**
   Don't move the c_subway_crowd.mov clip; it should start
   at 05:15 (check its start time in the Info window).

6. **In Video 1B, click and drag the** c_drivethrough_1.mov **clip**
   left to meet the other clips.

7. **Move the** c_drivethrough_2.mov **clip to the other track.**
   Select the clip in Video 1A, and drag it down to the Video 1B
   track. Drag it left to butt against the other clips.

8. **Click the time ruler at the position where the clips end in the**
   Video 1A track.
   Check the location in the Info window; the clips end at 18:05.
   If not, check back through the steps in this tutorial to see
   where you moved a clip incorrectly.

<TIP>
Check clip information in the Info window. Select the
c_man_papers.mov clip in Video 1A. In the Info window, you
see the Ending At location listed at 00:00:18:05.

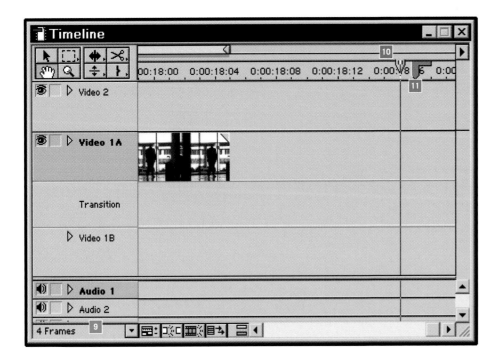

9. **On the Timeline, click the Time Zoom level to open the options list.**
   Choose 4 frames from the list. The Timeline zooms in to a closeup view of the contents.

10. **Click and drag the the time marker to 18:17.**
    Check the cursor position in the Info window to help you position it precisely.

<NOTE>
In the image, the time ruler is moved one frame left of the marker to show you the marker location clearly, and in fact is sitting at 18:16.

11. **Press * (the asterisk) on the number keypad to add a marker to the time ruler.**
    You use the marker location for positioning more clips in the next tutorial.

12. **Save the project.**
    You have clips in tracks Video 1A and Video 1B and have modified their positions. You rearranged clips in the tracks and moved clips from one track to the other.

<TIP>
Timeline markers are most commonly used for coordinating content on the Timeline, but you can also add markers to control Web pages. After the marker is added, double-click it to open the Marker dialog box. Type a Uniform Resource Locator (URL) to link to; you can also specify a specific frame. When the movie is output in a format such as QuickTime and played from a Web page, the embedded URL is recognized when the movie is played, and the page jumps to the URL embedded.

Tutorial
» Modifying the Storyboard

Now you have added the initial batch of clips to the Video 1A and 1B tracks. The second part of the movie also uses clips in the basic tracks. Rather than starting another storyboard, you can add more clips to the same Storyboard you created earlier. You work with the Timeline, Storyboard, and Project windows in this tutorial. Leave all windows open, and move or resize the windows on the screen as you work through the steps.

1. **Click the video bin in the Project window to display its contents.**
   Select the `project_footage.psq` file from the list of content files. A saved Storyboard file is listed in the active bin in the Project window. You originally created and saved the Storyboard file with the video bin in the Project window selected (active).

2. **Select the** `project_footage.psq` **file in the video bin.**
   Drag it to the Storyboard bin listed in the bins column of the Project window. When you automate a Storyboard to the Timeline, a Storyboard bin is added to the Project window, and copies of the clips are added to the bin. You have duplicate copies of clips in the project.

3. **Delete the duplicate clips from the video bin.**
   Select the clip and drag it to the Trashcan at the bottom of the Project window, or press Delete on the keyboard, or right-click the clip to open the shortcut menu and choose Cut. When you add a video clip to the Timeline, a small movie icon appears to the right of the clip name in the Project window. Audio clips show an audio wave icon (clips with both video and audio show both icons).

   Remove duplicates of the clips added to the Storyboard:
   `c_night.mov`
   `c_subway_crowd.mov`
   `c_night.mov`
   `c_subway.mov`
   `c_man_papers.mov`
   `c_drivethrough_1.mov`
   `c_drivethrough_2.mov`

   You have two clips remaining in this bin after removing the duplicates.

4. **Click the Storyboard bin in the Project window to display its contents.**
   Double-click the `project_footage.psq` file to open the Storyboard (you moved the Storyboard file in Step 2).

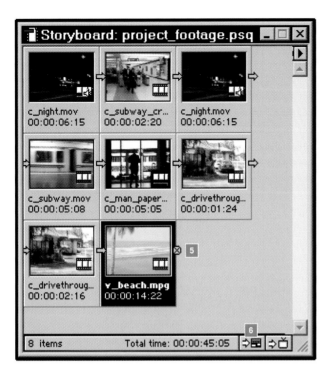

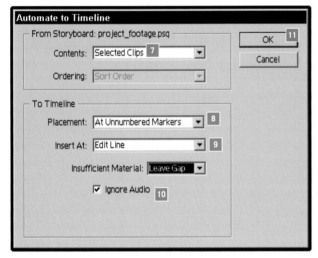

5. **In the Project window, open the view bin (within the beach bin).**
   Drag the v_beach.mpg clip to the Storyboard. Leave the clip selected in the Storyboard. You transfer this clip to the Timeline by itself.

6. **At the bottom of the Storyboard window, click the Automate to Timeline icon to open the Automate to Timeline window.**

7. **In the window, choose Selected Clips from the Contents dropdown menu.**
   You transfer only the selected clip added in Step 5.

8. **Choose At Unnumbered Markers from the Placement dropdown menu.**
   In the previous tutorial you added an unnumbered marker which you use now for placing the selected clip on the Timeline.

9. **For the Insert At option, choose Edit Line.**
   On the Timeline, the Edit Line is at the unnumbered marker's location. The other option is to insert the clip at the beginning of the Timeline.

10. **Click the Ignore Audio setting to select it.**
    The clip contains an audio track as well as video, but you won't use the audio in your project.

11. **Click OK.**
    The Automate to Timeline dialog box closes, and the v_beach.mpg clip is transferred to the Timeline. Arrange the windows on the screen so you can see the Timeline. Leave the Storyboard window open.
    Check the clip in the Timeline. It starts at the time marker location. The clip starts at 18:18 and ends at 33:09.

<TIP>
You can manage space on the Timeline using the Insufficient Material options. The default leaves gaps in the Timeline (you use the default in this tutorial). The second option is Fill to Fit, which means the selected clips will be stretched to fill gaps on the Timeline.

12. **On the Timeline, move the time marker to the 56:00 mark.**
    At this location, you add four more clips to the Timeline using the Storyboard.

<TIP>
Positioning the time marker and its edit line can be tricky. When you get close to the desired location, nudge the edit line one frame at a time back or forward with the left and right arrow keys on the keyboard.

13. **Your Storyboard window is still open, and the view bin (within the beach bin) is open in the Project window.**

    Add four more clips to the Storyboard. Drag these clips from the view bin in the Project window in this order and place them sequentially after the clips in the Storyboard:

    v_palms_sun.mpg

    v_garden.mpg

    v_drink.mpg

    v_palms_night.mpg

14. **When the clips are added to the Storyboard window, Shift + click each of the newly added clips to select them.**

15. **At the bottom of the Storyboard window, click the Automate to Timeline icon to open the Automate to Timeline window.**

16. **In the Automate to Timeline window, choose Selected Clips from the Contents dropdown menu.**

    You transfer the four clips selected in Step 14 to the Timeline.

17. **Choose Edit Line from the Insert At dropdown menu.**

    In Step 12, you moved the edit line along the Timeline to 56:00. The clips are added starting at that location.

18. **Change the Clip Overlap value to 0.**

    The default overlap is 15 frames. You arrange these clips in sequence without overlap.

19. **Deselect the Use Default Transition option.**

    The selected clips are placed in the Timeline end to end and don't require any transitions.

20. **Leave the Ignore Audio setting selected.**

    Although one of the clips in the group of clips you selected includes audio as well as video, you don't use the audio track in the project.

21. **Click OK.**

    The Automate to Timeline dialog box closes, and the clips transfer to the Timeline. Arrange the windows on the screen so you can see the Timeline.

    Check the clip positions in the Timeline. They start at the edit line location and end close to 01:30:00 (one and one-half minutes).

22. **Save the project and storyboard files.**

    Close the Storyboard. Your project now includes two groups of clips added to different areas. You added more clips to the Storyboard and then transferred the clips to the Timeline using different Automate to Timeline methods.

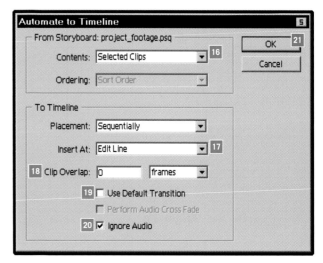

Tutorial
» Adding Clips Directly to the Timeline

You have now added several sets of clips to the Timeline using the storyboard method. This works fine for the Video 1A and Video 1B tracks, but doesn't apply to any of the superimposed tracks. Video 1A and Video 1B, along with the Transitions track, make up the basis of the A/B editing process. All other video tracks are called superimposed tracks, as they overlay — or superimpose — the basic video tracks. You must manually add clips to these tracks as the Storyboard process only applies to the Video 1 tracks. The default set of tracks in a project include one super track named Video 2. In this final tutorial of Session 2, you add clips to this track and adjust their speed from the Timeline. You work with the Timeline and Project windows, and check your progress in the Info window. Before you start the tutorial, arrange the three windows on the screen.

1. **In the Project window, open the video bin (within the city bin).**
   Select the c_staircase.mov clip from the video bin and drag it to the Timeline. Drop the clip into Video 2, with a start position at 01:23.

2. **On the Timeline, right-click the clip to open the shortcut menu.**
   Choose Speed to open the Clip Speed dialog box.

3. **In the Clip Speed dialog box, choose New Rate:.**
   The rate is shown as 100%. Change it to 110, and then click OK. The Clip Speed dialog box closes.

4. **Check the revised length of the clip in the Info window; its duration is 2:02.**
   On the Timeline, you see the length of the clip shortens. Increasing the speed makes the clip run faster, and decreases the duration.

5. **Select the c_traffic_light.mov clip in the Project window.**
   Drag the clip to the Video 2 track. Drop it into position to the right of the clip you added in Step 1.

<TIP>
Clips in the Timeline can be nudged right or left one frame at a time. Select the clip, and then press Alt + , (comma) to move it left one frame; press Alt + . (period) to move right one frame. Use the keyboard keys.

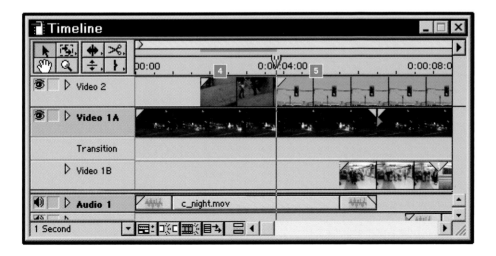

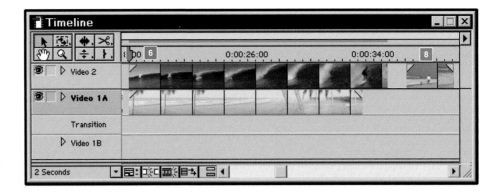

6. **In the Project window, open the sports bin (within the beach bin).**
Select s_surf2.mpg and drag it to Video 2 in the Timeline.
In an earlier tutorial you added a marker at 18:17. Drop the
s_surf2.mpg clip at approximately the marker position.

<NOTE>
The s_surf2.mpg is one of the clips you edit for length in an
upcoming session, so its exact position isn't critical at this time.
You can adjust its location on the Timeline when editing later.

7. **Right-click** s_surf2.mpg, **and choose Speed.**
When the Clip Speed dialog box opens, set the New Rate at
125%, and then click OK to close the Clip Speed dialog box.

8. **In the Project window, open the people bin (within the beach bin).**
Select b_woman_dog.mov and drag it to Video 2 in the
Timeline. Position it at the 36:04 mark. This clip is of the
proper speed, so you don't need to make changes.

<NOTE>
Don't worry about short gaps in the Timeline. Over the course of
the project you adjust and modify clip locations and lengths. In
this session the focus is the placement of clips on the Timeline.

9. **Add another clip to the Timeline sequence.**
   Click the view bin (within the beach bin) in the Project window to open it. Drag v_palms_rotate.mpg to Video 2 at the 41:15 mark. Check the clip's length in the Info window; you see it is 09:28.

10. **Right-click the clip and choose Speed to open the Clip Speed dialog box.**
    Set the New Rate at 80%, and then click OK. This is the first time you have decreased a clip's speed. On the Timeline, you can see the clip's duration has lengthened. Check the duration in the Info window, you see it is 12:13.

11. **Add another clip to Video 2.**
    In the Project window, open the beach bin and select the sports bin to open it. Drag s_surf_girl.mpg from the sports bin to Video 2 at the 55:01 mark.

12. **Add one final clip to the Timeline.**
    In the Project window, select b_girl_running_2.mov from the people bin (within the beach bin). Drag it to Video 2, and place it at the 01:16:19 mark.

13. **Save the project one last time.**
    Now you have superimposed clips added to your project. In this tutorial you added seven clips to the Video 2 track, referred to as a superimposed track since it is layered above the basic Video 1 tracks. The superimposed clips, along with those added through the Storyboard process, make up the Timeline.

To Storyboard or Not to Storyboard?

Clips are added to the Timeline either through the Storyboard or manually. Both options provide a visual display of what you are working with. It is simpler to use the Storyboard window if you are working only with basic tracks, because you can see the sequence of clips side-by-side. After you gain experience with the program, you likely will use both methods. Projects that use numerous superimposed layers are simpler to arrange manually (or in conjunction with the basic tracks laid down in the Storyboard window). If you are working on a simple A/B track project that can be reused a number of times with minor changes, such as a corporate presentation, you may find that saving and reusing storyboards is a timesaver.

» Session Review

This session covered the two different ways to add clips to a project. The Storyboard window, a new feature as of version 6.0, and the ever-popular drag-and-drop method are both ways to move clips from the Project window to the Timeline. This session also included lessons on working with clip durations, managing tracks in the Timeline, and moving clips on tracks.

Your project has an actual Timeline now! Granted, it doesn't look like a movie yet, but the video has a sequence. Your Timeline runs for one and one-half minutes and contains more than a dozen clips. As you scroll across the Timeline, you can see how the project segments take shape. The first section of the project contains street and city scenes. The second segment starts with the beach video, which you can see at the start of this session, and ends with the final image in this session, showing palm trees at night.

The following questions are to help you review the information from this session. The answers to the questions are in the tutorials noted in parentheses.

1. Can you change the way Premiere starts up? (See "Tutorial: Revising Program Startup Settings.")

2. Can you change the order of clips in the Storyboard window? (See "Tutorial: Working with a Storyboard.")

3. What information about a clip is shown in the Storyboard window? (See "Tutorial: Working with a Storyboard.")

4. Can you preview a clip sequence from the Storyboard window? (See "Tutorial: Working with a Storyboard.")

5. Can you save a storyboard? Where? (See "Tutorial: Working with a Storyboard.")

6. What is the default speed of a clip? (See "Tutorial: Setting Clip Durations.")

7. How are clip speed and duration related? (See "Tutorial: Setting Clip Durations.")

8. How should you express the duration of a clip? (See "Tutorial: Setting Clip Durations.")

9. Can you specify a Timeline location for clips transferred from the Storyboard? (See "Tutorial: Transferring Clips to the Timeline Automatically.")

10. What information is displayed in the Info window? (See "Tutorial: Adjusting Clips in the Timeline.")

11. Where is the Time Zoom control, and how is it used? (See "Tutorial: Adjusting Clips in the Timeline.")

12. What is the significance of a red arrow appearing on the margin of a clip when you move it in the Timeline? (See "Tutorial: Adjusting Clips in the Timeline.")

13. How can you tell a clip has been added to the Timeline when you are working in the Project window? (See "Tutorial: Modifying the Storyboard.")

14. Can a clip be added to a specific Timeline location from the Storyboard window? (See "Tutorial: Modifying the Storyboard.")

15. Can a clip be added to any track from the Storyboard window? (See "Tutorial: Adding Clips Directly to the Timeline.")

16. How can you move a clip precisely in the Timeline? (See "Tutorial: Adding Clips Directly to the Timeline.")

Part III
Basic Editing

Working with Clips

Session Introduction

When you look at the project you have created so far, you can see clips spaced and grouped in different ways along the Timeline. This is the basic set of clips that makes up much of the finished movie. Certain clips are the right length, but others must be shortened to fit in a particular location. One core function of Premiere is editing. In this session, you begin the editing process and learn to edit clips in the Clips window. You also learn how to adjust modified clips in the Timeline. You learn different ways to preview your work, including how to manually drag the edit line or scrub the Timeline as well as how to make a preview for a more complete test of segments of the Timeline. Finally, you learn how to add tracks and change the appearance of the Timeline.

TOOLS YOU'LL USE
Clip window, Play tools (Play, Stop, In to Out, Loop, Frame Forward, Frame Back), Timeline window, Select tool, time ruler, time marker, Monitor window, Next Edit and Previous Edit command, Target track menu, Track Options dialog box, Hide/Show Shy Tracks command

CD-ROM FILES NEEDED
Session 2 project file you created or the `session2.ppj` file from the CD-ROM

TIME REQUIRED
90 minutes

Tutorial
» Opening and Trimming Clips in the Clip Window

The Clip window is a convenient place to work with clips. You can view and review clips, adjust the length, and add different types of markers to assist you in clip placement. In this tutorial you trim clips you added to the project. Trimming is a key type of edit. Trimming a clip means changing its In and Out points. An untrimmed clip uses its first frame as its In point and its last frame as its Out point. Adjusting these points defines what parts of a clip you see in your finished movie.

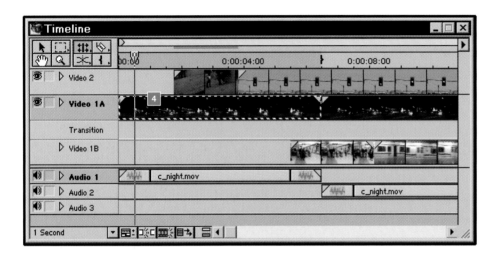

1. **Choose File→Open and navigate to the location you stored your project files.**
   You can also choose File→Open Recent Project and choose your project file from the list.

   <NOTE>
   If you didn't do the tutorials in Session 2, copy the session3.ppj file from the CD to your hard drive. Open the file and resave it as session3.ppj (or use another filenaming convention).

2. **Resave the project file as** session3.ppj.

3. **Choose Window→Timeline to open the Timeline.**
   Click the Time Zoom Level displayed at the lower left corner of the Timeline to open the menu. Choose 1 Second from the list. The time ruler is reset at a magnified rate. Using a higher magnification lets you see the content of the tracks more clearly.

4. **Double-click the first copy of the** c_night.mov **clip starting at 00:24 in Video 1A to open the Clip window.**

5. **Drag the time marker along the jog control to the right to manually advance the clip; drag left to manually reverse the clip.**
   When the current-time marker is at the start of the clip, the small bracket-like icon at the top left of the screen displays. This is the In point for the clip.

6. **Click Play to run the clip.**

7. **Click Stop when you have previewed the clip.**
   Stop when the time marker is close to or at 06:00.

8. **Use the Frame Forward and Frame Backward controls to move the time marker to the exact 06:00 position.**

9. **Click the Mark Out button.**
   When you set the Out point, you can see its icon marking the frame at the top right of the window. The Set Location bar changes from gray to solid yellow. The duration of the clip between the In and Out points displays below the Set Location bar, and the Apply button appears at the bottom of the window.

10. **Click Apply and close the Clip window.**

<NOTE>

Clip windows do not close automatically. Make sure to close them or you end up with dozens of open windows!

11. **In the Timeline, double-click the second copy of the c_night.mov clip in Video 1A starting at 06:24 to open it in the Clip window.**

12. **Click the time display and type the value** 416 **for the Out point.**

<TIP>

You can remove markers, including In and Out markers. Click the Marker icon in the Clip window, click Clear, and then choose the marker you want to remove from the list.

13. **Press Enter (Return) on the keyboard.**

    The timecode now reads 00:00:04:16.

<TIP>

The top of the Clip window shows the name of the clip, as well as its starting location in the Timeline.

14. **Click the Mark Out button.**

    The Out point icon displays at the top right of the window and the Set Location bar changes from gray to solid yellow. The Apply button appears at the bottom of the window.

15. **Read the clip length to be sure it is correct.**

    The duration of the clip between the In and Out points displays below the Set Location bar. The timecode below the Set Location bar now reads 00:04:17.

<NOTE>

Watch how clips are time-labeled in the Clip window. The In point may display a timecode of 00:00:00:00 or 00:00:00:01.

16. **Click Apply to transfer the In and Out point locations to the clip on the Timeline.**

17. **Close the Clip window to return to the Timeline.**

<TIP>

Make sure to open the Info window. Because it shows you clip location and duration, it is invaluable for editing and organizing.

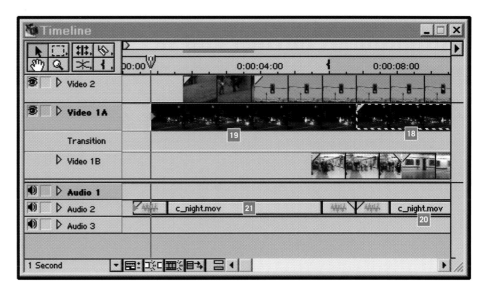

18. **Slide the second copy of the** c_night.mov **clip in Video 1A to the right along the Timeline to its final position starting at 06:24.**

19. **Slide the first copy of the** c_night.mov **clip in Video 1A to the right until it butts against the second copy.**
    The first copy of the c_night.mov clip starts at 00:24.

20. **Select the second copy of the** c_night.mov **audio clip in Audio 2.**
    Drag to align with the beginning of the c_night.mov video clip starting at 06:24.

21. **Select the first copy of the** c_night.mov **audio clip.**
    Drag it to Audio2 and butt it against the second copy. The audio clip starts at 00:09.

22. **Save the project.**
    You have trimmed your first clips! You trimmed the two copies of the c_night.mov clips in the Clip window and repositioned them on the Timeline. You moved the audio and video portions of the clips into their final positions on the Timeline.

Editing Space Options

A workspace is a layout of Premiere windows and palettes for specific purposes. There are two basic editing workspaces, as you learned in Chapter 1. They are A/B Editing and Single-Track Editing modes. In this book, you learn to use Premiere in the A/B Editing workspace. You can create and save your own workspaces as well.

1. **Organize the windows as you wish on the screen.**

2. **Choose Window➔Workspace➔Save Workspace.**

3. **You are prompted for a name. Name the workspace and click Save.**

< N O T E >
The first copy of the audio clip and the video clip have red arrows at their left margins indicating the tracks are out of sync. The arrows are also gone from the second copies of the audio and video tracks. Separate audio and video tracks display this arrow icon when their starting frames are different. It isn't important to have the tracks in sync in this case. In fact, the background sound starts before the video, which is an interesting effect.

Tutorial
» Setting Markers in the Clip Window

Sometimes you need assistance with deciding where you want to trim a clip. It may be obvious where to trim certain clips, but others need tweaking. A simple way to determine where to trim is to add markers as you view the clip. After the markers are in place, adjust them as necessary to get the right clip length, and then trim.

1. **Double-click the** c_man_papers.mov **clip in Video 1A starting at 12:11 to open it in the Clip window.**

2. **Click Play to play the clip.**
   Press * (the asterisk) on the numeric keypad when the play-back head reaches 00:27. A marker icon is displayed in the window.

3. **Click Play to resume the clip playback.**
   Now press * (the asterisk) on the numeric keypad when the playback head reaches 03:26 to add another marker.

4. **Click the Mark Out icon.**
   The Out point icon displays at the top right of the window and the Set Location bar changes from gray to solid yellow. The Apply button appears at the bottom of the window.

5. **Select the first marker.**
   Click the Marker Menu icon to open the menu, and then choose Go To➡Previous. The marker jumps back to the location of the first marker, and its indicator is displayed on the window.

6. **Click the Mark In icon.**
   The Set Location bar shortens. The new length of the trimmed clip is displayed as 3:00.

7. **Click Play In to Out on the controller to view the trimmed clip.**

8. **Click Apply to move the edits to the clip on the Timeline, and then close the Clip window.**

9. **On the Timeline, move the** c_man_papers.mov **clip into its final position on the Timeline at 12:11.**

10. **Trim 15 more clips!**
    Use the techniques you have learned so far in this session. The following table below lists the clips and the In point and Out point settings, their duration, and their starting location on the Timeline. Take your time with this exercise. An endpoint that doesn't need trimming is indicated with "x".

<N O T E>
The clips you have already edited are not included in this list. A full listing of all the clips in the movie as well as their durations and starting times is on the CD. Also, some of the clips aren't included in this list because they are edited using other methods in the next session.

11. **Save the project file.**
    You edited a clip using markers in the Clip window. The c_man_papers.mov clip is in its final location. You trimmed an additional 15 clips and repositioned them on the Timeline. In the next tutorial you check your edits using the Monitor window.

<T I P>
At the very least, save the file when you have finished the edits. I recommend you save your file much more often than that, perhaps after every edit. You never know when something will happen to your computer or work environment that creates a program error. You may lose work, and you will not be happy.

Table 3.1: Information for Editing Clips in Tracks 1A, 1B, and Video 2

Track	Clip Name	Duration	In Point	Out Point	Start Time
1A	v_beach.mpg	07:00	03:16	10:15	18:17
	v_palms_sun.mpg	02:26	x	02:25	1:19:26
	v_drink.mpg	02:23	04:21	07:13	1:23:23
1B	c_subway_crowd.mov	02:15	x	02:14	04:09
	c_subway.mov	03:17	x	03:16	06:24
	c_drivethrough_1.mov	01:16	x	01:15	10:11
	c_drivethrough_2.mov	01:04	00:17	01:20	11:27
	v_garden.mpg	02:22	04:21	x	1:21:21
	v_palms_night.mpg	04:04	01:08	05:11	1:25:26
V2	s_surf2.mpg	04:12	08:15	12:26	28:08
	b_woman_dog.mov	02:29	x	x	36:04
	v_palms_rotate.mpg	09:19	x	09:18	41:15
	s_surf_girl.mpg	03:09	03:00	06:08	55:01
	b_girl_running_2.mov	04:05	00:15	x	1:02:06

Tutorial
» Checking Clips in the Monitor Window

You can trim individual clips in the Clip window and see how and where you trimmed them. I am sure you have noticed the Monitor window that pops up whenever you click the time ruler in the Timeline. This window works in parallel with the Timeline and can be used for editing and trimming clips. You learn to edit clips in the Monitor window in the next session. For now, you get an introduction to the Monitor's functions and how to get around the Monitor window as you use it to check the edits you made in the previous tutorial.

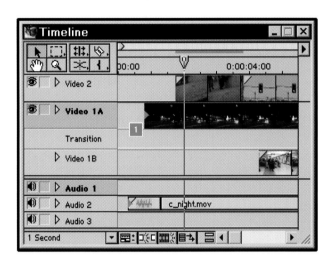

1. **Click the time ruler at the beginning of the first copy of the** c_night.mov **clip in track Video 1A.**
   The edit line moves to this location, which is at 00:24. The Monitor window opens. Arrange the windows on the screen so you can see both the Timeline and Monitor windows.

<TIP>
The Monitor window is part of the A/B Editing workspace. If you have closed the window, reopen it. Choose Window→Monitor.

2. **Read the time marker position on the Monitor window.**
   It also reads 00:24. Check the duration of your project's Timeline at this point, which is 1:30:00.

3. **On the Timeline, drag the time ruler until it is over the** c_stairs.mov **clip in Video 2. The** c_stairs.mov **clip starts at 01:23.**
   The exact time location isn't important as long as it is over this clip somewhere.

<NOTE>
You can move the time marker backward and forward in the Monitor window with both your mouse and the keyboard. On the Monitor window, click the right arrow to move forward one frame, and the back arrow to move backward one frame. On the keyboard, press the right arrow to move forward one frame, and the back arrow to move backward one frame.

4. **Check the Monitor window again.**

   This time you see the c_stairs.mov clip with an "X" icon
   at the top of the window, but don't see the c_night.mov
   image anymore. The Video 2 track is superimposed (in a
   higher track number) over the Video 1A and 1B tracks. The
   c_stairs.mov clip in Video 2 track has no transparency; all
   you see are the people running up the stairs and the street
   scene is hidden. The "X" icon means superimposed tracks are
   used. The icon also displays when you have added effects
   such as transparency or transitions.

5. **On the Monitor window, click the Previous Edit icon.**

   The time marker returns to the beginning of the c_night.mov
   clip. Moving backward through the project, the start of the
   c_night.mov clip is the previous edit from the location you
   chose in Step 3.

<TIP>

Control the position of the edit line on the Timeline using the controls in the Monitor window. In Step 5, the edit line jumps to the
first frame of the clip. As you become comfortable working with
two windows simultaneously, you develop methods of navigating in
both windows.

6. **Click the Next Edit icon.**

   The time marker on both the Monitor and Timeline windows
   jumps to the beginning of the c_subway_crowd.mov clip
   starting at 04:09. The monitor displays two clips simultaneously. You can see the content of both 1A and 1B.

7. **Click Next Edit again.**

   Continue throughout the movie checking the locations of your
   edited clips.

8. **Drag the time marker back to the beginning of your movie again.**

   You can drag the time marker in either the Monitor or the
   Timeline.

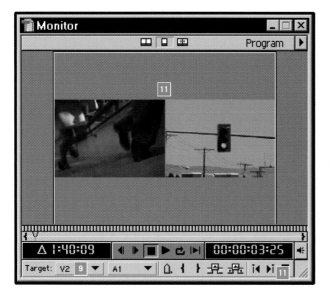

<NOTE>

If you experiment with the Monitor window, you sometimes see the same clip more than once, even if you click Next Edit. Look at the Timeline as you use the Monitor window to see what is happening. The Next Edit sequence includes clips in other tracks along with showing you the edits in the Target track. That is, the time marker jumps from edit to edit, regardless of track.

9. **Click the Target dropdown menu and select V2.**
   The Target track displays as V2, or Video 2. When you work in the Timeline, you can see all tracks simultaneously. In the Monitor window, you must specify the track you want to work with.

10. **Click the Next Edit icon.**
    The time ruler jumps to the beginning of the c_stairs.mov clip, which is the first clip edited in Video 2 (the Target track chosen in Step 9).

11. **Click Next Edit again.**
    The time ruler jumps again, and now you see the last frame of the c_stairs.mov clip and the first frame of the c_traffic_lights.mov clip, the location of the next edit on Video 2.

12. **Check the edits for the rest of this track as well.**
    You have checked the edits you made to the clips in the Timeline in the last tutorial. Rather than moving through the Timeline, selecting clips, and checking their information in the Info window, you used the Monitor window. You saw how the Monitor and Timeline windows are interrelated. You learned to quickly jump between edit locations and how to move through the Monitor timeline. You learned to choose Target tracks. In a later session you learn to edit in the Monitor window.

Tutorial
» Adding Tracks to the Timeline

Now you are going to do some preparation for the next session. The Timeline needs some more tracks. Though you can use dozens of audio and video tracks, you won't need that many!

1. **Click the Track Options Dialog icon.**
   The Track Options dialog box opens.

<NOTE>
You can access the Track Options dialog box through the Timeline window menu. Click the menu arrow, and then choose Track Options.

2. **Click Add.**
   The Add Tracks window opens.

3. **Add two more tracks.**
   Type 2 in the Video Tracks field.

<NOTE>
Premiere is capable of handling 99 audio and 99 video tracks. The program is capable — but is the average user?

4. **Change the Audio Track field to 0.**
   The default setting is 1 additional track.

5. **Click OK to close the Add Tracks window and return to the Track Options dialog box.**

6. **The additional tracks are added to the list.**
   Click OK to close the Track Options dialog box. The two new tracks have now been added to the Timeline and appear above the original tracks in Video 1 and Video 2. In the next session you add clips to the new tracks, named Video 3 and Video 4.

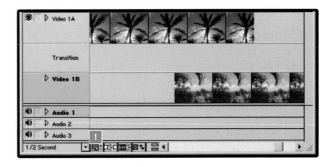

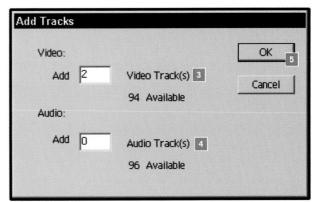

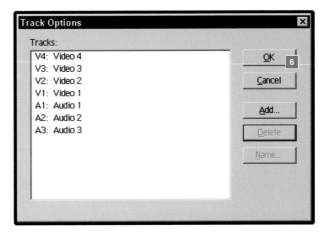

Tutorial
» Changing the Visibility of Tracks

Now that you have several video tracks in your project, you see how crowded the window can become. By the time you have finished assembling the project, you have a total of nine video tracks and four audio tracks. You can hide a track from view in the Timeline by setting the track as Shy. Throughout the sessions you change the layout of the Timeline by changing the shy state, that is, showing and hiding tracks. It is more convenient to hide tracks you are not working with to allow you to see the rest of the Timeline more clearly. You can hide both video and audio tracks. Hiding a track is not the same as turning a track on or off. The output of all tracks, both audio and video, can be toggled on or off. The content of a track that is turned off isn't included in exports or previews. Hiding a track doesn't have any effect on the content of your project. The same icon is toggled for track output and shy state. Video tracks use an eye icon, while audio tracks use a speaker icon.

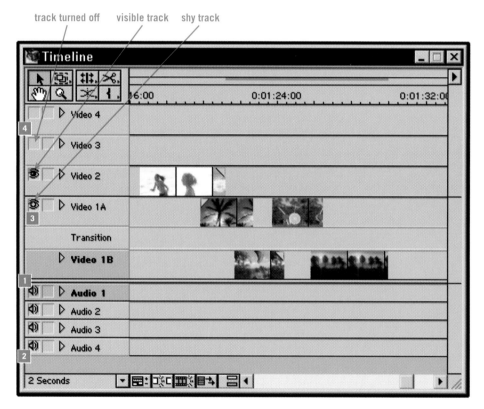

1. **Mark Audio 1 as Shy by changing its Shy State.**
   Ctrl + click (⌘ + click) the (the "speaker" icon). The icon changes to an outline of the speaker.

2. **Mark the remaining audio tracks as Shy.**
   Ctrl + click (⌘ + click) the sound icon for Audio 2, Audio 3, and Audio 4.

3. **Mark the Video 1A and Video 1B tracks as Shy.**
   Ctrl + click (⌘ + click) the eye icon for Video 1. Video 1A and 1B are controlled by the same visibility icon.

4. **Turn off Video 3 and Video 4.**
   Click the eye icon for each track. The eye icon disappears. The output for these two tracks is turned off.

tracks that are turned off are not hidden

5. Hide the tracks.

Click the Timeline menu and choose Hide Shy Tracks. The audio tracks set to Shy, and Video 1, also set to Shy, no longer display in the Timeline.

6. Display the shy tracks.

Click the Timeline menu and choose Show Shy Tracks. All shy tracks are visible again.

7. Change the Shy State of Video 1 track by using the same command you used to set the Shy State.

Ctrl + click (⌘ + click) the eye icon to toggle the Shy State off.

8. Hide the audio tracks again.

Click the Timeline menu and choose Hide Shy Tracks. The audio tracks are hidden from the Timeline again, while the Video 1 tracks remain visible. You won't be working with the audio tracks for several sessions. You can leave them hidden to save screen space. Display them if you are more comfortable viewing the entire project.

9. Save the project.

When you next open the project, the same tracks are hidden. You learned how to manage the visible tracks in the Timeline. Hiding tracks you are not working with is a useful way to organize the Timeline. Not only does it save space on the screen, but showing only those tracks you are working with makes it less confusing. When you work with 10 video tracks you see the value of using this process!

< T I P >

As long as the Hide Shy Tracks command is active in the Timeline menu, each time you toggle a track to Shy, it is hidden instantly.

< T I P >

The content or output of a track is not included in a preview or export of the Timeline when the track is turned off.

< N O T E >

You work with Video 1 in the next session. Follow the next steps to learn how to change the Shy Status of the Video 1 tracks back to visible.

» Session Review

In this session you learned one of the ways to edit your project's clips — how to adjust a clip's length in the Clip window using In and Out points. You learned how to add clip markers to pinpoint locations for setting locations in a clip, how to review the content of a track in the Monitor window, and how to add and work with tracks in the Timeline.

Your basic movie is taking shape. At this point you have most of the clips you need for Video 1A, Video 1B, and Video 2 tracks. The clips were edited to display the segment that best contributes to the overall movie you are building. Certain clips required a great deal of trimming, while others needed little or no trimming. The sample images in this session are a case in point. At the beginning of the session you saw the first frame of the `c_woman_dog.mov` clip. This clip required no trimming, however, the `s_surf2.mpg` clip required a lot of trimming to focus on the action. In the final image in this session you can see a frame from this clip. It looks exciting, and has a great sense of movement.

Here are some questions to help you review the information in this session. You can find the answer to each question in the tutorial noted in parentheses.

1. What is the difference between the first and last frames of a clip and its In and Out points? (See "Tutorial: Opening and Trimming Clips in the Clip Window.")

2. Can the first and last frames of a clip also be its In and Out points? (See "Tutorial: Opening and Trimming Clips in the Clip Window.")

3. What is a simple way to move the time marker in the Clip window to a precise time location? (See "Tutorial: Opening and Trimming Clips in the Clip Window.")

4. Can you remove markers after they are added in the Clip window? (See "Tutorial: Opening and Trimming Clips in the Clip Window.")

5. Why do certain clips show a red arrow at the left margin in their Timeline display? (See "Tutorial: Opening and Trimming Clips in the Clip Window.")

6. What keyboard shortcut can you use for adding markers to a clip? (See "Tutorial: Setting Markers in the Clip Window.")

7. What control plays only the portion of the clip marked with In and Out points in the Clip window? (See "Tutorial: Setting Markers in the Clip Window.")

8. How do you scrub the Timeline? (See "Tutorial: Checking Clips in the Monitor Window.")

9. Why do you sometimes see the same clip more than once when using the Next Edit feature in the Monitor window? (See "Tutorial: Checking Clips in the Monitor Window.")

10. How can you open the Track Options Dialog box? (See "Tutorial: Adding Tracks to the Timeline.")

11. How many tracks can you use in one project? (See "Tutorial: Adding Tracks to the Timeline.")

12. How can you tell if a track will be visible or played in your preview or finished movie? (See "Tutorial: Changing the Visibility of Tracks.")

13. Can a track be Shy and turned off at the same time? (See "Tutorial: Changing the Visibility of Tracks.")

Editing Clips

Session Introduction

In the last session, you started working with the movie clips. You learned to edit by defining a portion of a clip to use in your project. So far you learned to edit clips in the Clip window. As you have seen, making the clips fit into your project is a large part of getting the show on the road. In this session, you use more ways to edit your clips working in the Timeline, starting with a complex, multi-location edit. I also introduce a very important component of this book — the videos. This session and the sessions to follow are accompanied by a movie. Preview the movie before you start the session to see what you are doing. When you are finished working through the session, view the sample movie again and compare it to your movie. Yes, for the first time, you build a movie as well!

TOOLS YOU'LL USE
Timeline window, Project window, Clip window, Monitor window, In Point and Out Point tools (Timeline and Monitor windows), Extract controls (Monitor and Clip windows), Select tool, clip margin indicators (Timeline), Pan tool, Navigator, Ripple Edit command, Sync Mode, Target menu, Copy and Paste commands, Overlay command (Clip window)

CD-ROM FILES NEEDED
Session 3 project file you created or the session3.ppj file from the CD-ROM
surf_xtra.mpg from the extra video folder on the CD-ROM
session4.mpg preview file from the premiere_cc samples folder on the CD-ROM

TIME REQUIRED
90 minutes

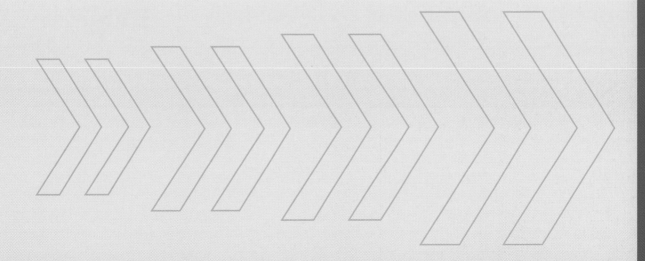

Tutorial
» Editing a Clip Using Multiple Windows

In the last session, you learned how to edit clips in the Clip window. You also saw how the Monitor window looks, and how to use some of its features. In this first tutorial, you use both these windows to perform a complex edit. First you trim the clip, and then you extract an interior section from the clip. Finally, you use the Timeline for positioning. You end up with two separate clips that make a total time of 01:20.

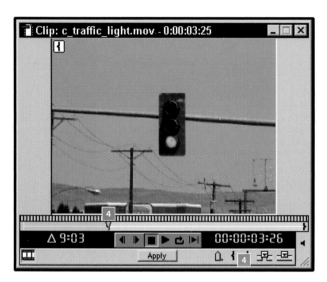

1. **Choose File→Open and navigate to the location where you stored your project files.**
   You can also choose File→Open Recent Project and choose your project file from the list.

<NOTE>

If you didn't do the tutorials in Session 3, copy the session3.ppj file from the CD to your hard drive. Open the file and resave it as session4.ppj (or use another filenaming convention).

2. Resave the project file as session4.ppj.

3. **Double-click the** c_traffic_light.mov **in Video 2 to open it in the Clip window.**
   You perform the edits in the Clip window. Although the original clip is nearly 13 seconds long, the finished edits result in a pair of clips of only 01:20.

4. **In the Clip window, move the time marker to 03:26.**
   Click the In point marker to set the In point. The clip length is now shown as 9:03.

<TIP>

When you adjust In and Out points in the Clip window, an Apply button displays at the bottom of the window. You can either click Apply each time it appears to transfer the changes to the clip in the Timeline, or wait until you have finished your edits and then click Apply before closing the Clip window.

5. **Move the time marker in the Clip window to 09:12.**
   Click the Out point marker to set the Out point. The clip length is now shown as 5:17.

6. **Click Apply to reset the length of the clip in the Timeline.**
   Do not close the Clip window yet.

7. **Move the time marker to 04:25 and press * (the asterisk) on the numeric keypad.**
   An unnumbered marker is added to the clip in the Clip window.

<TIP>

When you add a marker to the clip in the Clip window, a marker is added to the clip on the Timeline as well.

8. **Move the time marker to 08:22, and then press * (the asterisk) on the numeric keypad.**
   A second unnumbered marker is added to the clip in the Clip window. You use the two clip markers when you return to the Timeline to identify clip locations in the larger Timeline. Add the markers to the clip in the Clip window as you can see specific frames clearly; in the Timeline, move the edit line to the marker locations. The edits you make in the traffic light clip are precise, and identifying frames where colors change helps make the final clip sequence appear seamless.

9. **Close the Clip window.**
   On the Timeline, you see the shortened c_traffic_light. mov clip. You also see the two markers you added in the previous steps.

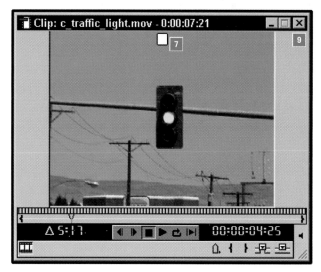

<TIP>

It is important that your time marker be in the correct location for making precise edits, so magnify the Timeline. Click the Time Zoom setting at the bottom left of the Timeline to open the menu list. Choose 8 frames (or less).

> 105

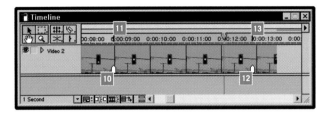

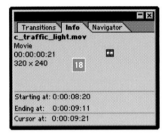

10. **In the Timeline, move the time marker to the location of the first clip marker in the** c_traffic_light.mov **in Video 2.**
    The clip marker was added at the 04:25 frame of the clip — in the Timeline the position is at 08:20.

<N O T E>
To make these images as clear as possible, I marked all but Video 2 as Shy, and then hid the tracks.

11. **In the Monitor window, click In point to set a new marker.**
    An In point marker appears on the time ruler of the Timeline.

12. **In the Timeline, move the time marker to the location of the second clip marker added to the** c_traffic_light.mov **in Video 2.**
    The marker is located at 12:17 on the Timeline.

13. **In the Monitor window click Out point to set a new marker.**
    An Out point marker appears on the Timeline's time ruler.

14. **Check the segment's length; it reads 3:27.**
    The Monitor window shows a small green bar over a portion of its Timeline, which is the length of the edited segment.

15. **Click Extract.**
    You have two separate clip segments. The segment of the clip you identified with Timeline markers in Steps 11 through 13 is removed from the clip. The remainder of the c_traffic_light.mov clip moves left to close the gap

created by removing the segment, a process called extraction. If you choose the other editing method available from the Monitor window (the icon to the left of the Extract icon), the edit is referred to a Lift edit. This means the Timeline segment bracketed by the Timeline markers is removed, and the gap remains.

16. **Choose Window→Info to open the Info window.**

17. **Select the first clip segment on the Timeline.**
    Check its length in the Info window. It is 00:29.

18. **Select the second clip segment on the Timeline.**
    Check its length in the Info window. It is 00:21.
    The combined time for the two segments is 01:20.

<N O T E>
These clips are not in their final Timeline locations. You do that in the next tutorial.

19. **Save the project.**
    You have completed a difficult edit. You started by identifying precise frame locations in the clip window and edited the c_traffic_light.mov clip for length. Then you worked with the Monitor and Timeline windows, adding In and Out points to the Timeline to isolate the segment for editing. You then completed an Extraction edit. What started as a long clip slowly showing a traffic light changing color is now a short clip showing the color change segments.

Tutorial
» Adjusting In and Out Points on the Timeline

Now you're going to do something completely different. You have completed a difficult type of editing. As a reward, here's how to do a simple type of editing. Until you have finished assembling the movie, you most likely will make small adjustments to clips here and there. A simple way to adjust the In and Out points of a clip is to do so directly in the Timeline.

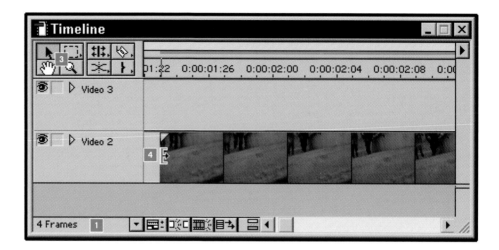

1. **On the Timeline, click the Time Zoom control to open the menu.**
   Choose the 4 Frames zoom level. You require a high magnification to visually edit clips on the Timeline.

2. **Move the Timeline toward the beginning of the project.**
   You are working with the c_staircase.mov clip.

3. **Choose the Select tool in the Timeline.**
   The Select tool changes to other tools on the Timeline depending on its location over a clip.

4. **Move the cursor slowly over the left edge of the**
   c_staircase.mov **clip.**
   The cursor changes to a red bracket and arrow, a margin adjustment tool.

5. **Try to click and drag the left margin of the clip.**
   The margin doesn't change, indicating the clip is showing its first frame.

<TIP>
You can see the margins of a clip in the Timeline. A gray triangle appears in the upper left corner of the frame, indicating the first frame of the clip is displayed.

6. **Scroll through the Timeline to the other end of the**
   c_staircase.mov **clip.**
   There is no gray triangle at the top corner of this end of the clip.

<NOTE>
Move through the Timeline using the scroll bar at the bottom of the window. You also can click the Pan tool (hand) in the Timeline toolbox and use it to drag the displayed portion of the Timeline forward and backward.

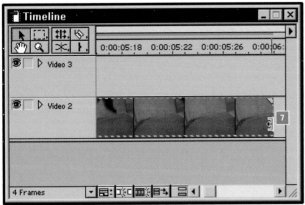

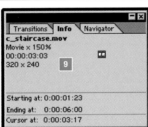

7. **Move the cursor over the clip.**
   When it changes to a red bracket and arrow, click and drag right. The full length of the clip is 04:07 (at a speed of 110%).

< N O T E >

If you want to see what you are doing from a "big picture" point of view, set the zoom level higher. If you are using a zoom factor such as 4 or 8 frames, click and drag beyond the right margin of the Timeline window. The window scrolls as it resizes the clip. Release the mouse, and then check the end of the clip. When you see the gray triangle at the top right of the frame, you have extended the clip to its full length.

8. **Right-click the clip and choose Speed to open the Speed dialog box.**
   Enter 150% as the speed value and click OK to close the dialog box.

9. **With the clip selected in the Timeline, check its length in the Info window.**
   Increasing the speed decreases the duration of the clip. It is 03:03.

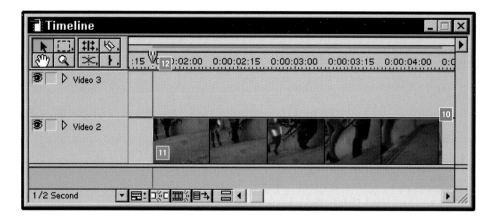

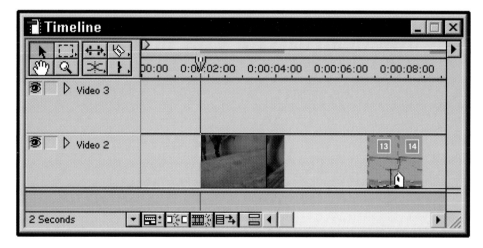

10. **Move the cursor over the end of the clip.**

    When it turns to a bracket and arrow icon, drag the end of the clip left. Watch the duration change in the Info window as you trim (shorten) the clip. Release the mouse when the duration is 02:25.

11. **Move the Timeline back to display the beginning of the clip.**

    Move the cursor over the end of the clip. When it turns to a bracket and arrow icon, drag the end of the clip right. Watch the duration change in the Info window as you trim the clip. Release the mouse when the duration is 02:16.

12. **Move the clip into its final location.**

    Click and drag the clip left (click on the body of the clip, not the end frames). Watch the Starting At time in the Info window as you move the clip. Release the mouse when the Starting At time is 01:23.

13. **Select the first copy of the** c_traffic_light.mov **clip and drag it left to start at 06:24.**

    Click on the body of the clip, not the end frames. Use the Starting At time in the Info window to guide positioning.

14. **Drag the second copy of the clip to butt against the first copy.**

    Use the Info window to assist in placing the clip. The end time for the second clip is 08:14.

15. **Save the project.**

    You have adjusted the c_staircase.mov clip endpoints directly in the Timeline. You also reset the speed and moved the clip into its final position in the project. Finally, you placed the traffic light clips in their final project locations.

Tutorial
» Trimming Clips on the Timeline

You can drag clips directly from the Project window to the Timeline and edit them in place. The simplest way is to move a few clips into place, edit and adjust them, and then go to the next group. In this tutorial, you add certain clips to the Timeline, edit them, and then use the Ripple Delete command to move them into position.

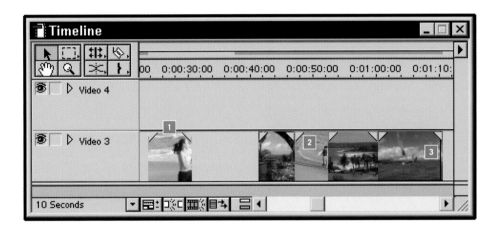

1. **Drag the following clips from the Project window to Video 3.**
   Use the Info window to assist you in placing the clips. Place the clips at the time listed in brackets. If no time is indicated, drag the clip to butt against the prior clip:
   b_girl_running_1.mov (23:21)
   v_garden2.mpg (41:15)
   b_couple.mov
   v_resort.mpg
   s_sail.mpg

2. **Change the speed of the** b_couple.mov **clip.**
   Right-click the clip and choose Speed to open the Clip Speed dialog box. Enter 200% as the speed value, and then click OK. These people walk way too slowly!

3. **Change the speed of the** s_sail.mpg **clip.**
   Right-click the clip, and then choose Speed to open the Clip Speed dialog box. Set the speed at 150%, and then click OK.

Table 4.1: Settings for Timeline Edits

Clip	Length	Move In point to read:	Move End point to read:	Final Duration
v_garden2.mpg	05:03	04:23	02:13	02:13
b_couple.mov	05:05	x	04:20	04:20
v_resort.mpg	07:29	05:20	01:28	01:28
s_sail.mpg	10:09	08:24	07:05	07:05

4. **On the Timeline, click the Time Zoom level.**

   Choose 8 Frames from the menu. Move the Timeline to show the end of the `b_girl_running_1.mov` clip in Video 3.

5. **Drag the end of the clip to shorten it to a final length of 05:29.**

   In the previous tutorial you learned the Selection tool converts to an editing tool when you move it over the ends of a clip on the Timeline. A clip with adjusted In and Out points displays a bracket and arrow cursor when you move over the end frame of the clip. A bracket with a double-ended arrow means you can move the endpoint in either direction to either shorten or lengthen the clip.

6. **Adjust the other clips you added.**

   Follow the settings shown in the table. Endpoints that should remain as is are indicated with an "x".

7. **Drag** `v_garden2.mpg` **to its final location at 41:15.**

   You added this clip to the Timeline at this location originally, but after moving the In point, you move it again.

8. **Right-click the space between the** `v_garden2.mpg` **and** `b_couple.mov` **clips.**

   The space on the Timeline is selected and a shortcut menu displays.

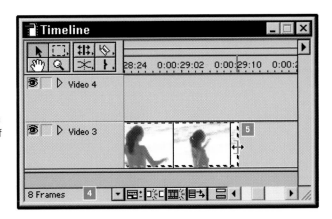

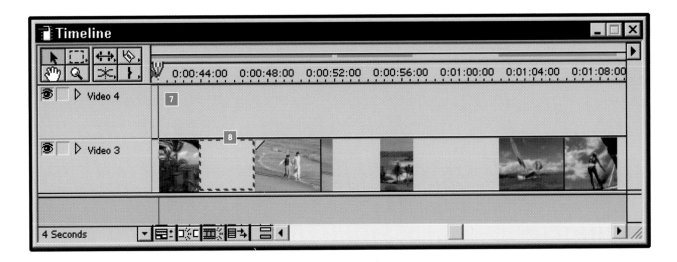

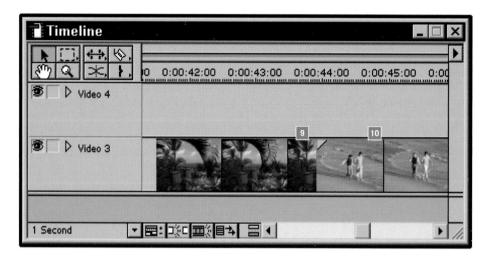

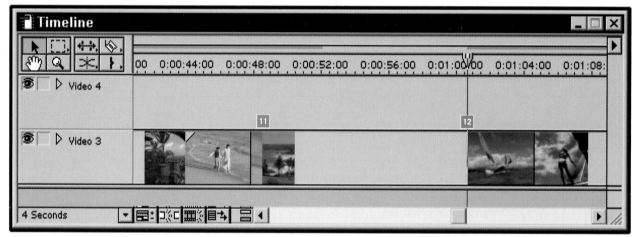

9. **Choose Ripple Delete.**

   The blank space is removed, and the two clips now butt one another on the Timeline.

<NOTE>

A Ripple Edit does just that — it ripples as it edits. This means that when you remove a space by shifting the next clip to close a gap, all the other clips in the track shift the same amount as well.

10. **Check the location of the** b_couple.mov **clips.**

    Select the clip in the Timeline and check its Starting At time in the Info window. It reads 43:28.

11. **Use the Ripple Delete between the** b_couple.mov **and** v_resort.mpg **clips.**

    Right-click the space between the two clips and Choose Ripple Delete.

    Check the final locations of the v_resort.mpg clip in the Info window. Its Starting At time is 48:18.

12. **Select the** s_sail.mpg **clip and drag it to its final location at 1:05:22.**

13. **Save the project.**

    Now you have added several more clips to the Timeline and edited them for length. You have also learned to use the Ripple Delete edit to move content in a track.

Tutorial
» Setting Precise In and Out Points

Here's a situation that can happen often: You have clips up to a certain point in time, and then you have more clips starting at another point in time. You know what you want to fit into the time gap, but not what particular part of a clip. You can change the clip length in the Timeline using In and Out Point tools. This tutorial shows you how to use these tools, along with Timeline markers, to add clips to your Video 4 track.

1. **Move the Timeline time indicator to 50:16.**
   Press (*) on the numeric keypad to add a marker to the Timeline. This marker identifies the location where the trimmed clip starts.

2. **Move the Timeline marker to 53:06.**
   Press (*) on the numeric keyboard to add a second marker to the Timeline. This marker identifies the location where the trimmed clip ends.

3. **Drag the** v_harbor.mpg **clip from the Project window to the Timeline to a start location of 46:16.**
   It is in the view bin (located within the beach bin).

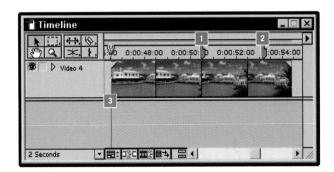

<TIP>
You don't have to use Timeline markers for this process. I have included them as guides for completing this tutorial.

4. **On the Timeline, click the Time Zoom Level to open the menu.**
   Choose a 4- or 8- frame view. You must magnify the Timeline to perform precise edits in the Timeline.

5. **Move the edit line to the marker at 50:16.**
   At a high magnification you clearly see the marker and can position the edit line accurately.

6. **Select the In point tool in the Timeline toolbox.**
   The In and Out Point tools share the bottom right location in the toolbox. Click and hold the tool displayed to open the subpalette. Select the tool, the subpalette closes, and the tool you chose displays in the toolbox.

7. **Move the tool over the clip in the Timeline.**
   Click the edit line at the marker location. The In point for the clip is reset and the frames prior to the edit line are removed from the Timeline.

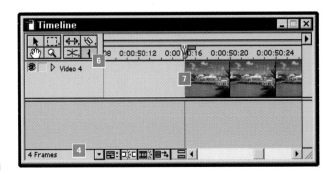

<NOTE>
You can also adjust the zoom value using the Navigator window. Choose Window→Navigator. The current view is outlined by a red box; drag the view left to zoom out and right to zoom in to the Timeline.

8. **Move the Timeline edit line to 58:08.**

9. **Select the Out Point tool in the Timeline toolbox.**
   Click and hold the In Point tool to open the subpalette. Click the Out Point tool to select it. Release the mouse and the Out Point tool is active (it displays in the toolbox).

10. **Move the tool over the clip in the Timeline.**
    Click the edit line at the marker location. The Out point for the clip is reset and the frames following the edit line are removed from the Timeline.

11. **Click the Selection tool in the toolbox.**
    Select the edited clip on the Timeline. Check the final clip length in the Info window. The clip is 02:20 long.

12. **Save the project.**
    You have edited a clip in the Timeline using the In and Out Point tools. This editing method, like the ones you used in previous tutorials, is not permanent. You can readjust the endpoints of the clip using the bracket and arrow icons.

13. **Take a short break.**
    Stretch, feed the cat, and come back for more editing.

More Ways to Edit Clips

For the most part, the methods and locations you use for editing clips depend on your personal preference, as well as the structure of your project. If you are in the finishing stages, you have to edit more cautiously than when you are doing the initial assembly.

The names of edits correspond to how a clip added to a track interacts with the clips before and after it in the track. Some have no effect on the overall length of the project, while others change the times.

These are the basic types of edits:

>> Rolling edit — This is used with two clips. Frames added or subtracted from Clip A are added or subtracted to Clip B. The program duration doesn't change.

>> Ripple edit — Adding or subtracting frames from a clip adds or subtracts frames from the entire project. You used this type of editing when you did ripple deletes in the Timeline.

>> Slip edit — This edit works with single clips and shifts the starting and ending frames of a clip forward or backward. This doesn't affect the length of the project, just the content of the clip that is visible in your project.

>> Slide edit — This edit works with clips surrounding a selected clip. Suppose you have three clips, Clip A, Clip B, and Clip C. If you use the slide edit tool with Clip B and drag left, the Out point of Clip A moves by the number of frames you move Clip B, and the In point of Clip C moves by the same number of frames. A slide edit doesn't affect the length of the project.

Tutorial

» Adding Clips and Tracks Simultaneously

Your project has a total of four video tracks containing most of the clips for your project. In this tutorial, you add clips, do more editing, and learn to add a clip and a track at the same time.

1. **Drag** s_boards.mpg **from the Project window to the Timeline.**
   The clip is in the sports bin (within the beach bin).

2. **Position the clip on Video 4.**
   Place the clip at 53:06 after the harbor clip you added in the last tutorial. The full clip runs for 07:27.

3. **Change the clip speed.**
   Right-click the clip, and then choose Speed. In the Speed dialog box, change the rate to 120%, and then click OK. The clip is now 06:17.

4. **Trim the clip using a method of your choice to a final length of 04:29.**
   Drag it to butt against the v_harbor.mpg clip. The focus of the s_boards.mpg clip is the woman in the black suit passing from left to right across the camera.

5. **Add the** s_jetski.mov **clip to the Timeline following the** s_boards.mpg **clip.**
   The clip is in the sports bin (within the beach bin). The full length of the clip is 11:00. When you add the clip to the Timeline in Video 4 the audio portion of the clip is added to the Timeline in Audio1.

6. **At the bottom of the Timeline, toggle the Sync Mode option to OFF.**
   The icon displays a link when the Sync Mode is ON. When the Sync Mode is on, audio and video portions of a clip are locked together.

7. **Delete the audio track of the clip.**
   Click the s_jetski.mpg track in Audio 1 and press Delete on the keyboard.

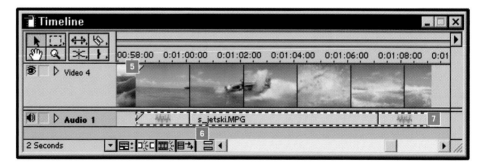

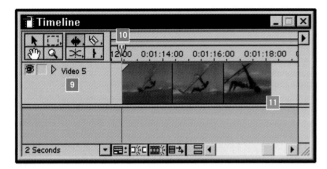

<NOTE>
When the sync mode is off, audio and video portions of a clip move separately. When the mode is on, the components are combined.

<TIP>
The focus of the s_jetski.mpg clip is the jetski, of course. Make sure to end the clip after the skier has passed and the shot is filled with water. Splashing water is a common theme in this project, and is used with effects later in the book.

8. **Trim the clip using a method of your choice to a final length of 04:23 and then butt it against the** s_boards.mpg **clip.**

9. **Select the** s_windsurf.mov **clip from the sports bin (within the beach bin) in the Project window.**
Drag it to the time ruler on the Timeline. Release the mouse. A new track, Video 5, is added, and the s_windsurf.mov clip is added to the track.

<TIP>
You can also drag the clip from the Project window to blank space at the bottom of the window to add a new track.

10. **The clip is added to the Timeline at the position you dragged the clip over the time ruler in Step 9.**
Drag the s_windsurf.mov clip to start at 1:12:12. Use the Info window to assist in positioning the clip.

11. **Trim the clip to a final length of 05:25 using the method of your choice.**
The full clip is 08:19 in length. Check the final length using the Info window.

12. **Save the project.**
You have added three more clips to the project. You learned to use the Sync Mode to separate the audio and video portions of a clip to delete extraneous audio. You also learned to add a clip and a track to the Timeline at the same time. Your project now contains six video tracks.

Tutorial
» Targeting the Location of a Clip

You can add clips to the Timeline using a combination of commands and windows. In this tutorial, you learn to set a location for adding a clip using the edit line in the Timeline and a target track set in the Monitor window. Arrange the screen to display the Monitor and Project windows. You also edit one more clip in this tutorial.

1. **Maximize or open the Monitor window.**
   Select V4 from the Target menu at the bottom left of the Monitor window.

<NOTE>
The Project window is always open; the Monitor window is open, closed, or minimized. To easily display the Monitor window, click the time ruler of the Timeline. The Monitor window displays in front of the Timeline. If you don't see the window, it has been closed. Choose Window→Monitor to open it.

2. **Move the edit line to 01:17:07.**
   Use the left and right arrow keys on the keyboard to nudge the edit line to the correct frame.

3. **In the Project window, open the sports bin (within the beach bin).**
   Right-click s_boards_2.mpg in the Project window to open the shortcut menu.
   Choose Overlay at Edit Line. The clip is added to the Timeline at the edit line location in the track you selected (V4) from the Target menu on the Monitor window.

<NOTE>
When the clip is added to the Timeline, the time marker jumps to the end of the clip, in this case to 01:22:07 (the clip is 05:00 long).

<NOTE>
You can adjust the time marker in either the Timeline or the Monitor window.

4. **On the Timeline, trim the clip to a final length of 03:25 using a method of your choice.**

5. **Delete the audio track of the clip.**
   The Sync Mode was toggled to OFF in the last tutorial, and the audio and video portions of the clip are separate units. This step is optional as it is repeated during the session on audio. Go ahead and remove the track now if you like — some people simply like a tidy Timeline!

6. **Save the project.**
   Your project contains one more clip, edited for length. You used the Monitor instead of the Timeline for placing the s_boards_2.mpg clip, and added the clip directly from the Project window using the Overlay at Edit Line command.

Tutorial
» Swapping Clips

Here's a common situation: You have added most of the clips to a project when you realize you should have put one clip in a different location, moved a different clip into another place, used another clip altogether, and so on. In this tutorial, you learn how to do these things with minimum amounts of time and frustration. You also see how to add a clip from the Clip window. This tutorial uses several windows, so you have to adjust window locations as you work through the steps.

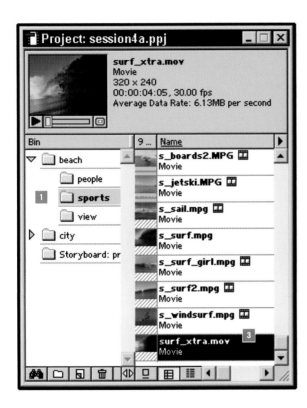

1. **Open the sports bin in the Project window (within the beach bin).**
   You add a clip to this bin.

2. **Choose File→Import File.**
   Browse to the location where you copied your project files.

3. **Select** surf_xtra.mpg, **and then click OK.**
   The file is added to your project and listed in the sports bin.

Replacing Placeholder Clips

Swapping a clip as described in this tutorial is not the same as replacing clips. Sometimes you don't have all the files you need when starting a project. In that case, create an Offline file by choosing File→New→Offline File and setting the characteristics for the file. You can work with this placeholder file until the actual footage is available. To replace a clip, select it in the Timeline or Project window and choose Project→Replace Clips. Locate the file you want to use and click OK to substitute the replacement file.

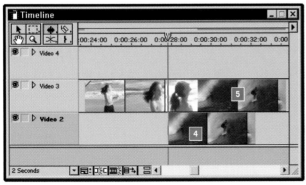

4. **Select the** s_surf2.mpg **clip in the Timeline.**
   Copy it (the clip starts at 27:25 in Video 2). Either press Ctrl + C (⌘ + C) or choose Edit→Copy.

<NOTE>
In an ordinary circumstance, you can merely select the clip, and then drag it to its final location. You use the original copy of the clip for another step.

5. **Click the empty space to the right of the** b_girl_running_1.mov **clip in Video 3.**
   Paste a copy of the clip. Either press Ctrl + V (⌘ + V) or choose Edit→Paste.

6. **Select the pasted clip in Video 3, and then drag it to Video 4 to start at 30:29.**

   When you paste the clip to the area indicated, you can see where it is. You can paste the clip to Video 4, however, it aligns itself against whatever clip comes earlier in the Timeline. This means you have to scroll to find the clip and move it. Selecting a blank space in the Timeline before pasting defines where the clip is pasted.

7. **Open or maximize the Monitor window.**

   Select Video 2 from the Target menu at the bottom left of the Monitor window.

8. **On the Timeline, move the time marker at the start of the original** s_surf2.mpg **clip.**

   This time location reads 27:25.

<**TIP**>

If you want to reposition the time marker in the Monitor window, turn off Video 3 on the Timeline first. Click the eye icon at the left of the track to turn off the track. This way you won't see the clips in Video 3 which overlay your subject clip.

9. **In the Project window, double-click the replacement clip** surf_xtra.mpg **located in the sports bin.**

   It opens in the Clip window.

10. **Preview the clip.**

    Its full length is 04:05.

11. **Click Overlay at the bottom right of the Clip window.**

    The clip drops into the Timeline at the edit line location you set in Step 8.

12. **Select the small portion of the original clip that remains, and then delete it.**

    It is located to the right of the edit line, which moved to the end of the replacement clip when you added it.

13. **Right-click the** surf_xtra.mpg **clip on the Timeline to open the shortcut menu.**

    Choose Speed to open the Clip Speed dialog box. Change the speed of the clip to 150%, and then click OK to close the dialog box.

14. **Move the** surf_xtra.mpg **clip to its final location at 28:24.**

    Use the Info window to place the clip precisely.

15. **Save the project.**

    You have added another clip to the project, and also to the Timeline. This time you used copy and paste commands for moving clips, and added a clip directly from the Clip window using the Overlay edit.

» Session Review

In this session, you learned many ways to edit clips. You learned how to combine edit types to achieve a particular goal; and how to use the Timeline, Monitor, and Clip windows for editing. You learned how to import extra clips and ways to replace clips in your project. You also learned a number of ways to adjust the In and Out points of a clip using different windows and tools.

You now have the video clips assembled for your entire project! Many are in their final locations; others are adjusted slightly when you learn to add effects. You now have five tracks in your project and have edited clips placed in all these tracks, such as the following s_windsurf.mpg clip. This is the first frame of the edited clip; the first frame of the unedited clip appears at the beginning of this session. The edited clip is treated to some very interesting effects later in the book.

If you review the sample movie for this session, you can see that there are still some black spots. Most of this black space is taken up by text added later in the project. Also note that many of your clips aren't visible. No need to panic — this is the nature of how a movie is made. Tracks are stacked one atop another, and only the uppermost layer is visible until effects are added.

Answer the following questions to help you review the information in this session. You can find the answers in the tutorial noted in parentheses.

1. What key on the numeric keypad can you use to add markers? (See "Tutorial: Editing a Clip Using Multiple Windows.")

2. What happens when you extract a portion of a clip? (See "Tutorial: Editing a Clip Using Multiple Windows.")

3. What appears on the endpoint of a clip when it is at its maximum length? (See "Tutorial: Adjusting In and Out Points on the Timeline.")

4. Can you adjust the In and Out points of a clip more than once in the Timeline? (See "Tutorial: Adjusting In and Out Points on the Timeline.")

5. What ways can you move the Timeline to view its contents? (See "Tutorial: Adjusting In and Out Points on the Timeline.")

6. Can you tell if a clip can be adjusted by moving the cursor over the end of the clip? (See "Tutorial: Trimming Clips on the Timeline.")

7. How does a Ripple Edit work? (See "Tutorial: Trimming Clips on the Timeline.")

8. How does the Navigator window work? (See "Tutorial: Setting Precise In and Out Points.")

9. Do you have to use the edit line in the Timeline to use the In and Out tools? (See "Tutorial: Setting Precise In and Out Points.")

10. Where in the Timeline do you drag a clip to add a new track? (See "Tutorial: Adding Clips and Tracks Simultaneously.")

11. What is the Target menu on the Monitor window used for? (See "Tutorial: Targeting the Location of a Clip.")

12. If you adjust the time marker in the Timeline, what effect does this have in the Monitor window? (See "Tutorial: Targeting the Location of a Clip.")

13. Can you add a clip to the Timeline directly from the Clip window? (See "Tutorial: Swapping Clips.")

14. Can you copy and paste clips in the Timeline? (See "Tutorial: Swapping Clips.")

» Other Projects

Make a second copy of the project. Use this copy to experiment with different editing techniques. Edit clips again using an alternate method. For example, if you edited a clip in the Timeline, use the Monitor window.

Session 5

Using Transitions

Session Introduction

If you have worked with presentation software such as PowerPoint, you have had an introduction to transitions, which is a method of graphically changing from one image to another. Unlike those found in presentation software, the Premiere transitions are highly customizable. You can vary their start times, end times, positions, and length; use them in combination; and even program some of them to create your own transitions.

The default set of tracks for your project include Video 1A and Video 1B and their Transition track. Transitions are used to transition the clips in Video 1A and Video 1B tracks. In this session, you add transitions to the project. You start with the transitions at the end of the project as these are simple transitions. You learn how to organize the Transitions palette, how to add transitions to the Timeline, how to adjust and configure transitions, how to use both video and still images with transitions, and how to use multiple transitions.

Before you start working on this session, open the sample file, session5.mpg in a player. The file includes one segment from the beginning of the project and two versions of the same segment from the end of the project. Preview the session5.mpg movie to see how different types of transitions look.

TOOLS YOU'LL USE
Transitions palette, transitions, Transitions dialog box, Zoom level control, Razor tool, edit line, Monitor and Clip windows, Duration command, Animate command, New Folder command (Transitions), render-scrub process

CD-ROM FILES NEEDED
Session 4 project file you created or the session4.ppj file from the CD-ROM
session5.mpg preview file from the premiere_cc samples folder on the CD-ROM
v_drink.tif file from the premiere_cc extra video folder on the CD-ROM (if you do not complete the Creating Stills from Video Clips tutorial)

TIME REQUIRED
90 minutes

Tutorial
» Managing Transitions

In this tutorial, you organize the Transitions palette so you can conveniently work on your project. Premiere offers 75 transitions for your designing pleasure — and for plenty of opportunity for creativity and confusion.

1. **Choose File→Open and navigate to the location where you stored your project files.**
   You can also choose File→Open Recent Project and choose your project file from the list.

2. **Resave the project file as** session5.ppj.

3. **Choose Window→Transitions.**
   The Transitions palette opens either with the last settings (if you have changed any settings) or with the default layout.

4. **Click the folder icon at the bottom of the palette to add a new folder.**
   Name the folder (for example, I named the folder premiere_cc). The folder is added to the bottom of the list of transition folders in the Transitions palette.

<NOTE>
To show you the folder contents in the figure, I dragged the subject folders to one location in the list. Your default settings have a different organization.

5. **Click the arrow to the left of the Dissolve heading to open the folder.**
   When the list of Dissolve transitions displays, drag Additive Dissolve to your new folder.

6. **Click the arrow to the left of the Iris heading to open the folder.**
   When the list of Iris transitions displays, drag Iris Square and Iris Round to your new folder.

7. **Click the arrow to the left of the Slide heading to open the folder.**
   When the list of Slide transitions displays, drag Push to your new folder. You have a set of four transitions in your custom folder now.

<NOTE>
If you didn't do the tutorials in Session 4, copy the session4.ppj file from the CD to your hard drive. Open the file and resave it as session5.ppj (or use another filenaming convention).

8. **Drag your folder from the bottom to the top of the palette folders.**
   When you open the Transitions palette, it always opens displaying the folders from the top of the palette down. If you leave your folder at the bottom of the list, you have to scroll down the list of folders to find your custom folder each time you open the palette.

9. **Click the arrow to the left of your custom folder's name to open your folder.**
   You see the four transitions listed in the folder.

10. **Click the arrow at the top right of the Transitions palette to open the Transitions menu.**
    Choose Animate from the menu. A checkmark displays before the Animate command. The icons in the Transitions palette animate, showing their basic effects.

<TIP>
You can leave the icons animated, or turn off the animation at any time. Click the arrow at the top right of the Transitions palette to open the Transitions menu. Click Animate again on the menu to toggle the animation off.

11. **Choose Window→Show Info to open the Info window.**
    The Info window displays information about transitions as well as clip information you have seen in previous sessions.

12. **Click one of the transitions from your folder.**
    The Info window displays the name and a description of the transition, as well as a larger animation. You have created a custom transition folder, learned to work with the Transitions palette, and used the Info window to read more information about transitions.

<TIP>
You often have to search through a number of folders to find the right transition to use. Here's a quick way to manage the contents of the Transitions palette. Choose Transitions→Expand all Folders, or Transitions→Collapse all Folders to open or close them respectively.

Showing and Hiding Transitions

Custom transition layouts are saved from session to session. Delete a custom folder by dragging it to the trashcan icon. The transitions are not removed; they're only hidden. A hidden transition shows the name of the transition in gray, italicized text. To restore a transition to its original condition, select a hidden transition, open the Transitions menu, and choose

Show Selected. You can hide individual transitions or whole folders.

Can't remember where you put a transition? Click Find Transition (the binocular icon), type the name of the transition, and then click Find. If the folder containing the transition you are searching for is open, the transition is highlighted; otherwise its folder is highlighted.

Discussion

Design Considerations

Premiere offers you 75 transitions — more if you consider the set of QuickTime transitions. This doesn't mean you use all of them at the same time! The range of transitions used in one movie depends on a number of factors, including the purposes of the transitions. If you use a transition for its traditional purpose (that is, changing from one visual to another), you limit the number of different types to about three. This doesn't include transitions that are used for specific purposes, such as the ones you use in the beginning of your project. This also doesn't include specific types of material in which the visual effect is the primary message, such as a music video. However, if you are building a training video, a limited number of transitions adds continuity to your project and focuses attention on the content of the video — as it should. Here are guidelines for choosing transitions.

» Match the tempo of transitions to the tempo of your project. This means the rate or rhythm of the activity in the video is matched by the characteristics of the transitions. If you are building a soft or smooth video, with lots of soft images and a similar color palette throughout, don't use sharp rectilinear transitions (transitions that use hard edges such as configurations of boxes or rectangles). They appear jarring and out of place. Instead, use dissolve transitions or mapped transitions that smoothly replace one image with another, which keeps with the style of the project.

» The transition is an appropriate length. Your eyes take about $\frac{1}{4}$ second to move from one side of the screen to the other. During that time, the content of the screen blurs as your eyes refocus. For this reason, make transitions last a minimum of $\frac{1}{4}$ second. For a video running at 30 fps, a good transition length is 77.5 frames in length.

» In a consistent production, use consistent transitions. Use the same length and type of transitions throughout. A set of three or four different transitions often is sufficient and can serve as visual cues to the viewer, along with transitioning visuals. For example, if you build a training video, you can use the same transitions to open major sections and subsections. These serve as cues to the viewer that information is changing.

» In a highly stylized production such as a music video, the rules do not always apply the same way. There are still rules, though! For example, you may use a transition that lasts three or four frames to add excitement. Add excitement rather than confusion by using similar transitions even for such short periods of time. Though you may use more than a handful of transitions for this type of project, use them in a consistent way. Here's another example: Suppose you are using a similar sequence of images several times in the same video. Use cuts and the same types of transitions for each block. The first sequence may use simple cuts and three transitions; the second sequence simple cuts and three other transitions; and so on.

» The key to good design is restraint. Spend time experimenting. Find what you need for your project, but stop when you find it. If the overall impression is something interesting, you have hit the right combination. If it seems jarring, out of place, confusing, or detracts from the content, keep looking.

Tutorial
» Inserting Transitions

Now that you have built a new folder to house the transitions for the project, it's time to add them. In this tutorial, you add the first of the transitions and you also learn how to save time when you use more than one copy of the same transition. You use the Info window to assist with placing the transitions on the Timeline. You used it in the last tutorial and it is still open. Move it to one side of the screen.

1. **Open the Timeline window.**
   Open or maximize the Info window and arrange the windows on the screen along with the Transitions palette.

2. **Drag the Additive Dissolve transition from your folder in the Transitions palette to the Timeline.**
   Drop it into the Transitions track below the v_palms_sun.mpg clip in Video 1A.

3. **Align the transition with the end of the** v_palms_sun.mpg **clip.**
   Click the transition to select it and drag. As you move the transition, you see vertical lines on either side of the transition that help you line it up with the v_palms_sun.mpg clip.

4. **Check the location of the transition in the Info window.**
   It has a duration of 01:01 and starts at 01:21:21.

5. **Double-click the Additive Dissolve transition in the Transition track.**
   The Additive Dissolve Settings dialog box opens in front of the Timeline window.

<TIP>
You need to zoom into the Timeline to precisely place an element, but the Timeline jumps back to the beginning of the project instead of zooming in at the location you want to see. Does this happen to you? If so, you can click the time ruler to move the edit line to the area of the Timeline where you are working. The zoom controls zoom in or out in relation to the position of the edit line.

6. **In the Additive Dissolve Settings dialog box, the Start and End pre-view areas show the letters "A" and "B".**
Click Show Actual Sources to show the project clips in the preview areas. The left preview area shows the clip in Video 1A; the right preview area shows the clip in Video 1B.

7. **Click the track selector arrow so it points downward.**
Downward is the default setting, but check the arrow to make sure. This means the transition starts from Video 1A and ends at Video 1B.

8. **Click OK to close the Addive Dissolve Settings dialog box.**

9. **In the Timeline, select the Additive Dissolve transition, and copy it.**
Either press Ctrl + C (⌘ + C) or choose Edit→Copy.

<TIP>
Transitions are treated like clips on the Timeline. You can copy, paste, and set the lengths (they have no formal In and Out points).

10. **Click the blank space to the right of the Additive Dissolve transi-tion already in place.**
This selects the blank area in the Transition track and defines a paste area.

11. **Paste a copy of the transition into the Transition track.**
Either press Ctrl + V (⌘ + V) or choose Edit→Paste. The tran-sition is copied to the Transition track.

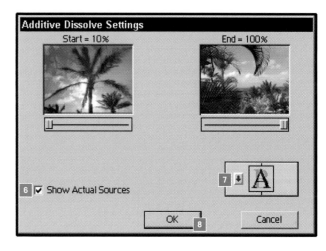

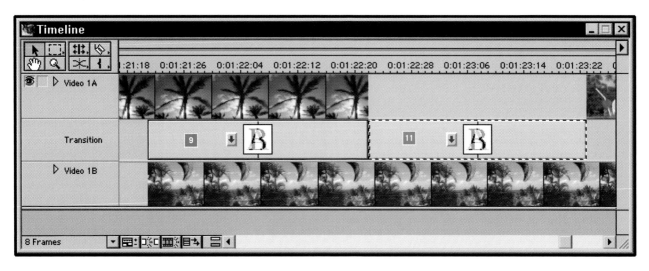

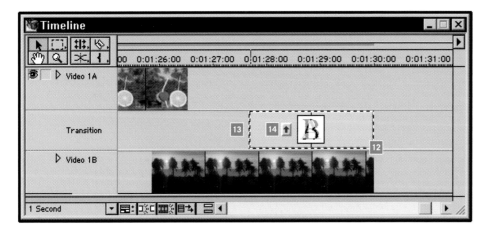

12. **Drag the copy of the transition in the track to the right until the end of it lines up with the end of the** v_palms_nite.mpg **clip at 01:30:00.**

13. **Hold the cursor over the left margin of the transition copy.**
When it turns to a bracketed arrow, drag the left margin. Check the transition's duration in the Info window as you drag the left margin. The final length of the transition is 02:10; its start time is 01:27:20.

14. **Click the direction arrow on the transition display to face upward.**
This copy of the transition starts from Video 1B and ends at Video 1A. You don't have to open the Additive Dissolve Settings dialog box to change the transition's direction.

15. **Save the project.**
Notice that there isn't a clip for the v_palms_nite.mpg clip to transition to. Instead, it fades to black at this point. In a later session you add a title in track Video 1A. The first type of transition is added to the project. You used the Additive Dissolve transition, and added a second copy using copy and paste commands from the Timeline.

<TIP>
When you use a high zoom factor, you can set the direction right from the Timeline. For certain transitions, you can change other settings here as well. Double-click the transition on the Timeline to open its dialog box to see the previews and access other settings.

Tutorial
» Creating Stills from Video Clips

Isn't this interesting? In a session about using transitions, I want you to make still images. This isn't out of place, though. One way you can control how transitions look and work is by combining video and stills. In this tutorial, you learn how to export a frame from a video clip as a still image. You use the still image with a transition in the next tutorial. Before exporting a frame, you trim the clip. This tutorial uses the Timeline, Monitor, and Info windows. Arrange the windows on the screen.

1. **Turn off all video tracks in the Timeline except Video 1A and Video 1B.**
   Click the Track Output (eye) icons at the far left of each track. When you export the frame, the content of visible tracks is exported; you only want to export the image in Video 1A.

2. **Move the edit line to the beginning of the** v_drink.mpg **clip at 01:23:23.**
   Add a Timeline marker (press (*) on the numeric keyboard) to mark the beginning of the clip. Use this marker to identify the start of the edited clip's location later in Step 9.

3. **Click Play on the Monitor window to play the clip.**
   Notice how the beginning of the clip isn't very steady. Click Stop to stop the clip when you have seen the difference between the unsteady and static portions.

4. **Add a Timeline marker at the 01:24:16 frame.**
   This is the frame identifying the end of the unsteady portion of the v_drink.mpg clip. You use this marker to identify the Timeline location for editing in later steps.

< N O T E >
The edit line is moved in the screen shot to show you the marker more clearly.

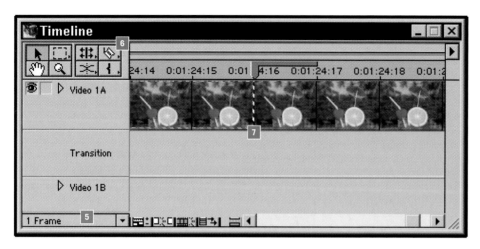

5. **In the Timeline, click the Time Zoom Level to open the menu.**
   Choose the 1 Frame magnification level, the maximum magnification level. You need to see the precise frame you cut in the next step.

6. **Select the Razor tool from the Timeline toolbox.**
   The top right selection in the toolbox is a set of three cutting tools. The default selection is the Razor tool, which cuts the content of a track. The other two tools are the Multiple Razor tool (which cuts through content in multiple tracks), and the Fade Scissors tool (used for adding pairs of control points on audio and video fade control rubberbands).
   Click the Edit line at the 01:24:16 marker location.

7. **Select the first segment (to the left of the Timeline marker).**
   Check the segment length in the Info window. The first segment is 23 frames long, beginning at 01:23:23. Select the second segment (to the right of the Timeline marker). Check the segment length in the Info window; the second segment is 02:00 long, beginning at 01:24:16.

8. **Select the first, shorter segment, and then press Delete.**
   The first segment containing the excessive motion is removed from the Timeline.

9. **Drag the remaining segment in the Timeline to start at the original clip start time of 01:23:23 (you placed a marker at this frame in Step 2).**

10. **Move the edit line to the last frame of the remaining clip.**
    The edit line identifies the frame for export.

11. **Choose File→Export Timeline→Frame.**
    The Export Still Frame dialog box opens. At the bottom left of the window read the default settings for Frame exports. The file type and frame size are listed.

12. **Click Settings at the bottom of the Export Still Frame dialog box.**
    The Export Settings dialog box opens.

< N O T E >

When you work with editing tools on the Timeline, In and Out points are added. Use these for positioning clip segments.

13. **Choose a file type from the File Type dropdown menu.**
Premiere defaults to the standard file type for your operating system. You can choose from several file types: TIFF, GIF, TARGA, and Windows Bitmap. Choose the file type you prefer to work with.

14. **Click Open When Finished to select it.**
When the export is finished, the clip opens in Premiere in the Clip window.

15. **Click OK.**
The Export Still Frame Settings dialog box closes and you return to the Export Still Frame dialog box.

16. **In the Export Still Frame dialog box, name the file and choose a location.**
Save the file in the same hard drive location as the other files in your project. The sample project uses the extra video folder as storage for this and other clips you create in later sessions.

17. **Check the settings.**
At the bottom left of the Export Still Frame dialog box, the file type you chose in Step 13 is listed.

18. **Click Save.**
The frame is exported and saved, and then opens in Premiere for viewing.

19. **Preview the clip in the Clip window.**
This is a static image clip, so the video controller isn't available.

20. **Click Duration at the bottom left of the Clip window to open the Clip Duration dialog box.**
The is shown as 05:00, which is the default still image clip duration. Click Cancel to close the Clip Duration dialog box.

21. **Close the Clip window.**

22. **Save the project.**
You edited the v_drink.mpg clip using the Razor tool to remove a shaky camera segment. You also exported a frame from the clip as a still image clip.

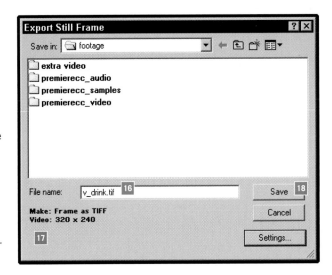

<NOTE>
I generally use TIF because the file size is much smaller than BMP. (Mac OS file types include PICT as a standard file type instead of BMP.)

When to Use Stills as Part of a Transition

Consider a couple of general reasons to use stills. A good example is when a defective segment of a clip is removed and it results in a clip that is too short. Use a still image clip to make up the length (this is what you did in the tutorial).

Sometimes your original clip is so short that using frames for transitioning leaves few frames to show action. Use a still image of the first and/or last frames for transitioning. This way, you won't lose any of the clip's action during the course of the transition.

Tutorial
» Adding Complex Transitions

In the previous tutorial, you created a still image to use for a transition. Now you add the still image clip to the project and use it for a customized transition. This tutorial uses two copies of the Iris Round transition. If you watch old-fashioned cartoons or silent movies, you have seen the Iris Round transition in action. Either a circle on the screen expands from black to show action, or the action shrinks into a circle and disappears to a black screen. This tutorial uses the Timeline, Project, and Clip windows.

1. **Open the view bin (within the beach bin) in the Project window.**
   You import the still image clip in the next step. Opening the view bin defines the location for the imported clip.

2. **Choose File→Import.**
   Browse to the location of the frame you exported and saved as a still image in the last tutorial and click Open. The image clip is added to the view bin.

3. **Double-click the** v_drink.tif **clip in the Project window.**
   The clip opens in the Clip window.

4. **Click Duration at the bottom of the Clip window to open the Clip Duration dialog box.**

< N O T E >

The simplest way to deal with a clip's duration is before you add it to the Timeline. The clip will use a short duration on the Timeline, while the default still clip length is 05:00. Rather than moving the clip to the Timeline and modifying it there, simply reset it in the Clip window. You can also right-click the clip in the Project window to access the Duration command.

5. **Type 00:23 and click OK to close the Clip Duration dialog box.**

6. **Close the Clip window.**

7. **In the Project window, select the** v_drink **still image from the view bin.**
   You can see the new duration setting in the clip summary at the top of the Project window.

8. **Drag the** v_drink **still image clip to the Timeline after the** v_drink.mpg **video clip.**

9. **Open the Transition palette, and open your folder.**
   Drag the Iris Round transition to the Timeline. Drop it in the Transition track between the v_garden.mpg clip in Video 1A and the v_drink.mpg clip in Video 1B.

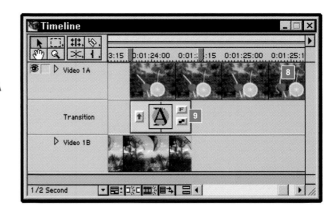

<TIP>
The transition often sizes itself according to the overlap between the clips in tracks Video 1A and Video 1B.

10. **Double-click the transition to open the Iris Round Settings dialog box.**

11. **Click Show Actual Sources at the bottom left of the dialog box.**
    Frames from the clips in Video 1A and Video 1B display in the Start and End preview areas.

12. **Toggle the forward/reverse selector to reverse.**
    It displays an R.

<NOTE>
The direction of the transition is different from the direction of the application. Click the track selector arrow to define the clip that begins a transition. Use the forward/reverse selector to define the direction to play the transition. Clips can go into or come out of another clip. In this case, the garden image goes into the center of the orange.

13. **In the End preview, drag the center point (the small square over-laying the image) to the center of the orange in the image.**
    Transitions such as the Iris Round have a center point that the transition occurs around. The center point of the transition is at the center of the screen by default. You can move the center point to any location on the screen.

14. **Click the anti-aliasing selector to High.**
    The default is Low; click the selector twice to cycle through Medium to High. Anti-aliasing refers to the smoothness of the edges of the transition. The higher the anti-aliasing setting, the smoother the edges of the transition appear.

15. **Click OK to close the Iris Round Settings dialog box.**
    The settings chosen in the dialog box are applied to the transition. You see the transition in action when making previews in later tutorials.

16. **Copy the transition.**
    When you close the Iris Round Settings dialog box, the transition is still selected on the Timeline.

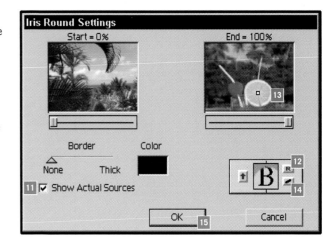

<TIP>
If you want a quick preview of how the transition looks, use the sliders in the transition's settings dialog box. Double-click the transition on the Timeline to open the dialog box. Drag the slider under the Start preview pane from 0% to 100%. You can see how the image changes. Make sure you return the setting to 0% before closing the dialog box. Otherwise, when you preview the transition again, you won't see anything change.

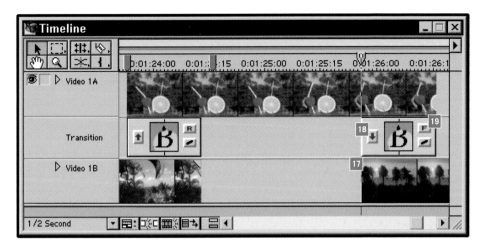

17. **Click the blank area to the right of the transition to select it.**
    Paste the copy into the Transition track. Drag the copy of the transition to the right along the Transition track so it lines up with the start of the v_palms_nite.mpg clip.

18. **Click the track selector arrow to point downward.**
    This changes the direction of the transition from the drink to the final scenic video.

<TIP>
If you cannot see the transition controls on the Timeline, you need to select a larger icon size. Click the Timeline menu arrow (the arrow at the top right of the Timeline window), and select Timeline Window Options. When the Timeline Window Options dialog box opens, choose the largest icon size. Click OK to close the dialog box. The Timeline displays larger icons, and the transition controls are now visible.

19. **Toggle the forward/reverse selector to forward.**
    It displays an F. When the transition plays, the palm trees scene will open from the center point of the orange slice in the drink image.

<TIP>
Double-click the second copy of the transition to open the dialog box. Preview the transition by dragging the sliders under the Start and End preview panes. Note how the transition expands from the center of the orange to the new scene.

20. **Save the project.**
    You added a pair of transitions to the project in this tutorial. You customized the Iris Round transitions to make the scenes change by coming in and out of an orange slice in the image.

Tutorial
» Previewing and Tweaking Content on the Timeline

Sometimes the best-laid plans go awry. In this tutorial, you learn how to render-scrub the Timeline for a better preview of the transitions. Oh no! Maybe the still should have been shorter; maybe the video should have been longer. Here's how to do some tweaking without redoing any work.

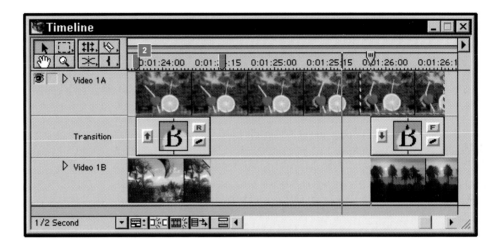

1. **Render-scrub the Timeline to view the effects in the Monitor window.**
   To render-scrub, Press Alt (Option) and drag the edit line in the time ruler. You see the content of the Timeline, complete with the transitions. If you scrub through the Timeline (drag the edit line across the time ruler), you see the uppermost layer of the project, but don't see any added elements such as transitions.

2. **Start the render-scrub before the first Iris Round transition, and end after the second copy of the transition.**
   Pay close attention to how the movie looks in the last few frames prior to the second transition. See how the straw rotates and stops? Three frames go by, and then the second transition starts.

Tweaking Options

You can tweak your layouts many ways. First, decide if it is worth changing at all. Next, look at your options. Certain modifications are much more time consuming than others. For example, in this tutorial, you reset the size of the still and lengthened the In point of the video leading up to the still image. This maintains the length and distribution of all the clips and transitions, so it is a simple, quick modification. You can also shift the other clips and transitions, or you can export the still image again, and then start over — which is not my first choice!

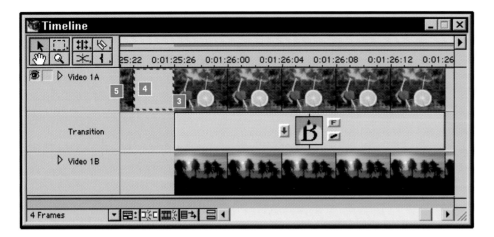

3. **Select the still image clip.**
   Click the left margin of the clip and drag it right. The clip snaps to a length that matches the start of the transition. The v_drink.tif clip is shortened leaving a gap between the still image clip and the video clip versions of v_drink.

4. **Click the gap in Video 1A between the two clips to select it.**
   Check the length of the blank space in the Info window. This space has a duration of 00:03, which is three frames.

5. **Click the v_drink.mpg video and drag the entire clip right to close the gap.**
   Don't just drag the right margin of the v_drink.mpg clip right to fill the gap. Your still image is shot from the last frame, so if you change the last frame, it no longer matches your still image.

6. **Click the left margin of the v_drink.mpg clip.**
   Drag it left to increase the length of the clip by 00:03, which is three frames. This adjusts the In point of the clip three frames, maintains the combined duration of the two clips, and doesn't distort the transition.

7. **Save the project.**
   You have previewed a portion of the Timeline using the render-scrub process. You repaired a flaw in the v_drink.mpg clip's motion by shortening the clip. To make the transition between the video and still image versions of the clip, you learned to extend the clip's duration at the start of the clip, rather than the region with the flaw, to maintain consistency between the last frame of the video clip and the still image clip.

<NOTE>
You can compare the transition created using the "correct" method used in this tutorial and the "incorrect method" (the caution described in Step 5). View the session5.mpg file. Both versions are included in this movie.

Tutorial
» Adding a Different Iris Transition

In this tutorial, you add one more type of Iris transition in the first section of the movie, and then you customize the transition. The Iris Square transition, as you may imagine, works in a similar fashion to the Iris Round transition, except the transition shape is square.

1. **Move the Timeline back to the location of the** c_man_papers.mov **clip, which is approximately the 12-second mark.**

2. **Drag the Iris Square transition from your folder in the Transitions palette to the Transition track between the** c_man_papers.mov **and the** c_drivethrough_2.mov **clips.**
   Line up the transition with the start of the c_man_papers.mov clip.

3. **Set the Iris Square transition's duration to 20 frames.**
   Click the right end of the transition and drag left. Check the duration in the Info window as you resize the transition.

<TIP>
You can resize a transition from either end; the content isn't variable, so where you resize it makes no difference.

4. **Double-click the Transition to open the Iris Square Settings dialog box.**

5. **In the dialog box, click Show Actual Sources.**
   An image of the man throwing paper shows in the Start preview area, the drivethrough shows in the End preview area.

6. **Move the transition's center point.**
   The center point is the small white square at the center of the Start preview. Drag the start location square to the upper right of the Start preview area. The center point defines the location on the screen where the transition opens and closes.

7. **Toggle the track selector arrow to point upward.**
   You see the clip images swap in the preview areas. This means the transition starts with the clip in Video 1B.

8. **Click the anti-aliasing selector to High.**
   Click the indicator twice to move from Low to High. The edges of the transition are smoother with anti-aliasing set to High (at a Low setting the transition edges are slightly jagged).

9. **Toggle the forward/reverse selector to forward.**
   It displays an F. This means the transition shows the clip in Video 1A as the Iris starts to open, gradually covering the clip in Video 1B.

10. **Click OK to close the dialog box and apply the settings.**
    Render-scrub through the transition portion of the Timeline. You see the transition occur in the Monitor window.

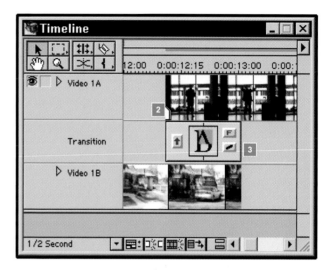

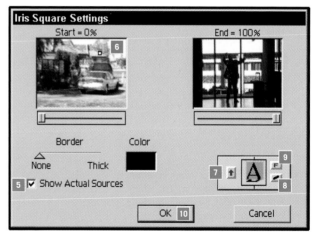

11. **Save the project.**
    You have added a Square Iris transition to your project. This transitions the car drivethrough clip to the man throwing paper. The square iris is a linear transition. The sharp angles of the transition are in keeping with the tone of the first segment of the project.

Tutorial
» Using Multiple Transitions

You aren't restricted to using one transition between a pair of clips, and the transitions don't have to actually transition clips. In this final transitions tutorial, you customize a pair of transitions that split the screen in the opening sequence of the movie. Because the only transition in your custom folder that hasn't been used is the Push transition, you can probably figure out what you use in this tutorial.

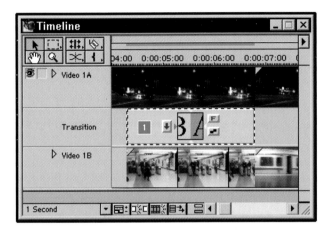

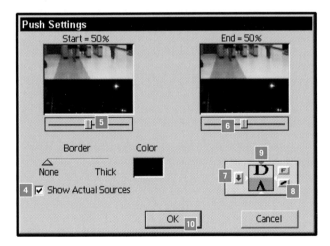

1. **Drag the Push transition from your custom folder to the Timeline.**
   Drop it into the Transition track above the `c_subway_crowd.mov` clip in Video 1B starting at 04:09.

2. **Resize the length of the transition to 02:15.**
   Make sure the transition extends for the length of the `c_subway_crowd.mov` clip (starting at 04:09 and ending at 06:24).

3. **Double-click the transition to open the Push Settings dialog box.**

4. **Click Show Actual Sources.**
   The actual clips' images load into the preview areas.

5. **Drag the Start slider to 50%.**
   Drag the slider below the Start preview area. The value in percent is shown above the preview.

6. **Drag the End slider to 50% using the same method as Step 5.**
   You have created a frozen transition. It is used for a split-screen effect but not for transitioning between clips. The beginning and ending of the transition look exactly the same and use the same settings.

7. **Toggle the track selector arrow to point downward.**
   This starts the transition with the clip in Video 1A.

8. **Click the anti-aliasing selector to High.**
   Click the indicator twice to move from Low to High.

9. **Click the edge selector arrow at the top of the sample to select it.**
   This sets the orientation for the transition, that is, the direction displayed on the screen. If you select one of the edge selector arrows on the left or right sides of the sample, the screen is split vertically.

10. **Click OK to close the Push Settings dialog box.**

11. **Copy the transition.**
    Paste it into the Transition track to the right of the first copy.

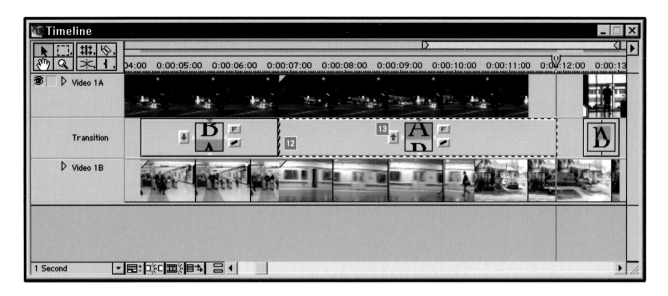

12. **Set the length of the second copy to 05:03.**

    The transition ends at 11:27, which is the same end point as the c_drivethrough_1.mov clip in Video 1B.

13. **Toggle the track selector arrow to point upward.**

    This starts the transition with the clip in Video 1B.

14. **Save the project.**

    You can preview these transitions to see the split-screen effect. The first pair of clips shows the traffic at night in the top half of the screen and people in the subway in the bottom half of the screen. The second pair of clips uses the same split-screen effect, but the traffic at night is in the top half of the screen and the subway plays in the bottom half of the screen. Note that the motion isn't centered — you see the feet of people, for example. This changes in the first session about animation.

» Session Review

This session covered working with transitions. You learned how to add different types of transitions to your project — from simple to customized to specialized. In the first tutorial, you learned how to work with the Transitions palette. Because so many transitions are available, this is a useful exercise. You learned how to add simple transitions and how to copy and paste rather than start new transition insertions for each copy of a transition. You also learned how to create a still to use for transitions, how to use the still for a transition, and then how to tweak it.

In this session, you also learned two of the most important things you can learn about Premiere: 1) In spite of all your planning and designing, until you see the finished product, you won't know how satisfied you are with the work; and 2) anything can be changed with minimal disruption to the rest of your project, as long as you work carefully and knowledgeably. You also learned how to use a different form of Iris transition. The session ended with using transitions that don't transition anything but instead are frozen and used for effect.

You added the transitions to your project and you learned to make attractive visual changes between clips, like the visual change in the following image. This is one of the frames using an Additive Dissolve transition. Compare it to the same frame shown at the beginning of this session. Doesn't this final image look more interesting?

Here are questions to help you review the information in this session. You can find the answer to each question in the tutorial noted in parentheses.

1. Can you add new folders to the Transition palette? (See "Tutorial: Managing Transitions.")
2. What methods can you use to find transitions in the palette? (See "Tutorial: Managing Transitions.")
3. What are the different ways you can use a transition in a project? (See "Discussion: Design Considerations.")
4. How many tracks can use transitions? (See "Tutorial: Inserting Transitions.")
5. In the Timeline, where do you paste a copied transition? (See "Tutorial: Inserting Transitions.")
6. How do you open the Transition dialog box from the Timeline? (See "Tutorial: Inserting Transitions.")
7. How do you select a frame to use for exporting as a still? (See "Tutorial: Creating Stills from Video Clips.")
8. What is the Razor tool and how do you use it? (See "Tutorial: Creating Stills from Video Clips.")
9. Is an exported still automatically added to your project? (See "Tutorial: Creating Stills from Video Clips.")
10. How can you do a quick preview to see how a transition will look? (See "Tutorial: Adding Complex Transitions.")
11. What is the difference between the direction of a transition and the direction the transition plays? (See "Tutorial: Adding Complex Transitions.")
12. How do you render-scrub a Timeline? (See "Tutorial: Previewing and Tweaking Content on the Timeline.")
13. How do you reset the length of a transition in the Timeline? (See "Tutorial: Adding a Different Iris Transition.")
14. How do you control the start and end points of a transition? (See "Tutorial: Using Multiple Transitions.")
15. Can a transition start and end at the same point? What is this called? (See "Tutorial: Using Multiple Transitions.")

» Other Projects

You used a limited number of transitions in this project. Spend time experimenting with the other transitions in the Transitions palette. Make sure the animation feature is activated (choose Transitions➜Animate Icons). Open a copy of the project. Using two clips, try different transitions. Preview the transitions in the Transitions dialog box or with a formal preview. Do you find any that are particularly interesting, particularly attractive, unattractive, or downright ugly? Think of projects in which different types of transitions would be appropriate.

Part IV
Working with Audio

Session 6

Preparing Audio Files

Session Introduction

In this session, you work with the audio in your project. You add numerous sound effect clips to the first segment, learn how to edit the clips, and learn how to use more than one copy of an audio track. You can put your newly gained video editing skills into practice with the audio clips, because many of the processes are the same. You also add new audio tracks to the project and manage the Timeline display.

All the clips you need for the first section of the project are on the CD. For the second section, you make your own custom soundtrack using a Premiere 6.5 plug-in. SmartSound Quicktracks was first introduced in version 6.0 and is expanded in Premiere 6.5. If you don't do the sound-track-building tutorial, a copy of the completed audio file is on the CD. The SmartSounds Quicktracks is a separate installation from the Premiere 6.5 installation. If you do not have it installed, run the Premiere 6.5 installation process again, and install the plug-in. You can work with audio two ways in Premiere: in the Timeline and in the Audio Mixer window. The Audio Mixer window is a feature first introduced in Premiere 6.0 and is designed for working in real-time. You work with it in Session 7. In this session, you work with audio in the Timeline.

TOOLS YOU'LL USE
Audio clip window, audio markers, In and Out markers, Add Tracks command,
Show/Hide Shy Track commands, Add Audio Track command, Timeline window,
SmartSound Quicktracks media and interface

CD-ROM FILES NEEDED
Session 5 project file you created or the session5.ppj file from the CD-ROM
Contents of the premierecc_audio folder from the CD-ROM
session6_gain sample.mpg file from the premierecc_samples folder on the
CD-ROM (for reference)
saucy.mpa file from the premierecc_samples folder on the CD-ROM (if you do
not complete the SmartSound tutorial)
session6.mpg preview file from the premierecc_samples folder (for reference)

TIME REQUIRED
90 minutes

Discussion

How and Why to Use Audio

Think about the last scary movie you watched, or the last science fiction or space epic. Now think what that movie would be like with the sound turned off. You can still see the door slowly open to allow the bad guy to enter, or a star going supernova in a blaze of fiery glory. But so much is missing.

That missing ingredient is sound. Sound has three primary functions in a movie. The first is to provide aural cues for events and activities, such as the ominous creaking of an opening door. Another function is to provide an overall mood for the movie. This is the role of the score. Imagine the scary movie with a light-pop sound track or a military march. It doesn't have quite the same impact, does it? Of course, there are exceptions to the rule. The evil villain may accomplish his nefarious deeds with a particular musical accompaniment. In that case, the music becomes a cue rather than a basic score.

The final sound function is to provide voices or narration. Since the advent of the "talkies" in the 1920s, you expect to hear actors say something when you see their lips move. Many applications use voiceovers as well, also known as narrations. Sometimes you see text on the screen accompanying the voiceover. Textual cues and voiceovers are often used together in training videos. In other types of videos, such as documentaries and movies in which a narrator is used as a tool for developing the plot or back story, the voice is rarely accompanied by text.

So how does this information apply to the task at hand? Your project has two very distinct elements — the city sequence at the start of the project, followed by the beach sequence. The opening sequence illustrates your prospective client's hurried and harried lifestyle. The sound for this segment should not be calm and tranquil. For this segment you build a score composed of several loops and edited segments of a drum track. The drum score is strident enough to contribute to the overall sense of irritation and anxiety conveyed by the video in the first segment of the project (without being annoying).

The segue to the second, vacation sequence begins with the sound of the ocean. This works as a trigger in the minds of the viewers and makes them begin to think about beaches and oceans before the first video even begins. A clever device, if I do say so myself.

Now consider the beach footage. What kind of music do you consider for the types of video you have assembled for the second half of the project? It can be energetic, because many videos of active water sports and activities are included. It can be light because this is a vacation. It also can be age-appropriate and current as well.

The people featured in the video clips are fairly young. Though an old tune like "Take Me Out to the Ball Game" would meet some of the criteria (that is, it is energetic and light), it certainly isn't current. With music, as with other elements of video design, your best responses occur when you tailor the sound track to the interests of your audience.

Match your movie's audio message to the overall message of the movie. Choose music and voices that appeal to the audience you are trying to reach. Audio and video content should match. Accompany soft images with soft music; use heavy drum-laden music for car chases and exploding planets.

Understanding Audio Characteristics

The same type of information always exists on an audio clip. Along with the file name and format, you see the rate, format, and bit depth settings. Rate (also known as sample rate) ranges from 5000 Hz (hertz) to 48000 Hz. A Hertz, by the way, is a unit of frequency (or cycle) in a sound wave of one cycle per second. Human ears normally hear a frequency of up to 20 kHz (20000 Hz or 20000 cycles per second). Better sound quality comes from a higher rate but also requires more processing time and storage space. Audio can be resampled to higher or lower rates (that is, a different rate can be defined). Audio can be upsampled, meaning the rate is increased, or downsampled, meaning the rate is decreased. Resampling requires more processing time.

Formats include mono and stereo. Music sounds best in stereo, while voiceovers work well in mono. Sound is recorded in two channels — left and right. Monaural sound (commonly referred to as mono sound) processes each channel separately, and stereo sound processes both channels simultaneously. Bit depth is either 8-bit or 16-bit and refers to the number of bits of data processed in a second. Voices have good quality with 8-bit sound and music usually sounds better at 16-bit depth.

Tutorial
» Preparing Audio Files

In the first session you imported individual files into your project. In this tutorial, you import audio files to your project as an entire folder. You also learn how to do simple editing from the Project window.

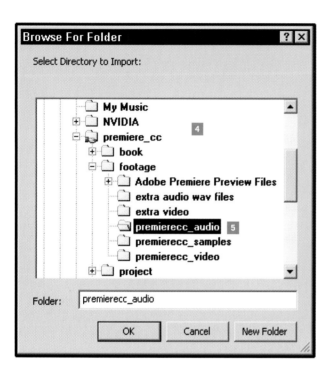

1. **Copy the contents of the premierecc_audio folder from the CD to your storage location.**

2. **Choose File→Open and navigate to the location where you stored your project files.**
   You can also choose File→Open Recent Project and choose your project file from the list. Open session5.ppj.

<NOTE>
If you didn't do the tutorials in Session 5, copy the session5.ppj file from the CD to your hard drive. Open the file and resave it as session6.ppj (or use another filenaming convention).

3. **Resave the project file as** session6.ppj.

4. **Choose File→Import→Folder.**
   The Browse For Folder dialog box opens. Navigate to the location where you stored the files.

5. **Choose the premierecc_audio folder and click OK.**
   The folder is added to the Project window.

<NOTE>
The audio files prepared for this project are in the .mpa format (MPEG audio format).

6. **Open the premierecc_audio folder in the Project window.**
   It contains seven sound clips:
   ```
   beat_heavy.mpa
   car.mpa
   cellphone.mpa
   crowd.mpa
   ocean.mpa
   phone.mpa
   truck_horn.mpa
   ```

7. **Click** car.mpa **to select it.**
   Basic information about the clip is displayed at the top of the Program window, including sound characteristics and file length.

8. **Double-click** car.mpa **to open it in a Clip window.**

9. **Resize the Clip window to view the full extent of the audio waveform.**

10. **Cycle through the zoom selector to display the audio waveform clearly.**
    Choose from four zoom settings; the display in the figure uses the second-from-maximum zoom factor.

11. **Click Play to run the clip.**
    Click Loop to play it repeatedly. Click Stop when you are familiar with the sound.

12. **Move the play head to 00:29.**
    Click into the Set Location area; use the forward and back keys to move forward or back one frame at a time; or use the Frame Forward or Frame Back buttons on the playback controller.

13. **Set the Out point for the** car.mpa **clip.**
    Click the Mark Out button.

14. **Check the length of the audio clip.**
    It is now 29 frames. The length is shown to the left of the playback controller on the Clip window.

15. **Close the Clip window.**
    You won't see any change in the clip information when you return to the Project window. Later, when you add the clip to the Timeline, you see it loads only the portion between the In and Out points.

16. **Trim the other audio clip using the same process.**
    The clip name and the frame at which to set the Out point are listed in Table 6.1.

17. **Save the project.**
    You have added seven sound clips to your project. You imported them using a single command. You learned to edit the clips for length by opening a Clip window from the Project window.

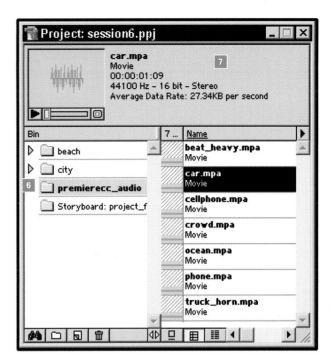

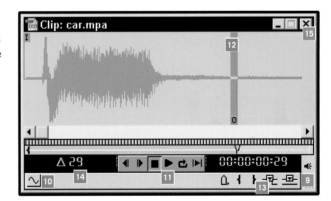

Table 6.1: Data for Trimming Audio Clips

Clip	Set Out Point at...
Cellphone.mpa	01:01
Crowd.mpa	05:01
Phone.mpa	01:00
Truck_horn.mpa	00:25

Tutorial
» Configuring the Timeline

You may ask why the Timeline needs to be configured. After all, you have been using it as it is to this point. However, you have been working mainly with video tracks. In this tutorial, you learn ways to reorganize the Timeline layout to make it simpler to do an all-audio session.

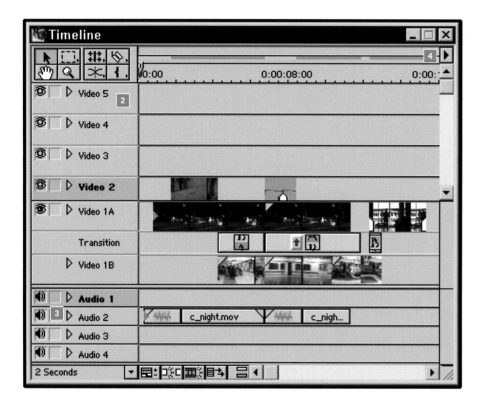

1. **Display all of the project tracks.**
   Click the Timeline menu and choose Show/Hide Tracks.

<NOTE>

Your project may have an alternate configuration of displayed, hidden, and turned off tracks depending on how you last left the project.

2. **Toggle the visibility of Video tracks 2, 3, 4, and 5 to Off.**
   Set the status of the tracks to Shy. Ctrl + click each track's Shy State icon. Leave Video 1 visible. You use this track as reference when placing audio clips.

3. **Make sure all audio tracks are visible.**
   If you have hidden any audio tracks in earlier sessions, remove the Shy status from the audio tracks. Ctrl + Click (⌘ + Click) the Shy State icon to toggle the Shy status off.

4. **Add one additional audio track.**
   Click the Timeline menu and choose Add Audio Track. It is added to the Timeline as Audio 4.

5. **Click the Timeline menu to open it and choose Track Options.**
   The Track Options dialog box opens.

6. **Select A1: Audio 1.**

   The default names of the tracks are numbered in sequence.

7. **Click Name.**

   The Name Track dialog box opens.

8. **Name the track "score".**

   Click OK to close the Name Track dialog box and return to the Track Options dialog box.

9. **Click OK to close the Track Options dialog box.**

   On the Timeline, you see the name of the first audio track changed to "score".

10. **Hide the shy tracks.**

    Click the Timeline menu to open it, and choose Hide Shy Tracks. On the Timeline, only Video 1A and Video 1B and the four audio tracks remain visible.

11. **Drag the Resize bar, which is the divider between the track labels and the tracks themselves, to display the entire track name.**

12. **Save the project.**

    You have configured the Timeline for an audio session. The video tracks required for reference (Video 1A and Video 1B) are visible, all other video tracks are hidden. You added another audio track and renamed Audio 1.

<NOTE>

This configuration is not carved in stone. In my experience, taking extra time to customize what you are viewing is always worth the effort. For a project in which I want to coordinate audio with contents of other video tracks, I toggle the other tracks on and off in addition to using markers (which is covered in a later tutorial).

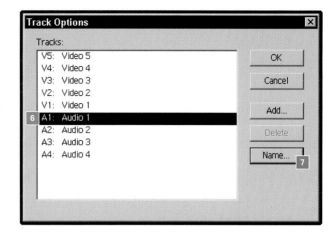

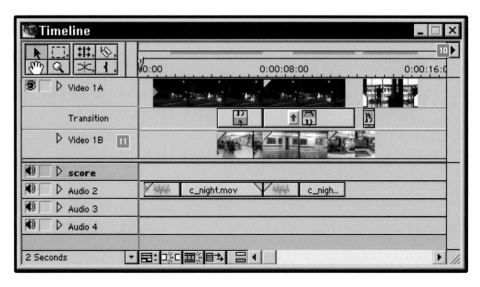

Tutorial

» Adding Trimmed Audio Clips to the Timeline

You have a total of four audio tracks at this point. Audio 1, which you renamed score track in the previous tutorial, is empty. You go back to that later to add the music score. In this tutorial you work with Audio 2, Audio 3, and Audio 4. Remember the audio component of the c_night.mpg clips? They are in Audio 2. In this tutorial, you organize them and add the audio clips you edited for length in a previous tutorial. You work with the Timeline, Project, and Info windows in this tutorial. Arrange the windows on the screen before you start.

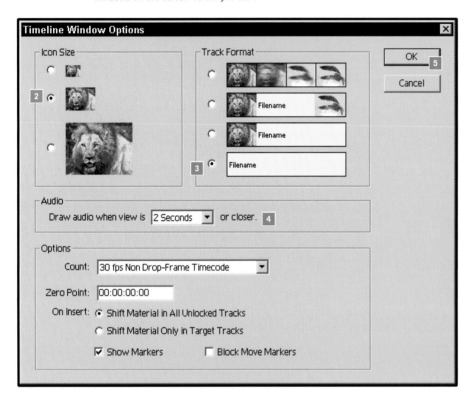

1. **Click the Timeline menu to open it and choose Timeline window options.**
   The Timeline Window Options dialog box opens.

2. **Choose a smaller Icon Size.**
   You are only working with audio and timecode, so the size of the tracks isn't important.

3. **Choose Filename from the Track Format options.**
   The Filename option displays only the clip's name. As you don't need to see the content of the video clips in Video 1, you don't need thumbnails for the video either.

4. **Choose the 2 Seconds option from the Audio dropdown box.**
   The two seconds option means any Timeline magnification at two seconds or less displays a waveform; over two seconds displays a straight line. You see major variations in the waveform at two seconds, but can zoom out of the Timeline enough to see larger sections, necessary for evaluating and reviewing your audio editing.

5. **Click OK to close the Timeline Window Options dialog box.**
   The changes to the Timeline are applied.

< T I P >
If you can't see the audio waveforms, click the arrow to the left of the track's name to open the track.

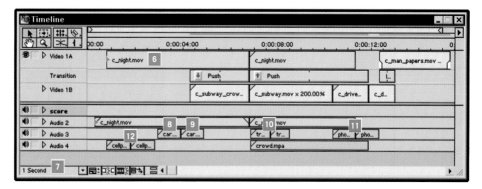

6. **Check and adjust the positions and timing for the** `c_night.mov` **audio clips in Audio 2.**
   Click the first copy to select it. The clip starts at 00:09 with a duration of 06:15. Click the second copy to select it and check its information. The second copy starts at 06:24 and has a duration of 04:17.

7. **Zoom in to the Timeline.**
   Click the Time Zoom Level and choose a zoom factor of one second or less. Unless you are at one second or less, you won't be able to read the names of the clips as you add them.

8. **Drag the** `car.mpa` **clip from the Project window to Audio 3.**
   Position the clip to start at 02:29 and check its position.

9. **Copy the** `car.mpa` **clip.**
   Click the blank track to the right of the clip and paste the second copy into the track.

10. **Drag the** `truck_horn.mpa` **clip from the Project window to Audio 3.**
    Position the clip to start at 06:24. Check its location in the Info window. Copy the clip. Paste a copy of the clip after the original clip just as you did in Step 9 for `car.mpa`.

11. **Drag the** `phone.mpa` **clip from the Project window to Audio 3.**
    Position the clip to start at 10:11. Again, copy and paste a second clip after the original.

12. **Drag the** `cellphone.mpa` **clip from the Project window to Audio 4.**
    Position the clip to start at 01:25. One last time here, paste a second copy after the original.

13. **Move the time marker in the Timeline to the beginning of the project.**
    Click Play in the Monitor window to listen to the sound effects you added.

14. **Save the project.**
    You configured the Timeline for working with audio. Your project contains a collection of sound effects now. The sound effects are still in their raw state.

<NOTE>
No hard and fast requirements exist for adding sound to tracks. If you are using multi-layered sound effects, such as those in the first segment of the project, the relative strengths of the sound are managed by fade controls.

Color Coding in the Timeline

When you have the visual icons turned off, as they are in this tutorial, you can readily see the content of the tracks is color-coded. A video track with an associated audio track is green, such as the `c_night.mov` tracks. Regular video clips are yellow, transitions are blue, and audio clips are aqua. Still images, though none are included in the project yet, are pink.

Tutorial
» Editing Audio Clips in the Timeline

The audio clips you added to the Timeline were edited for length in the Project window before you added them to the Timeline. In this tutorial, you edit a clip in the Timeline and add markers. You also learn how to adjust the appearance of the audio tracks.

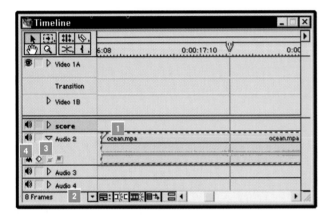

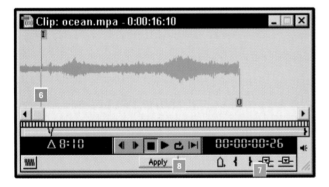

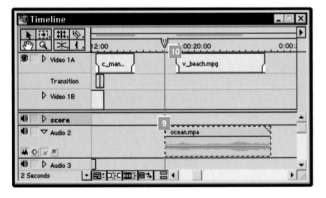

1. **Drag the** ocean.mpa **clip from the Project window to Audio 2 at approximately the 16-second mark.**
   The exact location isn't critical at this point as you move it into its final position after editing.

2. **Set the zoom level to 8 Frames.**
   You are editing the clip in the Timeline and need to see locations on the time ruler clearly.

3. **Click the arrow to the left of the Audio 2 label to open the track.**

4. **Toggle the show/hide audio waveform button to display the waveform.**
   You can see the audio wave displayed.

5. **Double-click the** ocean.mpa **clip to open it in a Clip window.**
   The original length of the clip is 09:06.

6. **Move the player head to 00:26 frames by dragging the slider under the waveform.**

7. **Click Mark In to set the In point, adding a green marker to the waveform and dropping the duration to 08:10.**
   The Apply button displays on the Clip window.

8. **Click Apply to transfer the settings to the Timeline.**
   Close the Clip window.

9. **In the Timeline, drag the** ocean.mpa **clip to its final location, starting at 17:20.**

10. **Move the edit line to 18:17 and press * (asterisk) on the numeric keyboard to add a marker to the Timeline.**
    This marker is used as a reference point for score and ocean wave tracks.

11. **Save the project.**
    You have added the sound of the ocean to your project. You edited the clip from the Timeline. You also added a marker that identifies an important location on the Timeline — in this case, the first video of the beach segment of the movie.

Tutorial
» Adjusting Audio Signal

Your project uses audio from a number of sources. Because neither you nor I recorded the clips, we have no control over the signal strength used. If you listen to the clips, you can hear differences in how loud or strong they sound. The loudness or strength of a clip is referred to as audio gain. In this tutorial, you adjust the gain of the clips so the sound strength is correct throughout the project.

1. **Move the Timeline back to the beginning of the project.**
   You worked with an audio clip from the beach segment of the project. Now you work with the clips in the city segment of the project.

2. **Right-click the first copy of the** c_night.mov **clip in the Timeline.**
   Choose Audio Options→Audio Gain. The Audio Gain dialog box opens.

3. **Click Smart Gain.**
   The Gain Value increases to 200%. Smart Gain adjusts the signal strength of a clip to a standard strength, equal to your computer's capabilities to a maximum of 200%.

4. **Click OK.**
   The Audio Gain dialog box closes.

5. **Using the Smart Gain feature, adjust the gain setting for the remaining audio clips you added:**
   c_night.mov (second copy)
   car.mpa (two copies)
   truck_horn.mpa (two copies)
   phone.mpa (two copies)
   cellphone.mpa (two copies)
   crowd.mpa
   ocean.mpa

6. **Save the project.**
   Now the gain is adjusted for all of your audio clips. The signal strength for the audio clips is consistent, which makes adjusting settings in later tutorials simpler and more predictable.

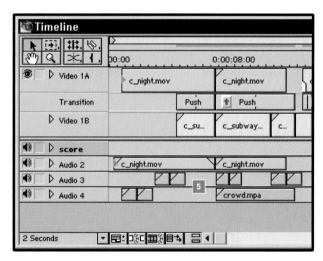

<NOTE>
You can manually enter a Gain value. Gain and Smart Gain yield the same outcome, that is, adjusting a clip's Gain. Smart Gain is standardized and produces a set of clips with an equivalent strength much more easily than experimenting with Gain settings manually.

The Difference Between Loudness and Volume

Gain adjusts the loudness of the clip, but this isn't the same as adjusting the volume. You can adjust the volume of various clips in a project to simulate clips of similar strength. The problem with this is clips that are captured at a low signal strength can distort before you can increase the volume loud enough to match your other clips. If you adjust the gain, you are starting from a common point and can adjust volumes throughout your project much more easily and predictably. The perfect example is a television program and commercials. You set the volume of your TV to a comfortable level. When the commercials begin, they seem much louder. They aren't really — their gain has been adjusted.

Tutorial
» Editing a Group of Clips in the Timeline

The last audio clip you add from the Project window is the drum beat for the first section. You use five copies of this clip and edit the clips to create a single score. You add the first clip, edit it, and then use the edited clip for the remaining elements.

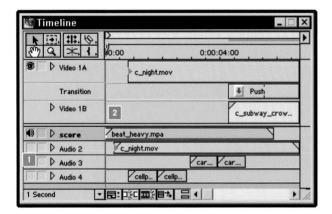

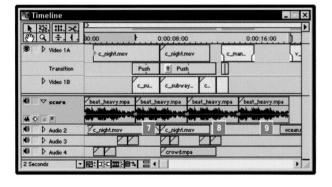

1. **Turn off Audio 2, 3, and 4.**
   Click the Speaker icon to the left of the tracks to turn them off. Like video clips you toggle between visible and invisible, audio tracks toggle between audible and silent. Audio 1 (score) remains audible. Isolating the track makes editing simpler when you work with multiple tracks in a project.

2. **Drag the** beat_heavy.mpa **clip from the Project window to the score track to start at 00:00.**

3. **Adjust the gain using the Smart Gain function.**
   Right-click the clip to open the shortcut menu. Choose Audio Options→Audio Gain. When the Audio Gain dialog box opens, click Smart Gain. Click OK to close the Audio Gain dialog box.

4. **Double-click the clip to open it in a Clip window.**
   Move the time location marker to 04:18. Use the arrow keys on the keypad or the arrows on the clip's controller to move the marker to the correct frame.

5. **Click Mark Out to set the Out point.**
   A red icon displays on the Clip window below the waveform. The Apply button appears at the bottom of the Clip window.

6. **Click Apply.**
   The edits are transferred to the clip on the Timeline. Close the Clip window.

7. **In the Timeline, copy the** beat_heavy.mpa **clip.**
   Paste a second copy into the score track. Butt it against the original clip.

8. **Paste a third copy into the score track.**
   Butt it against the second copy. The first three copies of the clip make a sound loop. That is, the sound repeats continuously across the three clips.

9. **Paste a fourth copy of the clip, and butt it against the third copy.**
   The first portion of the fourth copy adds to the sound loop. You edit the end of the clip to correspond with edits you do in later steps to a fifth copy.

10. **Double-click the fourth copy to open it in a Clip window.**

11. **Move the time marker to 03:10.**
    Click Mark In to move the In point. A green In point marker
    displays above the audio waveform. The Apply button appears
    at the bottom of the Clip window.

12. **Move the end point to the end of the clip at 05:26.**
    Click Mark Out to adjust the Out point. A red Out point marker
    displays below the audio waveform.

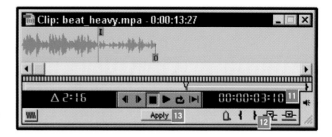

13. **Click Apply to transfer the edits to the clip on the Timeline.**
    Close the Clip window. Check the location on the Timeline.
    You have to adjust the clip position. Drag it to butt against the
    previous copy. The clip starts at 13:27, runs for 02:17, and
    ends at 16:14.

14. **Paste one final copy of the clip into the score track.**
    You have a total of five copies of the clip. Double-click the
    fifth copy to open it in the Clip window.

15. **Move the time marker to 03:11.**
    Click Mark In to move the In point. A green In point marker
    displays above the audio waveform. The Apply button appears
    at the bottom of the Clip window.

16. **Move the end point to 04:15.**
    Click Mark Out to adjust the Out point. A red Out point marker
    displays below the audio waveform.

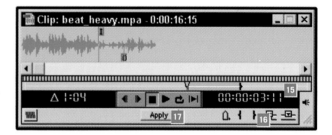

17. **Click Apply.**
    The edits are transferred to the clip in the Timeline. Close the
    Clip window.

18. **Drag the clip on the Timeline to butt against the previous copies.**
    Check the location on the Timeline. This final clip starts at
    16:14, runs for 1:05, and ends at 17:19. That this clip ends
    the frame before the sound of ocean waves crashing against
    the shore begins is no coincidence!

19. **Save the project.**
    You completed a complex audio edit sequence. From one short
    drum clip, you built a complete score. The drum loops through
    the first three copies of the clip and into the start of the fourth
    copy. You edited the fourth and fifth copies for two reasons —
    to make the music continue uninterrupted, and to produce the
    final length for the set of clips.

<NOTE>
When you crop a clip, you see two different values when you check
the lengths in the Clip window versus the Timeline. Check it for
yourself. Display the Info window. Select a clip on the Timeline and
double-click to open it in the Clip window. There is one frame difference in the lengths because the Info window counts the position
of a clip's first or last frame as well as the number of frames. Use
the values shown in the Info window to complete this tutorial.

Tutorial
» Making a Custom Sound Track

The final audio clip you need for the project is the score for the beach segment of the movie. You create this yourself with the SmartSound Quicktracks plug-in. A copy of this final custom clip is on the CD.

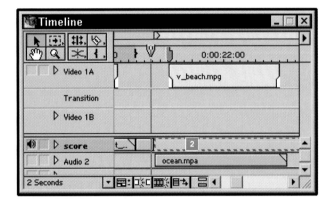

1. **Select the** premierecc_audio **bin in the Project window.**
   Your custom track is added to this bin.

2. **Click the score track in the blank area following the** beat_heavy.mpa **clips.**
   The beat_heavy.mpa clip sequence ends at 17:19.

3. **Choose File→New→SmartSound.**
   The SmartSound Quicktracks for Premiere interface opens.

4. **Click Start Maestro from the options on the interface.**
   A multi-step wizard opens.

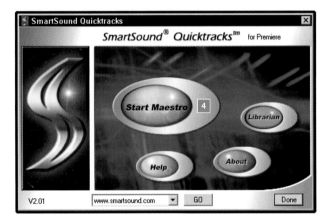

Installing SmartSound Quicktracks

You must have the SmartSound Quicktracks software installed to build the musical score for the beach segment of the project. Install the software from its CD-ROM, separate from the Premiere 6.5 installation disk. Close Premiere first. Put the SmartSound installation CD into your CD-ROM drive. On a Mac, double-click the Quicktracks Premiere icon on the desktop to install the program. On Windows, browse to the location of the CD drive, and double-click setup.exe. The program autoinstalls, and copies its files into your Premiere 6.5 plug-ins folder. Reopen Premiere. SmartSound appears as an option for new files.

5. **Choose Select By Style.**

   The first panel of the interface lists music according to a number of categories. You choose general music according to how the music will be used, for example, as background music, or according to other descriptions of the soundtracks, such as style or title.

6. **Click Next to open a panel categorizing music and sound effects according to a style such as classical or rock.**

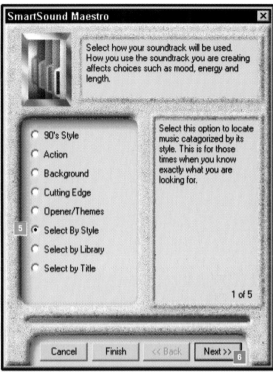

7. **Choose Specialty.**

   Specialty music options are global and eclectic types of music, appropriate for the beach scene in your movie.

8. **Click Next to open a panel with different sources of music in the specialty category.**

   The four choices vary in intensity and mood.

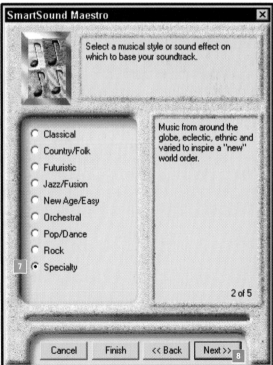

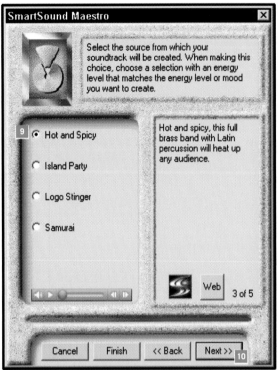

9. **Choose Hot and Spicy.**

   Hot and Spicy is a Latin-influenced piece of music featuring a brass band and percussion.

10. **Click Next to open the panel to define time characteristics for your custom track.**

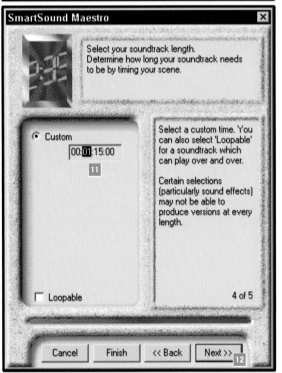

11. **Type a clip length of 01:15:00.**

    The default entry is 00:15. The program creates clip segments with approximately the length you typed in the custom value.

    < T I P >

    Your score is not loopable. If you want a track that can loop, click the Loopable box at the bottom of the panel. Loopable scores sound different from nonloopable scores in that the beginning and ending of the clip must blend seamlessly.

12. **Click Next.**

    This opens a panel listing a collection of soundtracks in the length range you entered. Each option is named.

    < T I P >

    You are prompted to put the SmartSound Quicktracks CD in your CD-ROM drive to access the source music.

13. **Choose Saucy from the list of soundtrack versions.**
    The clip's time of 01:15:01 displays.

14. **Preview the clip using the controllers.**
    Click the Play button to listen to the soundtrack.

15. **Click Finish.**
    The SmartSound Quicktracks interface closes and a Save the SmartSound dialog box opens.

16. **The clip is named SmartSound-Saucy.wav according to your selection.**
    Select your premierecc_audio folder to save the file into. Click Save to save the file and close the Save dialog box.

<NOTE>
The default audio format for your operating system is the only format available. You can modify the format in an external audio editing program.

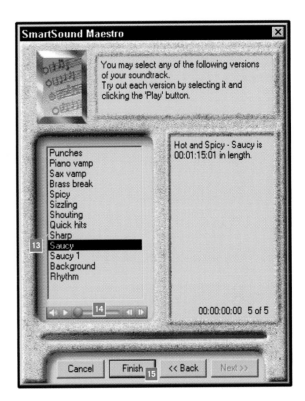

17. **In the Project window, open the premierecc_audio bin.**
    Select the SmartSound-Saucy clip.

18. **Drag the clip to the Timeline.**
    Place it in the score track at 18:17. This is the same time at which the v_beach.mpg clip begins.

<NOTE>
In the interest of saving hard drive and CD-ROM space, I substitute an mpa file for the wav file that is generated by the plug-in — the reformatted file is about 6 MB smaller.

19. **Save the project.**
    You added a sound track for the beach segment of the project. You worked with the SmartSound Quicktracks plug-in to build a custom musical score.

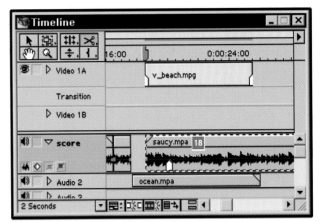

» Session Review

You finally have audio in your project, which certainly makes a difference doesn't it? This session introduced you to working with audio. It started with an introduction to how and why to use audio, and discussed how the sound track was chosen for the project. You learned how to edit audio clips, both in the Project window and in the Timeline, and how to adjust the signal strength of your clips to make further editing and effects easier to apply. This session showed you how to arrange the Timeline layout for ease of use. You also learned how to work with multiple copies of a clip. The CD-ROM contains a sample clip, session6.mpg, for the first 35 seconds of the project (35:11 to be precise). This sample includes the entire first section of the project and a part of the beach sequence. The last frame in the sample clip is the final image in this session. All clips in the sample are adjusted for gain.

You have not done any audio editing yet, except for trimming and setting the gain. As you listen to the sample or the audio from your project, you will notice the sound effects don't blend with one another. The clip which demonstrates this most clearly is ocean.mpa. The ocean sound is consistently loud and detracts from the musical score. The ocean sound ends partway through the b_girl_running_1.mov. The video at the final frame of ocean.mpa is shown in the image at the beginning of this session. You do more audio editing in Session 7.

This session contains a lot of information. Answer the following questions to review the information in this session. Answers to the questions are in the tutorial noted in parentheses.

1. What roles does sound play in a movie project? (See "Discussion: How and Why to Use Audio.")
2. Do you use different types of sound for different purposes? (See "Discussion: How and Why to Use Audio.")
3. How do you import the contents of an entire folder into your project? (See "Tutorial: Preparing Audio Files.")
4. When you trim a clip in the Project window, are the changes shown in the Project window? (See "Tutorial: Preparing Audio Files.")
5. How do you reset the Timeline to show only the names of the clips without an icon image? (See "Tutorial: Configuring the Timeline.")
6. How do you view the audio wave of a clip? (See "Tutorial: Adding Trimmed Audio Clips to the Timeline.")
7. Is there a difference between copying and pasting a clip in the Timeline, and dragging another copy from the Project window? When do you use one method rather than the other? (See "Tutorial: Adding Trimmed Audio Clips to the Timeline.")
8. What is the shortcut method of adding a marker to the Timeline? (See "Tutorial: Editing Audio Clips in the Timeline.")
9. How do you access the Gain dialog box? (See "Tutorial: Adjusting Audio Signal.")
10. Why must your clips have similar signal strengths? (See "Tutorial: Adjusting Audio Signal.")
11. Must all the audio tracks in a project be active? (See "Tutorial: Editing a Group of Clips in the Timeline.")
12. How do you isolate an audio track in the Timeline? (See "Tutorial: Editing a Group of Clips in the Timeline.")
13. Is a Quicktracks score automatically added to the Timeline? (See "Tutorial: Making a Custom Sound Track.")
14. How do you define a custom length for your score? (See "Tutorial: Making a Custom Sound Track.")
15. Are you able to choose an export format for the SmartSound score? (See "Tutorial: Making a Custom Sound Track.")

» Other Projects

This session explained how to work with one of the tracks from the SmartSound Quicktracks plug-in. Experiment with other music on the CD to find other music that may be appropriate for the video you are creating.

Record a voiceover to use with the project. Place it in a separate audio track. The script for the voiceover should describe or enhance what the viewer sees on the screen.

Editing
Audio Files

Session Introduction

In Premiere, you can work with audio two ways. In this session, you finish editing the sound files you added to your project. You learn how to work with the Audio Mixer window, and how to use other features in the Timeline window.

You may be one of those people who prefers to hear what you are working with, rather than interpreting it visually. For you real-time fans, Premiere provides an Audio Mixer window that allows you to adjust your project's sound as you listen to the clips. The Audio Mixer window uses an audio editing deck analogy. In this session, you learn to do some of the project audio edits in the Audio Mixer. Whether you work with the Audio Mixer or strictly in the Timeline is a matter of personal preference.

You use the Audio Mixer to adjust audio settings as you watch your video. The adjustments you make to a track transfer to the clips in the Timeline. The Audio Mixer window contains a set of controls that correspond with each track in your project, just like a big audio mixing deck. At the risk of stating the obvious, your computer comes with only one mouse, which means you cannot work with the Audio Mixer the same way as with a physical mixing deck. Instead, you can combine tracks using special controls. In your project, you use the Audio Mixer window to adjust the sound of certain clips.

At this point, the sound track of your project has been added to the Timeline, trimmed, and adjusted for gain. If you listen to the sound track for the project, it is quite rough. The sound is loud throughout; the volume of each clip is constant and doesn't blend with any other clips. The sound comes from the same source. By the end of this session the sound track will be finished except for some audio effects you add in Session 15.

TOOLS YOU'LL USE
Timeline window, In and Out markers, Show/Hide Shy Track commands, Audio Mixer window, Automation controls, pan/balance controls, volume fader, Pan Rubberband, Volume Rubberband, Fade Adjustment tool, Cross Fade tool, Scissors tool, Info window, Clip window

CD-ROM FILES NEEDED
Session 6 project file you created or the session6.ppj file from the CD-ROM
session7.mpg preview file from the premierecc_samples folder (for reference)

TIME REQUIRED
90 minutes

Tutorial
» Adjusting Volume for a Group of Clips

In this tutorial you adjust the volume of the score in the first section of your project using the volume rubberband and the fade tools. Remember that the score is made up of five copies of the drums_heavy.mpa clip.

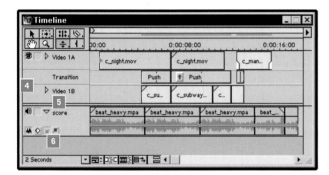

<NOTE>

If you didn't do the tutorials in Session 6, copy the session6.ppj file from the CD to your hard drive. Open the file and resave it as session7.ppj (or use another filenaming convention).

<NOTE>

You don't have to worry about trying to move the volume rubberband a specific distance below its current position to reach the specified volume value. You can drag below the limit of the track to set the value. When you release the mouse, the volume rubberband readjusts itself over the clip.

1. **Choose File→Open and navigate to the location you stored your project files.**
   You can also choose File→Open Recent Project and choose your project file from the list. Open session6.ppj.

2. **Resave the project file as session7.ppj.**

3. **Turn off Audio tracks 2, 3, and 4.**
   You are only working with clips in the score track and don't need to hear the sound from the other tracks.

4. **Hide all tracks except Video 1 and score tracks.**
   Set the tracks as shy, and choose Hide Shy Tracks from the Timeline menu. Now the tracks you turned off in Step 3 are hidden as well, giving you more room on the screen.

5. **Open the score track.**
   Click the arrow to the left of the track name to open the lower portion of the track.

6. **Click the red Display Volume Rubberband icon from the set of track icons.**
   You adjust the clip's volume using the rubberband

7. **Set the Timeline zoom factor to ½ Second.**
   Click the Time Zoom Level at the bottom left of the Timeline and choose ½ Second from the list to zoom into the Timeline. You need to see the time ruler clearly as you adjust the volume.

8. **Select the Fade Adjustment Tool icon from the Timeline toolbox.**
   Click the tool displayed in the third position of the bottom row to open the subpalette. Select the Fade Adjustment Tool to activate it. This tool adjusts the volume of the entire clip.

9. **Move the tool over the red volume rubberband until it displays an icon that matches the tool icon.**
   Press Shift and drag the red line downward. Stop when the display shows 71%. The rubberband and its two end handles move to the new volume setting.

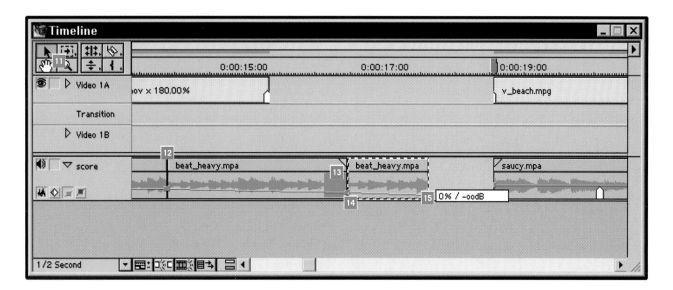

<NOTE>
You have the other audio tracks turned off at this point

10. **Set the volume rubberband to 71% on the second and third copies of the** `beat_heavy.mpa` **clip.**
    The first three copies of the clip produce a sequence of drum beats, and use the same volume. Leaving the clip volumes at 100% drowns out the sound of the other audio clips.

11. **Choose the selection tool in the toolbox.**
    Use the selection tool to add points to the rubberband.

12. **Move the tool over the handle at the start of the fourth clip until it displays a hand with a pointing finger.**
    Press Shift and drag downward. Stop when the display shows 71%. The left end handle moves to the new volume setting.

13. **Move the tool over the handle at the end of the fourth clip until it displays a hand with a pointing finger.**
    Press Shift and drag downward. Stop when the display shows 32%. The right end handle moves to the new volume setting.

14. **Move the tool over the handle at the start of the fifth clip until it displays a hand with a pointing finger.**
    Press Shift and drag downward. Stop when the display shows 32%.

15. **Move the tool over the handle at the end of the fifth clip until it displays a hand with a pointing finger.**
    Press Shift and drag downward. Stop when the display shows 0%.

16. **Preview the clip.**
    Move the edit line to the beginning of the project and press Enter. After you listen to the entire segment, press Enter again to stop the clip.

17. **Save the project.**
    In many projects (and in the second sequence of this one) the sound track usually fades in — gradually gets louder in volume. In this case, starting the sound track at full volume adds to the tension of the video, which is the intent. Because you use five copies of the clip to make the complete score for this segment, the sound is gradually decreased over the length of the five clips and finally fades out (gets quieter in volume or disappears completely).

Tutorial
» Working with Sound Effects

Now the score is set for the first segment. Several other tracks also contain sound effect clips. In this tutorial, you set the volume for these different sound effects. Along the way you get more practice with the fade tools and learn tips for using them.

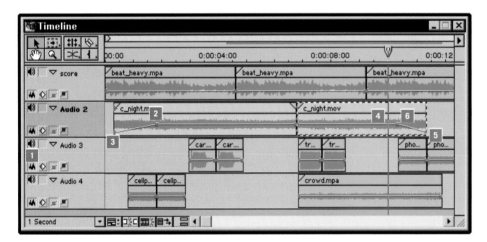

1. **Show Audio tracks 2, 3, and 4.**
   Open the Timeline menu and choose Show Shy Tracks. Make sure they are turned on. Toggle each track's Track Output icon (eye icon) to visible.

2. **Click the** c_night.mov **volume rubberband at 01:25.**
   A new handle is added to the rubberband.

<N O T E>
When you click the rubberband to add handles, you often move an entire segment by accident. Don't worry, that can be readjusted easily. Shift + click a handle to see the value. Drag up or down to the exact setting you want.

3. **Drag the start handle down to the bottom of the waveform display.**
   The first segment of the rubberband changes angle to stretch between the handles.

4. **Click the volume rubberband on the second copy of the** c_night.mov **clip with the selection tool at 10:00 to add another handle.**

<T I P>
To remove a handle, click and drag it either above or below the track margins. The rubberbands work like — rubberbands. That is, they stretch from a specific area, and then snap back into place. The selected handle is removed. You cannot remove the beginning and ending handles from a clip.

5. **Drag the end handle of the rubberband on the second copy down to the bottom of the waveform display.**

6. **Click and drag the handle you added at 10:00 horizontally to 10:11.**
   The handle slides along the rubberband to your desired position.

<N O T E>
You can place the handle at the precise location to start with, but then I wouldn't be able to explain how they slide!

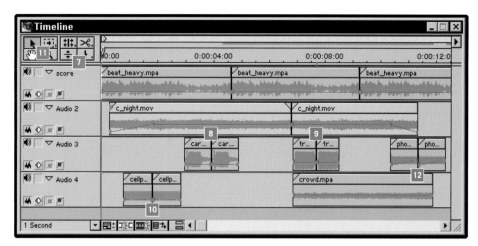

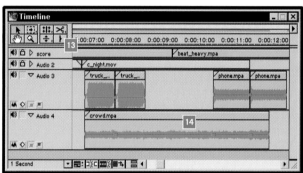

7. **Click the Fade Adjustment tool icon in the Timeline toolbox to select it.**

8. **Set the volume for both copies of the** `car.mpa` **clip in Audio 3 to 46%.**
   Move the Fade Adjustment tool over the red volume rubber-band until it displays an icon that matches the tool icon. Press Shift and drag the red line downward. Stop when the display shows 46%. The rubberband and its two end handles move to the new volume setting.

9. **Set the volume for both copies of the** `truck_horn.mpa` **file in Audio 3 to 75% using the method described in Step 8.**

10. **Set the volume for both copies of the** `cellphone.mpa` **file in Audio 4 to 52% using the method described in Step 8.**

11. **Choose the Select tool and add points to the rubberband.**

12. **Set the start volume for both copies of the** `phone.mpa` **clip in Audio 3 to 52%.**
    Move the Select tool over the start handle until it displays a hand with a pointing finger. Press Shift and drag downward. Stop when the display shows 52%. Set the end volume to 110% using the same method.

13. **Select the Fade Scissors tool from the Timeline toolbox.**
    Click and hold the top right icon in the toolbox until the sub-palette opens. Choose the scissors icon, which is used to add pairs of handles to the volume control rubberband.

14. **Move the cursor over the rubberband on the** `crowd.mpa` **clip, and then click when it changes to a pair of scissors.**
    Click the rubberband at these time locations: 07:21, 10:11, 11:11. The Fade Scissors tool doesn't cut the rubberband per se. What it does is add two points to the rubberband next to one another, which allows you to make sharp changes in volume.

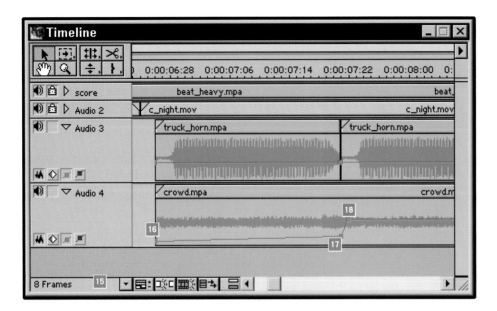

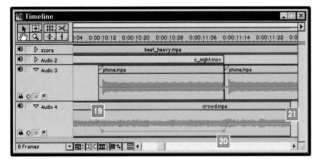

15. **Zoom in to the Timeline at the 8 Frames setting to better work with the pairs of handles added in Step 14.**

16. **Choose the Select tool from the Timeline toolbox.**
    Drag the start handle of the `crowd.mpa` clip down to 0% volume.

17. **Drag the first handle of the first pair of handles added in Step 14 to 25% volume.**
    The handle is located at 07:21 on the volume rubberband.

18. **Drag the second handle of the first pair located at 07:21 to 105% volume.**

19. **Move the Timeline view to the next pair of handles, located at 10:11.**
    Set the first handle at 105% volume and the second handle at 35% volume.

20. **Move the Timeline to the last pair of handles, located at 11:11.**
    Set the first handle at 35% volume and the second handle at 100% volume.

21. **Select the end handle of the `crowd.mpa` clip at 11:27.**
    Set the volume at 100% volume.

22. **Move the edit line to the beginning of the project.**
    Preview the sound track. You hear the volume increase quickly, decrease quickly, and then increase again.

23. **Save the project.**
    You used several methods for modifying volume, including manually adjusting handles, using the Fade Adjustment tool, and adding pairs of clips to create rapid volume changes using the Fade Scissors tool.

Tutorial
» Using the Audio Mixer

Most of the clips in the first section have now been adjusted for volume. In this tutorial, you learn how to set the Timeline for working with the Audio Mixer. Isolating a portion of the Timeline by setting In and Out markers makes previewing much faster as only the selected segment is previewed. You also learn how to run audio loops.

1. **Lock the audio tracks not in use.**
   Click the box immediately to the left of the track's name. A lock icon appears. Lock score, Audio 2, and Audio 4.

2. **Move the time marker to 10:00.**
   Click the In point tool on the Timeline toolbar to select it. Set the In point for the Timeline at the time marker.

<TIP>
Here's another easy way to set In and Out markers. Move the time marker to the desired location, and then right-click the time ruler. Choose Set Timeline Marker→In or Out.

3. **Move the time marker to 12:15.**
   Click and hold the In point tool on the Timeline toolbar to open the subpalette. Click the Out point tool to select it. Set the Out point for the Timeline at the time marker.

<NOTE>
You don't have to set In and Out markers when working with audio, but it saves a lot of time. In the Timeline, Monitor, Clip, and Audio Mixer windows you can choose a looping option. By defining In and Out markers, you define the portion of the Timeline you want to work with. If you work with a five-second segment, you don't need to preview or play the entire Timeline.

4. **Choose Window→Audio Mixer to open the Audio Mixer window.**
   The Audio Mixer contains a set of tracks that correspond to the same numbered or named track in the Timeline.

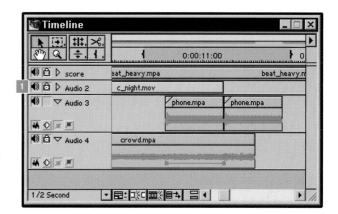

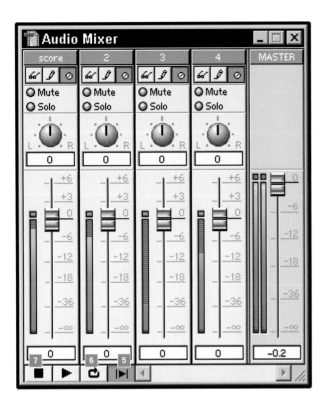

5. **Click the Play In to Out button to hear the segment of the Timeline between the end points.**

   Isolating the segment of the Timeline before you work in an area defines the portion of the Timeline that plays.

6. **Click the Loop button to run the segment of the Timeline repeatedly.**

   Only the portion of the Timeline defined in Steps 2 and 3 play.

7. **Click the Stop button to stop playback.**

   You hear the two copies of the phone.mpa clip playing in Audio 3. Now you are familiar with the sound of the clips. In the next tutorial you edit the clips in the Audio Mixer.

<NOTE>

The Master track shows one or two VU meters, depending on project settings. You are using stereo clips, so the Master track displays two VU meters. If you use mono clips, the Master track displays one VU meter. VU, by the way, stands for Volume Unit. The VU meters show relative volumes of the audio clips as they play. Most car, home, and computer sound systems have VU meter display options.

Tutorial
» Editing with the Audio Mixer

Many of the clips in the first section have now been adjusted for volume. In this tutorial, you edit a pair of clips using the Audio Mixer. Both clips start with a low volume level and end at a high volume level.

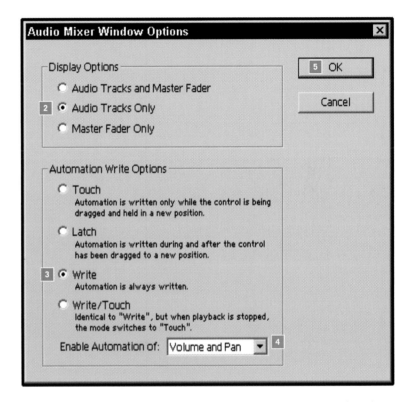

1. **Right-click anywhere on the Audio Mixer window.**
   Choose Audio Mixer Window Options to open the Audio Mixer Window Options dialog box.

2. **Choose Audio Tracks Only from the Display Options.**
   You do not set the overall sound level for the entire project, so you don't need to use either of the Master Fader options.

3. **Select Write from the Automation Write Options, which writes all adjustments you make with Audio Mixer controls to the clip on the Timeline.**
   The Automation Write Options determine *how* your real-time settings are transferred to the Timeline. Automation can be

written only while controls are being dragged (Touch); during and after a control is moved (Latch); or a combination of write and touch meaning animation is written as you adjust controls, and then switches back to a touch status when playback is stopped (Write/Touch).

4. **Choose Volume and Pan from the Enable Automation of menu.**
   You adjust both the volume and pan settings for the clips in this tutorial.

5. **Click OK.**
   The Audio Mixer Window Options dialog box closes.

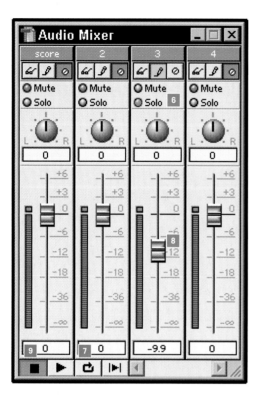

6. **In the Audio Mixer, click the Solo button to isolate the Audio 3 track.**

   The other tracks are automatically set to Mute. Isolate the track to hear the contents clearly. You can toggle Solo on and off and listen to the clip in combination with other tracks as you edit.

<NOTE>
Use the values cited in the following steps as an example. You likely can't duplicate these settings exactly using the Audio Mixer alone. You make final adjustments later.

7. **Click Loop.**

   The isolated portion of the Timeline plays repeatedly.

8. **Drag the thumb slider downward to approximately -10.0 dB (-9.9 is the closest Audio Mixer value).**

   Instead of using the slider, you can type the value. Click into the field and type **-10.0**. Press Enter. The closest dB value displays.

<NOTE>
A decibel is a value for measuring the intensity of sound. Decibels (abbreviated dB) measure sound pressure level on a logarithmic scale. A ten-decibel (dB) increase represents a doubling of sound level.

9. **Click Stop.**

   The segment of the Timeline stops playing. Move the Audio Mixer window to one side of the screen or minimize it to work in the Timeline.

Watching the VU Meter

Pay attention to the VU meter as you play clips in the Audio Mixer. A small, usually gray square sits above the colored volume bar. If the audio level of a track is set too high, it turns red, indicating that the sound will start to distort. This distortion is called clipping. On the other hand if the audio level is set too low, you hear excessive noise.

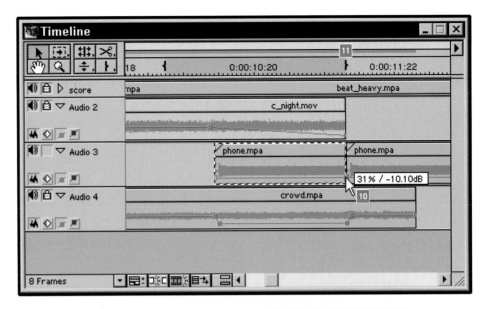

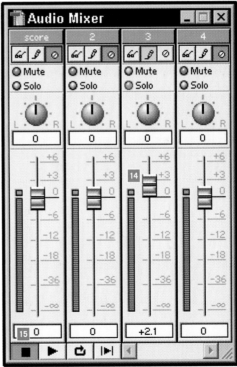

10. **In the Timeline, choose the Select tool from the toolbox.**

    Shift + click one of the end handles on the phone.mpa clips. The volume (as a percentage) and its decibel level are displayed. You can see a slight variation between the Audio Mixer value and the value shown in the Timeline. The volume in the Timeline changes in 1% increments and uses the dB level nearest the Audio Mixer setting.

11. **Click the Timeline ruler at 11:12.**

    Reset the Out point to this time location. This time location is the end of the first copy of the phone.mpa clip.

12. **Go back to the Audio Mixer window.**

    Right-click anywhere in the window. When the Audio Mixer Window Options dialog box opens, select the Latch Automation Write option. This write option transfers settings automatically to the Timeline during and after you drag the slider control to new settings.

13. **Click OK to close the Audio Mixer Window Options dialog box.**

14. **On the Audio Mixer, click Loop.**

    As the clip plays, drag the slider upward to a value of approximately 2.0 dB to adjust the clip's volume.

15. **Click Stop to stop the playback.**

    Move the Audio Mixer window or minimize it to return to the Timeline.

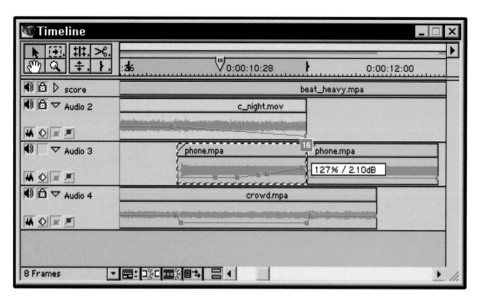

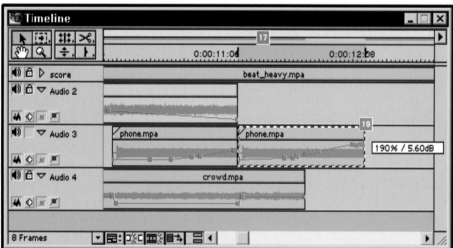

16. **Check the rubberband in the Timeline.**

    Shift + click the end handle of the rubberband on the clip. The volume in the example is 127% with a dB value of 2.10 dB.

17. **Reset the In and Out points on the Timeline once again.**

    Set the In point to start at the beginning of the second copy of the clip (at 11:12) and the Out point to end at the end of the clip (12:11).

18. **Repeat Steps 14 and 15 in the Audio Mixer.**

    You set the same values for the second copy of the phone.mpa clip. Close the Audio Mixer window.

19. **Shift + click the end handle of the rubberband on the clip in the Timeline.**

    The volume in the example is 190% with a dB value of 5.60 dB.

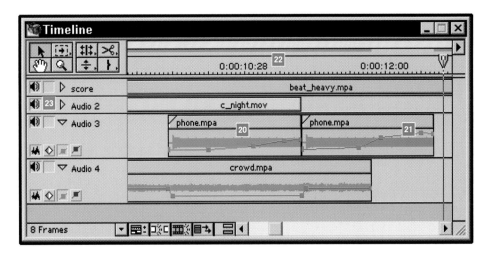

20. **Click and drag to remove extra handles from the first copy of the clip.**

Leave the two end handles as they are and remove extraneous handles from the rest of the clip. Leave three handles along the rubberband and slide or adjust them to approximately the positions shown in the example.

21. **Click and drag to remove extra handles from the second copy of the clip, leaving a total of five handles.**

Leave the two end handles as they are and remove extraneous handles from the rest of the clip. Leave three handles along the rubberband and slide or adjust them to approximately the positions shown in the example. In this second copy, raise the volume more sharply than the first copy.

22. **Right-click the time ruler.**

Choose Clear Timeline Marker➔In and Out.

<TIP>

You can leave the Timeline In and Out points or remove them. I generally remove them as a matter of course.

23. **Unlock the Audio tracks you locked in the last tutorial.**

Click the Lock icons to the left of the track names on the score, Audio 2, and Audio 4 tracks. The Lock icon toggles off.

24. **Move the edit line to the beginning of the project and preview the sound track.**

25. **Save the project.**

You adjusted the volumes of two clips using the Audio Mixer. You used real-time methods for transferring adjustments from the Audio Mixer to the Timeline as you listened and adjusted the clips. You removed extra handles from the clips in the Timeline. Now take a break! You completed a very complicated tutorial.

Ganging Tracks

Suppose you have a movie that moves from an exterior to an interior location. The sounds of nature or the street suddenly stop when the house door shuts. You can gang the tracks to adjust the volume levels for several tracks at once. Right-click a volume fader (a gray thumb control) and a list of gangs displays. Unlike those in West Side Story, this list of gangs is numerical. Choose a gang and the slider color changes to correspond with the gang. Add other tracks to a gang using the same method. Remove a track from a gang by choosing No Gang from the right-click menu list. You can set up several gangs for the same project. Controls in a gang work in unison; increasing the volume by 1dB affects the volume of all the tracks in the gang. The changes are relative. If the level of Track 2 is 2.0 dB and Track 3 is -1.0 dB, increasing the level by 1dB changes their levels to 3.0 and 0.0 dB, respectively.

Tutorial
» Balancing Clips

Think about what a car sounds like when it passes in front of you. First you hear the sound in your left ear. It increases in volume as it passes in front of you, at which time you hear it in both ears. It then gradually decreases in volume via your right ear, and then finally disappears. You can achieve this effect using the Pan/Balance rubberband, as well as other effects that transfer sound from left to right. In this tutorial you learn to set pan/balance. After isolating a portion of the Timeline, you work in the Audio Mixer, then return to the Timeline.

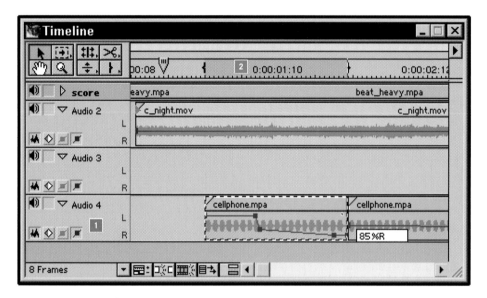

The Difference between Pan and Balance

In terms of what you hear, there really isn't any difference. The two terms refer to the type of channel content. Sound comes in two channels — right and left. A mono audio clip uses one channel, either left or right. Stereo sound uses both channels (which is why stereo is a fuller sound). You pan a mono clip from one channel to another, while you adjust the balance of the channels in a stereo clip.

1. **Click the Display Pan Rubberbands icon in Audio 4.**
   The Pan/Balance rubberband works in the same fashion as the Volume rubberband with one exception. A handle dragged to the top of the waveform moves the sound to the left channel exclusively (you hear it in your left ear only); the default is balanced (you hear it in both ears equally); and a handle dragged to the bottom of the waveform moves the sound to the right channel only (heard only in the right ear).

2. **Set the Timeline In and Out points to correspond with the first copy of the** cellphone.mpa **clip in Audio 4.**
   Set the In point at 01:01 and the Out point at 01:25.

3. **In the Audio Mixer, click the icon for Automation Write for Track 4.**
You don't have to open the Audio Mixer Window Options dialog box to choose a write setting.

4. **Click the Play In to Out button.**
The cellphone.mpa clip plays.

5. **Rotate the Pan/Balance dial to L.**
This balances the start of the clip to the Left track (you hear it in your left ear when wearing headphones).

6. **Replay the clip and rotate the dial to R.**
This balances the end of the clip to the Right track (you hear it in your right ear when wearing headphones). Close or mini- mize the Audio Mixer.

7. **Adjust the handles in the Timeline.**
Approximate the layout shown in the image.

8. **Shift + click the last handle to see the pan setting.**
The setting shows both the percentage and the channel.

9. **Select the first copy of the** cellphone.mpa **clip in Audio 4 and copy it.**

10. **Choose Edit→Paste Attributes.**
The Paste Attributes dialog box opens.

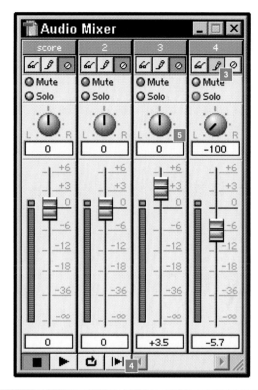

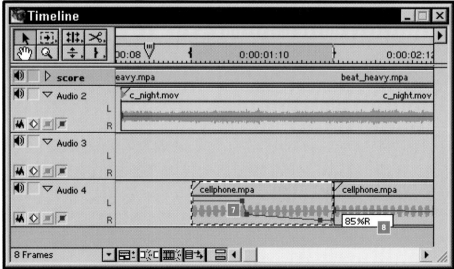

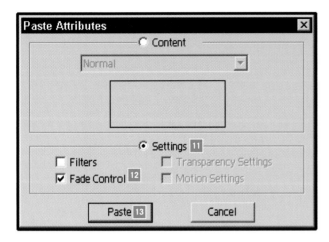

11. **Click Settings.**
    The Settings options activate.

12. **Select Fade Control.**
    This option identifies the fade controls in the copied clip.
    Pan/Balance are a type of audio fade.

13. **Click Paste.**
    The Paste Attributes dialog box closes.
    The Pan/Balance control settings are applied to the second
    copy of the cellphone.mpa clip.

14. **In the Timeline, adjust Balance settings for the clips listed in
    Table 7.1 as indicated.**
    Use either the Audio Mixer or the Timeline according to your
    preferences.

<TIP>
To duplicate the settings in another clip, use the Paste Attributes
command described in Steps 9 to 13.

Table 7.1: Balance Settings for Sound Effect Clips

Clip Name	Start	End
car.mpa	73% R	53% L
truck_horn.mpa	90% L	64% R

15. **Right-click the time ruler.**
    Choose Clear Timeline Marker➜In and Out.

16. **Move the edit line to the beginning of the project.**
    Preview the final score.

17. **Save the project.**
    You adjusted pan/balance effects in several sound effect clips.
    You learned to use the Paste Attributes command to quickly
    copy settings from one clip to another.

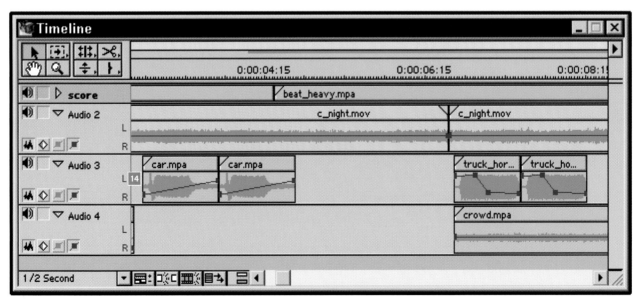

Tutorial
» Working with a Group of Audio Clips

In the last two sessions you learned to work with audio files. For the most part, you have been working with one tool or process throughout and then going to the next process and so on. In a real workflow, it isn't likely you would work in that type of fashion. You are more likely to work with clusters of clips, applying and modifying elements until you arrive at the finished product. In this tutorial, you isolate a portion of the Timeline. Essentially, you create a project within a project that makes previewing and editing much quicker. In the last two sessions you added In and Out markers to the Timeline to isolate segments for playback in the Audio Mixer. You set In and Out markers in this tutorial and prepare the tracks for the next editing tutorial.

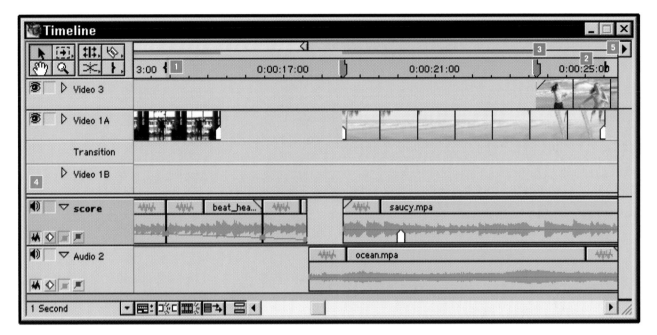

1. **In the Timeline window, move the edit line to 13:27.**
   Set the In point for the Timeline.

2. **Move the edit line again, this time to 25:15.**
   Set the Out point for the Timeline. These points isolate the portion of the Timeline you are going to work with, beginning with the fourth copy of the beat_heavy.mpa clip and ending after several seconds of the saucy.mpa score.

3. **Add a marker to the Timeline at 23:21.**
   Move the edit line to 23:21. Right-click the Timeline and choose Set Timeline Marker→Unnumbered. The marker identifies the first frame of the b_girl_running_1.mov clip.

4. **To isolate the tracks you work with, hide Audio 3 and Audio 4, and show Video 1 and Video 3.**
   You work with the audio clips in the score and Audio 2 tracks, and use the video clips in Video 1 and Video 3 as guidelines for audio adjustments.

5. **Click the Timeline menu, and choose Timeline Window Options.**
   When the Timeline Window Options dialog box opens, choose one of the visual Track Format options. Choose either of the thumbnail and filename options. Click OK to close the dialog box. On the Timeline, you see thumbnail icons of the video clips as well as their names. You worked with the filename display in the last several tutorials.

timeline segment

6. **Preview the segment of the Timeline.**
   Use the Monitor window or the Audio Mixer window depending on your preference. Regardless of which you use, because the In and Out points are set on the Timeline, you can isolate the portion you are working on. Use the Play In to Out or Loop options to play the segment.

7. **Play the segment several times.**
   Pay close attention to the overall sound, as well as the areas where clips start and end. In the next tutorial you make final adjustments to the audio segment defined in Steps 1 and 2. Up first, a discussion of the issues surrounding audio edits for this segment of the project.

Discussion
Making Audio Design Decisions

Before you can intelligently edit in Premiere, you have to make decisions as to what the final project should look and sound like. Of course, you won't know precisely how something looks or sounds until you actually experiment.

In the last tutorial, you defined a segment of the Timeline to use for editing. The segment, defined by In and Out points, is used for editing the clips that make up the transition between the two parts of the project as well as the beach audio clips. These clips were added and trimmed according to an overall project plan. This doesn't mean the decision-making process is complete.

In the final tutorial for this session (coming up next) you are going to do some final adjustments to the audio portion of the project. I think it is important for you to understand the questions asked and solutions developed rather than simply following a set of instructions. Here are the issues to consider:

1. Does the final `beat_heavy.mov` clip fade out fast enough?

2. Is there enough time before the `ocean.mpa` clip starts?

3. Should the `ocean.mpa file` fade in? If so, how fast should it fade in? Should it fade in as the `beat_heavy.mov` clip fades out? How loud should it be? When should it fade out?

4. The opening of the `saucy.mpa` clip is loud. Should it fade in? How fast or how slow? Should the clip be trimmed?

When you design your own projects, you regularly answer these kinds of questions. Whenever possible, consider the questions and decide on a plan of action before making changes in the Timeline. This saves you time and minimizes confusion.

Listen to the Timeline segment you set up in the last tutorial. What follows are the decisions I made for this project, which are executed in the next tutorial, and the reasons behind them. How would you answer the questions?

1. The `beat_heavy.mov` sequence is fine as it is. Shortening the final copy would have minimal effect and would likely require adjusting the copies that appear before it in the Timeline. This could be time-consuming and not worth the effort. Since the titles that are layered in this area haven't been added yet, there is no advantage to editing this section.

2. The `ocean.mpa` clip starts as the last drum clip ends. This is effective as an aural cue to what is coming up. However, it may be too sharp for the effect I am trying to achieve with the second segment of the clip — the introduction should be smoother. To solve this, I plan to move the `ocean.mpa` clip ahead in the Timeline.

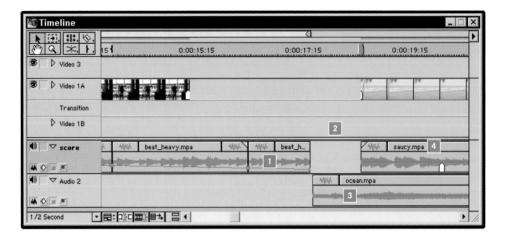

3. I decided the ocean wave clip should fade in and plan a crossfade between the drum and wave clips. The volume of the `ocean.mpa` clip needs to be evaluated after the crossfades are added. The clip will gradually fade out, but the exact location isn't determined until later in the process. It must coordinate with the content of the `saucy.mpa` clip itself and the beginning of the `b_girl_running_1.mov` clip; it depends on the solution to the fourth question.

4. The score starts loudly. Traditionally musical scores fade in, which means the forceful start of the score won't be heard clearly. At its default length, the clip is 1:15:01. If I remove the first chords from the clip (01:15), the final clip length is 1:13:16. This is still a sufficient length for the project. There is one more consideration with this clip after it is trimmed. Does the score coordinate with the action? I have to experiment with its start location on the Timeline to determine that.

Once the decisions are made, you can consider the approach. I decided nothing is to be done with the drum clips. The ocean waves clip will be moved so I can build a crossfade. The ocean waves clip also needs a fade-out, but before that can be accomplished, the `saucy.mpa` clip needs more trimming. Finally, the score and wave clips will be faded out.

Tutorial
» Fine-Tuning the Audio Tracks

The previous discussion outlined the planning and decisions required to edit the portion of the project that segues from the city to the beach segments. In this last tutorial of the session, you finish the audio editing for your project. You revisit the audio tracks only one more time in Session 15 to add some audio effects.

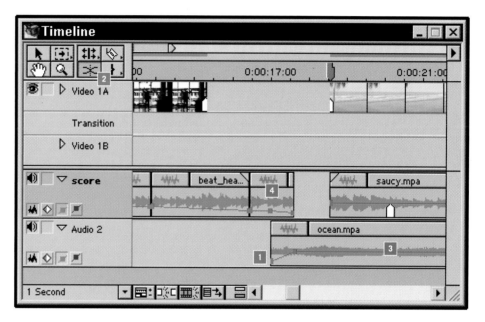

1. **In the Timeline, move the** ocean.mpa **clip left to start at 17:00.**
There is an overlap between the ocean.mpa and the final beat_heavy.mpa clips of 19 frames.

2. **Select the Cross Fade tool in the Timeline toolbox.**
The last tool used from the Fade tools subpalette was the Fade Adjustment tool. Click and hold the Fade Adjustment tool in the toolbox to open the subpalette. Choose the Cross Fade tool.

3. **Click the** ocean.mpa **clip with the Cross Fade tool.**
Clicking the clip selects the first clip in the crossfade pair (you don't see any changes on the Timeline or the clip at this point).

<TIP>
You can use this clip sequence or reverse it. Click the drum clip first, and then the wave clip. The tool works on a relationship between the clips.

4. **Move the cursor over the** beat_heavy.mov **clip.**
You see the cursor change to the Cross Fade tool. Click the beat_heavy.mov clip. The Cross Fade tool automatically adds handles to the clips and adjusts the volume fader. In the pair of crossfade clips, the beat_heavy.mov clip (earliest in the Timeline) begins to fade out at the same frame the ocean.mpa clip starts to fade in.

<NOTE>
Note in the pair of clips adjusted in Steps 1 to 4 that the volume levels you set earlier with the Fade Adjustment tool aren't changed.

5. **Double-click the** saucy.mpa **clip to open it in the Clip window.**
Play the clip to familiarize yourself with it.

6. **Move the time control in the Clip window to 01:16 and click Mark In to reset the In point.**
A green In point icon displays above the waveform. The Apply button appears at the bottom of the Clip window.

7. **Move the time control to 11:03 and press * (the asterisk) on the keyboard to add a marker.**
The marker location identifies a significant change in the rhythm of the clip and is used for final placement of the clip on the Timeline.

8. **Click Apply to transfer the edits to the clip on the Timeline.**

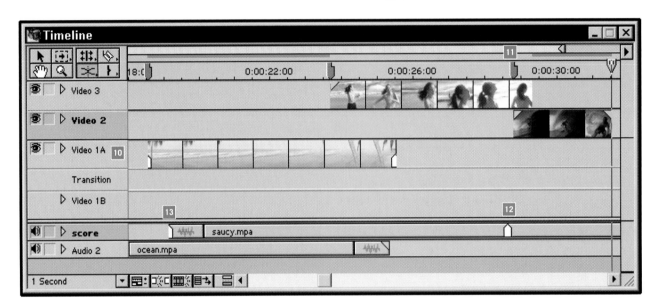

9. **Close the Clip window.**

10. **In the Timeline, show Video 1, 2, and 3.**
You need to see the clips in these tracks for final placement and editing of your audio clips.

11. **Move the edit line to 28:24 and click * (the asterisk) on the keyboard to add a Timeline marker.**
The marker identifies the beginning of the surf_xtra.mpg clip.

12. **Slide the** saucy.mpa **track left until the marker you added at 11:03 in Step 7 aligns with the new Timeline marker set at the start of the** surf_xtra.mpg **clip in the last step.**

13. **Check the** saucy.mpa **clip start time — the clip starts at 19:10.**
The markers you worked with in the last several steps were both on the Timeline and in an individual clip. Identifying an important location in a clip is a useful way to align clips on the Timeline. If a clip has important sound changes or visual changes, use clip and Timeline markers together to synchronize sound and action accurately.

14. **Save the project.**
This is a good time to save your work. You made some precise clip edits and added markers to the clip and Timeline. These tasks are complex and time-consuming, and you don't want to lose your work in the event of computer problems.

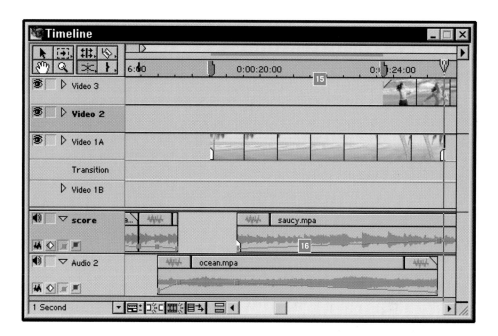

15. **Set new Timeline In and Out markers.**
Set the In point at 16:14 and the Out point at 30:00. Preview the segment.

16. **Click the** ocean.mpa **clip with the Cross Fade tool, and then click the** saucy.mpa **clip to create a crossfade between the two.**
This crossfade solves all the layout and fading problems described in the discussion. The sound of the waves gradually fades out as the music fades in, and coincides well with the clip of the girl running along the beach. The segment before the crossfade (at full volume) is a good introduction to the beginning of the v_beach.mpg clip.

17. **Move the Timeline to the end of the project.**

18. **Choose the Select tool and click the volume rubberband on the** saucy.mpa **clip in the score track at 01:31:15 to add another handle.**

19. **Drag the end handle down to fade out the** saucy.mpa **clip.**
The fade ends the score for your project.

20. **Save the project.**
You created a sophisticated segue between the two parts of the project. The drum score of the city segment fades out as the sound of the waves crashing on the beach fades in. You set the location of the soundtrack for the beach segment based on specific points in clips rather than an arbitrary location on the Timeline. Good work!

» Session Review

This second session on audio editing showed you how to handle, modify, and manage the clips in a project. You learned how to adjust volumes for single clips or groups of clips. You had an introduction to the Audio Mixer and learned how it is used for adjusting volume and pan/balance settings. You leaned how to organize the Timeline for efficiency and how to work with Timeline markers to isolate segments of the project. A discussion on the design decision process explained certain issues and possible solutions involved in finishing a sound track. Finally, you learned how to adjust and edit tracks to coincide with specific components of your project. The image that opened this session shows the location in the Timeline where the most intensive editing began; the final image shows the location in the Timeline that was a key frame in the decision-making process.

Here are questions to help you review the information in this session. You'll find the answer to each question in the tutorial noted in parentheses.

1. How do you display the volume rubberband on the Timeline? (See "Tutorial: Adjusting Volume for a Group of Clips.")

2. How does the Fade Adjustment tool work? How do you select the tool? (See "Tutorial: Adjusting Volume for a Group of Clips.")

3. How do you set the volume of a clip at a handle to a precise volume percentage? (See "Tutorial: Adjusting Volume for a Group of Clips.")

4. What does the Fade Scissors tool do? How do you select the tool? (See "Tutorial: Working with Sound Effects.")

5. Why do you use the Fade Scissors tool on the volume rubberband rather than adding handles by clicking the rubberband with the Select tool? (See "Tutorial: Working with Sound Effects.")

6. Can you hear volume edits made for a clip in the Clip window? (See "Tutorial: Working with Sound Effects.")

7. How do you lock tracks on the Timeline? (See "Tutorial: Using the Audio Mixer.")

8. What is the advantage of setting In and Out points on the Timeline? (See "Tutorial: Using the Audio Mixer.")

9. What are the different Automation Write Options available for the Audio Mixer? How are they different? (See "Tutorial: Editing with the Audio Mixer.")

10. Is there a difference in the information displayed about a clip's volume in the Timeline when using the Audio Mixer to set the volume? What is the difference? (See "Tutorial: Editing with the Audio Mixer.")

11. How do you adjust the Pan/Balance for a clip in the Timeline? (See "Tutorial: Balancing Clips.")

12. Can Pan/Balance be adjusted in the Audio Mixer? How? (See "Tutorial: Balancing Clips.")

13. How do you add a marker to the Timeline? (See "Tutorial: Working with a Group of Audio Clips.")

14. How do you set a crossfade between two clips on the Timeline? (See "Tutorial: Fine-Tuning the Audio Tracks.")

15. Can you use Timeline and clip markers together? When should you use them together? (See "Tutorial: Fine-Tuning the Audio Tracks.")

» Other Projects

In this session, you learned how to edit audio using both the Timeline and the Audio Mixer. Experiment with a copy of the project. Adjust the volume and pan/balance settings using the Audio Mixer. Use different combinations of writing options and see how the different writing options work.

The audio clips are arranged and edited a specific way in the project. Experiment with different clip arrangements and edits. Use a separate copy of the project or add extra audio tracks for experimentation. Make sure to turn off the tracks you are not using.

Part V
Creating and Animating Titles

Working with Titles

Session Introduction

What goes into the average movie or television program? Obviously, video and audio. You generally see effects as well. Have you ever seen a movie or a television program that doesn't have credits? Not likely.

Aside from credits, text is used other ways in a video project. A project whose primary purpose is to provide information is usually accompanied by varying amounts of text. Suppose you wanted to make a video on how to catch a fish. What elements can you use? You can use close-up shots of someone actually performing the tasks involved, such as baiting a line. You can use a voiceover to describe the action as it happens. You can also use a text system for reinforcing the content.

The titles must be just that — titles — not paragraphs. Leave the talking to the narrator. The goal is to reinforce what the narrator says, not to provide a transcript. At the end of the piece, you can again use scrolling text to list the folks who worked on the video.

Until Premiere 6.5, the Title window was fairly limited in its capabilities. The new Title Designer window offers templates, drawing tools, extensive layout options, text effects, and motion options. In addition, dozens of Adobe fonts ship with the program and can be used both with Premiere and with other programs.

You need to build two titles for the first segment and a collection of titles for the second segment. Some of the titles are static, while others are part of an animated title sequence you work with later in the book. You build two types of graphic titles. The opening segment of the video uses sequences of red bars moving horizontally and vertically. These are simple graphic titles. The second segment uses a mask for one clip sequence. You build the rectangular graphic used for the mask in the Title window as well.

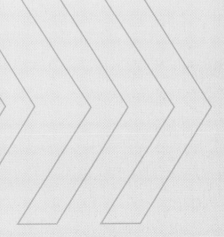

TOOLS YOU'LL USE
Timeline window, Monitor window, Project window, Title Designer window, Horizontal Text tool, Text Selection tool, Rectangle tool, Rounded Rectangle tool, Arrange commands, Align commands, Position commands, Transform commands, text properties, stroke properties, Style menu, Templates menu, video display controls

CD-ROM FILES NEEDED
Session 7 project file you created or the session7.ppj file from the CD-ROM
Nine .prtl files from the extra video folder on the CD-ROM (if you do not complete the title building tutorials)
session8.mpg preview file from the premierecc_samples folder (for reference)

TIME REQUIRED
90 minutes

Tutorial
» Creating a Static Title

The first titles you create are the pair used in the city segment of the project. In this tutorial, you learn the basics of the Title Designer window. You create the first title and save a style to use for the second title.

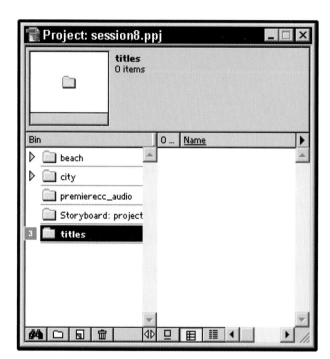

1. **Choose File→Open and navigate to the location where you stored your project files.**
   You can also choose File→Open Recent Project and choose your project file from the list. Open session7.ppj.

   <NOTE>
   If you didn't do the tutorials in Session 7, copy the session7.ppj file from the CD to your hard drive. Open the file and resave it as session8.ppj (or use another filenaming convention).

2. **Resave the project file as** session8.ppj.

3. **Create a new bin in the Project window.**
   Click the new folder icon at the bottom of the window to open the Create Bin dialog box. Name the bin "titles" and click OK to close the Create Bin dialog box.

4. **Choose File→New→Title to open the Adobe Title Designer window.**

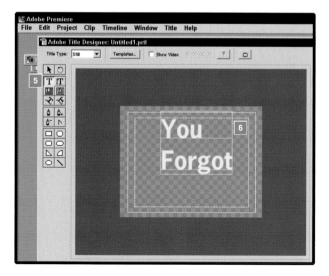

5. **Select the Horizontal Type tool.**
   Click with the tool on the layout to display the vertical I-beam. The initial layout for the text isn't important, because you adjust its size and position later.

6. **Type the text for the first title:** You Forgot.

7. **Click the arrow to the left of Properties.**

This opens the Properties dropdown list.

8. **Click the Font dropdown list and choose Antique Olive Bold Condensed.**

If you do not have this font installed on your computer, find a similar font.

<TIP>

Antique Olive is one of the Adobe fonts shipped with Premiere 6.5. The set of fonts are installed automatically when you install the program.

9. **Change the Font Size to 90.0, and the Aspect to 125%.**

Click the default value to activate a text field and type the new value; or hold the mouse cursor over the default value shown. When it changes to a double-end arrow, drag left (to decrease the value) or right (to increase the value).

<TIP>

You can visually preview fonts. From the main program menu, choose Title→Font Browser and scroll through the list to find the font you want to use. Click OK.

10. **Click the checkbox to the left of the Fill heading to activate the settings.**

Click the dropdown arrow to the left of the checkbox to display the settings options.

Use these Fill settings:

Fill Type Solid

Color white (RGB value of 255/255/255)

100% Opacity

11. **Click the checkbox to the left of the Shadow heading to activate the settings.**
Click the dropdown arrow to the left of the checkbox to display the settings options. Use these Shadow settings:
Color: Black (RGB value of 0/0/0)
Opacity: 100%
Angle: 150.0%
Distance/Size/Spread: 4.0

12. **Right-click the title to open the shortcut menu.**
Choose Position→Horizontal Center to align the title horizontally.

13. **Right-click the title again.**
Choose Position→Vertical Center to align the title vertically.

14. **Click New Style to save the title layout.**
The New Style dialog box opens.

15. Name the style.

I use an abbreviation for this book, pr_cc. If you are working on a large project you may want to use a more descriptive name.

16. Click OK to close the New Style dialog box.

A sample of the style is added to the Title Designer style list.

17. Click Close.

A Save dialog box opens asking if you want to save the file.

< T I P >

You can save a title by choosing File➜Save from the main program menu. Because you have to close the window anyway, the method I describe saves you one step.

18. Browse to the location you are storing the project files.

Name the file "you_forgot" and click Save. The Title Designer window closes.

< T I P >

It is simple to name a file and forget to check the hard drive location. If that happens with a title file, check in the Premiere 6.5 installation directory on your hard drive. This is the default storage location for Premiere files.

19. In the Project folder, click the new title in the titles bin.

View the details at the top of the Project window.

20. Save the project.

You have created your first title, one of the pair of titles used at the end of the first segment of the project. You also created a text style, which you use in the next tutorial to create the second title.

< T I P >

Name a title file according to its contents. For example, the title content reads "You Forgot". Use that as the file name as well. You can keep track of a large number of titles in a project much more simply if you use descriptive names.

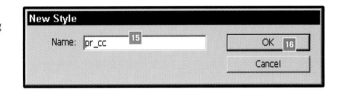

Discussion

Designing the Perfect Title

What makes a title "right" for a project? There are several elements that contribute to a good title: text, background, element placement, and type of display. These elements may or may not seem obvious. Let's have a look.

Text characteristics include font, style, size, and color. Text comes in many shapes and sizes. If you look through the fonts on your computer or online font sites, you see hundreds of different fonts. Finding that perfect font isn't always easy. How you define a font as "perfect" varies from project to project and also from medium to medium. You are working with online, computer, or television display options. Variations among the different media exist, but use these points as a general guideline:

» Don't use an overly elaborate font for transferring information. Decorative fonts are very difficult to read. Save elaborate fonts for conveying a mood. (Have you ever seen a good Dracula movie that didn't use Gothic-style titles? Me neither.) Use a font that is clear and legible for blocks of text or credits.

» Use a font that is heavy enough to be legible but not so heavy that it is illegible. Some fonts look attractive on a printed page, particularly those that are cursive, like handwriting. The problem is the strokes are often very thin and disappear when seen on screen. At the other end of the spectrum, big fat balloon fonts, which can also look interesting on a printed page, look like indistinguishable blobs on the screen.

» Choose a font that is in keeping with the tone of your project. The fonts used in the beginning segment are different than those you will use in the second segment. Why? Because each font creates a different mood. The titles in the first segment contribute to the sense of anxiety created by other elements of the video (that is, the sound track, graphic titles, video, and stills). You would certainly not use the same type of font for a beach scene. Instead, the fonts contribute to the laid back, fun mood of the second segment.

» Use an appropriate size for your titles. Font size corresponds with the distance the viewer is from the screen. Font size also depends on the size of the project output. A full-screen display can use a smaller-sized font more readily than a tiny 160×120 pixel display. Make the text fit without crowding; if the text is used as a subtitle, make it small enough to display the image. If the text is a caption, it should be smaller yet.

» Choose the font color carefully. Color is very emotion-laden. It can be used with positive effects and with negative effects. Use a high-contrast color (black on white for example) for the text when either legibility or tension is the prime consideration. You can use a font that blends more with the background or background imagery for elements such as titles. Be careful of color choice for certain uses. A television broadcast, for example, requires using a smaller color gamut (range of colors) to prevent optical illusion. If you have ever seen an image on television where the color, especially red, seems to be vibrating or bleeding, you have seen an example of poor color selection.

Title backgrounds can be anything from solid colors to video. The choices depend on the purpose of the title and how it fits in with your entire project's titling. Opening credits for a movie usually overlay titles on video, and closing credits are usually scrolling text on a solid background. Why the difference? Opening credits are designed to pull the viewer into the scene and create interest. These credits are usually limited to the name of the movie and the important people involved. Closing credits are lists of names and functions designed for reading, and likely fulfilling legal requirements.

Title elements are placed differently on the screen depending on their importance. Subtitles for foreign language films are always in fairly small text on the bottom third of the screen. This allows the viewer to see the action along with the text. Major titles, on the other hand, are most often placed over anything else on the screen. You can use one of dozens of effects and transitions to change a title's visibility. Sometimes titles are the major elements in the project. Several years ago, I animated a 3000-year-old Egyptian love poem. The text in that case was as important as the animation.

The final factor to consider is how the title is displayed. Titles can be static or animated in some way. Common types of title animation are scrolling and crawling text. Scrolling moves vertically and crawling moves horizontally.

Any and all of these guidelines can be ignored with dramatic effect in the hands of skilled designers. The movie *Seven* ran the credits backward. Running credits in reverse is jarring and disturbing, and extremely effective in this film, which is in itself jarring and disturbing.

Using Safe Title Displays

Use the Show Safe Titles option for title layouts if you plan output to television. The two safe title areas are drawn over your title, and identify the action-safe zone (outermost line) and the title-safe zone (innermost line). Television screens are not flat and do not display the entire content of a frame. Use the layout guides to prevent losing your text or motion due to the screen characteristics. Make sure your text and graphics remain within the boundaries.

Tutorial
» Creating a New Title from a Style

You have created the first title and also saved a style. In this tutorial, you use the style to create a second title, and then modify a portion of the title for impact. In this tutorial, note the alternate layout for the Styles section of the Title Designer window.

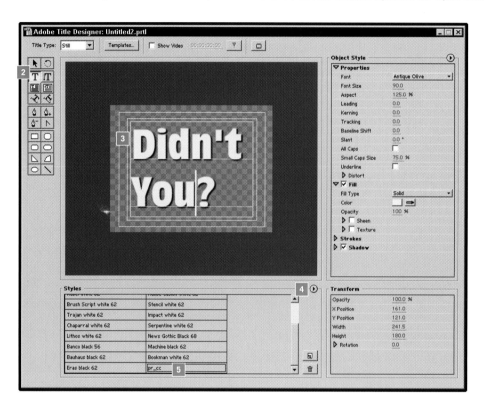

1. **Choose File→New→Title to open the Adobe Title Designer window.**

2. **Click the Horizontal Type tool.**
   Click with the tool on the layout to display the vertical I-beam. The initial layout for the text isn't important because you adjust its size and position later.

3. **Type the text for this title:** Didn't You?

4. **Display the Styles by name.**
   Click the Styles menu arrow and choose Text Only.

5. **Click the** pr_cc **style to apply it to the text.**
   The settings you created and saved as a style in the last tutorial are applied to the text.

<TIP>
It isn't necessary to change the Styles layout; I included this step to show you how the layout was changed as shown in the figure.

Title Conversion

Premiere 6.5 uses the .prtl file format for titles created in the Title Designer window. All previous versions of Premiere used the .ptl file format for titles created in the Title window. You can import titles from previous versions into Premiere 6.5 and use them at will. You cannot edit these older titles in the Title Designer. Instead, double-click a .ptl file to open the old Title window.

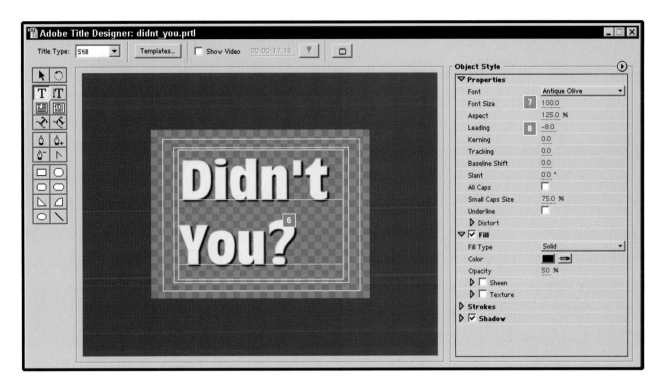

6. **Select the question mark at the end of the title with the Horizontal Text tool.**
   Click on the screen to the left of the "?" and drag to select the question mark.

7. **Increase the font size for the selected "?" to 100.0.**

8. **Reset the Leading to –8.0.**
   The larger font size drops the baseline. Don't worry about the text's position. You adjust it in the next step.

9. **Right-click the title to open the shortcut menu.**
   Choose Position→Horizontal Center. Right-click the title again. Choose Position→Vertical Center.

10. **Click Close.**
    The Save dialog box opens. In the Save dialog box, name the title "didnt_you", and store it in the same location as your other project files. Click Save to close the dialog box.

11. **Save the project.**
    You have created the second title for the project based on a custom style. You also combined different font sizes in the same title.

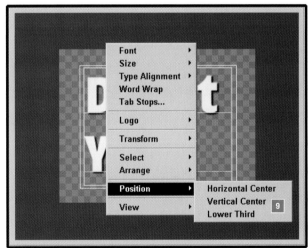

Tutorial
» Adding Titles to the Timeline

You have built the titles for the first section of the project. In this tutorial, you add them to the Timeline and set fades. Use the Info window to assist in placing clips correctly. Choose Window➜Info to open the window. Arrange windows on the screen to display the Timeline, Info, and Project windows.

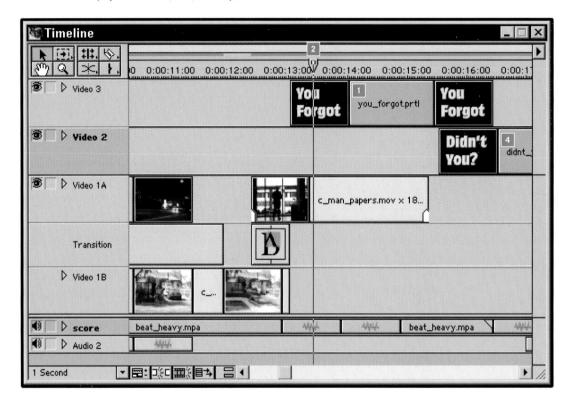

1. **Select the** `you_forgot.prtl` **file from the titles bin in the Project window.**
   Drag it to Video 3 in the Timeline window.

2. **Position the clip to start at 13:01.**
   Use the Starting at time in the Info window to place the clip correctly.

3. **Set its duration to 03:13.**
   Right-click the clip and choose Duration. Enter **313** in the Duration field and click OK.

<TIP>
You can also drag either end of the clip to change its duration as you have done in previous sessions; use the duration setting in the Info window as a guide.

4. **Drag the** `didnt_you.prtl` **clip from the titles bin in the Project window to Video 2.**

5. **Position the clip to start at 15:16.**
   Set its duration to 02:02 as described in Step 2.

<NOTE>
Look at the locations of the second title clip and the last copy of the `beat_heavy.mpa` clip. The titles end at the same time the score for the first segment finishes. Not a coincidence!

6. **Choose Window➜Monitor to open the window.**
   Arrange it on the screen with the other windows. Shift + click the time ruler to show the title overlaying other clips in the Timeline. View the layers in the Monitor window.

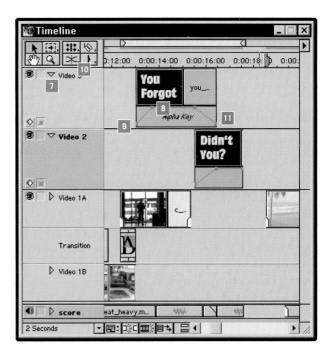

<NOTE>
Titles are created with a transparent background by default.

7. **Click the arrows to the left of the Video 2 and Video 3 tracks to open them.**

   The red rubberband you see is the fade rubberband. The title's transparency setting, Alpha Key, is written on the bottom portion of the clip.

8. **Click the Selection tool in the Timeline toolbox.**

   In the you_forgot.prtl clip, click the fade rubberband at 13:21 to add a handle.

9. **Click the handle at the beginning of the clip and drag down to the bottom of the track to set the fade to 0%.**

<TIP>
These handles and rubberbands work the same way as the ones you used for the audio clips.

10. **Select the Cross Fade tool in the Timeline toolbox.**

    If the Cross Fade tool is not displayed, click and hold the Fade tool displayed to open the subpalette, and select the Cross Fade tool.

11. **Click the title in Video 3, and then the title in Video 2 to create a crossfade.**

    The crossfade uses the overlapped frames' duration to fade out Video 3 and fade in Video 2.

<NOTE>
You may wonder why the last title doesn't fade out but ends abruptly instead. This cut to black was done for effect. When you preview the clip, you see the second title cut to black, and then for a second (29 frames, to be exact) the screen is black and you hear the sound of the ocean. That's when the beach video clip begins. If you wish, experiment with adding a fadeout for the last title. I think a direct cut is more effective.

12. **Save the project.**

    You have now added titles complete with fades to the first part of the project.

How to Maintain Your Titles' Transparency

A title is used like any other type of visual project component. That is, you can use it as content for the Video 1 tracks or place it in the superimposed tracks starting at Video 2. The default title construction uses a transparent background. If you drag a title into Video 1, and then move it to another track, the transparency is lost. To reset it, follow these steps:

1. **Select the clip in the Timeline**

2. **Right-click to open the shortcut menu, and then choose Video Options→Transparency.**

3. **In the Transparency Settings dialog box, click the Key type dropdown menu.**

4. **Select Alpha Channel.**

5. **Click OK to close the dialog box. Your title's transparency is reset.**

Tutorial
» Customizing Title Text

The second segment of the project uses titles as well. In this tutorial, you make more titles in the Title Designer window using other text features such as strokes and custom fills. These titles are added to the project in a later session.

1. **Move the Timeline edit line to 29:00.**

2. **Choose File→New→Title.**
   The Title Designer window opens.

3. **Click Show Video.**
   You see the image of the young lady running on the beach.

<TIP>
Once you click Show Video, a frame of the Timeline displays behind the title. In Step 1 you set the edit line location at 29:00, which is the default location shown when you click Show Video. To show any frame in the project, click the time indicator next to the Show Video checkbox and type the desired frame location, or click and drag the displayed time left to move toward the beginning of the project or right toward the end of the project. Use frames from the project to match color in the title. Viewing actual frames also helps to place titles in precise locations.

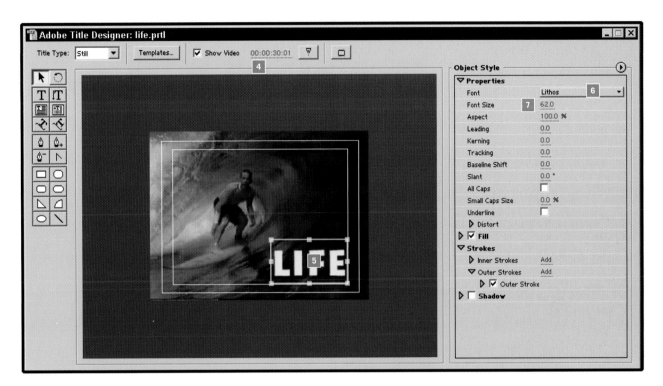

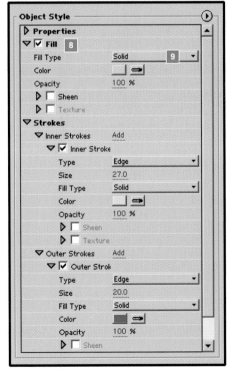

4. **Drag the time slider to approximately 30:00.**

   Now you see the image of the surfer. You select a stroke color from the surfboard, so make sure the frame you chose displays it clearly.

5. **Select the Horizontal Text tool.**

   On the right side of the screen, type **LIFE**. Position the title in the lower right portion of the screen.

6. **Click the Font dropdown list and choose Lithos→Black (or a similar substantial font).**

7. **Set the font size to 62.**

8. **Click the checkbox to the left of the Fill heading.**

   Open the Fill selection menu by clicking on the arrow to the left of Fill.

9. **Choose Solid from the Fill Type menu.**

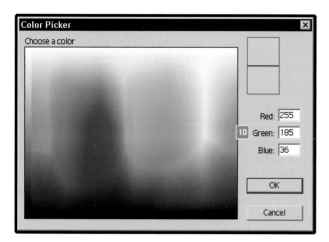

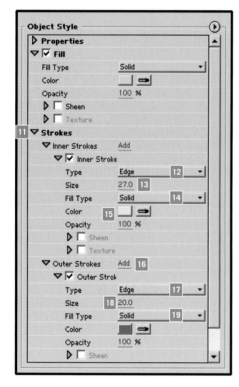

10. **Click the color swatch to open the Color Picker.**
    Set the color to RGB=255/185/36. Click OK to close the Color Picker. The text is now a gold color.

11. **Click the arrow to the left of the Strokes heading to open a sub-menu.**
    Click Add to add an Inner Stroke. Click the arrow to the left of the Inner Strokes heading to display the Inner Stroke settings.

12. **Select Edge from the Type menu.**
    You add a stroke around the edge of the text for added interest.

13. **Set the Size to 27.0.**

14. **Choose Solid from the Fill Type menu.**

15. **Click the color swatch to open the Color Picker.**
    Set the color to RGB=255/223/72. Click OK to close the Color Picker. A yellow stroke is added to the text.

16. **Click Add to add an Outer Stroke.**
    Click the arrow to the left of the Outer Strokes heading to display the Outer Stroke settings.

17. **Select Edge from the Type menu.**
    You add a stroke outside the edge of the text for contrast.

18. **Set the Size to 20.0.**

19. **Select the Eyedropper tool next to the color swatch.**
    The cursor changes to an eyedropper. Move the eyedropper over the image. You can see it changes color as it samples different pixels in the image. Select a red color from the surfboard. The sample uses RGB = 175/0/40.

20. **Close the Title Designer window.**
    In the Save dialog box, name the title file "Life" and click Save.

21. **Save the project.**
    You have created another title using strokes for added interest and font weight. You used custom colors, and chose one color from the image itself.

Tutorial
» Duplicating Project Titles

In the previous tutorial, you learned how to make a title using custom colors and strokes. You probably noticed that you weren't instructed to make a style from the file. In this tutorial you learn to duplicate a title to make two more project titles. The images in the tutorial show random frames from the Timeline behind the text.

1. **Double-click the** `life.prtl` **file in the titles bin of the Project window.**
   The Title Designer window opens.

2. **Double-click the text to select the text box and activate the Horizontal Text tool.**

3. **Select the "LIFE" text in the text box and replace it with** IS A.

4. **Choose File→Save As.**
   Name the file `is_a.prtl`. Click Save, but don't close the Title Designer window as you use it again.

5. **Press the Shift key and drag the title left across the screen to line up the text with the Safe Title Margin.**
   The Shift key constrains the motion so the title doesn't move vertically. You set the final location in Step 7.

6. **Select the text and type** BEACH **over the "IS A" text.**

7. **Nudge the text box back to the right as far as it goes before wrapping.**

<TIP>
When the text box reaches the Title Safe border, its text wraps to the next line. Control this fine movement using the arrow keys to nudge the text box one pixel left or right. If it wraps as you are nudging right, press the left arrow key to reposition it.

8. **Create a style from the text.**
   In the Styles area, click the Style menu and choose New Style. Name the style "beach" and click OK. The new style is added.

9. **Choose File→Save As.**
   Name the file `beach.prtl`. Click Save and close the Title Designer window.

10. **Save the project.**
    You made two copies of the titles for the second segment of the project.

Tutorial

» Creating Titles from Templates

The text titles are nearly complete. You have completed the phrase "Life is a Beach". It's true, isn't it? In this tutorial you make the last title for the sequence. This time you use one of the templates supplied with Premiere 6.5.

1. **Choose File→New→Title to open the Title Designer window.**

2. **Deselect the Show Video option.**
   You work with the Title Designer templates which include their own backgrounds.

3. **Click Templates.**
   The Templates window opens.

4. **In the Templates window, choose Travel→Tropical→**`trp title.prtl`.

5. **Click Apply.**
   The Templates window closes and the template's image and text displays in the window.

6. **In the Title Designer window, click the subtitle text block and press Delete.**

7. **Delete 2 of the 3 title text blocks.**
   You choose which one should remain. The final text is repositioned.

8. **Select the text in the remaining text box and type** FIND YOURS.

9. **Apply the beach style you added in the last tutorial.**
   Click the style from the Styles menu at the bottom of the window. The text changes to the beach style.

10. **Move the text box to right-align with the Safe Title margin.**
    Right-click the title to open the shortcut menu. Choose Position→Lower Third. The text moves to the lower third of the screen.

11. **Save the title as** `end.prtl`.
    Close the Title Designer window.

12. **Save the project.**
    You have made the final title for your project. You used a template and applied a custom style created in a previous tutorial.

Tutorial
» Using a Title in the Video 1 Track

Wait until you see what happens with the title you built in the last tutorial! It is truly lovely. In this tutorial, you add the template-based title to Video 1. Remember that transitions can be used with clips in Video 1A and Video 1B tracks. You add a transition to complete the ending of your movie.

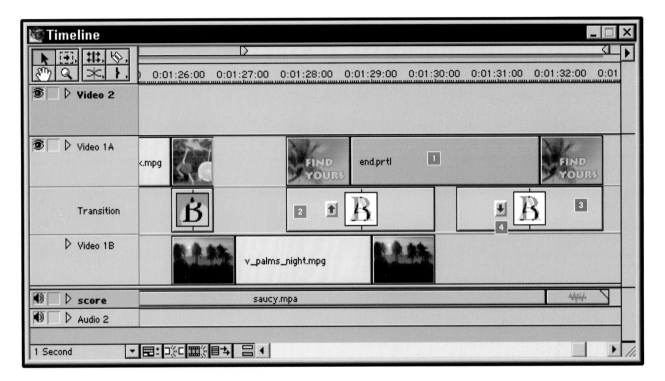

1. **Drag the** end.prtl **file from the titles bin in the Project window to Video 1A.**
   Start the clip at 01:27:20. Leave the default duration of 05:00.

2. **Copy the Additive Dissolve transition from the Transition track.**
   It is located below your title clip.

3. **Click the Transition track to the right of the first transition, and paste the Additive Dissolve copy.**
   Drag the copy right to align it with the end of the end.prtl title clip.

4. **Click the arrow to set the direction of the transition downward.**

5. **Preview the clip.**

6. **Save the project.**
   You added the template-based title to the end of the project. You used a transition to finish the fadeout of your movie.

<NOTE>
This portion of the Timeline is included in the session8.mpg preview file.

Tutorial
» Creating Graphic Titles

The first portion of the movie uses a set of animated red horizontal and vertical bars numerous times for effect. In this tutorial, you create these two bars. Each is a graphic title. You won't be adding these to the project at this time.

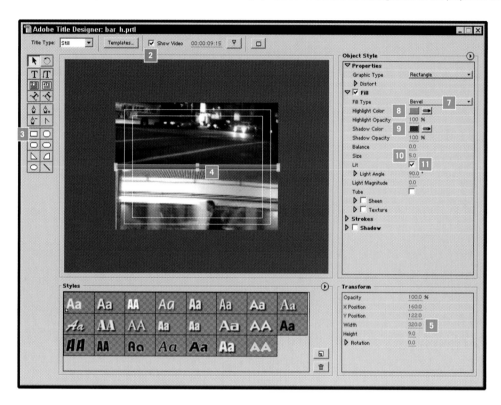

1. **Choose File→New→Title to open the Title Designer window.**

2. **Click Show Video.**
   Slide the Timeline indicator to approximately 09:15. The frame displayed on the screen shows the split screen image, which is important for locating the title you make in the next steps.

<TIP>
The horizontal bar title you are creating in this tutorial is animated at various positions throughout the first section of the movie and is used as a divider between the split screen segments. Set the title graphic into the correct position for the split screen. When you animate the titles in the next session, you only have to animate those copies of the title moving at different levels. This saves a lot of time.

3. **Select the Rectangle tool.**

4. **Draw a rectangle over the screen that extends the width of the screen.**
   The precise size isn't important.

5. **In the Transform panel, click the displayed Width value.**
   Type **320** to resize the rectangle to 320.0 pixels wide. Click the displayed Height value and type **9** to resize the rectangle to 9.0 pixels high.

<TIP>
The decimal values are added automatically.

6. **Right-click the rectangle and choose Position→Horizontal Center; repeat and choose Position→Vertical Center.**

7. **Click the checkbox left of the Fill heading to activate it.**

   Click the arrow to the left of the checkbox to display the Fill settings. Choose Bevel from the Fill Type list.

8. **Click the Highlight Color swatch to open the Color Picker window.**

   Choose a red color (the sample uses RGB = 205/0/5). Click OK to close the Color Picker window.

9. **Click the Shadow Color swatch to open the Color Picker window and choose a dark purple (the sample uses RGB = 68/0/40).**

   Click OK to close the Color Picker window.

10. **Set the Size at 5.0.**

11. **Select Lit.**

    This setting creates the illusion of a light source.

12. **Choose File→Save.**

    Name the file `bar_h.prtl` and click Save. You have created the first graphic title for the project. Don't close the Title Designer window.

13. **Select the rectangle.**

14. **Rotate the rectangle 90 degrees.**

    Use the Rotation slider setting. Click the value to the right of the Rotation heading (it displays 0.0) and type **90**.

<TIP>
Another way you can enter the 90 degree rotation is to click the arrow to the left of the Rotation heading and use the Rotation control or right-click the rectangle and choose Transform→Rotation.

15. **Reset the length of the rectangle to 240 pixels.**

    Click the Width control and drag it to 240 or type the value.

16. **Center the rectangle vertically on the screen.**

    To do this, set its X Position (horizontal) at 6.0.

17. **Choose File→Save As to open the Save As dialog box.**

    Name the file `bar_v.prtl` and click Save. The dialog box closes. You have created a second version of the graphic bar title. Close the Title Designer window.

18. **Save the project.**

    Your project now includes both horizontal and vertical versions of the graphic bar title.

How to Define a Location on the Screen

The location of content on a frame is defined by basic geometry. The horizontal axis, (the x-axis) and the vertical axis (the y-axis) divide the screen into quadrants. The center of the screen, where the axes intersect, has coordinates 0, 0. The number of pixels along each axis depend on the size of the project. You are working with a frame size of 320 x 240. Therefore, there are 320 pixels along the x-axis and 240 pixels along the y-axis. The center of the screen is located 160 pixels from the left (or right) and 120 pixels from the top (or bottom).

<TIP>
Because the rectangle is centered on the screen, you can also adjust the X Position (horizontal location of the rectangle's center) to 160.0 pixels and the Y Position (vertical location of the rectangle's center) to 120.0 pixels.

Transform		
Opacity	100.0 %	
X Position	6.0	16
Y Position	120.0	
Width	240.0	15
Height	9.0	
▷ Rotation	90.0	14

Tutorial
» Building Graphic Mattes

In the final tutorial for this session, you make yet another graphic title. However, this title is different in that it is never used as is in the project. Seems like a pointless exercise doesn't it? To the contrary — this graphic image is used in a later session as a special type of transparency for a section of the video. Using this title as a matte allows portions of one track to show at the same time the portions of another clip show.

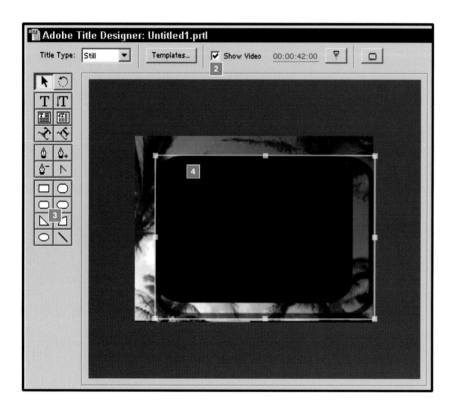

1. **Choose File→New→Title to open the Title Designer window.**

2. **Click Show Video.**
   Slide the Timeline indicator to approximately 42:00 or select the time displayed and type "4200".

<TIP>
If the palm tree video is not displayed, check the visibility of the tracks in the Timeline. This clip is in Track 2; you may need to turn off Track 3.

3. **Select the Round Corner Rectangle tool.**

4. **Click and drag the cursor over the screen to draw a rectangle.**

<NOTE>
The safe areas are turned off to show the content more clearly. Right-click inside the Title Designer work area and choose View→Safe Title Margin. Repeat and choose View→Safe Action Margin. The margins are deselected and disappear from the screen.

5. **Click the arrow to the left of the Properties label to display the Properties settings.**

   Set the Fillet Size at 15.0%. Click the displayed value and type **15** or drag the value to 15.0. This setting controls the corners' rounding.

6. **Click the checkmark to the left of the Fill heading to select the option, and click the arrow to the left of the checkbox to display the Fill settings.**

   Click the Color swatch to open the Color Picker. Set the color to black (RGB = 0/0/0) and click OK to close the Color Picker.

7. **Adjust the rectangle size in the Transform panel at the bottom right of the Title Designer window.**

   In the Transform panel, check the size of the rectangle. Set the width to 265 pixels and the height to 190 pixels.

8. **Copy and paste the rectangle.**

   At this point, you have to take my word for it! You can't see the second copy of the rectangle yet unless you drag it to another location in the window. It is located directly above the first rectangle.

9. **Reset the size of the rectangle to 295 pixels wide and 211 pixels high.**

10. **Set the opacity to 0% in the Fill settings.**

    The rectangle is transparent. It's difficult to work with transparent objects! Don't panic, you add a visible stroke to the rectangle in the next steps.

11. **Open the Strokes menu by clicking on the arrow to its left.**

    Click Add to add an Inner Stroke. Click the arrow to the left of the Inner Stroke heading to open its property settings.

12. **Use the default Edge type.**

    Set the Size to 8.0 pixels. Now you can see a border surrounding the transparent rectangle.

13. **Decrease the opacity to 60%.**

    The stroke appears gray on the screen.

14. **Right-click over the visible stroke.**

    Choose Arrange➜Send to Back from the shortcut menu.

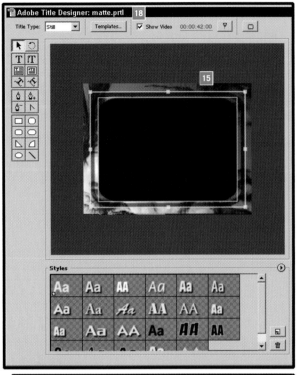

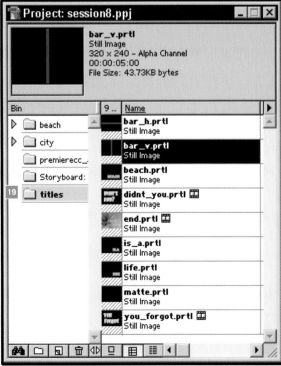

15. **Group select both rectangles.**
    Click the outline rectangle to select it, and then press Shift and click the solid rectangle. Both rectangles are now selected.

16. **Right-click the group and choose Align Objects→Horizontal Center.**
    Repeat and choose Align Objects→Vertical Center. The two rectangles are positioned directly over one another horizontally and vertically, making the border created by the second rectangle equidistant from the first solid black rectangle.

17. **Right-click the group and choose Position→Horizontal Center.**
    Repeat and choose Position→Vertical Center. The two rectangles are positioned at the horizontal and vertical centers of the screen.

18. **Save the title as** `matte.prtl`.
    Close the Title Designer window.

19. **Click the titles bin in the Project window.**
    You have a total of nine titles in all; three have icons indicating they have been added to the Timeline.

20. **Save the project.**
    Now you have created the graphic matte, you have completed the title design and construction for the project.

» Session Review

In this session, you learned how to create a variety of titles. You were introduced to the design concepts involved in title construction. You built both text and graphic titles. You learned how to save time duplicating a series of similar titles and how to make sure the titles were consistent by saving styles. You learned how to create titles from a template. You also learned how to add titles to the Timeline, both into superimposed tracks and the Video 1 tracks. What a difference titles can make! The image at the beginning of this session shows the last video clip of the project. The final image in this session shows the same portion of the Timeline, but this time you can see how much different it looks when dissolving into a closing title.

Answer the following questions to help you review the information in this session. You can find the answer for each question in the tutorial noted in parentheses.

1. How do you align titles in specific locations? (See "Tutorial: Creating a Static Title.")

2. How do you save a text style? (See "Tutorial: Creating a Static Title.")

3. How do you choose the correct font for a project? (See "Discussion: Designing the Perfect Title.")

4. What elements do you have to consider when designing titling? (See "Discussion: Designing the Perfect Title.")

5. Can you combine more than one size of font in the same title? (See "Tutorial: Creating a New Title from a Style.")

6. Does a title clip behave the same as a footage clip in the Timeline? (See "Tutorial: Adding Titles to the Timeline.")

7. How do you set the transparency for a title in the Timeline? (See "Tutorial: Adding Titles to the Timeline.")

8. How do you add strokes to title text? (See "Tutorial: Customizing Title Text.")

9. How do you use the content of the Timeline as guides in the Title Designer window? (See "Tutorial: Customizing Title Text.")

10. Do you have to make a text style to duplicate a title? (See "Tutorial: Duplicating Project Titles.")

11. How do you access templates to use for your titles? (See "Tutorial: Creating Titles from Templates.")

12. How do you use titles in the basic Video 1 tracks? Is it different than other types of footage? (See "Tutorial: Using a Title in the Video 1 Track.")

13. Is there a difference between creating titles that use text and titles that use graphics? (See "Tutorial: Creating Graphic Titles.")

14. How do you rotate a graphic element in the Title Designer window? (See "Tutorial: Creating Graphic Titles.")

15. Can you create titles or graphics that are used for other purposes? (See "Tutorial: Building Graphic Mattes.")

16. How do you change the opacity of an element in the Title Designer window? (See "Tutorial: Building Graphic Mattes.")

17. How do you align title elements? (See "Tutorial: Building Graphic Mattes.")

» Other Projects

Watch TV (yes, this is a real project!). Look for the credits and the opening title sequences. Pay attention to the different titling elements and consider how and why they were used in the particular situation. Are the titles effective? Ineffective? An afterthought? Do they contribute to the mood of the program? How?

The project uses a small number of Title Designer features. Experiment with the title window capabilities in the project and for other projects.

Session 9
Creating
Animation

Session Introduction

This session is the first of two devoted to animation. Animation in Premiere is different than what you may think of when you read the term. Premiere is not designed as a full-blown animation program. Though you can do traditional animation in Premiere (and I have in the past), the question is why would you? Computer animation requires sophisticated Timeline capabilities, parent-child relationship capabilities, and the use of numerous other features. Premiere doesn't provide those types of tools simply because it isn't designed as an animation program.

If you can't make a cartoon in Premiere, what do you animate? Everything you add to the project as well as elements you create (such as titles) can be animated. Premiere has a separate Motion Settings window to design animation for a clip. Within this window, you can set a motion path for a clip to follow. This motion path can vary from a smooth slide across a screen to a complicated and convoluted path like a falling leaf.

You have several tools to use for building animation. First and foremost is the Timeline (the Motion Settings window has its own). You can modify characteristics of the clip for any point specified along the Timeline. These animation options include location, rotation, zoom, and distortion of the clip. You can also control the speed of the clip through the Motion Settings window's Timeline using delay settings, motion options, and smoothing.

You use the graphic titles created and stored in your project in Session 8 to create much of the animation used in the opening sequence of the project. Review the sample from this session or the finished project to see what you build. In addition to learning certain basics of animating in Premiere, you also gain lots of experience organizing and working with large numbers of similar clips. Also in this session, you learn how to create a type of preview called Print to Video, which gives you a good view of your work.

TOOLS YOU'LL USE
Timeline window, Show/Hide tracks command, Info window, Effect Controls window, Motion Settings window, Create New Alpha command, Preview window, Motion path, Motion timeline, Motion timeline markers, motion path coordinates, Print to Video command

CD-ROM FILES NEEDED
Session 8 project file you created or the session8.ppj file from the CD-ROM
Session9.mpg preview file from the premierecc_samples folder (for reference)

TIME REQUIRED
90 minutes

Tutorial
» Changing Clip Size and Position

This tutorial introduces you to the Motion Settings window. The Motion Settings window can be used to resize and reposition clips. In this tutorial, you work with a clip from the first section of the project.

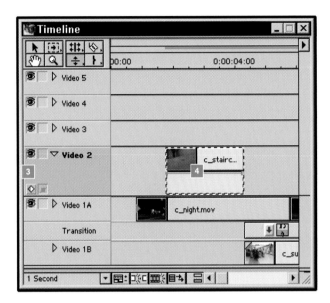

1. **Choose File→Open and navigate to the location where you stored your project files.**
   You can also choose File→Open Recent Project and choose your project file from the list. Open session8.ppj.

<NOTE>
If you didn't do the tutorials in Session 8, copy the session8.ppj file from the CD to your hard drive. Open the file and resave it as session9.ppj (or use another filenaming convention).

2. **Resave the project file as session9.ppj.**

3. **Hide all the audio tracks and show all the video tracks.**

4. **Select the** c_staircase.mov **clip in Video 2, which starts at 01:23.**

5. **Right-click the clip to open the shortcut menu.**
   Choose Video Options→Motion. The Motion Settings window opens.

<NOTE>
You can also access the Motion Settings for a clip from the Effect Controls window. Select the clip on the Timeline and choose Window→Effect Controls. When the Effect Controls window opens, click Motion to open the Motion Settings window.

preview window   motion timeline   timeline marker   motion path

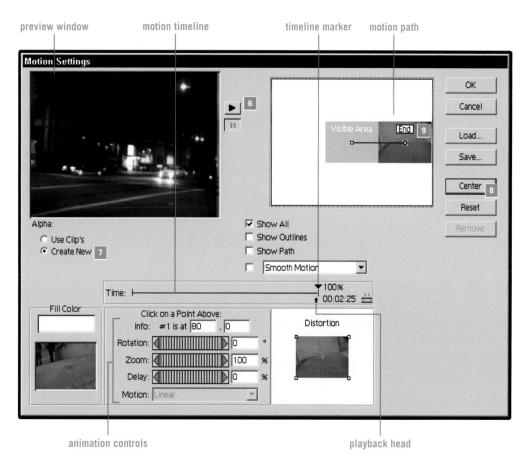

animation controls   playback head

6. **Click Play to view the clip.**
You see the clip moving from left to right across the Preview window. Click Stop when you are finished viewing the clip.

7. **Click Create New to create an alpha channel for the clip.**
Clips are created with a transparent background layer, referred to as an alpha channel. The c_staircase.mov clip, like other video clips, has an alpha channel of the same dimensions as the video (320 × 240 pixels). You resize the video clip later in this tutorial, which means the size of the video changes, but the size of the alpha channel remains the same. If you use the clip's alpha channel, your resized clip is shown against a solid white background that fills the screen — the size of the default alpha channel. Choosing the Create New option adds an alpha channel that changes in size as you resize the video clip.

8. **Click Center to move the Start frame to the center of the screen.**
In Step 6 you saw the clip move from left to right across the screen. You need the clip static and centered on the screen.

<NOTE>
When the Motion Settings window opens, the Start frame is selected.

9. **Click the End frame in the motion path area.**
It appears as a small square. When you click it, it is labeled as End.

10. **Click Center again to move the end frame to the center of the screen.**
Now the clip is in a static location for its duration and you can begin its animation. Test the motion in the Preview area. The clip doesn't move.

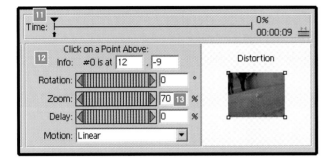

How the Motion Settings Coordinates Work

Keyframe location coordinates work in a standard geometric fashion. The horizontal axis (the x-axis) and the vertical axis (the y-axis) divide the screen into quadrants. The center of the screen, where the axes intersect, has coordinates 0, 0. Moving to the upper right quadrant makes the x-axis value positive, and the y-axis value negative. For example, 10, -10. Moving to the upper left quadrant makes both the x-axis and y-axis values negative. A keyframe in the bottom left quadrant has a negative x-axis value, and a positive y-axis value. Finally, a keyframe in the lower right quadrant has positive values for both axes.

11. **Click the 0% position on the Timeline.**

    When you selected and centered the End position in the Motion path area, the 100% position on the Timeline is selected.

12. **Set the location settings by typing new values into the fields.**

    Info: #0 is at 12, −9.

    The image moves upward and to the right in the motion path area of the window.

<TIP>

Be careful moving around the settings in this window. Don't press Enter after adding a new value or time marker. Doing so closes the window. Instead, click another field or press Tab to move the cursor to another field.

13. **Set the Zoom value to 70%.**

    The image decreases in size. You see the image's top and right edges are even with the top and right edges of the Visible Area (the gray square in the motion path display).

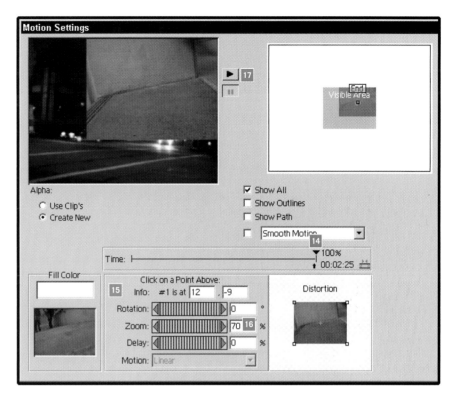

14. Click the 100% position on the Timeline.

You change the setting for the end of the clip as well.

15. Set the location settings by typing new values into the fields.

Info: #1 is at 12, –9.

The End image moves up and right.

16. Set the Zoom value to 70%.

The End image shrinks to fit within the top and right margins of the Visible Area.

17. Click Play.

After the clip has cycled through its Timeline, click Stop. You can see the clip has moved to the upper right of the window and is static throughout its length. Its size also remains constant for the duration of the clip.

18. Click OK.

The Motion Settings window closes. A red horizontal bar displays over the lower part of the clip's thumbnail image in the Timeline. This indicates motion settings have been applied.

< T I P >

If you open the Video 2 track, you can see the label Alpha Key. This label refers to the alpha setting you added in the Motion Settings window.

19. Save the project.

Your first clip with modified motion settings is complete. You changed the size and location of the clip. Where the original clip filled the screen, the modified clip sits in the upper right portion of the window, making up the first part of the split screens you work on in this session.

Tutorial
» Reusing Animation Settings

The c_traffic_light.mov clips also require resizing. These clips were edited in the Timeline using extraction edits. As a result, there are two clips that make up the traffic light sequence. You set motion settings for the traffic light clips similar to the settings you created for the c_staircase.mov clip in the last tutorial. Rather than setting each clip's location and size individually, this tutorial shows you how to reuse the settings.

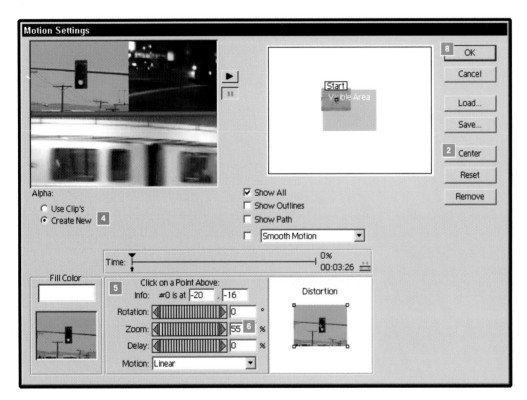

1. **Right-click the first copy of the** c_traffic_light.mov **clip.** Choose Video Options➔Motion from the shortcut menu to open the Motion Settings window.

<NOTE>
Although you haven't added it in the tutorials, the image shows one of the horizontal bar titles. I added it so you can see how changing the clip size and position correlates with the bar titles when you add them in the next tutorials.

2. **Click Center to move the Start frame to the center of the screen.** The image of the clip moves to the center of the screen in the motion path area.

3. **Select the End frame in the motion path area and click Center to move it to the center of the screen.** The clip is now static. That is, it remains stationary at the center of the screen for its duration.

4. **Make sure the Create New option for the Alpha setting is selected.** As you learned in the last tutorial, the default alpha for the video clip won't change sizes as you resize the clip, resulting in a solid white background behind the resized video clip.

5. **At the 0% position on the Timeline, set the location to –20, –16.** The image moves to the upper left of the screen.

6. **Set the zoom to 55%.** The image is resized. Its top and left edges now match the top and left edges of the gray Visible Area in the motion path area.

7. **Click the 100% position on the Timeline.**
   Set the location to –20, –16, and the zoom to 55%. The Start and End frame images now overlay one another in the motion path area.

8. **Click OK.**
   The Motion Settings window closes. You see the red horizontal bar across the c_traffic_light.mov clip in the Timeline indicating custom motion settings.

9. **Copy the** c_traffic_light.mov **clip on the Timeline.**

10. **Select the second copy of the** c_traffic_light.mov **clip.**
    You will paste custom attributes to this copy of the clip.

11. **Choose Edit→Paste Attributes.**
    The Paste Attributes window opens.

12. **Choose Settings in the Paste Attributes dialog box.**
    All four settings are selected by default. You are pasting only the Motion Settings option. As the copied clip has none of the other attributes selected (filters, fade control, or transparency) you can leave these selections.

13. **Click Paste.**
    The Paste Attributes dialog box closes.
    The settings from the first clip are now applied to the second clip.

14. **Check that the settings have transferred to the clip.**
    You will see the red line indicating Motion Settings are applied.

<TIP>
You may or may not see an Alpha Key indicator on the clip. It is applied with the Motion Settings.

15. **Save the project.**
    You have modified two more clips to use for the split screen effect in the first segment of the project. You learned to reuse settings created for one clip with another clip.

<NOTE>
You can also use video effects to trim the clip for the same final effect, but resetting the clip's dimensions in the Motion Settings window is much quicker.

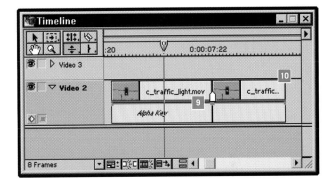

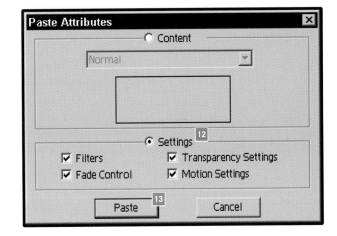

Discussion

Working with Large Numbers of Similar Clips

It is not uncommon to have numerous copies of the same clip in a project. In this project, you are going to work with over 30 copies of the horizontal and vertical bar titles you made in the last session. That seems daunting, and it certainly can be. It also seems very time-consuming, and it can be that as well. The key to saving time and sanity is organization. This discussion outlines a method I have used many times that works. A lot of work and thought is still involved, but it is organized chaos. The steps outlined here are used as the basis for the upcoming tutorials.

1. First add an extra work track or two. Tracks can be easily added and removed. Use them as a holding area.

2. Write out what you want to do. Physically write it out on a piece of paper. Some projects are designed with written and drawn storyboards. If you have one, use it as a place to start. If not, make lists of what you want. It helps to have a copy of the project content before you start that you can refer to repeatedly as you assemble your list. As you mark up clip info, you can see patterns develop, such as clip coordinates for animating.

3. Decide where to start. In this project, the bar titles are used both as animations and also to define vertical and horizontal split screens. Start from any location that must be matched precisely to simplify both design and construction. In this project, clips are added on a track-by-track basis. In your own projects, without a predetermined layout, start with locations that must be matched, and then add other copies of the clips that can use variable locations.

4. Look for common characteristics among elements. Consider the horizontal bar title. It was created to overlay the screen split between two pairs of clips and can be used as a static clip for that purpose. The static clip's position is taken care of. Looking at the final project, you can see two other positions for the horizontal bar — both above and below the location of the original. This means you need two copies of this clip with alternate motion path settings. What about the vertical bar title? It appears in the middle of the screen in its static state. This is the correct position for one of the vertical split screen segments (although its length must be adjusted). It also has versions moving across the screen at various locations. Although there are six location requirements for the vertical and horizontal bar, it isn't necessary to re-create the animation six times.

   For example, you may need a copy of the vertical bar that moves across the screen in one second and another copy that moves across the screen in half that time. You can create two sets of motion settings for two copies of

the clip, or you can add the settings to one copy and use a half-second duration for a second copy to achieve the faster motion results with no extra
work.

5. Preplan the stacking order. Clips are layered one on top of the other, starting
    with Video 2. A clip in Video 2 is behind a clip in Video 3. This determines
    the locations of certain clips in the project. There is no rule for clip layout; it
    depends solely on how the clips look when overlaid in numerous tracks. In
    this project, the copies of the bars used for framing split screens are set
    behind the copies of the clips in motion.

6. Test and retest. Render-scrub the Timeline many times as you assemble the
    clips, and use Print to Video previews. Make quick tests in the Motion win-
    dow as you add clips by using the Show All setting. The Show All setting
    displays the contents of the Timeline for all tracks below the one you are
    working in. You can easily see the effect of the animation you are designing
    for a clip without having to leave the Motion Settings window.

I used the set of steps outlined here as the basis for designing the tutorials. Of
course, you add clips to a project that is already designed. If you do the complete
design yourself, though you don't know the final layout, you have an idea of what
you want to accomplish. You can still use the steps with only minor variations.

Tutorial
» Using Titles as Horizontal Frames

There are many copies of the bar title clips used in the project. If you look at the session sample, you can see a number of split screens. In addition to using the bar titles for animation, you also use them for frames. In this tutorial, you lay down some of the framework by modifying the horizontal frame elements and adding them to the project. Make sure you have the Info window displayed for this and subsequent tutorials. You need the duration and start location information to correctly place the clips.

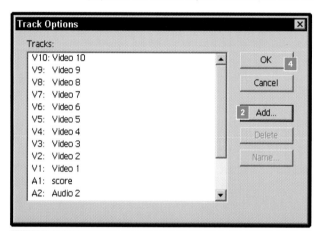

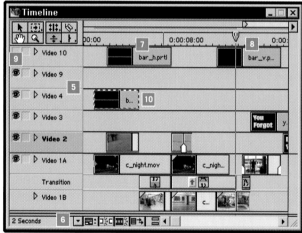

< N O T E >
Video 9 and 10 are only holding areas and are removed after all the clips are in place. You don't need Video 9 displayed for this tutorial, but displaying it acts as a visual separation between the tracks you are working with and the storage track (Video 10).

< T I P >
To quickly position the horizontal bar clip, select it in the Timeline and slowly drag left. It snaps into position aligned with the end of the stairs clip.

1. **Click the Timeline menu to open it, and choose Track Options.**

2. **Click Add in the Track Options dialog box.**
   This opens the Add Tracks window.

3. **In the Add Tracks dialog box, type** 5 **in the Video tracks available field.**
   Click OK to close the window. You see V1 to V10 listed in the Track Options dialog box.

4. **Click OK to close the Track Options dialog box and return you to the Timeline.**

5. **In the Timeline, turn off Video tracks 5, 6, 7, and 8.**
   Hide those tracks not being used. If you are doing a preview or render-scrub of the Timeline, the content is still visible.

6. **Set the zoom level to 2 Seconds.**
   At a zoom level of 2 Seconds, you can see the Timeline clearly and see enough of its length to easily add clips without having to move the visible portion of the Timeline.

7. **Drag** bar_h.prtl **from the titles bin in the Project window to Video 10.**
   You use this clip as the master copy of the bar_h.prtl clip.

8. **Drag** bar_v.prtl **from the titles bin in the Project window to Video 10.**
   You use this clip as the master copy of the bar_v.prtl clip.

< T I P >
Place the two clips in the viewing area of the Timeline in the region you are going to use the copies. This saves time later and allows you to see what you have to work with.

9. **Turn off Video 10.**
   You are using this track as a storage area, but don't want it shown in previews.

10. **Copy the** bar_h.prtl **master clip in Video 10.**
    Paste it into Video 4 above the c_stairs.mov clip. Set its duration to 03:11, and position the clip to start at 00:20.

11. **Choose Window➞Show Effect Controls.**

    The Effect Controls window opens.

12. **Click Motion Setup on the Effect Controls window.**

    The Motion Settings window opens.

<NOTE>

You may be wondering why you add the clips to Video 4 rather than Video 3. In the next tutorial you see why. Tracks stack one on top of the other from lower to higher tracks. When you add the vertical bar clips to Video 3 in the next tutorial, the clip edge is covered by the horizontal bar clips you add here. You then layer the animated bars above these framing clips.

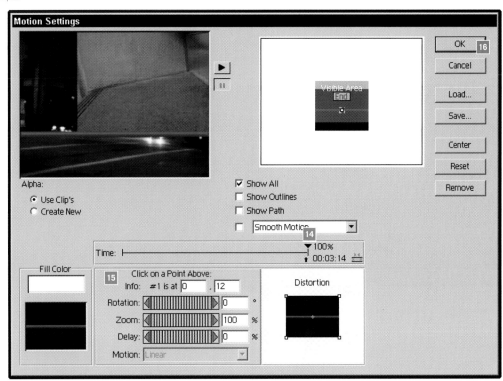

Combine Palettes for Convenience

Look at the previous image of the Effect Controls window. It is combined with the Info window in the same palette. You need to access both the Motion Settings and the Info window repeatedly and frequently. To combine the palettes, choose Window➞Show Effect Controls and Window➞Show Info. Drag the window tabs to separate them from their default palette groups, and then drag one over the other to combine them into another palette. Combining palettes is a good habit to develop for organizing what you need for specific types of tasks.

13. **In the Motion Settings window, set the 0% location coordinates to 0, 12.**

    The image moves downward in the motion track area.

14. **Click the 100% point on the Timeline.**

15. **Set the #1 location coordinates at 0, 12.**

    The image moves downward in the motion track area. Now the clip is set at a constant location throughout its duration.

16. **Click OK to close the Motion Settings window.**

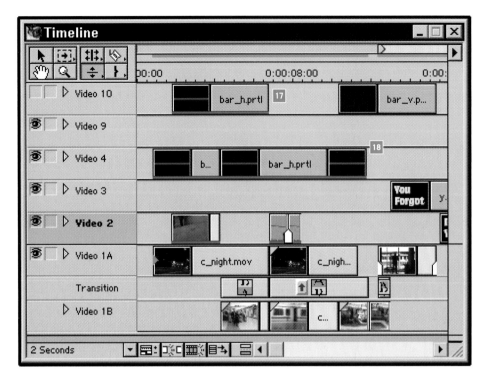

17. **Copy the master** `bar_h.prtl` **clip in Video 10.**

18. **Paste the** `bar_h.prtl` **copy into Video 4 to start at 04:07.**
    Extend the duration to 07:12 (the clip ends at the same time as the transition between Video 1B and Video 1A).

<TIP>

Remember you can change the length of a title clip by dragging either end. Right-clicking the clip and choosing Duration is even simpler. Because you are working with so many clips of varying lengths, typing a duration saves time.

19. **Click Motion Setup on the Effect Controls window.**
    The Motion Settings window opens.

20. **Click Center to move the Start frame to the center of the screen.**
    Click the End frame in the motion path area to select it, and click Center again to move the end frame to the center of the screen. The clip is static.

21. **Click OK to close the Motion Settings window and return to the Timeline.**

22. **Save the project.**
    You have a total of 10 video tracks in the Timeline. You added "master" copies of the horizontal and vertical bar clips to Video 10: a track you use as a holding area. You added the horizontal bars to the project for use as a frame in the split screen segment of the movie.

Understanding Motion Settings Timeline Coordinates

The Timeline in the Motion Settings window is different than the main Premiere Timeline. Although both display time visually, the Motion Settings Timeline display uses several ways to express information at any single point. You have experience with 0% and 100% locations on the Timeline. These two percentages are the same as the Start and End frames of the clip. Selecting the Start frame of the clip displays both Info: #0 and 0%. This means at the start of the clip, the first location marker is at 0% of the clip's duration. Selecting the End frame of the clip displays both Info: #1 and 100%, which means the second marker is at 100% of the clip's duration and any settings changed at this location apply to the clip at location #1. You can only select a location on the Motion Settings Timeline based on percentage of duration. The Info markers are used to identify altered clip settings such as zoom or distortion. In later tutorials you learn to add additional points to the Timeline and adjust the duration using delays.

Tutorial
» Using Titles as Vertical Frames

In the last tutorial, you organized the layout and added the framing copies of the horizontal bar title. In this tutorial you add the framing copies of the vertical bar title.

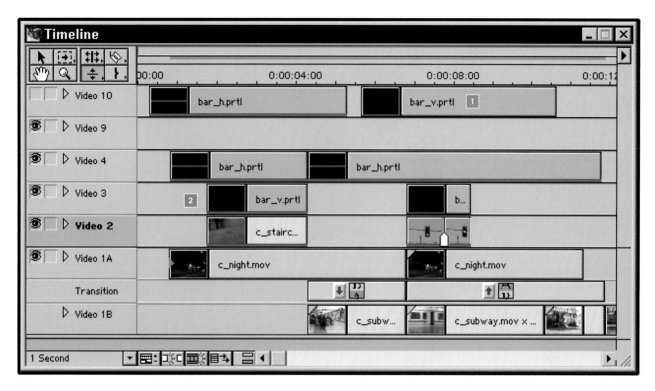

1. **Copy the master** bar_v.prtl **clip in Video 10.**

2. **Paste it into Video 3.**
   Set the duration and position to match the
   c_staircase.mov clip in Video 2.

3. **Open the Motion Settings window.**

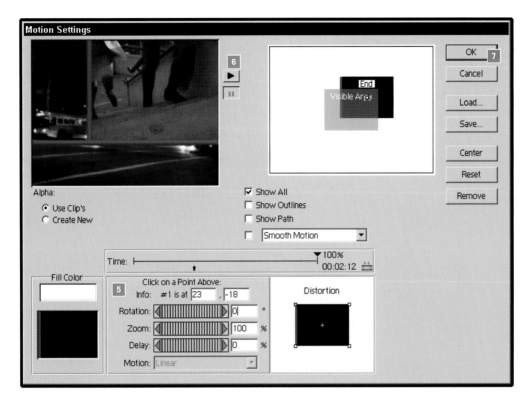

4. **Set the location coordinates for the 0% position to 23, –18.**
   The image of the clip moves upward and to the right in the motion path area.

5. **Set the location coordinates for the 100% position to 23, –18.**
   The image of the clip moves upward and to the right in the motion path area.

6. **Preview the clip in the Motion Settings window.**
   You can see the horizontal bar overlap the vertical bar, and none of the clip in the upper right corner of the screen is visible outside the margins of the bars.

7. **Click OK.**

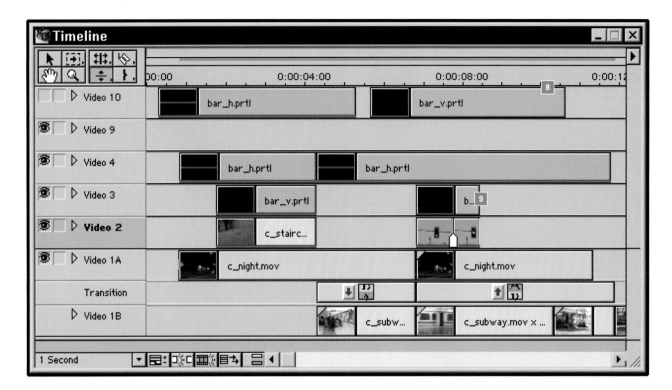

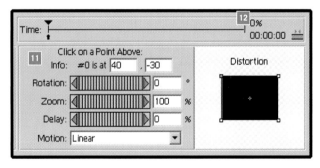

8. **Copy the master** `bar_v.prtl` **clip in Video 10.**

9. **Paste the clip into Video 3.**
   Move it into position to start at 06:19 (with the first part of the `c_lights.mov` clip) and set its length at 01:16 (to end even with the second part of the `c_lights.mov` clip).

10. **Open the Motion Settings window.**

11. **Set the #0 location coordinates for the 0% position to 40, –30.**
    The image of the clip moves upward and to the right in the motion path area.

12. **Set the #1 location coordinates for the 100% position to 40, –30.**
    The image of the clip moves upward and to the right in the motion path area.

13. **Click OK to close the Motion Settings window and return to the Timeline.**

14. **Save the project.**
    Your project has two vertical bar clips added. These clips are positioned in the Motion Settings window to use as frames between video clips in the split screen segment of the movie.

< T I P >

It is sometimes difficult to figure out how the numbering system works for adjusting the coordinates. Change one coordinate value and see which way the clip moves. Readjust until you have the final position.

Tutorial
» Animating Horizontal Title Bar Clips

Now you have the static title copies added and the locations for the bars defined. You can use these coordinates as a starting point for animating a number of other copies of the horizontal title. In this tutorial, you animate two copies of the horizontal bar title.

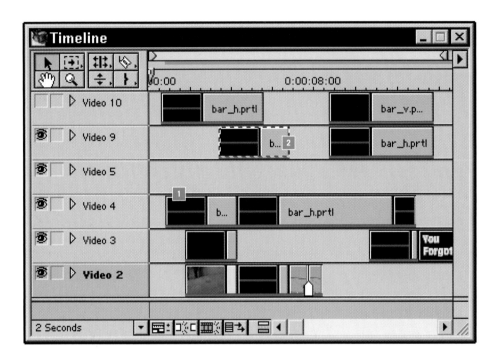

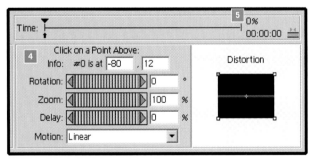

1. **Select the first copy of the** `bar_h.prtl` **clip in Video 4 and copy it.**

2. **Paste a new copy into Video 9.**

3. **Open the Motion Settings window.**

4. **Set the #0 location coordinates for the 0% position to –80, 12.**
   The image of the clip moves downward and outside the left margin of the Visible Area in the motion path area.

5. **Set the #1 location coordinates for the 100% position to 80, 12.**
   The image of the clip moves downward and outside the right margin of the Visible Area in the motion path area.

<NOTE>
The animation moves the bar across the screen from left to right. A value of –80 means the clip starts just to the left of the screen; a value of 80 means it ends just at the right of the screen.

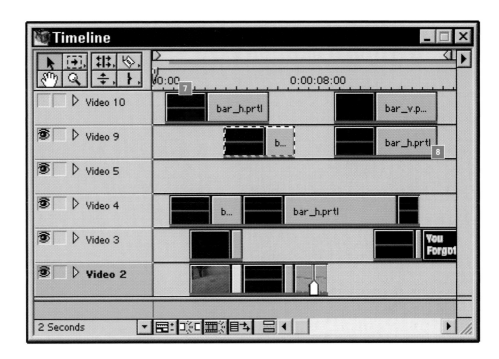

6. **Click OK.**

7. **Select the master copy of the** bar_h.prtl **clip in Video 10 and copy it.**

8. **Paste it into Video 9 following the other clip added in Step 2.**

9. **Open the Motion Settings window.**

10. **Set the #0 location coordinates for the 0% position to –80, 0.**
    The image of the clip moves outside the left margin of the Visible Area in the motion path area.

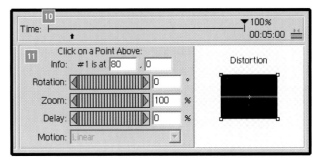

11. **Set the #1 location coordinates for the 100% position to 80, 0.**
    The image of the clip moves outside the right margin of the Visible Area in the motion path area.

12. **Click OK to close the Motion Settings window.**

13. **Save the project.**
    You have added two more copies of the horizontal bar clip, and customized the motion settings for each. One clip moves left to right across the center of the screen while the other moves from left to right across the screen below center.

14. **Take a break.**
    Although you are more than halfway through the session, the next tutorial is complex. You must be able to concentrate.

Tutorial
» Adding Animated Horizontal Bars to the Timeline

In this tutorial, you add collections of animated horizontal clips to the Timeline. They add movement to the project as well as entry and exit points for the static copies of the clips. You set them up in the Video 9 track using copies of the master clips as well as other clips you have already added. The set of clips you add in this tutorial uses simple animation.

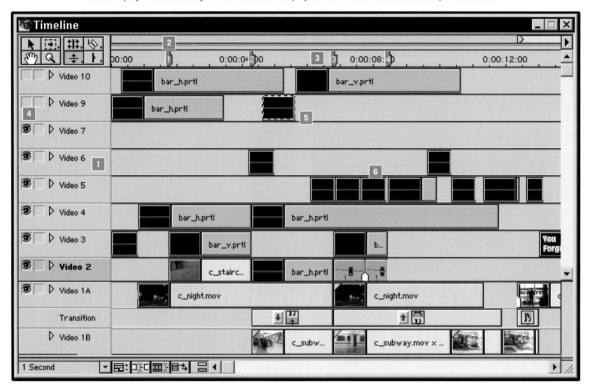

1. **In the Timeline, show Video 5, 6, and 7.**

2. **Add Timeline markers for reference.**
   Move the Timeline edit line to 01:18. Right-click the Timeline and choose Set Timeline Marker→1.

3. **Set three additional numbered Timeline markers using the process described in Step 2.**
   Set the markers at these locations to place them at the positions where the split screens begin and end:
   Marker 2 at 04:07
   Marker 3 at 06:09
   Marker 4 at 08:11

4. **Turn off Video 9.**
   You are using it as a staging area and don't want the contents to interfere with your layout.

5. **Copy the first** bar_h.prtl **clip in Video 9 and paste it into a blank area of Video 9.**
   Shorten the clip you just pasted to approximately 01:00 (you adjust the copies later) and copy it.

<TIP>
Use a blank area in a track that is larger than the duration of the clip you are pasting. This keeps tracks from shifting.

6. **Paste twelve copies of the** bar_h.prtl **clip you copied in Step 5.**
   Add the copies to the Timeline and adjust their lengths. Render-scrub through the Timeline to see your progress. The track, start time, and duration for the clips added to the Timeline are listed in Table 9.1.

7. **Open the Motion Settings window to check the coordinates of the remaining** `bar_h.prtl` **clip in Video 10.**
   Delete the clips from Video 9 you worked with in Steps 5 and 6. One copy of the `bar_h.prtl` clip remains. This clip uses −80, 0 and 80, 0 as its end coordinates (that is, the animation shows the bar moving from left to right across the center of the screen).

8. **Drag the** `bar_v.prtl` **clip further along the Timeline out of the area you are working with.**

9. **Adjust the length of the remaining** `bar_h.prtl` **clip in Video 9 to approximately 01:00 and copy the clip.**

10. **Paste copies to the Timeline according to Table 9.1.**
    Render-scrub through the Timeline to see your progress. The track, start time, and duration for the clips are listed in Table 9.2.

11. **Render-scrub through the Timeline to see the final layout.**

12. **Save the project.**
    You added markers to the Timeline to identify areas where static horizontal and vertical bar clips were placed in an earlier tutorial. You added twelve copies of one version of the `bar_h.prtl` clip and eleven copies of another version of the same clip.

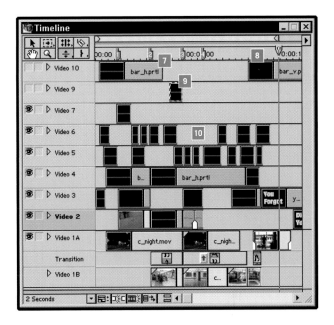

<TIP>

To save time and figure out what you have to work with when using multiple copies of a clip, copy and paste as many copies as you think you will use into a working track. If the duration of a clip is less than the space you want to move the clip into, drag the clips one by one to their locations, and then resize them. If the clip is too lengthy, resize it before moving it to prevent dislodging other clips.

Table 9.1: Layout for the Horizontal Bar Animation Using Coordinates −80, 12 to 80, 12

Track	Start Time	Duration
2	04:07	02:12
3	00:00	00:20
4	04:07	07:12
5	06:02	00:18
5	06:22	00:14
5	07:15	00:14
5	08:11	01:11
5	10:08	00:17
5	11:08	01:03
5	12:15	00:12
6	04:04	00:19
6	06:22	00:17

Table 9.2: Layout for the Second Horizontal Bar Animation Using Coordinates −80, 0 to 80, 0

Track	Start Time	Duration
3	10:16	02:08
4	11:19	01:03
5	00:15	01:03
5	02:19	01:03
6	00:08	00:20
6	02:19	00:14
6	03:12	00:14
6	05:07	01:03
6	11:02	01:03
6	12:15	01:03
7	01:16	01:03

Tutorial
» Printing to Video

In this tutorial, you learn how to use an output format called Print to Video. It is a format used to export your Timeline to video-tape. You may be wondering why a tutorial on printing to video appears in a session on animation; there is a good reason. In the absence of videotape, Print to Video produces a preview on a black screen. This is a handy way to watch your movie as it progresses. Print to Video uses the Project Settings.

complete preview area   partial preview area

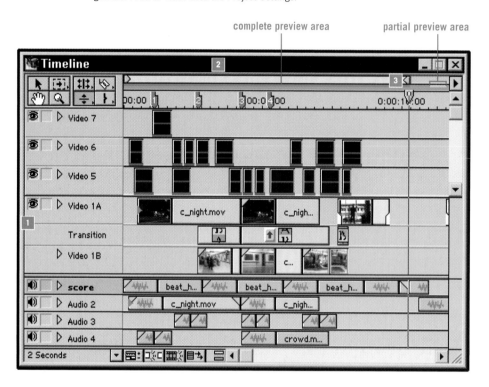

Building Preview Files

Create a preview for all of your project or a defined work area and, until you make changes in your Timeline, you have a complete preview as indicated by the blue/green bar under the work area bar. Areas of the preview are deleted as you make changes. When this occurs, you see patches of another color in the blue/green bar indicating a break in the preview. When you have made changes and want to build another preview, the remaining preview areas are reused with only the changed areas rebuilt.

1. **Make sure the tracks you want to preview are displayed in the Timeline.**
   Turn on Video 1 to Video 7 and Audio 1 to Audio 4.

2. **Double-click the work bar area to move the bar to the visible portion of the Timeline.**
   You are working with the first section of the project, so you don't need to preview the entire Timeline.

3. **Drag the end of the work area bar to approximately 16:10.**
   Take care moving the work area bar. If you drag the ends, you can resize the length of the bar. If you drag within the bar, you can reposition it at its current length along the Timeline.

4. **Choose File→Export Timeline→Print to Video.**
   The Print to Video dialog box opens.

5. **Leave the default settings and click OK.**

   A Building Preview window opens, which shows the progress of the build.

<NOTE>

Experiment with the other Print to Video settings to see their effects. You can set the movie to play at full size, double its size from your working version, or set it in a loop.

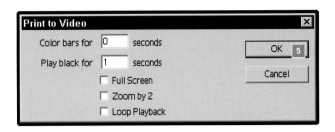

6. **Follow the preview build in the Preview Build window.**

   Press Stop to interrupt the build. Otherwise, let it complete the build.

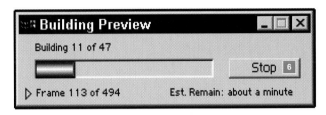

7. **The work area of the Timeline is shown against a black screen.**

   The default Print to Video settings include a Loop setting. When you finish watching the preview, press Esc to return to the program window.

8. **Save your project.**

   You didn't add any elements to the project in this tutorial. Instead you created and saved complete previews of the first segment of the movie using the Print to Video export option.

Managing Preview Files

Preview files are stored in designated video and audio preview files that are created when you install Premiere. Many files are created for one project. When you open a project containing previous previews, you are prompted for the location of one of the preview files, named with very long numeric strings. Search for preview files using the last three digits. You can choose to skip the previews, which means all previews for the new work session are built from scratch. The preview files have been removed from the session project (ppj) files. You must generate the files on your machine using your resources and storage locations.

» Session Review

This session finished much of the beginning section of your project. The image at the beginning of this session shows the clip of a couple running up a staircase. Contrast that one with the final image in this session. Here you see the resized clip as well as some of the bar titles in action. This ending clip is significantly more interesting. In the next session, you add the animated vertical bars for even more impact.

In this session, you learned how to work with simple animations. You learned how to use the Motion Settings window to resize a clip and change its position. You learned how to use the same clip as both a static element and also as an animation.

You learned a lot about working with large numbers of similar clips. I think this is an important lesson to learn, because repetitive elements are a very common design device. I gave you information about how to organize a project that uses dozens of copies of the same clip, and I hope this method proves useful for you in the future. You also learned how to make a print to video preview of your project for a finished view of your work. The Print to Video method is simple to use, and playing your project against a black background lets you concentrate on the content without distraction from windows and dialog boxes. Besides that, it just looks good!

The questions below will help you review the information in this session. You can find the answer for each question in the tutorial noted in parentheses.

1. How do you preview clips in the Motion Settings window? (See "Tutorial: Changing Clip Size and Position.")
2. Where can you see the motion path for your animation? (See "Tutorial: Changing Clip Size and Position.")
3. How do you resize a clip in the Motion Settings window? (See "Tutorial: Reusing Animation Settings.")
4. How can you tell a clip has motion settings applied when you view it in the Timeline? (See "Tutorial: Reusing Animation Settings.")
5. What is one of the simplest ways to streamline adding clips to the Timeline tracks? (See "Discussion: Working with Large Numbers of Similar Clips.")
6. What areas should you consider first when planning a project using large numbers of the same clips? (See "Discussion: Working with Large Numbers of Similar Clips.")
7. How does the stacking order of tracks work? (See "Tutorial: Using Titles as Horizontal Frames.")
8. Can you set a clip to play outside the visible screen area? (See "Tutorial: Using Titles as Vertical Frames.")
9. For a project sized at 320 × 240 pixels, what coordinates mean a clip is placed outside the left margin of the visible area? (See "Tutorial: Animating Horizontal Title Bar Clips.")
10. For a project sized at 320 × 240 pixels, what coordinates mean a clip is placed outside the right margin of the visible area? (See "Tutorial: Animating Horizontal Title Bar Clips.")
11. What are some uses of Timeline markers? (See "Tutorial: Adding Animated Horizontal Bars to the Timeline.")
12. How do you prevent the content of a track from shifting when adding another clip to it? (See "Tutorial: Adding Animated Horizontal Bars to the Timeline.")
13. How do you set the work area bar in the Timeline window? (See "Tutorial: Printing to Video.")
14. How can you tell what areas of the Timeline have current previews? (See "Tutorial: Printing to Video.")

» Other Projects

This session used a limited number of variations on the basic clips for practical reasons. Experiment with setting more coordinates for the clips.

If you have experience with Adobe After Effects, try building part of this sequence in that program. You will be able to add much more fine motion to the animation.

Building Complex Animations

Session Introduction

In the last session you added many copies of the horizontal bar clip to the project which created very effective animation using simple clip animations. In this session, you add the vertical bar title clips to the project. Again, you are working with a large number of clips. While the process of adding all the bars may seem tedious, it's worth it. The many red bars in motion give the movie an edge. I promise this is nearly the end of the red lines for this project!

You learn new processes as you animate the vertical bar clips. You learn how to add a delay to a clip's Timeline. You also learn more how animation works and how the time values on the Motion Window Timeline translate to time values on the project Timeline.

Later in the session, you work with the colorful beach titles you created. As you work with these titles, you learn how to add rotations and distortion and other settings to the clip along with the settings you are already familiar with. The animation for each text title is designed to coordinate with the action in the underlying clips.

One thing that may become apparent is how long it can take to create animations and how complex they can become. Fortunately, a process for saving and reusing animation exists, and you learn that process in this session as well.

TOOLS YOU'LL USE
Timeline window, Show/Hide tracks command, Info window, Effect Controls window, Motion Settings window, Create New Alpha command, Preview window, Motion path, Motion timeline, Motion timeline markers, motion path coordinates, delay settings, motion characteristic settings, smooth motion options, distortion options, rotation settings

CD-ROM FILES NEEDED
Session 9 project file you created or the session9.ppj file from the CD-ROM
Session10a.mpg and Session10b.mpg preview files from the premierecc_samples folder (for reference)
beach.pmt from the extra video folder
life.pmt and is_a.pmt from the extra video folder (for reference)

TIME REQUIRED
90 minutes

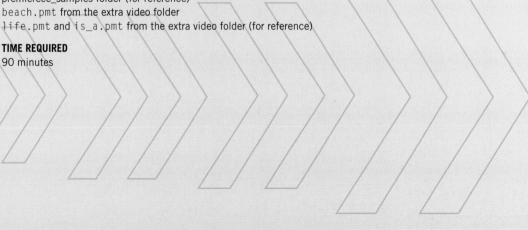

Discussion

Understanding Motion Settings

Working in the Motion Settings window is not intuitive, especially if you have little experience working with keyframes and timelines — the basic elements of animation. You are already familiar with timelines. Keyframes are points added to the Timeline to control settings. Add a keyframe to the Timeline, and set the characteristics for the animation at that point in time. Add another keyframe along the Timeline, and adjust the settings, and so on. The animation is created as the Timeline moves from one keyframe to the next. When you open a clip in the Motion Settings window, you have two initial keyframes — the Start and End frames of the clip are automatically defined as keyframes.

Up to this point, you have used basic settings such as location, zoom, and Start and End points. The tutorials in this session use settings you worked with in the last session, as well as more advanced animation settings such as rotation, distortion, and delay. As you work on the tutorials, refer back to this discussion for pointers on working with the Motion Settings window.

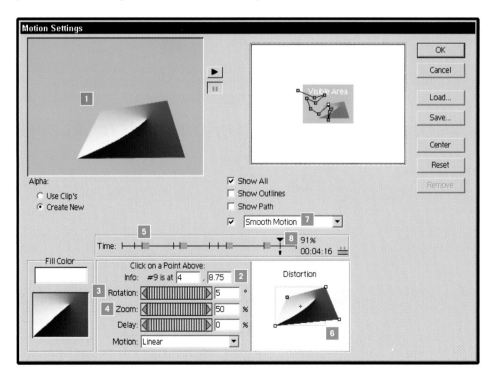

Translating Pixels

The Motion Settings window uses a timeline similar to the major program timeline with one major difference — the entire timeline applies to just one clip, rather than all the clips in your project.

1. The coordinates you set in the Motion Settings window refer to the sample image used in the window. The window is 80 × 60 pixels. When you move your animation to your project, the animation scales up as well. The project you are building is based on a size of 320 × 240 pixels. This means each pixel of movement in the Motion Settings dialog box translates to a 4-pixel movement in the finished animation.

2. How can you achieve the much sought after perfect animation? You can set locations using decimal places. A coordinate set as 8.75 in the Motion Setting window translates to 35 pixels on the finished animation in a project sized at 320 × 240 pixels (8.75 × 4 = 35 pixels).

Using Tools

You can use rotation, zoom, delay, and distortion tools in your animations.

3. Objects can be rotated between keyframes in a range from −1440 degrees to 1440 degrees. This is equal to eight complete rotations.

4. Use the zoom tool to resize a clip. You modify the size of a clip in a range from 0 to 500 percent. The clip is invisible at 0 percent, and five times normal size at 500 percent. The zoom tool is an effective way to simulate 3-D motion. You used this tool to resize clips to play them over another clip in the last session.

5. Set a delay to pause the motion of a clip for a specified length of time. The distance between any keyframes you add and any delay you set cannot equal more than 100 percent, which is equivalent to the length of the clip. If a delay is set at a keyframe added at the 80 percent mark, it cannot be longer than 20 percent of the length of the clip. When setting delays for a Timeline with multiple keyframes, the length of the delay between keyframes cannot be longer than the distance in time between the two keyframes.

6. Distortion is used to create the appearance of organic movement or 3-D motion. Work with this tool carefully. No tools for placement assistance such as guidelines exist in the Distortion section of the Motion Settings window, and you cannot enter any values manually. You must instead develop a pattern for changing distortion settings. You learn a systematic method for distorting a clip later in the session as you work through the Creating Title Animation Using Distortion tutorial.

Smoothing Options

Rotation, direction, and distortion can appear irregular in how they are applied to your animation. Use the Smooth Motion options to even out the changes. The Smooth Motion options range from Smooth Motion, which provides the smallest amount of smoothing, to Averaging-High, which provides the greatest amount of smoothing.

7. Experiment with the Smooth Motion settings to see how they work. You generally need a complex animation to see the effect of using different smoothing options. Certain prebuilt motion settings (such as leaves moving) modify the clip sufficiently on a keyframe-by-keyframe basis so you can see the difference.

Coordinating your Work

You work with keyframes on both the main Timeline and the Timeline in the Motion Settings window. A keyframe identifies a particular point in time.

8. Settings you modify apply to a selected keyframe. The settings you apply to one keyframe do not carry over to the next keyframe.

Tutorial
» Using Animation Delays

In this tutorial, you animate the vertical bar title clip and add it to the Timeline. Unlike the horizontal bar animation, the vertical bar animations are more complex and use delays. You use different animation settings applied to two copies of this clip. In the first segment of the project, you built a number of split screen sequences. You created horizontal bar frames for the split screens in earlier tutorials. There are two split screen sequences where the top half of the screen is further split into two segments. In this tutorial, you work with two vertical bars. Using the Motion Settings window, you create animation using a delay, or pause in the motion. At the completion of the tutorial, the vertical bar clips appear to sweep across the screen from the left, stop for a period of time, and then move out of view to the right.

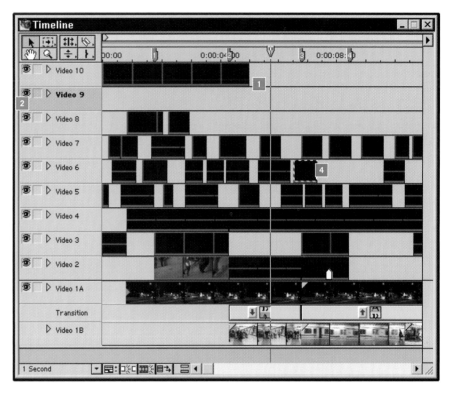

1. **Delete all content from Video 9 and 10 except for the** bar_v.prt1 **clip in Video 10.**
   The bar_v.prt1 clip is the master clip for this tutorial.

2. **Turn on Video 9.**
   The track was turned off in earlier tutorials.

3. **Copy the** bar_v.prt1 **clip in Video 10 and paste the copy into Video 9.**
   Set its duration to 00:20.

4. **Move the clip into its final location starting at 06:12 in Video 6.**

5. **Open the Motion Settings window.**
   Right-click the clip and choose Video Options➔Motion.

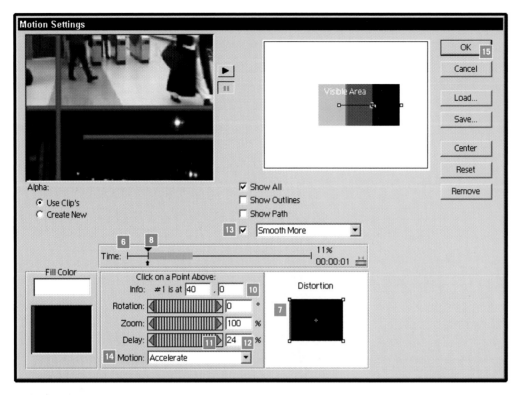

6. **Click on the Timeline at 0% to select the Start frame.**
   Set the 0% location coordinates at –10, 0.
   The vertical line is slightly out of the Visible Area (the gray box in the motion path area of the Motion Settings window).

7. **Click on the Timeline at 100% to select the End frame.**
   Set the 100% location coordinates at 82, 0. The vertical line ends up at the right margin of the visible area and disappears with the next frame of the project.

8. **Move the cursor just above the Timeline.**
   When the cursor changes to a downward arrow, click to add a keyframe marker. The marker appears as a vertical line cutting through the Timeline. You have been working with default settings, and changing settings only at the Start and End frames of the clip at 0% and 100% locations on the Timeline. The Start and End frames are the default keyframe markers for a clip.

9. **Slowly drag the marker left or right to 11%.**
   You see the percentage value at the right of the Timeline changes as you move the marker.

10. **Set location coordinates for this marker to 40, 0.**
    Note the keyframe marker is shown as #1 in the Info area.

11. **Click the right Delay slider.**
    The slider controls look like control sliders on electronic equipment. Click the left arrow to decrease the value, click the right slider to increase the value. As you click an arrow, the arrow is highlighted, and the slider is animated. The control's value changes in the box to the right of the slider.

12. **Hold the slider until the delay is 24%.**
    The delay is shown on the Timeline as a lavender bar. You can only add as much delay as time remaining from the marker. In this case, because the delay starts at 11%, you can add anything up to 89% delay. The location of the marker plus delay cannot equal more than 100%.

13. **Check the Smooth option to select it.**
    Click the dropdown list and choose Smooth More. These settings control how fluid the path of the bar is as it animates. There are five options, ranging from a small amount of smoothing, named Smooth Motion, to a large amount of smoothing named Averaging-High.

14. **Click the Motion dropdown list and choose Accelerate.**

    Linear motion is the default, which means motion is applied to the Timeline in an even fashion. Accelerated motion means that the animation gradually speeds up along the Timeline between keyframes.

15. **Click OK to close the Motion Settings dialog box.**

16. **Render-scrub the portion of the Timeline.**

    The clip was added at 06:12; a render-scrub from 06:00 to 08:00 shows the clip in its entirety as well as a few frames before and after. Watch the vertical bar carefully. It sweeps across the screen, stops, seems to deposit the short vertical frame, and then continues across the rest of the screen.

17. **Save the project.**

    You have completed a complex animation and need to save the settings.

18. **The** bar_v.prt1 **clip you have been working with is still selected in the Timeline starting at 06:12 in Video 6.**

    Copy the clip. Paste it into Video 6 starting at 01:08.

19. **Open the Motion Settings window again.**

<NOTE>

The Timeline pauses at the keyframe for the length of time set in the Delay control. When the clip plays, the animation starts and then stops at the keyframe you added at 11%. After 24% of the clip's duration passes, the animation continues. That is, for a ten second clip the first 1.1 seconds will play. The animation then pauses for 2.4 seconds. Whatever settings you have specified display for that 2.4 second time period. Then the animation continues for the remaining 6.5 seconds.

<TIP>

If you prefer, you can use the Print to Video option instead and watch the animation.

<NOTE>

The marker numbers change as you add keyframes to the Timeline. The Start frame is always identified as #0. Keyframes are numbered sequentially as you add them along the Timeline and renumber themselves if you add additional keyframes. For example, you added a keyframe at 11% which is identified as #1. If you added another keyframe at 5%, that marker would become #1 and the keyframe at 11% becomes #2.

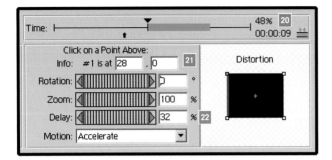

20. **Move the keyframe marker you added in Step 8 to 48%.**
    Move the cursor over the marker. When it changes to a pointing finger, slowly drag the marker right. Stop when the percentage value at the right of the Timeline shows 48%.

21. **Set the location coordinates for #1 to 28, 0.**
    The animation for this clip pauses at a different location on the screen than the copy you worked with earlier in the tutorial.

22. **Set the delay to 32%.**
    Click the Delay control's right arrow to increase the value.

23. **Click OK to close the Motion Settings window.**

24. **Render-scrub the portion of the Timeline.**
    The clip was added at 01:08; a render-scrub from 01:00 to 03:00 shows the clip in its entirety as well as a few frames before and after. Watch the vertical bar carefully. It moves right across the screen, stops, seems to deposit a short vertical frame, and then continues across the rest of the screen.

25. **Save the project.**
    You animated a copy of the vertical bar clip. The vertical bar appears at the left of the screen, sweeps across the screen, and stops for a period of time. After the pause, the bar continues across the screen and disappears to the right. You copied the clip and changed the animation settings for the second copy.

<NOTE>

You can see the completed animation for this portion of the project in session10a.mpg.

Tutorial
» Animating Vertical Bars

This is the final tutorial that uses red bars of any kind. In this tutorial, you add a sprinkling of vertical bar animations to the project. You have only one clip to create and copy. Like many of the horizontal bar title clips you added earlier, you can use your own sense of design when adding these clips. The track, start time, and duration are listed for the clips added.

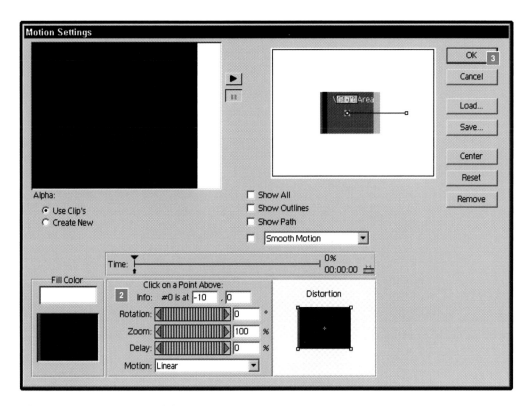

1. **Open the Motion Settings window for the** `bar_v.prt1` **clip in Video 10.**

2. **Click on 0% in the Timeline.**
   Change the starting location coordinates (at 0%) to –10, 0. Look at the image of the clip in the motion path section of the window. You see the red vertical bar is aligned just outside the left margin of the gray Visible Area.

3. **Click OK to close the Motion Settings window.**

<NOTE>
You use a number of identical short clips in this tutorial; all copies of the `bar_v.prt1` master copy you work with in Steps 2 and 3. The default motion path for any clip starts at –80 and ends at 80 on the horizontal axis. This means the entire frame of the clip passes across the screen from left to right. By decreasing the length of the path the vertical bar clip travels, you can estimate the timing of the motion more precisely. The location set in Step 2 places the vertical bar one frame out of view to the left of the screen. When you set the duration for copies of the clip later in the tutorial, you know that the vertical bar is visible on-screen after the first frame.

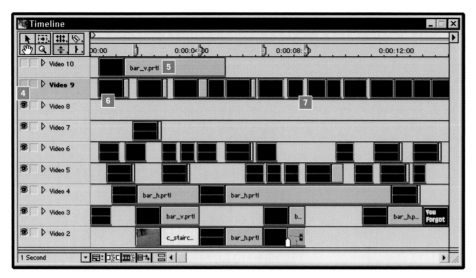

Table 10.1: Layout for the Vertical Bar Animation

Track	Start Time	Duration
5	00:00	00:05
5	02:01	00:08
5	04:15	00:17
6	01:08	00:20
6	06:12	00:20
7	00:04	00:10
7	00:15	00:13
7	03:00	00:12
7	03:23	00:22
7	05:08	00:17
7	06:19	00:17
7	07:18	00:18
7	08:20	00:18
7	10:00	00:12
7	10:14	00:12
7	11:06	01:08
7	13:00	01:04
8	01:05	00:20
8	02:05	00:17

<NOTE>
The keen observer will notice that a blank black space appears in the top half of the split screen in the session10a.mpg file from 11:08 to 12:08. Not to worry! This is taken care of in Session 15.

4. **Turn off Video 9.**
   You are using this track for a staging area in this tutorial, and don't want the contents to be visible as you render-scrub later in the tutorial.

5. **Copy the** bar_v.prtl **clip in Video 10.**

6. **Paste a copy into Video 9.**
   Set its duration to approximately 01:00. You adjust the clips for final length in Step 8.

7. **Copy the shortened** bar_v.prtl **clip in Video 9.**
   Paste 18 more copies of the bar_v.prtl clip into Video 9. This is the total number of copies of the clip you distribute.

8. **Drag the 19 copies to the locations as listed in Table 10.1.**
   Set the durations and start times as indicated. It will take some time and effort to move these clips and set their locations and durations. Work carefully. It is worth it though. You will be pleased with the result — the bars in motion add a cool edgy look to the project.

9. **Delete all clips from Video 9 and Video 10.**
   Even though you have emptied the tracks, don't delete them. You use them again for more title placement activity.

10. **Render-scrub through the Timeline to view the clips in action, or use the Print to Video preview.**

11. **Save the project.**
    You added nineteen vertical bars throughout the first segment of the project, adding motion, color, and excitement. Now take a well-earned break!

Tutorial
» Adding Titles

In this tutorial, you get the second segment of the Timeline ready to work with the title clips. You move three clips to organize the Timeline and set two markers in the score. Finally, you get the copies of the titles into their starting locations. Make sure to open the Info window to assist in placing clips in this tutorial.

1. **Show Video 1 to Video 5 and Audio 1 (score).**
   Check that the tracks are turned on as well. The eye icons display for video tracks, and the speaker icon displays for the audio track.

2. **Select the** s_jetski.mpg **clip in Video 4 starting at 58:04.**
   Move the clip to Video 3 to start at 57:10.

3. **Select the** s_boards2.mpg **clip in Video 4 starting at 01:17:22.**
   Move the clip to Video 3 to start at 01:17:22.

4. **Select the** s_windsurf.mpg **clip in Video 5 starting at 01:12:09.**
   Move the clip to Video 4 to start at 01:12:09. The clips are repositioned.

5. **Double-click the** saucy.mpa **audio score clip to open it in the Audio Clip window.**

<NOTE>
The markers are used along with the action clips to decide where to place the title clips. For example, the beach.prtl clip starts at the same time as a fairly dramatic change in the music occurs, which also coincides with the point in the s_windsurf.mpg clip when the surfer's hair touches the water. This makes for a cohesive and dramatic use of media.

6. **In the Audio Clip window, move the player head to 46:01.**

7. **Click the Marker icon to open the Marker Menu and choose Mark→1.**
   A gray numbered marker icon displays above the waveform. The Apply button appears at the bottom of the Clip window.

8. **Move the player head to 56:19.**

9. **Open the Marker Menu again and choose Mark→2.**
   A gray numbered icon displays above the waveform.

10. **Click Apply.**
    The 1 and 2 markers are added to the soundtrack file saucy.mpa. The two markers designate specific changes in the music.

11. **Close the Clip window to return to the Timeline.**

12. **Select the** life.prtl **clip from the titles bin in the Project window.**
    Drag the clip to the Timeline. Place it in Video 5 starting at 55:02. Set its duration to 07:00.

13. **Select the** is_a.prtl **clip from the titles bin in the Project window.**
    Drag the clip to the Timeline. Place it in Video 5 starting at 01:08:09. Set its duration to 04:00.

14. **Select the** beach.prtl **clip from the titles bin in the Project window.**
    Drag the clip to the Timeline. Place it in Video 5 starting at 01:14:21. Set its duration to 06:00.

15. **Save the project.**
    You made some changes in the Timeline in preparation for animating more title clips. You moved three video clips into their final locations. Then you added two markers to the audio clip for coordinating title placement. Finally, you added the three titles to the Timeline.

Tutorial
» Creating Title Animation Using Distortion

In this tutorial, you animate the `life.prtl` title. You learn how to use more of the motion settings in the Motion Settings window. Using the Distortion settings along with settings you have used in previous tutorials, you make the title appear to move with the action. If you haven't read the discussion on Motion Settings at the start of this session, review it before working through this tutorial. Doing so helps you to understand what you are working with.

1. **Select the** `life.prtl` **clip in Video 5 in the Timeline starting at 55:03.**

2. **Choose Window→Effect Controls to open the Effect Controls palette.** Arrange the palette on the screen with the Timeline.

3. **Open the Motion Settings window from the Effect Controls palette.** You can click the blank square to the left of the Motion title, or you can click Setup to the right of the Motion title. The Motion Settings window opens. After settings are applied, you see an *f* in this box. Toggle the motion settings off by clicking the box to toggle the *"f"* off. Once settings have been applied, reopen the Motion Settings window by clicking Setup.

<NOTE>
When you open the Effect Controls palette and select a clip in the Timeline, you may see a message that reads *Edit line is outside of clip*. The location of the Timeline's edit line isn't important for working with motion settings, but this is important in a later session when you add effect keyframes to clips on the Timeline.

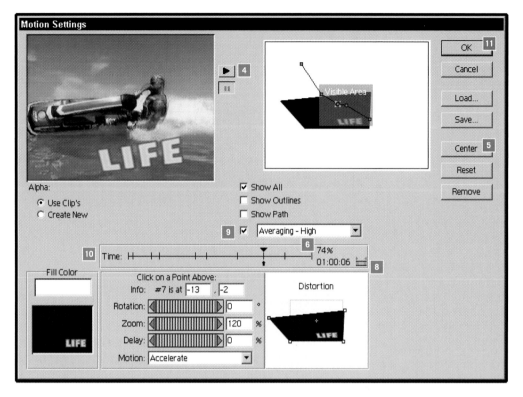

4. **In the Motion Settings window, play the clip several times.**
   Press Stop when you are familiar with the underlying clips.

5. **Click the Start position on the Motion Settings window Timeline to select the Start keyframe.**
   Click Center. In the motion path area you can see the image of the frame moves to the center of the screen.

6. **Click the End position on the Motion Settings window's Timeline to select the End keyframe.**

7. **Click Center again.**
   In the motion path area you can see the image of the frame moves to the center of the screen.

8. **Click the time measure on the Timeline to toggle to the program Timeline count.**
   The default setting shows the two red arrows touching one another in the center. This means the Timeline only works with the values of the clip (in this case from 00:00 to 07:00). The time settings you use here relate to the larger Timeline (from 55:02 to 1:02:02). Because the markers relate to major Timeline positions, you have approximate locations for correlating animation with Timeline activity, such as transparency and fades.

9. **Select Smooth Motion and choose Averaging-High from the drop-down menu.**
   You apply a great number of variable settings in this motion path. Smoothing the motion makes the changes from one configuration more fluid and less jerky or abrupt. Due to the extreme changes throughout the animation, use the highest amount of smoothing, Averaging-High.

   <NOTE>
   In the Motion column, L = linear; A = accelerate; D = decelerate.

10. **Add keyframes and settings to the animation:**
    At keyframe 0 (55:02), set the coordinates at 35,20 and the zoom at 10%
    At keyframe 1 (55:06), set the coordinates at 0,0 and the zoom at 40%
    At keyframe 2 (56:00), set the coordinates at 0,0 and the zoom at 100%
    Set the remaining keyframes according to the settings listed in Table 10.2. Use the distortion images as a guide.

11. **Click OK to close the Motion Settings window.**
    Check in the Effect Controls window — the *"f"* now appears in the box to the left of the Motion heading.

Table 10.2: Motion Settings for the "Life" Title Clip

Keyframe	Time	Coordinates	Rotation	Zoom	Motion	Distortion
3	56:06	0,0	0	100	D	
4	57:16	0,0	0	100	D	
5	58:02	0, 0	0	100	L	
6	59:05	0, 0	-8	100	A	
7	1:00:06	−13, −2	0	120	A	
8	01:01:01	−37, −15	-5	180	A	
9	01:02:02	−67, −60	0	300	—	—

12. **Render-scrub the Timeline from approximately 55:00 to 01:03:00 to see the animation or Print to Video to preview the clip.**

13. **Save the project.**
    This tutorial was a lot of work! You animated the first title in the beach segment of the project. You used many motion settings to create the illusion that the titles move with the action.

< N O T E >
You can see the completed animation for this portion of the project in session10b.mpg.

Tutorial
» Using Rotation to Animate a Title Clip

In this tutorial, you animate the is_a.prtl title. Much of the animation centers on rotation settings, but you use other settings as well. You also learn how to save motion settings for an animation. As you apply the settings, see how each contributes to a particular type of motion.

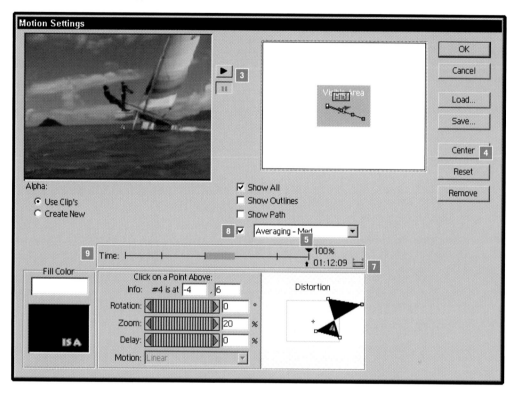

1. Select the is_a.prtl clip in Video 5 in the Timeline starting at 01:08:12.

2. Click the checkbox to the left of the Motion heading on the Effect Controls window or click Setup to the right of the heading on the Effect Controls window to open the clip in the Motion Settings window.

3. Play the clip several times.
   Click Stop when you are familiar with the movement in the underlying clips.

4. Click the Start position on the Motion Settings window Timeline to select the Start keyframe.
   Click Center. In the motion path area you can see the image of the frame moves to the center of the screen.

5. Click the End position on the Motion Settings window's Timeline to select the End keyframe.

6. Click Center again.
   In the motion path area you can see the image of the frame moves to the center of the screen.

7. Click the time measure on the Timeline to toggle to the program Timeline count.
   Like the title you animated in the last tutorial, the title you work with in this tutorial uses a series of keyframes and different settings. Using the program Timeline count gives you approximate locations for correlating animation with Timeline activity, such as transparency and fades.

<TIP>
To see the underlying clips, make sure Show All is selected.

8. **Select Smooth Motion and choose Averaging-Medium from the dropdown menu.**
   This animation uses less distortion than the one you did in the last tutorial. It needs smoothing, but not quite as much.

9. **Add keyframes and settings at the time locations listed in Table 10.3.**

10. **Set the delay for keyframe 2 to 16%.**

11. **Set the distortion for keyframe 4 (at 100%).**
    Use the layout in the figure as a guide. The distortion actually has the top left point, which is blue, pulled across the top right point, which is white. This allows the text to be shaped in a sharp point.

12. **Click OK to close the Motion Settings window and return to the Timeline.**
    An "f" now appears in the box to the left of the Motion heading in the Effect Controls palette, indicating the clip has applied motion settings.

13. **Render-scrub the Timeline from approximately 01:08:00 to 01:13:00 to see the animation or Print to Video to preview the clip.**

14. **Save the project.**
    You animated the second of the titles in the beach segment of the movie. Like the last tutorial, you used many of the motion settings. The main effect for this animation is based on rotation.

<NOTE>
You can see the completed animation for this portion of the project in session10b.mpg.

Saving Motion Settings

Sometimes you need to save motion settings, especially if you plan to use a complex animation in more than one project. After the animation settings are complete, click Save. Locate the storage folder you want to use, name the file, and click Save. If you are working with an animation that you plan to use for several clips within a single project, you can copy the clip in the Timeline, and then paste the motion settings into the other clips using the Paste Attributes command. After the settings are applied to a clip, you can change them when necessary for that clip.

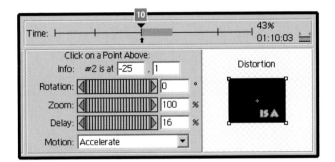

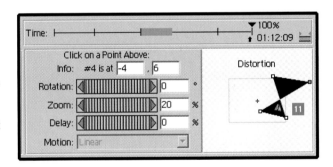

Table 10.3: Motion Settings for the "Is A" Title Clip

Keyframe	Time	Coordinates	Rotation	Zoom	Motion
0	01:08:09	29, 18	10	35	L
1	01:09:04	13, 12	-8	45	A
2	01:10:03	-25, 1	0	100	A
3	01:11:16	-25, 1	0	100	D
4	01:12:09	-4, 6	0	20	D

<NOTE>
In the Motion column, L = linear; A = accelerate; D = decelerate.

Tutorial
» Applying a Motion File to a Clip

In this final tutorial of this session, you animate the beach.prt1 title. Rather than create the settings from scratch, you use the existing beach.pmt file, which is included with the other project material. Whether you create and save settings yourself, use settings imported from other resources such as the file on the CD, or use one of the prebuilt motion settings files shipped with Premiere, motion files are a simple way to re-create and reuse settings. Rather than trying to re-create duplicate motion settings for a number of clips, you save the settings as an external file that can be reused as necessary.

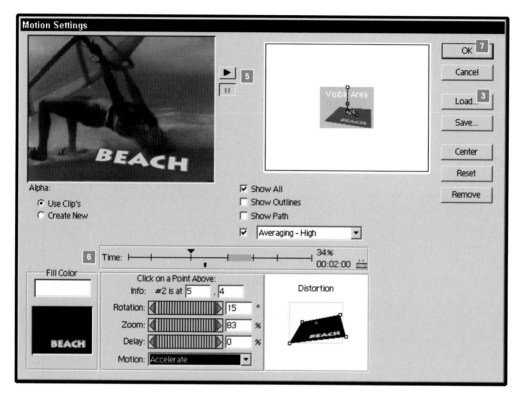

1. **Select the** beach.prt1 **clip in Video 5 in the Timeline starting at 01:14:27.**

2. **Open the clip in the Motion Settings window.**

3. **Click Load.**

4. **Browse to the location where you store your project files.**
   Select the beach.pmt file and click Open. Motion files are saved with a .pmt extension.

<NOTE>
Premiere ships with a set of motion files, which are installed with the program installation. They are in the Motion folder which is within the Premiere program folder.

5. **Play the clip several times.**
   Click Stop when you finish viewing.

6. **Move through the keyframes in this title.**
   At each keyframe you see settings applied from the beach.pmt file for the location, rotation, zoom, delay, and distortion. Can you see how the motion is created?

7. **Click OK to close the Motion Settings window and return to the Timeline.**

   Although you didn't manually create the settings for this title, the *"f"* now appears in the box to the left of the Motion heading in the Effect Controls palette, indicating the clip has applied motion settings.

<TIP>

For work in future projects, remember to save and reuse settings whenever possible. Animations can be lengthy to create as you have learned.

8. **Render-scrub the Timeline from approximately 01:14:00 to 01:21:00 to see the animation or Print to Video to preview the clip.**

9. **Save your project.**

   You animated the third title in the beach segment of the movie. The title used many motion settings like those you added manually in the last two tutorials. Unlike the last two tutorials, this title used prebuilt settings.

» Session Review

In this session you added multiple copies of the vertical bar graphic title. You used copies of the clip both as frames and motion titles. Using many copies of the clip moving at different speeds adds color and and edgy look to the city segment of the movie.

Much of the session concentrated on working with advanced motion settings and the colorful titles from the beach segment of the movie. Animating the title to appear to move along with the motion, as you can see in the final image in this session, enhances the sense of movement in a very cool way. You learned to add multiple keyframes to the Motion Settings window's Timeline, how to use combinations of settings, including location, rotation, zoom, delay, and distortion to create very interesting motion effects for the titles in the beach segment of your movie, and how to apply preconfigured motion settings to a title. Animation can be saved from one clip and then reused over and over, both in the same project and for other projects. You can even share motion settings files with other Premiere users.

The following questions help you review the information in this session. The answer for each question is in the tutorial noted in parentheses.

1. How are the coordinates in the Motion Settings Timeline different from those in the main Timeline? (See "Discussion: Understanding Motion Settings.")

2. How large or small can you resize a clip in the Motion Settings window? (See "Discussion: Understanding Motion Settings.")

3. How do you add Smooth Motion settings to your animation? (See "Discussion: Understanding Motion Settings.")

4. Can you move a clip outside the visible area in the Motion Settings window? If so, how? (See "Tutorial: Using Animation Delays.")

5. How do you determine the amount of delay to use in an animation? (See "Tutorial: Using Animation Delays.")

6. Do you adjust the Start and End animation locations for a short clip? When? (See "Tutorial: Animating Vertical Bars.")

7. How can you use markers in a clip to organize the location of other clips? (See "Tutorial: Adding Titles.")

8. Do you have to move the edit line of the Timeline within the margins of a clip to use the Motion Settings window? (See "Tutorial: Creating Title Animation Using Distortion.")

9. When would you use the clip time rather than the Timeline time in the Motion Settings window? (See "Tutorial: Creating Title Animation Using Distortion.")

10. Do clips run at the same speed in the Motion Settings window as in the Timeline? (See "Tutorial: Creating Title Animation Using Distortion.")

11. How are keyframes numbered along the Motion Settings window Timeline? (See "Tutorial: Creating Title Animation Using Distortion.")

12. How do you change the Timeline count option in the Motion Settings window? (See "Tutorial: Using Rotation to Animate a Title Clip.")

13. Can you save motion settings? If so, how? (See "Tutorial: Applying a Motion File to a Clip.")

14. Can you change settings after you apply a motion settings file to a clip? If so, how? (See "Tutorial: Applying a Motion File to a Clip.")

» Other Projects

Create other types of animations for the titles — both the text titles and the vertical bar graphic titles.

Create and save custom motion settings.

Apply some of the prebuilt motion settings files. They are located on your hard drive in the Motion folder which is located inside the Premiere folder.

Part VI
Adding Transparency and Video Effects

Session 11

Adding Transparency to Clips

Tutorial: **Adjusting Fade Levels for a Group of Clips**

Tutorial: **Fading Clips**

Tutorial: **Creating Crossfades**

Discussion: **Key Types**

Tutorial: **Adjusting Transparency Using Luminance**

Tutorial: **Using the Screen Transparency Key**

Tutorial: **Adding Alpha Channels to Clips**

Session Introduction

In this session, you start work on the clips' transparency settings. The first type of transparency you use is fade levels. You adjust the fade level, or opacity of a clip using handles on the opacity rubberband. In this session, you go back to the red vertical and horizontal bar title clips and adjust fade levels. You also start working with the fade levels for the beach segment clips.

You have already worked with transparency. The titles you made in an earlier session are created with a transparent background. You overlay the text on other clips without having to deal with a background. Though that is one of the most common uses of transparency, it is certainly not the only type. Transparency types are referred to as keys. You can key out or remove specific color from clips based on color ranges you choose. A key identifies pixels in an image that matches color or brightness levels, and makes those pixels transparent or semitransparent.

Video and certain image formats are composed of three grayscale images, one each of red, green, and blue. These are referred to as RGB color. An alpha channel is a fourth type of channel and defines transparent or opaque areas of an image or frame — the image channels are referred to as RGBA color. Programs like Premiere, Photoshop, and After Effects use this fourth channel to superimpose contents of one clip over another clip. Premiere has several different alpha channel keys. You can also base keying on luminance of an image rather than transparency. Luminance is another common type of key where darker and lighter values are used for defining transparency. Darker values are transparent; brighter areas are opaque.

Regardless of the type of transparency you choose for a clip, it only works in the superimpose (super) tracks. A project contains one super track by default — Video 2. You can add up to 97 more super tracks. As you can imagine, experimentation is required to achieve the perfect effect.

TOOLS YOU'LL USE
Timeline window, Show/Hide tracks command, Info window, Effect Controls window, Transparency Settings window, background viewing options, Luminance key, Screen key, Alpha Channel keys, settings sliders, opacity rubberbands, Cross Fade tool, Fade Adjustment tool, Maintain Aspect Ratio command, Paste Attributes command, Paste Attributes Again command, Motion settings window

CD-ROM FILES NEEDED
Session 10 project file you created or the session10.ppj file from the CD-ROM
Session11a.mpg and Session11b.mpg preview files from the premierecc_samples folder (for reference)
Zoom_Left.pmt from the extra video folder (this is a duplicate of the prebuilt file installed with Premiere)

TIME REQUIRED
90 minutes

Tutorial
» Adjusting Fade Levels for a Group of Clips

In this first tutorial, you fade some of the many, many red horizontal and vertical bar titles you created in previous sessions. Rather than working through them one by one, you set several levels and then duplicate the effect for other bars. You don't change opacity for all the clips. Some remain 100% opaque, and you don't change the opacity of the bars used as frames for clips.

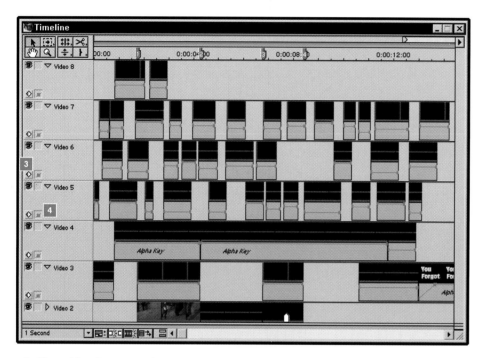

1. **Choose File→Open and navigate to the location where you stored your project files.**
   You can also choose File→Open Recent Project and choose your project file from the list. Open `session10.ppj`.

<NOTE>
If you didn't do the tutorials in Session 10, copy the `session10.ppj` file from the CD to your hard drive. Open the file and resave it as `session11.ppj` (or use another filenaming convention).

2. **Resave the project file as** `session11.ppj`.

3. **Hide all tracks except Video 2 to Video 8.**
   Limit the number of visible tracks in the Timeline to those you are working with to save screen space.

4. **Display the opacity rubberbands for Video 2 to Video 8.**
   Click the arrow to the left of the track's name to expand the track and display the rubberbands.

<NOTE>
I have collapsed different tracks in the images in this tutorial to make the numbered areas of the Timeline easier to identify. As you are working, keep Video 2 to Video 8 tracks expanded.

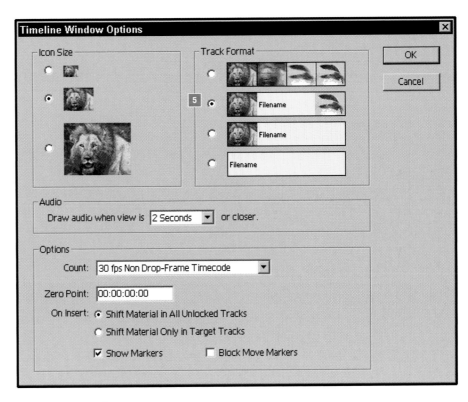

5. **Click the Timeline menu and choose Timeline Window Options.**
   Choose a track format that displays the clip image. Click OK
   to close the Timeline Window Options dialog box and reset the
   appearance of the Timeline.

<NOTE>

Change Timeline layouts as you work on different tasks. You are
familiar with zooming in and out of the Timeline to make it easier
to see the clips. You work with numerous bar title clips in numerous tracks in this tutorial. To make it simpler to identify a clip visually, use a Timeline display that shows the clip images. Don't use
the display option that lists only the file name, as many clips are
too short to display the full name. Don't use the display option that
shows a string of thumbnail images. That option takes too long to
redraw on the screen when you zoom in or out or move the
Timeline. The remaining two options, those showing both title and
either one or two thumbnails, are right for the work you are doing.

How Transparent is Transparent?

**Each clip you are working with is a single colored bar. The effect
you are trying to create is a simple variation in transparency. Alter
the transparency by 10 to 20 percent increments to produce a
noticeable effect. Because the clips are in motion, your eye can
barely see the difference between 80 and 85 percent opacity,
while the difference between 60 and 80 percent is quite
noticeable.**

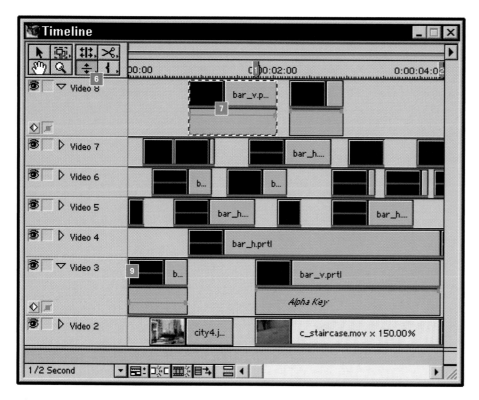

6. **Select the Fade Adjustment tool from the toolbox.**

   If the Fade Adjustment tool is not the active fade tool, click and hold the fade tool displayed to open the subpalette. Click the Fade Adjustment tool to select it. It is now the active tool and displays in the toolbox.

7. **Press Shift and drag the opacity rubberband down to 80% for the first** bar_v.prtl **clip in Video 8 starting at 00:20.**

   There is no rule for a start location when you are doing a sequence of tasks like the copy and paste processes you work with in this tutorial. I chose the first clip in Video 8 as that track has the fewest bar clips in it. Using the clip in Video 8 as the starting clip, I know that once I have changed this clip I don't have to think about the content of that track as I work with the remaining tracks.

<TIP>

As you gain experience with Premiere you will develop your own methods of working with large numbers of similar clips.

8. **Click the Select tool in the toolbox.**

   Select and copy the clip. The copied clip has 80% opacity. You paste the opacity setting from the copy to a group of clips listed in Table 11.1. Steps 9 through 11 apply to the first clip from Table 11.1; Step 12 is used for the subsequent clips listed in the table.

9. **Select the first clip listed in Table 11.1 (the clip starting at 10:16 in Video 3).**

   Choose Edit→Paste Attributes. The Paste Attributes dialog box opens.

10. **Click Settings to activate the options at the bottom of the dialog box.**

    Deselect all options except Fade Control.

11. **Click OK to close the Paste Attributes dialog box.**

    In the Timeline, you see the opacity rubberband for the clip you selected in Step 9 (starting at 10:16 in Video 3) is set at a lower opacity level.

12. **Select the next clip listed in Table 11.1 (the clip at 07:15 in Video 5).**

    Choose Edit→Paste Attributes Again. The opacity rubberband is set at a lower level.

<TIP>

The Paste Attributes Again command is a real timesaver. Once you have copied a clip and used the Paste Attributes dialog box to define the settings you want to paste, you don't have to open the dialog box again. The Paste Attributes Again command is active until you change settings.

13. **Repeat Step 12 with the remaining clips listed in Table 11.1.**

<NOTE>

The clip fades are based on a somewhat random selection process. You can alter the opacity of the clips in any order you prefer. Keep in mind that the vertical and horizontal titles should not use the same fade at the same time, and clips following one another shouldn't use the same opacity.

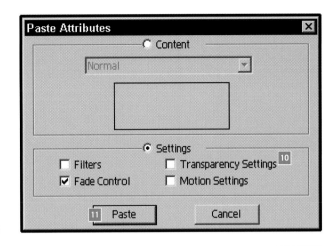

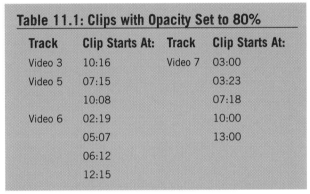

Table 11.1: Clips with Opacity Set to 80%

Track	Clip Starts At:	Track	Clip Starts At:
Video 3	10:16	Video 7	03:00
Video 5	07:15		03:23
	10:08		07:18
Video 6	02:19		10:00
	05:07		13:00
	06:12		
	12:15		

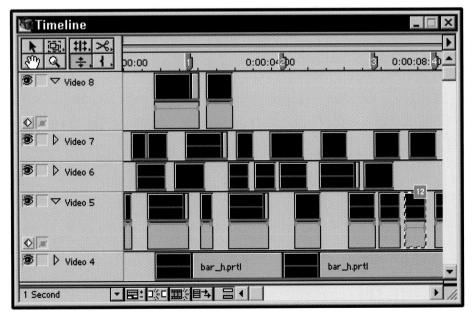

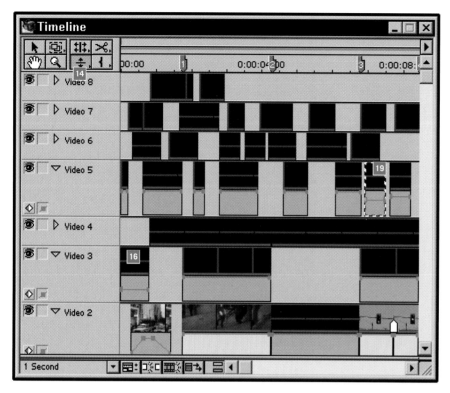

14. **Select the Fade Adjustment tool in the toolbox, and drag the opacity rubberband slider for the** `bar_h.prtl` **clip starting at 02:05 in Video 8 to 60%.**
    Use this clip as the start point for the group of clips. Now this clip's opacity is adjusted, you are finished working with the clips in Video 8, leaving you only five tracks to worry about!

15. **Click the Select tool in the toolbox, and select the** `bar_h.prtl` **clip you worked with in Step 14. Copy the clip.**
    You paste the 60% opacity setting from the copy to the clips listed in Table 11.2. Steps 16 through 18 pertain to the first clip from Table 11.2.

16. **Select the clip starting at 00:00 in Video 3.**
    Choose Edit→Paste Attributes. The Paste Attributes dialog box opens.

17. **Click Settings to activate the options at the bottom of the dialog box.**
    Deselect all options except Fade Control.

18. **Click OK to close the Paste Attributes dialog box.**
    In the Timeline, you see that the opacity rubberband for the clip you selected in Step 16 is set at a lower opacity level.

19. **Select the next clip listed in Table 11.2 (the clip starting at 11:19 in Video 4).**
    Choose Edit→Paste Attributes Again. The opacity rubberband is set at a lower level.

20. **Repeat Step 19 with the remaining clips in Table 11.2.**

Table 11.2: Clips with Opacity Set to 60%

Track	Clip Starts At:	Track	Clip Starts At:
Video 4	11:19	Video 7	00:15
Video 5	06:22		05:08
Video 6	00:08		06:19
	04:04		11:06

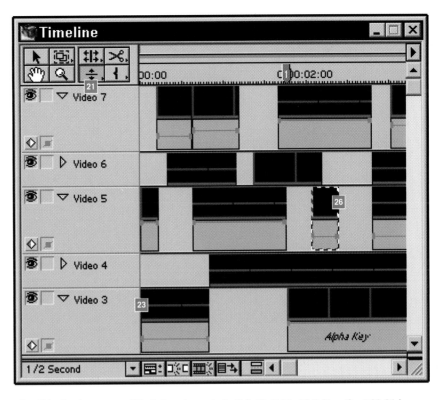

21. **With the Fade Adjustment tool, drag the opacity slider for the**
    bar_v.prtl **clip starting at 00:04 in Video 7 to 40%.**
    Use this clip as the starting point for the group of clips with
    40% opacity.

22. **Click the Select tool in the toolbox. Select and copy the**
    bar_v.prtl **clip you modified in Step 21.**
    The copied clip has 40% opacity. You paste the opacity set-
    ting from the copy to the clips listed in Table 11.3. Steps 23
    through 25 pertain to the first clip from Table 11.3. Follow
    Step 26 for the rest of the clips in the table.

23. **Select the first clip listed in Table 11.3 (the clip starting at 00:00**
    in Video 3).
    Choose Edit→Paste Attributes. The Paste Attributes dialog box
    opens.

24. **Click Settings to activate the options at the bottom of the**
    dialog box.
    Deselect all options except Fade Control.

25. **Click OK to close the Paste Attributes dialog box.**
    In the Timeline, you see the opacity rubberband for the clip
    you selected in Step 16 (starting at 00:00 in Video 3) is set at
    a lower opacity level.

26. **Select the next clip listed in Table 11.3 (the clip at 02:01 in**
    Video 5).
    Choose Edit→Paste Attributes Again. The opacity rubberband
    is set at a lower level.

27. **Repeat Step 26 with the remaining clips in Table 11.3.**

Table 11.3: Clips with Opacity Set to 40%

Track	Clip Starts At:	Track	Clip Starts At:
Video 3	00:00	Video 6	01:08
Video 5	02:01		11:02
	02:19	Video 7	10:14
	04:19		
	08:11		
	12:15		

28. **Preview the segment you modified (approximately the first 14 seconds of the project).**

    You see the bar titles moving across the screen. Using three opacity settings along with 100% opacity adds to the sense of movement.

29. **Save the project.**

    You worked with both horizontal and vertical bar titles, adding different levels of opacity. Imagine how long this tutorial would take if you had to manually set each clip's opacity. Using the Paste Attributes and Paste Attributes Again commands you learned to work with settings for large numbers of clips quickly and consistently.

<TIP>

The clip rubberband shows you the opacity level. To read the opacity value Shift + click the opacity rubberband with the fade adjustment tool to display the value.

What the Transparency Terms Mean

Several terms are used when talking about basic transparency edits. Fade levels refer to the opacity level of the entire clip, which can range from 0 to 100 percent. A fade refers to changing the opacity between two handles on the opacity rubberband. A crossfade decreases the opacity of one clip while increasing the opacity of another at the same time. You can create crossfades manually or with the Cross Fade tool.

Tutorial
» Fading Clips

In this tutorial, you fade two of the clips you worked with in the last tutorial to finish the moving bars montage. This final step helps to end the first segment of your project more smoothly. The last copies of the vertical and horizontal bars fade from view as they move across the screen.

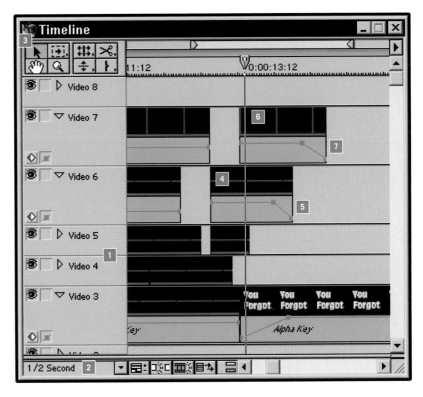

1. **Collapse Video 4 and Video 5.**
   You don't work with Video 4 and Video 5 in this tutorial, but you use them again in the next. Rather than hide the tracks, collapse them. Your Timeline displays six tracks in total, so there is enough room on the screen to work with the four remaining expanded tracks.

2. **Zoom in to ½ second.**
   Click the Time Zoom level at the bottom left of the Timeline. When the menu opens, choose ½ second.

3. **Click on the selection tool in the Timeline toolbox.**

4. **Select the last clip in Video 6.**
   This is a copy of bar_h.prtl starting at 12:15. You set the clip's opacity level to 80% in the previous tutorial.

5. **Click the opacity rubberband at 13:11 to add a handle.**
   Drag the end handle down to 0%. The opacity rubberband drops from 80% at the handle location to 0% at the end handle.

6. **Select the last clip in Video 7 — a copy of** bar_v.prtl **starting at 13:00.**
   You set the clip's opacity level to 80% in the previous tutorial.

7. **Click the opacity rubberband at 13:20 to add a handle.**
   Drag the end handle down to 0%. The opacity rubberband drops from 80% at the handle location to 0% at the end handle.

8. **View the fades in the Monitor window as you render-scrub through the Timeline.**

   As you drag the edit line in the Timeline, the Monitor window opens. You may have to reposition the windows on the screen to see both the Timeline and Monitor windows entirely. You may prefer a slightly different location for the handles that start the final fades for the two clips. I like the arrangement described, even though the handles don't correlate with either the clips' locations or the fade-in of the "You Forgot" title clip.

9. **Save the project.**

   You added fades to both the last horizontal and vertical bar clips in the project. The fades finish the bars montage in the first segment of the project by gradually fading the two clips from view as they move across the screen.

Tutorial
» Creating Crossfades

In this tutorial, you set up some fades and crossfades for clips in the first part of the beach segment. For some you use the Cross Fade tool, for others you adjust the levels manually.

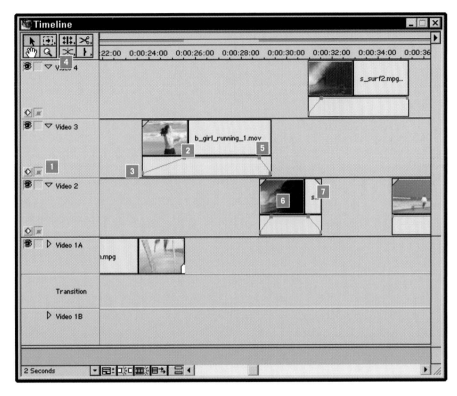

1. **Display the opacity rubberbands for Video 2, Video 3, and Video 4.**
   You are working with clips in these tracks in this tutorial.

2. **Add a handle to the** `b_girl_running_1.mov` **clip rubberband at 25:17.**
   You cannot use a crossfade between a superimposed clip and a clip in Video 1; you must manually fade the clip.

3. **Drag the start handle of the** `b_girl_running_1.mov` **down to 0%.**
   The clip of the woman running down the beach gradually fades in and replaces the beach scenery clip in Video 1A. Because the beach scenery clip is in Video 1A, it has no transparency setting and therefore you can't fade-out the clip.

4. **Select the Cross Fade tool in the Timeline toolbox.**

5. **Click the** `b_girl_running_1.mov` **clip in Video 3 with the Cross Fade tool.**
   The clip is selected as the first clip in a crossfade pair. You don't see a change in the cursor.

6. **Click the** `surf_xtra.mpg` **clip in Video 2.**
   As you move the tool over the clip, the cursor displays the Cross Fade icon. When you click, a handle is automatically added to the `b_girl_running_1.mov` clip at 28:24. The `b_girl_running_1.mov` clip gradually fades out as the `surf_xtra.mpg` clip fades in. The `surf_xtra.mpg` clip has a handle automatically added at 29:10. The `surf_xtra.mpg` clip fades in from the start handle to the new handle. The crossfade occurs over 16 frames.

7. **Click the** `surf_xtra.mpg` **clip in Video 3 with the Cross Fade tool.**
   The clip is selected, and set as the first clip in a crossfade pair.

> 279

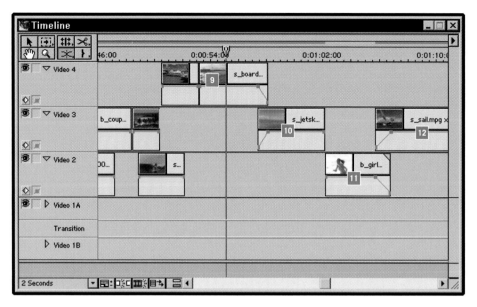

<TIP>
Remember that crossfades are created between a pair of clips in Video 2 and higher. Which clip of the pair you select first and which you select second doesn't matter. The crossfades are the same length as the number of overlapped frames between the clips. In the pair of clips you worked with in Steps 5 and 6, the overlapped area is 16 frames.

8. **Click the** s_surf2.mpg **clip in Video 4 with the Cross Fade tool to complete the crossfade.**
   As you move the tool over the clip, the cursor displays the Cross Fade icon. The surf_xtra.mpg clip gradually fades out as the s_surf2.mpg clip fades in. Handles are added to both clips; the surf_xtra.mpg clip has a handle at 30:29, which is the start of the s_surf2.mpg clip; the surf2.mpg has a new handle at 31:17, which is the same frame as the end of the surf_xtra.mpg clip.

9. **Click the** s_boards.mpg **clip in Video 4 starting at 53:06 with the Cross Fade tool.**
   The clip is selected, and set as the first clip in a crossfade pair.

10. **Click the** s_jetski.mpg **clip in Video 3 with the Cross Fade tool to complete the crossfade.**
    Handles are added to both clips. The s_jetski.mpg clip fades in from the start to the handle added at 58:05. The s_boards.mpg clip fades out from the handle added at 57:13 to the end.

11. **Click the** b_girl_running_2.mov **clip in Video 2 starting at 01:02:06 with the Cross Fade tool.**
    The clip is selected, and set as the first clip in a crossfade pair.

12. **Click the** s_sail.mpg **clip in Video 4 with the Cross Fade tool to complete the crossfade.**
    Handles are added to both clips. The b_girl_running_2.mov clip fades out from the handle added at 01:05:22 to the end. The s_sail.mpg clip fades in from the start to the handle added at 01:06:25.

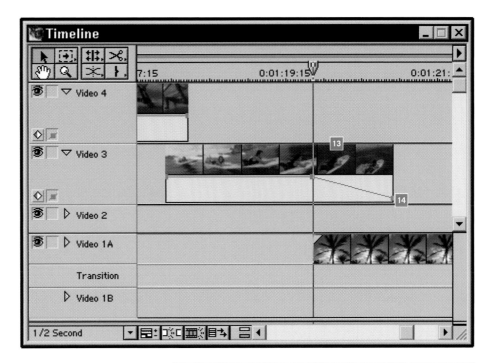

13. **Add a handle at 01:19:26 to the** s_boards2.mpg **clip rubberband in Video 3.**
    The handle is added to the opacity rubberband at the same frame as the v_palms_sun.mpg clip starts in Video 1A.

14. **Drag the end handle down to 0%.**
    You must create the fade-out for the s_boards2.mpg clip manually as the v_palms_sun.mpg clip is in Video 1 and can't have fades or crossfades applied.

15. **Test the crossfades you have created.**
    Build a preview, print to video, or render-scrub through the Timeline.

<TIP>
Feel free to move clip handles to change the length of the fades. For longer crossfades, you can adjust the lengths of the clips.

16. **Save the project.**
    You completed several crossfades in this tutorial. You used the Cross Fade tool to create crossfades, and set some fades manually when the Cross Fade tool couldn't be used, that is, when one of the clips in a pair is in Video 1.

<NOTE>
Quite a few clips do not have any fade adjustments. Some of these clips will not have fades attached; others have fades adjusted after you apply transparency keys.

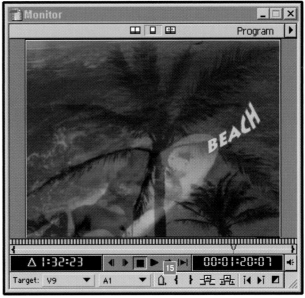

Discussion

Key Types

Premiere includes a range of key types in the Transparency Settings window. You can select any of 15 different keys to use in a project. Certain keys are easily understood, others are more complex, and others seem very similar to one another. How do you decide which one to use?

Certainly the key to deciding on a key (no pun intended) is to define the effect you are trying to achieve using the characteristics of the clips you are working with. For example, certain keys can be used for very dramatic color compositions and effects, while others are used to superimpose segments of one image on top of another.

There are several categories of keys. This discussion covers two commonly used categories — alpha channel keys and brightness keys. Alpha channel keys create transparency for clips containing an alpha channel; brightness keys add transparency based on pixel brightness. Other categories are discussed in later sessions.

Alpha Channel Key

The alpha channel, as described in the introduction to this session, is a separate grayscale image that defines image transparency and opacity. Alpha channels can be straight alpha (meaning the transparency is stored in the alpha channel only) or premultiplied (the background color of the image is also blended into the image). Use the Alpha Channel key for straight alpha channel images or clips. All titles created in Premiere use a straight alpha channel.

Black Alpha Matte and White Alpha Matte Keys

Premultiplied alpha channels have a colored background blended into the alpha channel. The left image shows the original clip. Using a Black Alpha Matte key, shown in a magnified view in the center image, creates a halo around the content of the clip. The image on the right, shown against a white background, shows the clean edge produced by the White Alpha Matte key.

Luminance Key

Luminance works on the darkness or lightness value of a pixel. Darker colors are transparent and brighter colors are opaque. The Luminance key works well for keying out dark areas in a clip, particularly in high-contrast clips. The left image (a) shows the underlying clip, the central image (b) shows the overlying clip; the image on the right (c) shows the results of applying the Luminance key.

Set a Luminance key using two controls — threshold and cutoff. Threshold refers to the range of values that become transparent. The left image (d) shows a clip with both threshold and cutoff values set at 0. Only the overlying butterfly clip is visible. The underlying solid blue matte clip doesn't show through as no pixels have been designated as transparent. The middle image (e) shows the effect of changing the Threshold to 100 and leaving the cutoff value at 0. The higher the threshold value, the wider the range of transparency. The entire pixel value range of the butterfly is now available for transparency. Once you have defined the range, set the opacity for the selected areas using the cutoff setting. In the right image (f), much more of the butterfly is blue as the cutoff value is increased to 60. The higher the value, the wider the range of transparency. A higher cutoff value increases transparency. That is, once you define the range of pixel values that become transparent, change the cutoff value to define *how* transparent the pixels become.

Multiply and Screen Keys

These two keys also work on the luminance of a clip and can create some very interesting effects. The Multiply key always produces output darker than the original; the Screen key always produces lighter output. The image on the left shows the clip before a key is applied. The central image shows the Multiply key, and the right image shows the Screen key. The same pink/yellow gradient shown earlier is used in these examples.

Multiplying creates areas of transparency that correspond to darker pixel values in the underlying clip. Screening produces areas of transparency corresponding to the lighter pixel values in the underlying clip. You can adjust the amount of transparency by changing the cutoff setting. Unlike the Luminance key which is based on the darkness of a pixel, the Screen key is based on the lightness of pixel values. A higher cutoff setting produces less transparency.

  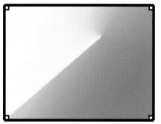

Tutorial
» Adjusting Transparency Using Luminance

In the discussion on keys it mentioned how transparency can be based on the pixel brightness of a clip, also known as lumi-nance. In this tutorial, you add a still image clip to the first section of the project and use a Luminance key.

1. **Open the stills bin in the Project window (located within the city bin).**
   Select the city4.jpg clip.

2. **Right-click the** city4.jpg **clip in the Project window to open the shortcut menu.**
   Choose Duration. In the Clip Duration dialog box, set the dura-tion to 01:05 and click OK. The new duration is shown with the other information about the clip.

3. **Drag the clip to Video 2 in the Timeline starting at 00:09.**
   The clip ends at 01:14.

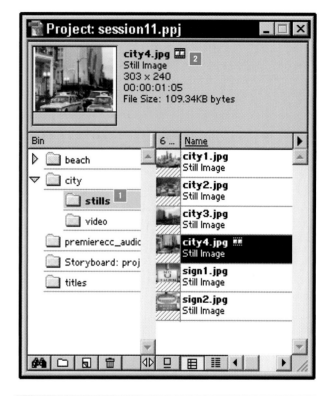

4. **Choose Window→Show Effect Controls to open the Effect Controls window.**

5. **Click the box to the left of the Transparency heading.**
   This opens the Transparency Settings dialog box.

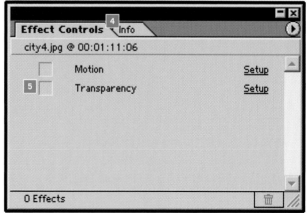

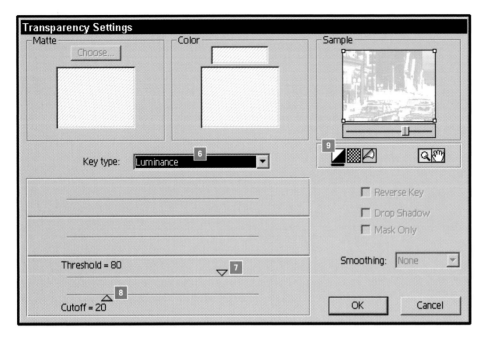

6. **Click the arrow to open the Key type menu.**
   Select Luminance from the Key type menu.

7. **Drag the slider to set the Threshold to 80.**
   Choosing a high value such as 80 identifies a broad range of brightness values in the image that will become transparent as you see in Step 11.

8. **Set the Cutoff to 20.**
   The still image is very dark overall. A low cutoff displays the underlying video while still allowing the city still to be distinguishable.

9. **Click the background option.**
   This places a white background behind the clip. You can click the black/white background option to toggle between black and white for better visibility. You can see how transparent the clip is based on the amount of white visible in the sample window.

10. **Select the underlying image display option.**
    You can see the underlying clip as well as the clip you are working with.

11. **Drag the slider to preview the clip.**
    The underlying track for the city4.jpg clip on the Timeline is blank until the c_night.mov clip starts at 00:24. Unless you drag the slider to preview the clip, you won't see the transparency effect. Sliding the preview slider shows the traffic in the background clip through the dark portions of the still image.

12. **Click OK to close the Transparency Settings window and return to the Timeline.**
    Leave the clip selected in the Timeline. When the Transparency Settings dialog box closes, the name of the transparency key displays below the opacity rubberband of the clip on the Timeline.

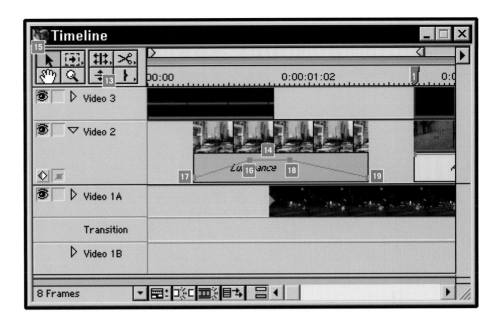

13. **Select the Fade Adjustment tool in the Timeline toolbox.**
    If another fade tool is displayed in the toolbox, click and hold the fade tool displayed until the subpalette opens. Then select the Fade Adjustment tool.

14. **On the Timeline, drag the opacity rubberband for the** `city4.jpg` **clip to 80%.**

15. **Click on the selection tool in the Timeline toolbox.**

16. **Add a handle at 00:20.**
    When you create the fade in the next step, the handle defines the end point of the fade.

17. **Drag the start handle down to 0%.**
    The clip gradually fades in from the start frame at 00:09 to the handle at 00:20.

18. **Add a handle at 00:28.**
    When you create the fade in the next step, the handle defines the point where the fade begins.

19. **Drag the end handle down to 0%.**
    The clip gradually fades out from the handle at 00:28 to the end frame at 01:14.

20. **Save the project.**
    You added a still image to the Timeline. You set its transparency using the Luminance key, which allows the city video to show through portions of the still image. You adjusted the overall transparency for the clip, and finished the editing by fading the clip in and out.

Tutorial
» Using the Screen Transparency Key

In addition to luminance settings, there are also screen and multiply options that work on the relationship between the brightness of a clip and the underlying image. In this tutorial, you add another clip to the project and set its transparency using the Screen key. Also, remember that empty space in the Video 2 track? Here is where you start to fill it.

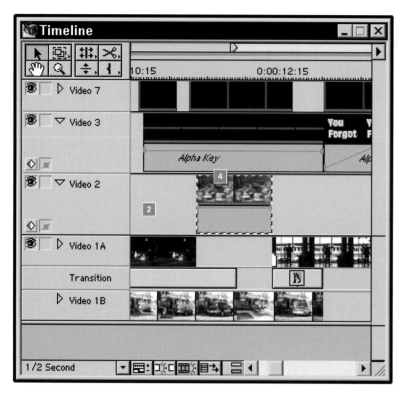

1. **In the Project window, select the** city2.jpg **clip from the stills bin (within the city bin).**

2. **Drag the** city2.jpg **clip to the Timeline.**
   Place it after the traffic light clips in Video 2 (starting at 08:14).

3. **Right-click the** city4.jpg **clip in the Timeline to open the shortcut menu. Choose Duration.**
   In the Clip Duration dialog box, set the duration to 01:00 and click OK to close the Clip Duration dialog box.

4. **Adjust the starting time on the Timeline.**
   Move the clip to start at 11:11.

5. **Open the Transparency Settings dialog box.**
   Click the box to the left of Transparency on the Effect Controls panel, or right-click the clip and choose Video Options→ Transparency.

6. **In the Transparency Settings dialog box, select Screen from the Key type dropdown menu.**

7. **Move the Cutoff slider to 95.**

   The city2.jpg image is light in color. A high cutoff value identifies a small range of pixels that become transparent based on their lightness. Since the image is overlaid on a split screen using both a dark and light underlying image, using a cutoff value that is too low makes the city2.jpg image and its underlying images indistinct.

8. **Click OK to close the Transparency Settings window.**

9. **In the Timeline, add a fade handle to the opacity rubberband of the city2.jpg clips at 12:03.**

   When you create the fade in the next step, the handle at 12:03 defines the point where the fade begins.

10. **Drag the end handle to 0%.**

    The clip gradually fades out from the handle at 12:03 to the end frame at 12:11.

11. **Save the project.**

    You add the first clip to fill in the blank space in Video 2. The city2.jpg clip uses a Screen key for blending it with the split screen video on underlying tracks. You set the cutoff to a high value to show the two underlying video clips. You set a fade handle and faded out the clip.

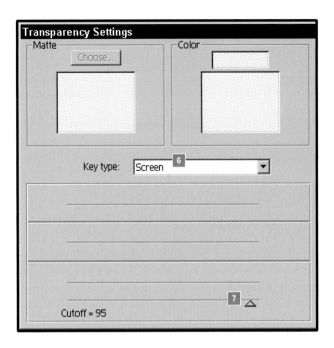

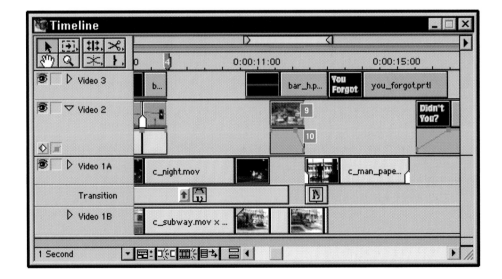

Tutorial
» Adding Alpha Channels to Clips

In this tutorial, you work with two more clips you add to that blank space in Video 2. Again, you use still images. You edit the two clips in their entirety in this tutorial. That is, you add them to the Timeline, set their durations, and add transparency. When that is done, you adjust the aspect ratios of the clips and top them off with animation.

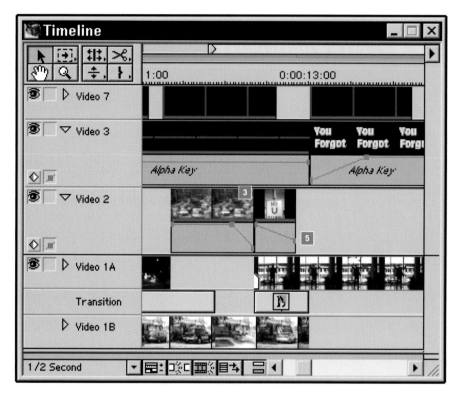

1. **Open the Project window.**
   Right-click the `sign1.jpg` clip in the stills bin.

2. **Select Duration and set the clip length to 00:15.**
   You can see the new value listed in the clip details.

   <TIP>
   This is a short clip. To view it easily, zoom in to one second or less.

3. **From the Project window, drag the** `sign1.jpg` **clip to Video 2 in the Timeline.**
   Place it after the `city2.jpg` still image (starting at 12:11).

   <NOTE>
   Don't move the clip into this location unless the duration is adjusted. The default length for the clip is five seconds. If you see

a set of semi-transparent arrows when you drag the clip into a blank space, don't release the mouse because the clips for the entire Timeline will be adjusted if you drop the clip in that location.

4. **Right-click the clip to open the shortcut menu.**
   Choose Video Options→Maintain Aspect Ratio. The thumbnail is centered horizontally on the image with black margins to the left and right. The `sign1.jpg` clip does not conform to the aspect ratio for the rest of the project because the image is taller than it is wide. When the image is added to the project, it is changed to the 4:3 ratio named in the Project Settings. This command restores the proper dimensions of the image.

5. **Drag the end opacity rubberband handle to 30%.**
   You add a gradual fade to the clip. It starts at 100% opacity and fades out to 30% opacity.

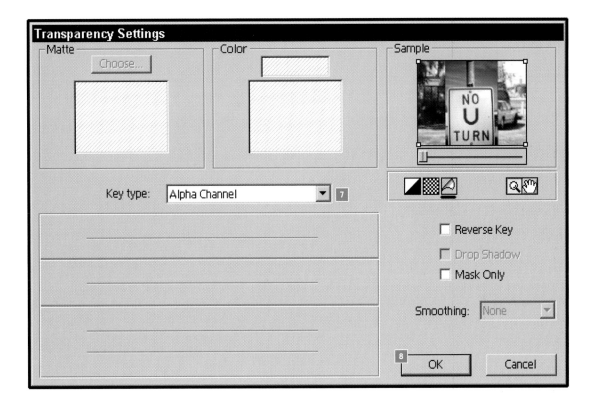

6. **Open the Transparency Settings window to add transparency to the clip.**
   Right-click sign1.jpg and choose Video Options→ Transparency or click the box to the left of the Transparency heading on the Effect Controls window. The sign1.jpg clip needs an alpha channel to create transparency in the animation you add starting with Step 9.

7. **Select Alpha Channel from the Key type menu.**
   The black margins to the left and right of the image disappear and the underlying track is visible in the Sample area of the Transparency Settings window.

<NOTE>
The Black Alpha Matte key also works.

8. **Click OK.**
   The Transparency Settings window closes.

9. **Open the Motion Settings window.**
   Click the box to the left of the Motion label on the Effect Controls window, or right-click the clip and choose Video Options→Motion Settings.

To Resize or Not to Resize

In this tutorial, you adjusted the aspect ratio of the two image clips. If you look at the city4.jpg clip used in an earlier tutorial, you see its size is 303 x 240 pixels (not 320 x 240 pixels). In a quest for perfection, you would resize the clip to conform with project size or use the Maintain Aspect Ratio command like you did in this tutorial. I recommend you do nothing to the city4.jpg clip for several reasons. If you use the Maintain Aspect Ratio command, unattractive black bars are added to the city4.jpg image margins. The difference between the clip width and project width is so slight you can't see any distortion in the image. Balance the outcome of changing aspect ratios such as dealing with blank space at the clip's margins against the distortion the clip displays if you don't change the aspect ratio.

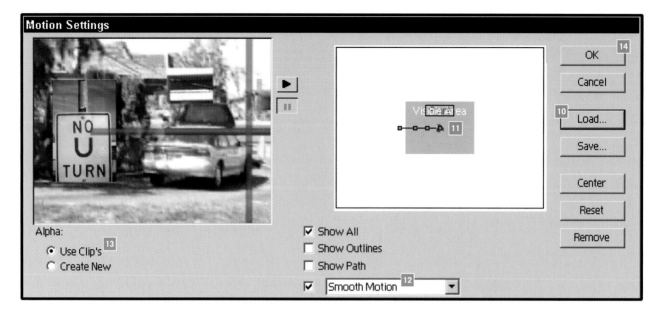

10. **Click Load to open the Load Motion Settings dialog box.**
   Locate the folder on your hard drive containing the motion preset files. The motion presets are installed with Premiere and are located in a folder named Motion. The Motion folder is inside the Premiere program folder on your hard drive. A copy of the preset file is also in the extra video folder if you prefer.

11. **Select the** Zoom_Left.pmt **file from the Motion folder.**
   Click Open. The Load Motion Settings dialog box closes, and you return to the Motion Settings window. The preset file is loaded into the Motion Settings window.

<TIP>
You can see the Zoom_Left.pmt file's settings. The Timeline now contains four keyframes. If you preview the clip, you can see the sign appearing at the center of the screen and moving left as it increases in size.

12. **Select Smooth Motion.**
   The preformatted motion settings use a number of changes in distortion and position that create jerkiness. Use the Smooth Motion option to blend the changes and make the animation more even.

13. **Select Use Clip's under Alpha.**

14. **Click OK.**
   The Motion Settings window closes.

15. **In the Project window, right-click the** sign2.jpg **clip and reset its duration to 00:15.**
   The location the clip is placed into on the Timeline is of much shorter duration than the default clip length of 05:00.

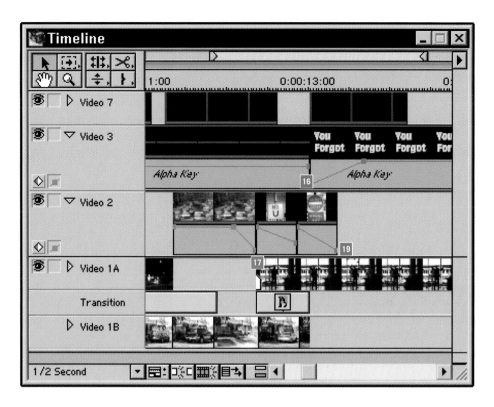

16. **Drag** `sign2.jpg` **to the Timeline.**
    Place it after the `sign1.jpg` clip in Video 2 starting at
    12:26.

17. **Select the** `sign1.jpg` **clip and copy it.**
    You are going to transfer the settings you added to the
    `sign1.jpg` clip to the `sign2.jpg` clip.

18. **Select the** `sign2.jpg` **clip.**
    Choose Edit➔Paste Attributes. The Paste Attributes dialog box
    opens. Click Settings and then click Paste. In previous tutori-
    als you deselected some of the settings. In this case, leave all
    settings to have them pasted automatically — filters, fade
    controls, transparency, and motion settings.

<TIP>
Leave the four setting types selected. The `sign1.jpg` clip doesn't
contain any filters (video effects) for you to copy. You do have fade
controls, transparency, and motions settings that are pasted from
the `sign1.jpg` clip.

19. **Drag the end opacity rubberband handle down to 0%.**
    This is the only difference in settings between the two sign
    clips. Fade-out the `sign2.jpg` clip to 0%. The `sign2.jpg`
    clip appears at nearly the same time as the start of the first
    title clip You Forgot. A fade-out to 0% makes a smoother tran-
    sition to the title clip's fade-in.

20. **Preview the movie segment.**
    Render-scrub or Print to Video the segment approximately
    from 12:00 to 14:00 to see both sign clips in action.

<NOTE>
Instead of using the same motion path for the second clip, you can
substitute the right perspective path instead. Again, make sure to
choose Smooth Motion. I tried both options, as well as some custom variations on the path, and found using the same perspective
provides a good balance to the opening Iris Square transition.

21. **Save the project.**
    You added two still images to the project and edited them in
    their entirety. You adjusted their aspect ratio settings. You
    added fade controls. You also added transparency to the clips
    and finished the edits by adding motion setting to the clips.

» Session Review

In this session, you learned a method to modify a collection of clips using several fade levels and the Paste Attributes/Paste Attributes Again commands. You also added some fade-out and fade-in effects to clips throughout the project, both manually and using the Cross Fade tool.

The latter part of the session showed you how to work with some common types of transparency keys. You can review your progress against the sample movies on the CD. The first, `session11a.mpg`, shows the completed first segment of the movie; `session11b.mpg` shows the portions of the second segment that have fades applied.

Notice that the tutorials are becoming more complex. That is, in addition to working with one specific process or task, you now combine different processes such as applying keys and adding motion. Not only is it important for you to learn how to use the program, but it is also important for you to learn efficient ways to apply different processes to the same clip.

Look at the final image in this session, which shows the faded horizontal bar titles. You can also see one of the static images you added in this session. Because the clip has a Transparency key and motion added, it doesn't look very static!

Answer the questions below to review the information in this session. The answer for each question can be found in the tutorial noted in parentheses.

1. Where is the fade adjustment tool located? How do you use it? (See "Tutorial: Adjusting Fade Levels for a Group of Clips.")

2. What is the difference between the Paste Attributes and the Paste Attributes Again commands? (See "Tutorial: Adjusting Fade Levels for a Group of Clips.")

3. How can you display the precise value of a fade on the Timeline? (See "Tutorial: Adjusting Fade Levels for a Group of Clips.")

4. Is there a rule for placing handles to fade-in or fade-out a clip? (See "Tutorial: Fading Clips.")

5. Can you use the Cross Fade tool for clips in any track? (See "Tutorial: Creating Crossfades.")

6. How do you know how much of a clip will be used for a crossfade? (See "Tutorial: Creating Crossfades.")

7. How does an alpha channel create transparency? (See "Discussion: Key Types.")

8. What is the difference between a straight alpha channel and a premultiplied alpha channel? (See "Discussion: Key Types.")

9. What is the difference between the Screen and Multiply keys? (See "Discussion: Key Types.")

10. What two settings are required for using the Luminance key? How do they work? (See "Tutorial: Adjusting Transparency Using Luminance.")

11. How do you preview the effect of your settings in the Transparency Settings window? (See "Tutorial: Adjusting Transparency Using Luminance.")

12. What characteristic of a clip does the Screen key use to create transparency? (See "Tutorial: Using the Screen Transparency Key.")

13. Does the Screen key produce a darker or lighter effect? (See "Tutorial: Using the Screen Transparency Key.")

14. Can different keys produce the same effect? (See "Tutorial: Adding Alpha Channels to Clips.")

15. When is it important to consider the aspect ratio of a clip? (See "Tutorial: Adding Alpha Channels to Clips.")

» Other Projects

You modified the fades added to the bar titles in the first segment, but only three opacity levels were used. Vary the fades added to the bar titles in the first segment. View the bar titles segment to see if any of the clips would benefit from a fade-in or fade-out.

Working with Transparency

Session Introduction

In the last session, you started adjusting transparency settings for some clips in your project. You completed many of the fade adjustments for the project. You also used a few transparency keys.

So far you have used transparency keys that work with alpha channels and brightness levels. A number of color keys designate specific colors or color ranges as transparent. Layering clips one on top of another, and blending them using different keys and fades is called superimposition. Your project primarily uses superimposed clips.

The matte keys add a lot of visual punch to a project. You can use the alpha channel of one clip to affect the transparency of another clip. This is referred to as a matte. You can also use a moving matte to display another clip. This is called a traveling matte.

Before you begin the tutorials there is a discussion about the types of transparency which were not covered in the last tutorial. This gives you an understanding of the work you do in this session. The tutorials only apply to clips in the beach segment of the project. You add a copy of a clip at the end of the project and work with the matte title you created earlier. You then apply it to several clips in the middle of the beach segment, and work with a variation of another title at the beginning of the beach segment — in that order. Wait until you see what you build!

TOOLS YOU'LL USE
Timeline window, Info window, Effect Controls window, Transparency Settings window, background viewing options, Image Matte key, Track Matte key, settings sliders, Magnifying Glass tool, hand tool, opacity rubberbands, Cross Fade tool, fade adjustment tool, Paste Attributes command, Paste Attributes Again command, Motion settings window, Title Designer window, font properties, fill properties, stroke properties, rectangle tool, fill properties, Crawl/Roll options, crawl settings

CD-ROM FILES NEEDED
Session 11 project file you created or the session11.ppj file from the CD-ROM
Session12.mpg preview file from the premierecc_samples folder (for reference)
beach_xtra.mpg from the extra video folder
life2.prtl from the extra video folder (if you do not build the title in the tutorial)
matte2.prtl from the extra video folder (if you do not modify the title in the tutorial)

TIME REQUIRED
90 minutes

Discussion

Color-Based and Matte Keys

Color-based keys are used for both composites and superimposing; matte keys are used for creating visually rich superimpositions.

Chroma Key

The Chroma key is used to select a color range for transparency. You can key out a background from a clip using a range of one color, called the target color. In the following example, the first image shows the clip before the key is applied. The pale blue of the sky is defined as the target color by sampling it with the eyedropper in the Color sampling window. The similarity setting defines how many other colors are set as transparent in addition to the pale blue selected. The higher the number, the more transparency results. The sample uses a similarity set to 16. The transparent area includes shades of green as well as the sky. The higher the setting, the larger the range of color that becomes transparent. When the color range is defined, the clip is blended with the clip below it on the Timeline (a solid pink matte) using the blend setting. The higher the blend setting, the more faded the foreground image (the trees) and the brighter the background image (the pink color matte). Use the threshold and cutoff sliders to control the visibility of shadow in the image. In the example, both settings remain at their default value of 0 as shadows aren't prominent in the image. Finally, use smoothing to adjust the amount of anti-aliasing applied to the boundaries between keyed out areas and the opaque areas of the clip. In this case, Smoothing was set to High. Use the Chroma key for removing a background that uses a range of shades of one color.

  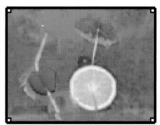

RGB Difference Key

The RGB Difference key is similar to, but less complex, than the Chroma key. In the examples, the image on the left shows the underlying clip; the center image shows the original clip. You select a range of colors to key out and adjust Smoothing; in this case, the similarity slider is set to 10. Selecting a blue color from the sky produces the image on the right, which now looks like the palm trees have the beach in the background. You can't blend the image or adjust shadows. This key works well for removing bright backgrounds such as the sky.

Blue Screen, Green Screen, and Non-Red Keys

True green and blue are used as keys for defining transparency. Often, the Green and/or Blue keys are used for movie effects. The superhero appears to fly across the city at night, but the actor is actually suspended from a set of cables in front of a green or blue screen. When the video is composited, the blue screen background color from the superhero video is keyed out, or made transparent and placed on top another layer of video showing the city. On a less dramatic level than flying superheroes, the following images show the effect of a Blue Screen key. The left image shows the sign with its blue background. When the Blue Screen key is applied, the blue background is made transparent and shows the underlying image. The right image shows the sign with a replacement background. In this case, the underlying clip is the same solid pink clip shown earlier.

The Non-Red key is also used for green and blue backgrounds. In addition to making either green or blue transparent, the Non-Red key allows for blending. It also reduces fringing around the edges of opaque objects. Use this key (instead of the Green Screen or Blue Screen keys) to control blending.

Image Matte Key

The Image Matte key produces transparency based on a still image. In the following set of images, the image on the top left is a clip that will have the Image Matte key applied to it. It is placed on the Timeline in the track above a solid green clip, which is on the top right. When an image matte is applied to a clip, black areas in the image become transparent, white areas remain opaque, and gray becomes transparent based on its depth (dark gray is more transparent than light gray). The image on the bottom left shows the clip with the matte applied to it. You can reverse the key in the Transparency Settings window using the Reverse Key option. This means the black areas remain opaque, and the white areas become transparent. In the image on the bottom right, you can see how the letters are transparent and reveal the green layer below.

Generally a grayscale image is used for image mattes because it is simpler for Premiere to calculate transparency from a standard number of shades of gray than from millions of colors. Colored images remove color from the underlying clip based on color value calculations. This means the equivalent amount of gray in a color is calculated and used for transparency. Color value calculations are similar to photocopying something colorful in black and white. Pale lavender photocopies as pale gray while brick red photocopies as dark gray. You work with this key in the project using a black and white title clip.

Difference Matte

The Difference Matte key often is used to key out a static portion of a clip, such as a person walking across the screen. In the following example, the yellow ball in the first image (on the left) is animated. A frame of the background is saved and used as a formal Difference Matte. It can be used with either the central figure or the background. The example uses the background. Selecting the Reverse Key option saves a frame of the foreground image instead. The Difference Matte key is based on a pixel comparison frame by frame. Matching areas become transparent, so the entire background becomes transparent, allowing the content of the track underneath to show, as seen in the image on the right. You use this key in your project to blend pixels.

Track Matte

The Track Matte key is used to create a matte in motion. When both the original clip and the underlying clip are in motion, it is called a traveling matte. Clips are placed in adjacent tracks in the Timeline, and the clip defined as the matte affects the visibility of the underlying clip. You can use either a motion or a still clip as a matte. Like the Image Matte key, use of a color image removes color from the underlying clip depending on the amount of gray in the image's colors. Unless this is the effect you are trying to achieve, use a grayscale image. You use this key in your project.

Tutorial
» Using a Color-Based Transparency Key

In Session 5 you created a still image from the last frame of the clip showing a fruit-laden tropical drink. You used the still for the transition to the next clip. In this tutorial, you use another copy of that clip and add a key to it. You will use the Blue Screen key, removing some of the background from the drink clip and showing the palm trees in the underlying clip. Adding the still image clip and the transparency key enhances the transition from the last clip that shows the palm trees at night to the final clip.

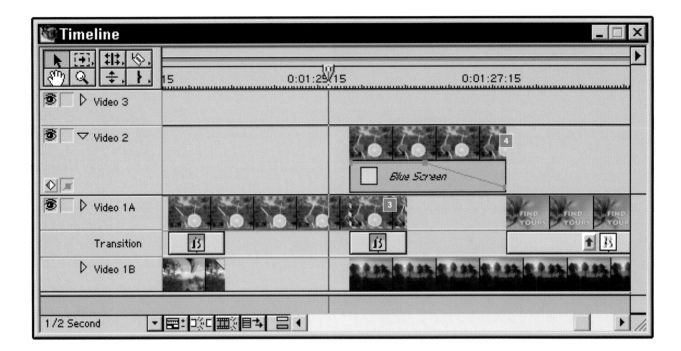

1. **Choose File→Open and navigate to the location where you stored your project files.**
   You can also choose File→Open Recent Project and choose your project file from the list. Open session11.ppj.

   <NOTE>
   If you didn't do the tutorials in Session 11, copy the session11.ppj file from the CD to your hard drive. Open the file and resave it as session12.ppj (or use another filenaming convention).

2. **Resave the project file as** session12.ppj.

3. **Copy the** v_drink.tif **clip located in Video 1A starting at 01:25:26.**

4. **Paste the copy into Video 2.**
   Set the clip duration to 01:24. Move the clip to start at 01:25:26.

5. **Right-click the clip and choose Video Options→Transparency.**
   The Transparency Settings window opens.

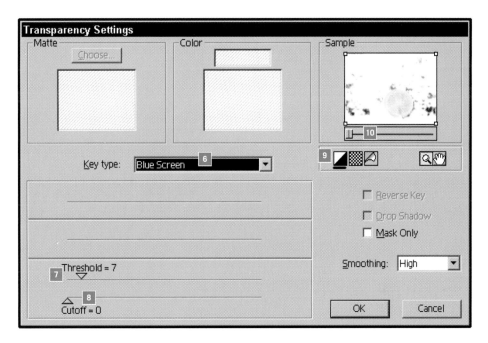

6. Select Blue Screen from the Key type menu.

7. Set the Threshold to 7.

The goal is to have only the orange slice visible against the palm trees in the underlying clip. At a low level, such as 7, only the bright yellows of the orange (and some of the cherry reds) are visible.

8. Leave the Cutoff at its default setting of 0.

Adjusting the Cutoff to a higher level makes the orange brighter and more opaque; the goal is to make the fruit translucent.

9. Select the white background display option.

Use a white background to clearly display the transparent areas.

10. Preview the clip.

Against the white background you can clearly see what elements of the still image are visible. That is, you see the orange and some of the cherry.

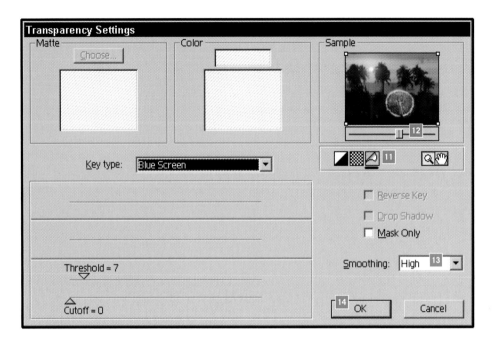

11. **Select the underlying image display background and preview the clip again.**

12. **Drag the preview slider to show how the clip overlays the palm tree background.**

    You can see the translucent orange displayed over the palm trees in the latter part of the preview. The first part of the preview shows the translucent orange appearing from within the iris round transition applied to the clips underlying the still image clip on the Timeline.

13. **Set Smoothing to High.**

    The edges of the orange slice are smoothed and produce less defined boundaries. This contributes to the overall translucency of the clip.

14. **Click OK.**

    The Transparency Settings window closes. The transparency key name displays below the opacity rubberband. You can see this in the first image in this tutorial.

15. **Save the project.**

    The Blue Screen transparency key works well for making the fruit translucent. The Green Screen and Non-Red keys also create a similar effect. I wanted to see the orange slice and not the straw, and the Blue Screen key is the only one that produces this specific effect. You can try them all.

Tutorial
» Preparing Clips for an Image Matte

In this tutorial, you organize the clips that use the Image Matte key. You assembled and edited clips in the first four sessions of the project so you would have something to see throughout the length of the movie. In this session you adjust clips for length and move the clips into their final locations. You also do an experiment with the matte you created in the previous titles session. Use the Info window to assist in adjusting clips.

1. **Hide all tracks except Video 2 and Video 3.**
   You are working only with a group of clips in these two tracks. Hiding other tracks gives you more screen room.

2. **Extend the** v_palms_rotate.mpg **clip in Video 2.**
   Lengthen the clip to 11:08. Drag the right edge of the clip right to extend the clip. The left end of the clip is at its end point.

3. **Slide the** v_garden2.mpg **clip in Video 3 left to start at 38:23.**

4. **Move the** b_couple.mov **clip in Video 3 left to butt against the** v_garden2.mpg **clip.**
   It starts at 41:06.

5. **Move the** v_resort.mpg **clip in Video 3 left to butt against the** b_couple.mov **starting at 45:26.**

<TIP>
The clips in Steps 3 to 5 are in their final locations.

6. **Select the** v_garden2.mpg **clip in Video 3 starting at 38:23.**
   Right-click the clip and choose Video Options→Transparency to open the Transparency Settings dialog box.

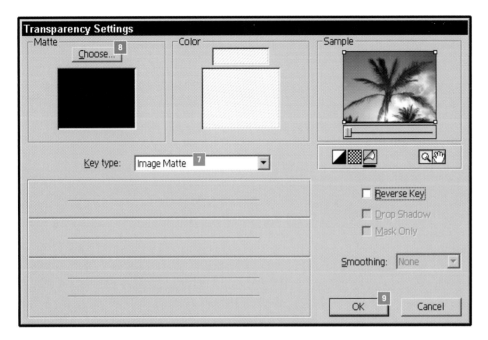

<TIP>
Even though the clip is included in the project, you can't select it directly from the Project window.

7. **Select Image Matte from the Key type menu.**

8. **Click Choose.**
   In the Load Matte browser window that opens, locate the matte.prtl clip you created and click Open. The matte appears as a solid black box in the Matte preview box. An obvious problem exists with the matte file. If you refer back to the discussion in this session, can you determine the problem? Here's a hint: It concerns the way the matte title is constructed and what colors become transparent.

9. **Click OK.**
   The Transparency Settings window closes.

10. **Render-scrub through the Timeline or make a preview of this segment of the Timeline.**
    You won't see anything except the lovely palm trees swaying in the breeze, which is nice, but not the effect you are looking for. The goal was to use an image matte that would allow portions of both the clips in Video 2 and Video 3 to show at the same time.

11. **Save the project.**
    You adjusted and moved a sequence of clips into their final positions on the Timeline. You also added an image matte to a clip, but it didn't work. In the next tutorial, learn how to fix the image matte to produce the effect.

Tutorial
» Creating an Image Matte

Have you figured it out? The matte title you created in the titles session used two black rectangles placed over a transparent background. Remember that mattes define black areas as transparent. What happened here is that black is defined as transparent, and the transparent areas of the title remain transparent. The end result — nothing. To use this title as a matte, you have to create some opaque areas.

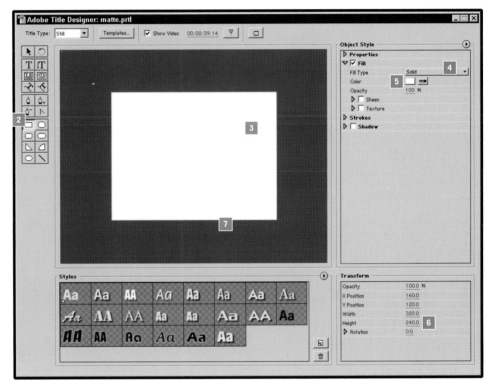

1. **Double-click the** matte.prtl **clip in the Project window to open it in the Title Designer window.**

<NOTE>
If you do not complete this tutorial, a copy of the finished clip is on the CD in the extra video folder. The CD file is named matte2.prtl.

2. **Select the rectangle tool.**

3. **Draw a rectangle covering the entire screen.**
   You color this rectangle to create opaque areas for the matte.

4. **Click the checkbox to the left of the Fill heading to activate the Fill settings.**
   Click the arrow to the left of the checkbox to display the settings. Select the Solid fill from the Fill Types list.

5. **Set the color to white (RGB 255/255/255).**
   Click the color swatch to open the Color Picker and enter the RGB values. Click OK to close the Color Picker.

6. **Set the dimensions of the rectangle to 320 pixels by 240 pixels.**

7. **Center the rectangle vertically and horizontally.**
   Right-click the rectangle to open the shortcut menu and choose Position→Horizontal Center; right-click again and choose Position→Vertical Center.

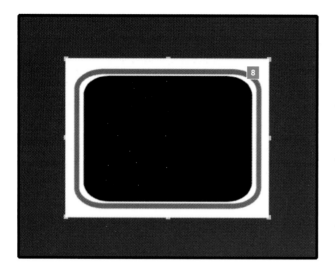

8. **Right-click the rectangle to open the shortcut menu.**
   Choose Arrange→Send to Back. The white rectangle moves behind the black rectangle and black rectangle outline.

9. **Choose File→Save As.**
   Name the title `matte2.prtl`. It is suitable for using as a matte.

10. **Select the** `v_garden2.mpg` **clip in Video 3.**
    Right-click the clip and choose Video Options→Transparency to open the Transparency Settings window.

11. **Click Choose.**
    In the Load Matte browser window, locate the `matte2.prtl` clip you created and click Open. The new matte displays in the Matte window and shows in the Sample preview window.

12. **Preview the clip.**
    The purpose of the matte is to show a video clip centrally on the screen surrounded by a border of another video clip. The palm trees in Video 2 are displayed centrally, while the garden clip is a border around the edges. The palm trees in Video 2 should be the border clip. The important part of the composite should be the garden clip, not the palm trees.

13. **Click the Reverse Key.**
    The Reverse Key setting flips the opacity setting. Now the majority of the screen displays the garden clip (also seen through the semi-transparent outer rectangle), and the outside margins of the screen show the palm trees.

14. **Click OK to close the Transparency Settings window.**

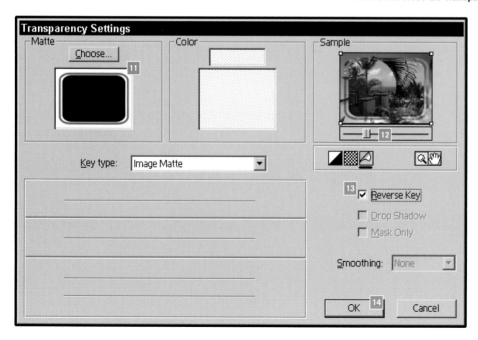

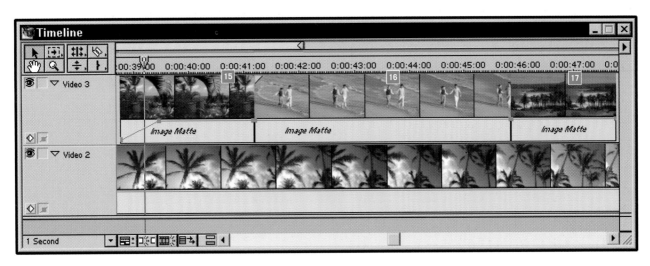

15. **Copy the** v_garden2.mpg **clip in the Timeline.**

16. **Select the** b_couple.mov **clip starting at 41:06 in Video 3.**
    Choose Edit→Paste Attributes to open the Paste Attributes
    dialog box. Select Settings, deselect all options but
    Transparency Settings and click Paste to apply the image
    matte settings to the clip.

17. **Select the** v_resort.mpg **clip starting at 45:26 in Video 3.**
    Choose Edit→Paste Attributes Again to paste the image matte
    settings to the clip.

18. **Preview the movie segment from approximately 38:00 to 48:00.**
    Admire your work.

<NOTE>
Some of the content inside the rectangle is similar in color to the
rotating palm tree background clip. You add an effect to the background clip in a later session to make it more distinctive.

19. **Save the project.**
    You modified the image matte title clip to create areas of
    opacity. You replaced the original image matte clip in the
    Transparency Settings window. As the opaque and trans-
    parency areas were reversed, you used the Reverse Key setting
    to flip the images showing the clips in Video 3 centrally sur-
    rounded by the palm trees clip from Video 2.

Tutorial
» Converting a Title to a Track Matte

In this tutorial, you reuse one of the titles you used in an earlier session. You modify the title to make it more functional for use as a track matte. You also add crawling animation in the Title Designer window. With the addition of motion, the track matte becomes a traveling matte.

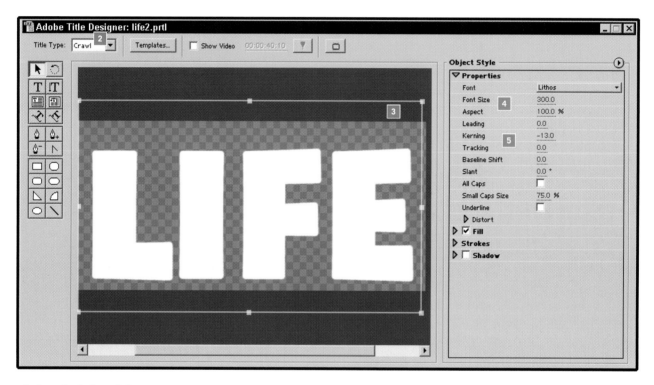

1. **Open the Project window.**
   Open the titles bin. Double-click life.prtl to open it in the Title Designer window.

<NOTE>
If you do not complete this tutorial, the finished clip, life2.prtl is on the CD in the extra video folder.

2. **Select Crawl from the Title Type menu.**
   Crawling text moves from left to right across the screen. The size of the crawl depends both on the size of the text, any spaces you add before or after the text, and other crawl settings explained in more detail later in the tutorial. Rolling text, the other option, moves text vertically across the screen.

3. **Choose the select tool and select the title.**

4. **Click the arrow to the left of the Properties panel to display the settings.**
   Change the font size to 300.

5. **Set the Kerning to –13.0.**
   Kerning defines the spacing between characters. You need the letters as close as possible but still legible. When you use the title as a matte, the video of the underlying layer shows through the letters.

<NOTE>
You can adjust the kerning between individual pairs of selected letters. Select the Text tool and click on the text. Move the I-beam to the letters, drag to select, and then adjust the kerning. When you deselect the text, the kerning setting now displays only dashed lines. This indicates there is more than one setting used. You can use the same process with other properties as well, such as font size or aspect.

6. Click the checkbox left of the Fill heading to activate it.

Click the arrow to the left of the checkbox to display the Fill settings.

7. Choose the Solid fill type, which was selected from the original text.

8. Set the text color to white (RGB = 255/255/255).

< T I P >

Rather than click the color swatch to open the Color Picker, click the eyedropper tool and click one of the white boxes used for text settings.

9. Open the Inner Strokes panel.

Deselect all Inner Strokes.

10. Open the Outer Strokes panel.

Deselect all but one of the Outer Strokes; it doesn't matter which stroke you leave selected.

11. Choose these settings for the stroke:

Type — Edge
Size — 10.0
Fill Type — Solid
Color — White
The text for this title is very large. Adding a stroke helps smooth the edges of the letters.

12. From the Premiere menu headings, choose Title→Roll/Crawl Options.

The Roll/Crawl Options dialog box opens. These settings determine how fast the text moves.

13. Type 10 into the Pre-Roll field.

Pre-Roll is the number of frames at the beginning of the title that appear motionless before the animation starts.

14. Type 15 into the Post-Roll field.

Post-Roll refers to the number of frames at the end of the title that display after the animation stops.

15. Type 0 into the Ease-In field, and 5 into the Ease-Out field.

Ease-In refers to the number of frames you need to get the title moving at regular speed. Ease-Out refers to the number of frames you need to stop the title. 0 starts the title moving at normal speed, and 5 means the title slows down to its stop position over 5 frames.

16. Click OK to close the Roll/Crawl Options dialog box.

17. Choose File→Save As.

Name the title life2.prtl. Close the Title Designer window. The new title is added to the project. You modified a title clip to use as a track matte, resized and moved the letters, changed the stroke on the letter, and added a crawl animation to the text.

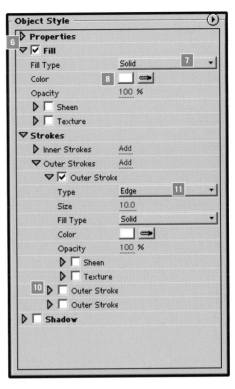

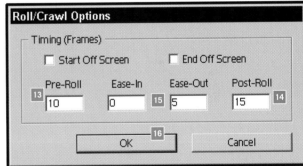

Using Roll/Crawl Settings

Here's something for future reference. You can set an attractive text crawl using the Start Off Screen and End Off Screen settings. If you use these settings with a track matte, you may see a vertical transparent bar corresponding to the width of the screen (if a title extends 640 pixels and the project is 320 pixels wide, the bar appears half-way thought the title). Remove the settings. Add several spaces before and after the text to simulate the same effect. Save the title with a different name as Premiere won't save modified roll/crawl settings with the same file name.

Tutorial
» Adding the Title Track Matte

The beginning of the beach sequence is — a beach. You then see a happy person running down said beach. In this tutorial, you add zip to your project using the animated title you created as a track matte.

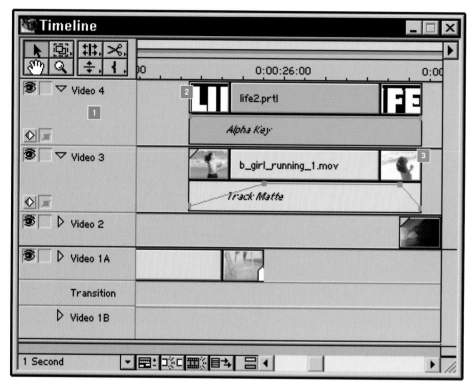

1. **Display Video 4.**
   Drag the life2.prtl clip from the Project window to Video 4.

2. **Place the** life2.prtl **clip above** b_girl_running_1.mov **in Video 3.**

3. **Set the duration to 05:19 to correspond with the** b_girl_running_1.mov **clip in Video 3.**
   Move the cursor over the end of the clip and drag until the life2.prtl clip is the same length as the clip in Video 3.

4. **Select the** b_girl_running_1.mov **clip.**
   Right-click and choose Video Options→Transparency to open the Transparency Settings window.

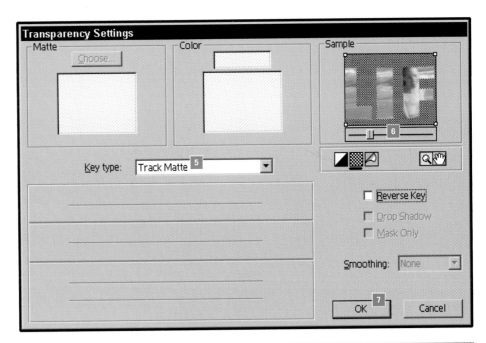

5. **Choose Track Matte from the Key type menu.**

6. **Preview the clip.**

   As you drag the slider below the Sample window, you can see the title slowly moving and the girl running along the beach through the letters.

<NOTE>

In the image you can see a black and white background behind the text. This is the checkerboard background (the center option). Any preview background displays the preview clearly in this clip.

7. **Click OK.**

   The Transparency Settings window closes.

8. **Preview the movie segment.**

   Notice the clip looks fine until the beach clip ends, and then all you see is black surrounding the text cutouts. Also notice that the letters look irregular and rough. In the following tutorial, you take care of both these issues.

9. **Save the project.**

   Your project has an animated title used as a track matte. The text crawls across the screen and the video showing the girl running down the beach plays through the text.

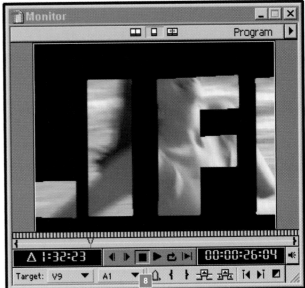

Tutorial
» Completing the Track Matte Background

The track matte looks interesting until the beach clip ends, and then the text is surrounded by black. In this tutorial, you add another clip to Video 1 to take care of the black space.

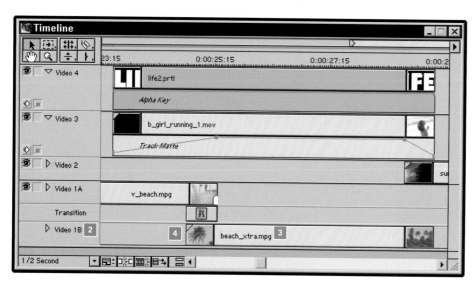

1. **Choose File→Import→File and locate your project folder.**
   Select beach_xtra.mpg from the extra video folder and click Open.

2. **Drag the** beach_xtra.mpg **clip to Video 1B.**

3. **Edit the clip to a final duration of 04:10.**
   Double-click the clip to open it in the Clip window and set In and Out points. Choose any segment of the clip you like.

4. **Position the clip to start at 25:00.**
   The clip starts before the end of the beach clip and ends at the same time the track matte clips end.

5. **Open the Dissolve folder in the Transitions palette.**
   Drag the Cross Dissolve to the transition track.

6. **Move the transition into position between the Video 1A and 1B clips.**

7. **Preview the segment.**
   You see the beach_xtra.mpg clip instead of the black areas you saw in the earlier preview.

8. **Right-click the** life2.prtl **clip in Video 4 to open the shortcut menu.**

9. **Choose Video Options→Transparency to open the Transparency Settings window.**

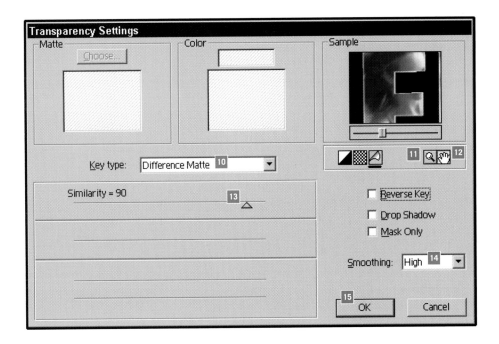

10. **Choose Difference Matte from the Key type menu.**

11. **Zoom in to the Sample.**
    Click the magnifying glass tool and click the Sample image. You want to see the edges of the letters clearly.

<TIP>
Hold the Alt key and click with the tool to zoom out of the Sample image.

12. **Click the hand tool to select it.**
    Click the Sample image and move it to show the top edges of the letters.

13. **Set the Similarity to 90.**
    A frame of the title clip is used as a matte for itself. With a high similarity setting, the matte smooths out some of the rough edges around the letters.

14. **Set Smoothing to High.**
    A high level of smoothing blends the edges of the letters even more.

15. **Click OK to close the Transparency Settings window.**

16. **Preview the clip again.**
    Notice how smooth the letters display against the backgrounds. When you set the transparency key for this clip, you use a copy of itself as its matte. The key compares a copy of the matte to itself. When the similarity is set at a very high level, the rough edges smooth out.

17. **Save the project.**
    You added an additional clip to the project to fill in a black gap that appears during the playback of the title matte and its underlying clips. You completed the title matte clip by adding a difference matte to blend pixels at the edges of the letters, and smoothing the letters.

> 315

» Session Review

At the start of this session, I explained that you would work with other transparency keys and produce very interesting effects. For example, the image that opens this session shows a couple walking along a beach. At the same frame, shown in the last image in this session, you can see how much impact transparency keys have. The couple is still walking along the beach, but this clip is playing inside another clip, also in motion.

You learned to use a range of transparency keys, how to create and modify images to use as image or track mattes (in this case, titles), and how to animate a title inside the Title Designer window.

Understand that sometimes when you make a change, it has further impact on other parts of your project. You saw this while working with the track matte. Not only did you have to create and apply the matte, but you then had to modify the content of other tracks.

The following questions are provided to help you review the information in this session. Answers for each question are found in the tutorial noted in parentheses.

1. What is the difference between the Chroma and the RGB Difference keys? (See "Discussion: Color-Based and Matte Keys.")

2. What are Blue and Green Screen keys commonly used for? (See "Discussion: Color-Based and Matte Keys.")

3. Can you use colored images for image mattes? Does it make a difference? (See "Discussion: Color-Based and Matte Keys.")

4. How can you display backgrounds in the Transparency Settings window? Are there different options? Is one better than another? (See "Tutorial: Using a Color-Based Transparency Key.")

5. How do you preview a clip in motion in the Transparency Settings window? (See "Tutorial: Using a Color-Based Transparency Key.")

6. Can any title be used as an image matte? (See "Tutorial: Preparing Clips for an Image Matte.")

7. When an image is used as a transparency matte, how do you see black? (See "Tutorial: Creating an Image Matte.")

8. Can you change transparency settings so the areas that are opaque and the areas that are transparent are reversed? If so, how? (See "Tutorial: Creating an Image Matte.")

9. What is the difference between crawling and rolling text? (See "Tutorial: Converting a Title to a Track Matte.")

10. What is the difference between Pre-Roll and Post-Roll settings? (See "Tutorial: Converting a Title to a Track Matte.")

11. Do animated titles always require Ease-In and Ease-Out frame settings? (See "Tutorial: Converting a Title to a Track Matte.")

12. Can a track matte be in motion? (See "Tutorial: Adding the Title Track Matte.")

13. Can you see the effects of key settings up close in the Transparency Settings window? (See "Tutorial: Completing the Track Matte Background.")

» Other Projects

Experiment with other transparency keys. Try different keys with the same clip.

Experiment with other source materials for your image matte. Try using an imported image.

Experiment with the keys using colored mattes. How do the different settings affect the clips and produce the final color?

Moving from Transparency to Video Effects

Session Introduction

In this session, you work with transparency keys. You use the Chroma key for a new clip. You add luminance to the clip showing a woman and dog running on a beach in the early part of the beach segment. In addition to adding the Luminance key, you add a color matte behind the same clip to give it some color interest, and then add an effect to the color matte to complete the look. You add a Ramp effect, which comes from After Effects and is new to Premiere 6.5. By the way — a ramp isn't something skateboarders use! A Ramp effect is the proper name for using a color gradient as an effect.

You work with other video effects in this session as well. As you learn in this and the following session, video effects have many different forms. Premiere ships with 79 effects, though there are actually more than that. One effect called QuickTime is actually a set of 15 effects. Premiere uses numerous After Effects effects, identified by an icon next to the effect's names in the Video Effects panel. You can also use other After Effects effects in Premiere.

In this session, you work with effects that enhance clips by correcting color, size, and even direction. As you have worked with Premiere you have learned that there is usually more than one way to achieve an effect or outcome. You can use different transparency settings to produce similar effects or different transitions to produce similar effects. You see how comparable effects processes work in this session. For example, you tint two clips using the Tint effect. For another clip you use the Luminance key and color matte process to do much the same thing, but with more control over color.

TOOLS YOU'LL USE
Timeline window, Info window, Effect Controls window, Transparency Settings window, Chroma key, Luminance key, settings sliders, Magnifying Glass tool, opacity rubberbands, Cross Fade tool, Motion settings window, Title Designer window, Video Effects palette, Effect Controls palette, Ramp effect, Horizontal flip effect, Tint effect, Crop effect

CD-ROM FILES NEEDED
Session 12 project file you created or the session12.ppj file from the CD-ROM
life3.prtl from the extra video folder (if you do not complete the tutorial)
life3.pmt from the extra video folder
Session13.mpg preview file from the premierecc_samples folder (for reference)

TIME REQUIRED
90 minutes

Tutorial
» Layering Animated Titles

The beginning of the beach segment shows a woman running down a beach with the text title superimposed. That looks fine, but it can still be more interesting. In this tutorial you modify a title to layer over the other images.

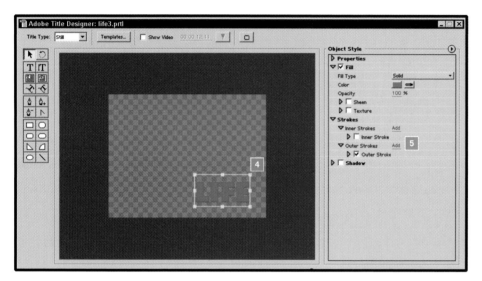

<NOTE>
This tutorial describes how to create another title. If you prefer to use a prebuilt file, import the life3.prtl file from the extra video folder on the CD, and then continue from the next tutorial.

1. **Choose File→Open and navigate to the location where you stored your project files.**
   You can also choose File→Open Recent Project and choose your project file from the list. Open session12.ppj.

<NOTE>
If you didn't do the tutorials in Session 12, copy the session12.ppj file from the CD to your hard drive. Open the file and resave it as session13.ppj (or use another filenaming convention).

2. **Resave the project file as** session13.ppj.

3. **Double-click the** life2.prtl **clip in the Project window (in the titles bin) to open it in the Title Designer window.**

4. **Click on the select tool in the toolbox and select the text.**

5. **Click the arrow to the left of the Strokes heading to open the Strokes panel.**
   Click the arrow to the left of the Inner Strokes heading to open the panel. Deselect Inner Stroke. An outer stroke is also applied to the text. You can leave this intact to give the text extra weight.

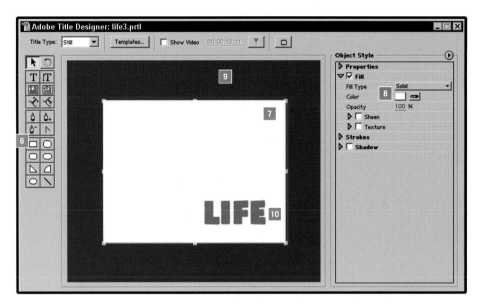

6. **Click on the rectangle tool in the toolbox to select it.**

7. **Draw a rectangle the size of the screen (320 x 240 pixels).**
   Use the Transform settings at the bottom right of the Title Designer window to assist in sizing the rectangle.

8. **Click the checkbox to the left of the Fill heading to activate the settings.**
   Click the arrow to the left of the checkbox to display the Fill settings. Set the color to white (RGB = 255/255/255).

9. **Right-click the rectangle and choose Position→Horizontal Center.**
   Repeat and choose Vertical Center. The white rectangle is placed at the center of the screen.

10. **Right-click the rectangle and choose Arrange→Send to Back.**
    The rectangle is placed behind the text.

11. **Choose File→Save As.**
    Save the file as life3.prtl. Store the file in the titles bin in the Project window.
    You have made another title by modifying an existing title file. You layer the title over other tracks in the next tutorial.

Tutorial

» Adding Motion and Transparency to the Title

Now you have built or imported the new title. In this tutorial, you add motion to your new title using a prebuilt set of motion settings from the extra video folder on the CD. Finally, you apply the Chroma key to the title clip.

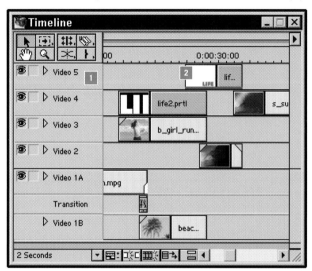

1. **Drag the** `life3.prtl` **title from the titles bin in the Project window to Video 5 in the Timeline.**

2. **Set its duration to 03:20, and its starting position at 27:27.**

3. **Open the Motion Settings window.**
   Right-click the clip on the Timeline and choose Video Options→Motion.

4. **In the Motion Settings window, click Load.**
   Browse to the location where you stored the project files. Choose `life3.pmt` and click Open. The motion settings file is applied to the clip. The clip has a new alpha channel. The smoothing is set on Averaging-High as there is no distortion in the clip, but it needs smoothing. Also note the Timeline settings include a significant delay to control the speed of the clip.

5. **Click OK and the Motion Settings window closes.**

6. **On the Timeline, right-click the** `life3.prtl` **clip.**
   Choose Video Options→Transparency to open the Transparency Settings window.

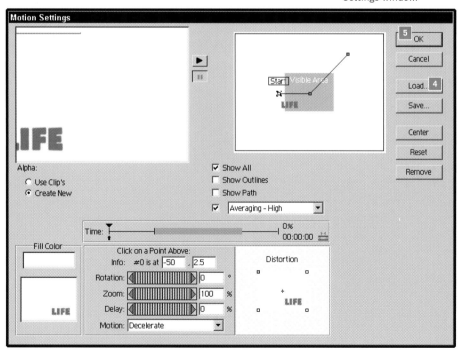

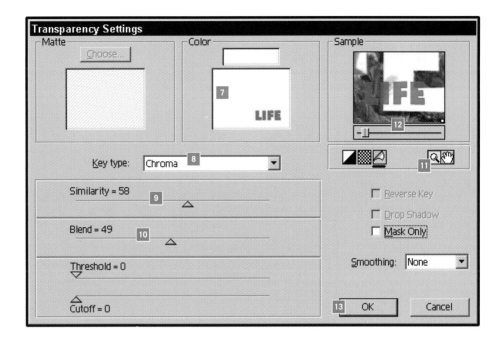

<NOTE>
The text is placed at an x-axis value of 2.5. Remember that each pixel displayed in the Motion Settings window converts to four pixels on the screen in the project? This means the text sits ten pixels (2.5 x 4) above the center of the screen. Setting the text at this value places the text within the space of the larger letters of the title in Video 4

7. **Move the cursor over the image of the clip in the Color sample window.**
   It changes to an eyedropper. Click the background. This defines the white background as the transparent color.

8. **Choose Chroma from the Key type menu.**

9. **Set the Similarity setting to 58.**
   The clips underlying this title on the Timeline are varied in coloration. At a similarity setting of approximately 58, you see the text clearly throughout the duration of the clip.

<TIP>
As you make and adjust the settings, preview the clip in the Sample window to see how it looks over different parts of the clip.

10. **Set the Blend setting to 49.**
    Like the Similarity setting, the Blend setting is affected by the underlying clips' coloration. At a setting of approximately 49, the text blends with the underlying clips while still remaining legible.

<NOTE>
Leave the Threshold and Cutoff settings at their defaults of 0. These settings affect shadows, which are not used in this title.

11. **Zoom in to the Sample window to view the effects of the settings clearly.**

12. **Preview the clip by dragging the slider.**

<NOTE>
Leave the Smoothing set to None. Experiment with the settings. Notice that the Low and High smoothing settings make the text indistinct and remove the crisp edge from the letters.

13. **Click OK.**
    The Transparency Settings window closes.

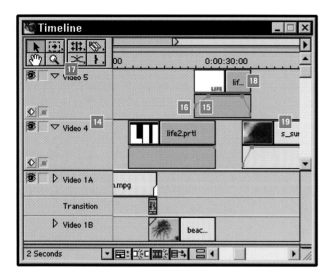

14. **In the Timeline, open the Video 4 and Video 5 tracks.**
    Click the arrows to the left of the tracks' names to display the
    bottom portion of the clips. Click the red Display Opacity
    Rubberband icons to display the rubberbands.

15. **Add a handle to the** life3.prtl **clip in Video 5 at 28:24.**
    Click the Select tool in the Timeline toolbox and click the
    opacity rubberband.

<T I P>
Use the Info window to place the handle at the correct frame.

16. **Drag the start handle down to 40%.**
    The clip starts at 40% opacity and increases to 100% opacity
    at the handle.

17. **Select the Cross Fade tool in the Timeline toolbox.**
    If the Cross Fade tool is not active, click and hold the fade
    tool displayed to open the subpalette. Click the Cross Fade
    tool to select it.

18. **Click the** life3.prtl **clip in Video 5 with the Cross Fade tool
    to set it as the first clip of a crossfade pair.**

19. **Click the** s_surf2.mpg **clip in Video 4 to complete the
    crossfade.**
    A handle is automatically added to the life3.prtl clip in
    Video 5 at 30:29; the clip fades to 0% from the handle to the
    end handle. Another handle is automatically added to the
    s_surf2.mpg clip in Video 4 at 31:17; the clip fades in
    from 0% at the start handle to 100% at the new handle.

20. **Preview the segment from approximately 27:00 to 32:00.**
    Notice how the depth and translucency of the text color
    changes depending on the background.

21. **Save the project.**
    You worked with the title clip you added to the project in the
    last tutorial. You added a prebuilt motion settings file to the
    clip. You added transparency using the Chroma key. You have
    also added crossfades to complete the edits for this clip.

Tutorial
» Adding Luminance to a Clip

Move a little further along the Timeline now. In this tutorial, you add transparency to the clip showing the woman and dog running on a beach. After applying the Luminance key to the clip, you then add more depth of color with a color matte.

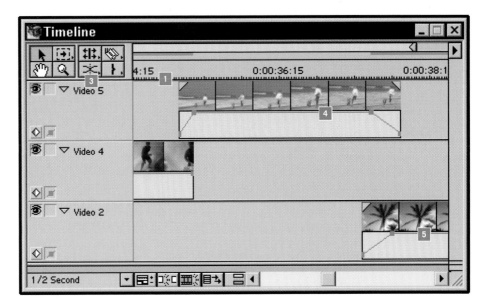

1. **In the Timeline, move the** b_woman_dog.mov **clip from Video 2 to Video 5 to start at 35:05.**
   Although you can move the clip to Video 3, you need that track for a color matte you are adding later.

2. **Open Video 2 and Video 5.**
   Click the arrow to the left of the tracks' names to display the lower portion of the track. Click the red opacity rubberband icon to display the rubberband.

3. **Select the Cross Fade tool from the Timeline toolbox.**
   If you are continuing this tutorial from the last, the Cross Fade tool is the active fade tool.

4. Click on the b_woman_dog.mov clip in Video 5 with the Cross Fade tool to set it as the first clip of a crossfade pair.

5. **Click on the** v_palms_rotate.mpg **clip in Video 2 to complete the crossfade.**
   A handle is automatically added to the b_woman_dog.mov clip in Video 5 at 37:18; the clip fades to 0% from the handle to the end handle. Another handle is automatically added to the v_palms_rotate.mpg clip in Video 2 at 38:04; the clip fades in from 0% at the start handle to 100% at the new handle.

6. **Select the** b_woman_dog.mov **clip in Video 5.**
   Right click the clip in the Timeline and choose Video Options→Transparency to open the Transparency Settings window.

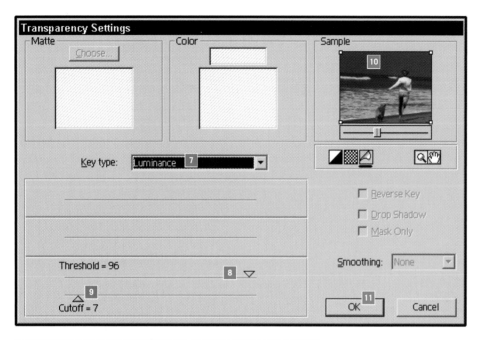

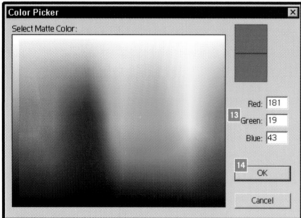

< N O T E >
This is the only matte in the project, so I left the default name color matte. When saved, it is automatically added to the Project window. Store it in the titles bin. A color matte is an internal file in Premiere, and can't be exported or stored in a folder.

7. **Select Luminance from the Key type menu.**

8. **Set the Threshold to 96.**
   A high Threshold value creates a great deal of transparency in the clip, which is the desired effect.

9. **Set the Cutoff to 7.**
   A low value retains the visibility of the figures in the clip. If the Cutoff is set too high, the woman and dog become too transparent to see clearly.

10. **Preview the clip in the Sample window.**
    Notice how dark the clip looks in the sample. The clip is superimposed over Video 1 and Video 2, which are both blank at this location in the Timeline (they appear black). You perk up the clip shortly.

11. **Click OK to close the Transparency Settings window.**

12. **Choose File→New→Color Matte.**

13. **In the Color Picker, type the RGB value of 181/19/43.**
    The color matte uses the same value as the red used for the text in the project.

14. **Click OK.**
    At the prompt, name the matte and click OK.

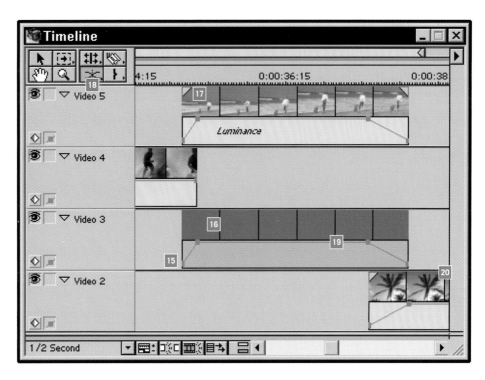

15. **In the Timeline, drag the matte to Video 3.**
    Set its duration to 02:29. It starts at the same time as the b_woman_dog.mov clip in Video 5 at 35:05.

16. **Click the Select tool in the Timeline toolbox.**
    Click the rubberband to add an opacity rubberband handle to the matte in Video 3 at 35:11. Drag the start handle to 0%.

17. **Add an opacity rubberband handle to the** b_woman_dog.mov **clip in Video 5 at 35:11.**
    Drag the start handle to 0% to fade the clip in from 0% at the start handle to 100% at the new handle.

18. **Select the Cross Fade tool in the toolbox.**
    If you are continuing this tutorial from the last, the Cross Fade tool is the active fade tool in the toolbox.

19. **Click the color matte in Video 3 with the Cross Fade tool to set it as the first clip of a crossfade pair.**

20. **Click the** v_palms_rotate.mpg **clip in Video 2 to complete the crossfade.**
    No additional handles are added to this clip as they were added when the first crossfade was constructed. A new handle is added to the color matte in Video 3 at 37:18.

<TIP>
You can also copy the clip in Video 2 and then use the Paste Attributes command. To reuse the Cross Fade tool is faster because you have it selected. Nothing changes when you click the clip in Video 2 the second time. Because both the clip in Video 5 and the color matte are the same duration at the same time on the Timeline, the crossfade is applied only to the color matte.

21. **Preview the segment.**
    You see the woman and dog running on the beach is colored with a red tint. The clip fades out as the palm trees clip fades in.

22. **Save the project.**
    You added the final transparency setting for this project to a clip. You used luminance to control the amount of transparency in the clip showing the woman and dog on the beach. You used a solid red matte in a lower track which blends with the beach clip. In the next tutorial, you change the red matte using a video effect.

Discussion
Video Effect Categories

As I mentioned in the introduction to this session, there are 79 effects that ship with Premiere. How do you decide what effect or effects to use? The answer is with careful planning, consideration of your overall design goals, and experimentation. It is important to work with effects to see what they can do and how they can be modified. The Video effects palette contains 14 categories of effects. You can see sample images to give you a basic idea of how each category of effect works. In each example, the original image is shown to the left, and the modified image to the right. Here's a brief rundown.

Adjust effects: These are used to correct imported images or clips. You can adjust and balance color and levels using several methods. The image shows the Color Balance effect. The green and blue channels were adjusted.

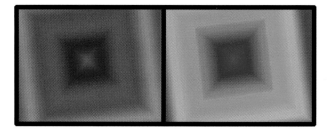

Blur effects: These decrease the contrast level between pixels to soften images. Blurs can be based on factors including channels, luminance, and pixel averages. The image shows a Fast Blur effect.

Channel effects: These are used to manipulate color by creating controlled blends between tracks. The effects in this category modify color or color channels based on color values, calculated color values, or transparency. The image shows the Channel Blend effect. Color channels are blended between layers, in this case the black and white swirl and the underlying green background.

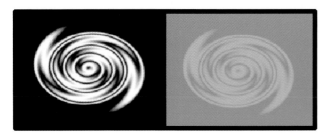

Distort effects: These alter the geometry of an image. Distortion effects work with control points to control the changes. The effects work on the edges of images or alter the entire image. The effects use controls to define the amount and direction of distortion. The image shows the Ripple effect.

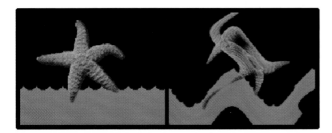

Image Control effects: These modify color information in a clip. Color can be corrected, replaced, or removed. The sample shows the outcome of the Color Replace effect, which replaced a gold color in the original image with a dark purple color.

Perspective effects: These simulate depth by adding shadows or edges that appear to make an image float against another image or background. The starfish appears to be floating in space over a pale blue background. The Basic 3D effect was used to create this image.

Pixelate effects: These fracture the appearance of an image into a collection of cells of different shape and size. The image uses the Crystallize effect.

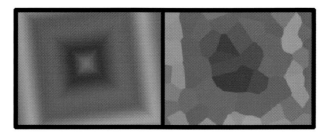

QuickTime effects: These use a separate dialog box. The collection includes 14 effects ranging from sharpening to color tinting to adding fire or lens flares. The image shows the QuickTime Lens Flare effect.

Render effects: These create calculated images such as lens flares or lightning, as shown in the image. In this session you work with the Ramp effect, which is a calculated image that creates a color gradient. The images are based on different algorithms that produce an image over an underlying layer (clip in a track). The underlying layer may or may not be included with the effect.

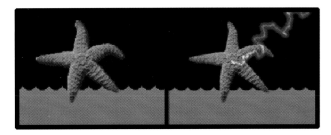

Sharpen effects: These change the contrast level between pixels like the blur effects. Sharpen effects, such as the Sharpen Edges effect shown in the image, increase the contrast between pixels.

Stylize effects: These work two ways: They displace or alter pixels, and they manipulate the color palette of an image. The image shows the Tiles effect, which is an altered pixel effect.

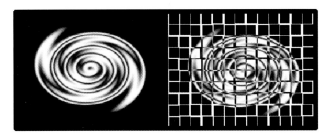

Time effects: These produce dramatic effects. A clip in a track is used as a time standard, and the effect shows changes over time superimposed over one another. The image shows the Time Echo effect. As the swirl in the clip rotates, several layers of the swirl at different points in time appear on the screen at the same time.

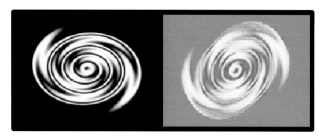

Transform effects: These change the appearance of a clip on the Timeline by modifying what is visible and how it is displayed. These effects can be used for corrections, such as cropping (shown in the image) or flipping clips.

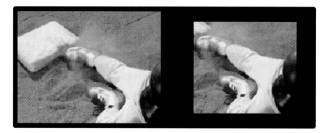

Video effects: These are used to correct clips for broadcast distribution. In the image, the NTSC colors filter has been applied. The colors appear muted.

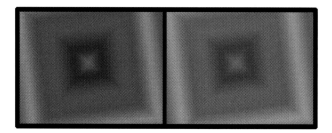

Tutorial
» Adding the Ramp Video Effect

You work with your first video effect in this tutorial, even though it isn't the simplest effect to use. This is a reasonable location to apply the Ramp effect so the tutorials follow a logical workflow. You add a color gradient or ramp to the color matte you added in the previous tutorial. As I mentioned in the introduction to this session, this kind of ramp has nothing to do with skateboards. Instead, it refers to a color ramp, where a color identified in one location gradually becomes a different color in another location. The Ramp effect, a calculated image, is one of the Render effects.

1. **Open the Video Effects palette.**
   Open the Render folder.

2. **Select the Ramp effect.**
   Drag the effect to the `color matte` clip in Video 2 in the Timeline. As you drag the effect over a clip, you can see the image of the clip is inverted (the colors reverse). This highlight identifies the clip that receives the effect if you release the mouse. When an effect is applied, the Effect Controls window opens automatically.

3. **In the Effect Controls window, click the Start Color eyedropper.**
   Click the color matte in the Timeline to quickly copy the color.

4. **Click the End Color swatch.**
   Type the RGB values of 193/222/245, and then click OK.

5. **Click the Start of Ramp crosshairs to change the Start of Ramp location.**
   The crosshairs are used to define x- and y-coordinates for an effect.

What Happened to the Solid Red Matte?

The Ramp effect is a rendering filter (another name for an effect). This means the original content of the clip remains as is, and changes are made to it based on the algorithms of the selected filter (in this case creating a gradient). The gradient has its own values for color and distribution. In essence, it sits on top of the matte; for this reason, the underlying matte can be any color. I chose one of the colors from the actual ramp to make it simpler to understand. The only time the matte color is important is if you use the Blending feature to blend the ramp colors with the underlying matte color.

6. Choose Window→Monitor to open the Monitor window.

Click the image in the monitor window to the left of top center (the default location for the ramp start). The location used in the sample is 108, 14.

<TIP>

Your positions don't have to be exact. In fact, they are difficult to copy exactly using the crosshairs. The coordinates are listed on the Effect Controls panel to the right of the crosshairs. You can click the coordinates and type the exact values used in the sample.

7. Click the crosshairs to change the End of Ramp location.

8. Click the image in the monitor window to the right of bottom center (the default location for the ramp end).

The location coordinates used in the sample are 239, 232.

9. Turn off Video 5 in the Timeline.

10. Render-scrub the Timeline to display the ramp (gradient).

11. Drag the Ramp Scatter slider to approximately 38.5.

You can also click the underlined value and type the new value. This disperses the color distribution in the ramp and gives an interesting grainy look to the ramp. Scatter is important when you create a ramp for online distribution when the frame rates are dropped and resolution is low. Scattered pixels decrease the appearance of color banding, which can occur with gradients. As a gradient changes across the screen you see definite bands of color rather than a smooth blend of color.

12. Preview the segment.

The clip still shows the woman and dog running on the beach, but now the background is colored, gradually changing from red in the upper left to blue in the lower right of the screen.

13. Save the project.

You added a complex video effect. The Ramp effect, one of the rendering effects, calculates color and generates an image, in this case a red/blue color gradient.

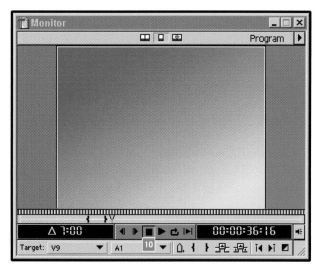

Tutorial
» Flipping the Action for Effect

You finally finish the segment of the woman and dog running on the beach in this tutorial. In the previous tutorial you added a Ramp effect (filter). The colors were chosen based on other colors in the project. The red Start of Ramp color is used in the text throughout the project, and the blue End of Ramp color is taken from the sky in the clip that follows the matte in the Timeline. The ramp colors look good and work well, but they don't enhance the subject matter in the clip. It's time to fix that.

1. **Open the Video Effects palette.**
   Open the Transform folder.

2. **Drag the Horizontal Flip effect to the** b_woman_dog.mov **clip in Video 5 starting at 35:05.**
   When an effect is added to a clip, a green line displays along the top border of the clip in the Timeline.

3. **In the Effect Controls palette, toggle the effect off and on to see the difference.**
   Notice an absence of options or settings for the Horizontal Flip effect in the Effect Controls panel. This is one of the effects that is absolute. The clip is either flipped or it isn't, so you don't customize any settings. You cannot see the Flip effect in the Timeline view of the clip; it is visible only when previewing or making a render-scrub of the Timeline.

Using the Video Effects Palette

In Session 5, you learned how to manage the Transitions Palette. Use the same processes and techniques for the Effects palettes as well. You can organize and hide effects, create folders to customize the contents, and search for effects. The Effects palettes include a menu. Like the Transitions Palette menu, you use commands to work with folders and to show or hide effects.

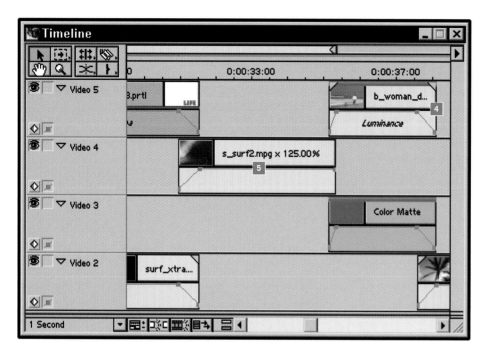

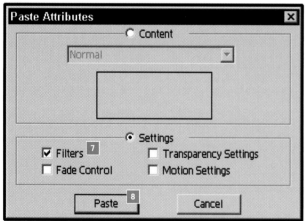

4. **Copy the** b_woman_dog.mov **clip in Video 5 in the Timeline.**

5. **Select the** s_surf2.mpg **clip in Video 4 starting at 30:29.**

6. **Choose Edit→Paste Attributes.**

7. **In the Paste Attributes window, choose Settings.**
   Deselect all settings except Filters.

8. **Click Paste.**
   The Paste Attributes window closes. The action in this clip is flipped horizontally as well.

9. **Preview the Timeline segment including both clips edited in this tutorial, from approximately 30:00 to 39:00.**
   Both clips now run as mirror images of their originals. That is, the woman and dog now run from right to left on the beach. This orientation works well with the color ramp you added in the previous tutorial. The surfer now moves from right to left.

10. **Save the project.**
    You added the same effect to two clips. The Horizontal Flip effect reverses the direction of the action in the clips.

Tutorial
» Correcting and Modifying Color Using Effects

In this tutorial, you work with the pale and faded-looking opening beach clip. You use Adjust and Image Control effects to correct the color of the clip. You also learn to work with multiple effects on the same clip. Sometimes you must experiment to determine what you need to use. Other times you can predict what you need to use and add the effects at once, and then adjust them individually. You use this second approach in this tutorial; that is, effects are rendered in the order they are added. Arrange the Timeline window and Effect Controls palette on the screen.

1. **Open the Video Effects palette.**

2. **Open the Adjust folder.**
   Drag the Brightness & Contrast effect to the v_beach.mpg clip in Video 1A on the Timeline. The effect is listed in the Effect Controls palette.

<TIP>
When the Effect Controls palette opens, ignore it and add the other effects first; then return to the palette.

3. **Open the Image Control folder.**
   Drag the Color Balance (HLS) effect to v_beach.mpg clip in Video 1A on the Timeline. The effect is listed in the Effect Controls palette.

4. **Drag the Gamma Correction effect from the Image Control folder to** v_beach.mpg **clip in Video 1A on the Timeline.**
   The effect is listed in the Effect Controls palette.

<NOTE>
If you open the Video 1A track on the Timeline, you can see the effects are arranged in a menu. You work with this menu in the next session.

> **337**

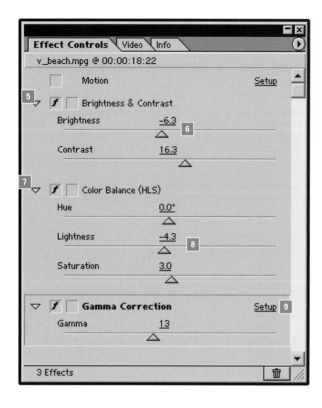

5. **Click the arrow to the left of the Brightness & Contrast effect heading to display the settings.**

6. **Set the Brightness & Contrast effect options.**
   You can either drag the sliders or click the underlined value and type a new value:
   Set Brightness to -6.3
   Set Contrast to 16.3.
   The brightness is decreased and contrast is increased. The Brightness & Contrast effect adjusts the tonal ranges of the clip.

7. **Click the arrow to the left of the Color Balance (HLS) effect heading to display the settings.**

8. **Set the Color Balance (HLS) effect options.**
   Set Lightness to -4.3
   Set Saturation to 3.0.
   The HLS Color Balance effect modifies color based on the HLS (Hue/Lightness/Saturation) color model. Hue, which specifies the color scheme for the image, is unchanged. The clip is darkened slightly by decreasing the Lightness setting; the color is made more intense by increasing the Saturation setting.

<NOTE>
There is another Color Balance effect in the Adjust effects folder. If you are more comfortable working with RGB color values than HLS values you may prefer to use that effect.

9. **Click Setup to the right of the Gamma Correction effect.**
   The Gamma Correction Settings window opens. You can use the Setup window to evaluate changes as you make adjustments.

10. **Drag the slider to a Gamma value of 1.3.**
    The Gamma value of an image is the relative brightness of the midtones of an image. Gamma values have no effect on either shadows or highlights. Increasing the Gamma value darkens the mid-gray levels (midtones) giving more fullness to the image.

11. **Click OK to close the Gamma Correction Settings dialog box.**

12. **Preview the clip.**
    The color is much more rich and full with the settings you applied.

13. **Save the project.**
    You added three color correction effects to the same clip in this tutorial. You adjusted the color in the beach clip. The original clip was very pale and indistinct; the corrected clip is much more vibrant.

Tutorial
» Tinting Clips

In the previous session, you added a second background clip behind the "Life" track matte. You return to that clip and tint it using another Image Control effect. The same effect with different settings is applied to several clips. The Tint effect alters color information using luminance (yes, the same as transparency). The luminance of each pixel is mapped to selected colors. You can use this effect for clips in any track, but it is especially useful for clips in Video 1 that can't use transparency settings.

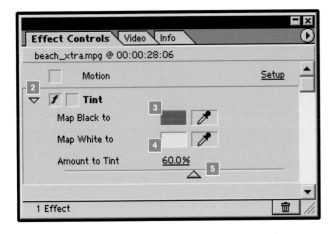

1. **Drag the Tint effect from the image Control folder in the Video Effects palette to the** beach_xtra.mpg **clip in Video 1B of the Timeline.**
   The Tint effect is added to the Effect Controls palette.

2. **Click the arrow to the left of the Tint label on the Effect Controls palette to display the Tint effect settings.**

3. **Click the Map Black to color swatch and type an RGB value of 90/100/75.**
   Dark pixels are mapped to the color chosen in the Map Black to swatch.

4. **Click the Map White to color swatch and type an RGB value of 200/230/255.**
   Light pixels are mapped to the color chosen in the Map White to swatch.

5. **Drag the Amount to Tint slider to approximately 60%.**
   The higher the value, the more intense the tint becomes.

6. **Return to the Timeline, and toggle Video 3 and Video 4 off.**
   You can't view the clip in the Monitor window with overlying tracks displayed.

7. **Preview the tinted clip in the Monitor window.**
   Render scrub through the Timeline time ruler over the beach_xtra.mpg clip. In the Monitor window you see the tinted clip.

8. **Turn on Video 3 and Video 4 tracks.**
   Render-scrub through the Timeline to preview the clip again. Notice how the background is still obviously a forest of palm trees, but it is much less obtrusive now and doesn't detract from the track matte.

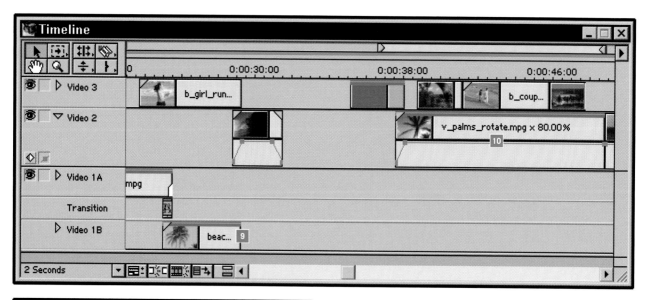

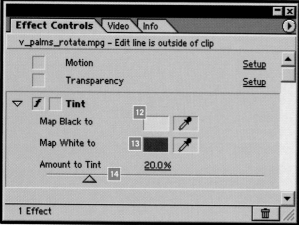

9. In the Timeline, copy the `beach_xtra.mpg` clip from Video 1B starting at 25:00.

10. Select the `v_palms_rotate.mpg` clip in Video 2 on the Timeline starting at 37:18.

11. Choose Edit→Paste Attributes, and paste the Filter to the `v_palms_rotate.mpg` clip.
The Tint effect is added to the clip's Effect Controls palette.

12. In the Effect Controls palette, change the Map Black color to RGB = 193/222/245.
This is the same shade of blue you used in the Ramp effect added to the color matte in the earlier tutorial.

13. Change the Map White color to RBG = 66/73/12.
This is a shade of green selected from the palm trees.

14. Change the Amount to Tint to 20%.
The dark/light tints are reversed. That is, the black in the image is mapped to a light blue color; the white in the image is mapped to a dark green color. A small amount of tint produces the desired muted look.

15. **Preview the clip.**
    The v_palms_rotate.mpg clip is a background clip, dis-
    played behind the track matte and foreground video. The tint
    mutes the colors of the palm trees and sky slightly, making the
    foreground video more dominant.

16. **In the Timeline, move back to the first segment of the project and
    select the** c_staircase.mov **clip in Video 2, starting at
    01:18.**

17. **Choose Edit→Paste Attributes Again.**

18. **In the Effect Controls palette, change the Map Black color to
    RGB = 68/0/40.**
    This is the same shade of purple used for the shadow in the
    horizontal and vertical bar titles.

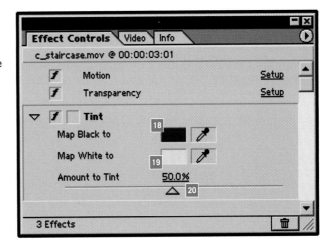

19. **Change the Map White color to RBG = 255/213/135.**
    This is a color from the street video. It was selected from the
    lights washing the building behind the bus.

20. **Change the Amount to Tint to 50%.**

21. **Preview the clip.**
    The dark and light colors in the c_staircase.mov clip are
    replaced by shades of yellow and purple, making the clip coor-
    dinate with the background street clips and the bar title clips.

22. **Save the project.**
    You have used the Tint effect for three different clips in the
    project. You tinted two background palm tree clips to make
    them more subdued. You tinted the clip showing the couple
    running up the stairs at the start of the movie to make it coor-
    dinate better with the other layers in the video.

Tutorial
» Cropping the Content of Clips

In the final tutorial of this session, you use the Crop effect on two clips at the end of the movie. The clip of the tropical drink and the final clip of palm trees at night both need trimming.

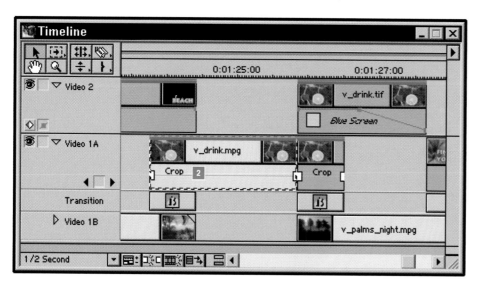

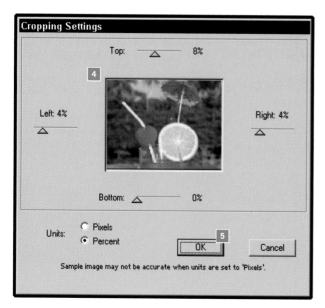

1. **Open the Transform folder in the Video Effects palette.**

2. **Drag the Crop effect to the first copy of the** v_drink.mpg **clip in Video 1A starting at 01:23:18.**

3. **Click Setup in the Effect Controls palette to open the Cropping Settings dialog box.**
   Make sure Percent is chosen in the Units area. If you select Pixels instead of Percent, your edits may be inaccurate.

4. **Adjust the crop settings to:**
   Crop Left 4%
   Crop Top 8%
   Crop Right 4%

5. **Click OK.**
   The Cropping Settings dialog box closes.

6. **Copy the** v_drink.mpg **clip in Video 1A.**

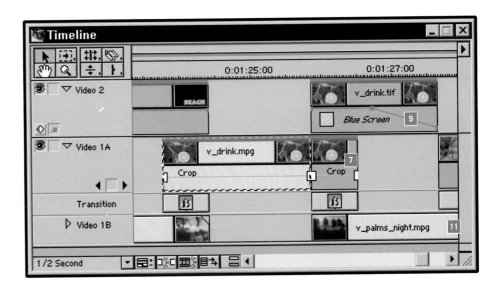

7. In the Timeline, select the v_drink.tif clip next to the first copy in Video 1A.

8. Choose Edit→Paste Attributes, and paste the filter to this clip.

9. Select the v_drink.tif clip in Video 2 starting at 01:25:20.

10. Choose Edit→Paste Attributes Again to paste the crop settings to this copy of the clip.

11. Select the v_palms_night.mpg clip in Video 1B starting at 01:25:20.

12. Choose Edit→Paste Attributes Again to paste the crop settings to the clip.

13. Open the Effect Controls palette.

14. Adjust the crop settings.
    Crop Left 20%
    Crop Top 0%
    Crop Right 20%
    Crop Bottom 20%

15. Preview the Timeline segment.
    Both the tropical drink and palm tree clips are more evenly centered on the screen.

16. Save the project.
    You added the Crop effect to three clips. Two copies of the v_drink clip were cropped, as was the final clip of palm trees at night.

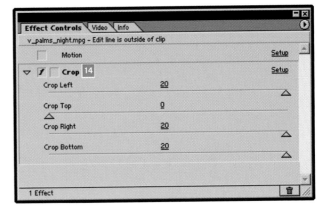

< T I P >

You can also click Setup to open the Cropping Settings dialog box to see the image as you are cropping.

» Session Review

In this session, you finished most of the transparency work needed to complete your project. You added Chroma and Luminance effects to clips. You leaned how to add a solid color matte to your project to serve as a background for a clip with luminance-based transparency and how to modify the matte by adding a Ramp effect to it. The final image in this session shows the same frame from the beginning of the session at the end of the session's activities. What a difference!

It is very important that you experiment with the effects. Certain effects are similar in their application and results and others are wildly different, or just wild! Most effects can be modified in some way, such as with configurable parameters, or custom colors. Other effects are absolute in that they are applied or they are not applied.

You learned how to apply more than one effect to the same clip and how to change the tint of a clip, which adds interest and blocks of color to your project. You also learned to copy and paste effects from one clip to another to speed up your workflow. Finally, you learned how to crop clips and reuse the settings for other clips.

Here are questions to help you review the information in this session. The answer to each question is in the tutorial noted in parentheses.

1. How do you modify the arrangement of layers in a title? (See "Tutorial: Layering Animated Titles.")
2. Can you define a color as transparent when working with the Chroma key? If so, how? (See "Tutorial: Adding Motion and Transparency to the Title.")
3. Do you necessarily have to adjust the Threshold and Cutoff settings for the Chroma key? When are these settings used? (See "Tutorial: Adding Motion and Transparency to the Title.")
4. What do the transparent portions of a clip display when using the Luminance key? (See "Tutorial: Adding Luminance to a Clip.")
5. How do you create a color matte? How is it stored? (See "Tutorial: Adding Luminance to a Clip.")
6. What types of effects alter an image's geometry? (See "Discussion: Video Effect Categories.")
7. What kinds of effects are used to color correct and balance images? (See "Discussion: Video Effect Categories.")
8. How do you adjust the start and end color locations for the Ramp effect? (See "Tutorial: Adding the Ramp Video Effect.")
9. Why would you increase the Ramp Scatter value? (See "Tutorial: Adding the Ramp Video Effect.")
10. What kinds of effects are absolute? What does that mean? (See "Tutorial: Flipping the Action for Effect.")
11. Can you see the outcome of a Horizontal Flip effect in the Timeline? (See "Tutorial: Flipping the Action for Effect.")
12. Can you use more than one effect on the same clip? (See "Tutorial: Correcting and Modifying Color Using Effects.")
13. Is there a specific order for rendering effects? (See "Tutorial: Correcting and Modifying Color Using Effects.")
14. Can effects be used with clips in Video 1A and Video 1B? (See "Tutorial: Tinting Clips.")
15. How do the selected Map Black and Map White colors relate to the luminance of a clip? (See "Tutorial: Tinting Clips.")
16. Do you use pixels or percentage as the form of measurement for cropping clips? Why? (See "Tutorial: Cropping the Content of Clips.")

» Other Projects

Experiment with different Ramp effect colors and settings. Can you see how changing the coordinates alters the direction?

Use a clip that requires a lot of correction. Experiment with the correction-type effects (such as those in the Adjust and Image Control folders) to see how they work. Try them in combination. Adjust their order in the Effect Controls panel list. Is there a difference in the appearance of the clip based on the effects' order?

Working with Keyframes and More Video Effects

Session Introduction

This session is all about wow. It's the icing on the cake. It's the sprinkles on the sundae. Pick a cliché and it likely applies!

You have certainly learned by now that Premiere is a powerhouse program. It can do so many types of editing and uses a wealth of options for managing and editing a clip. In the last session, you learned to apply effects to manage elements like color, contrast, tint, and so on. These types of effects are most often used to correct a clip rather than to add a special effect to it.

In this session, you work with numerous effects, many of which are keyframed. Notice the gray diamond icon next to the opacity rubberband icon on the Timeline. When you click this, you see a pale blue line instead of the red rubberband line. This blue line is used for keyframing. Keyframes are points added to a clip to control the activity of an effect. Each keyframe can have its own collection of settings for an effect. While the clip plays, the effect settings change as each keyframe is reached. In essence you have a Timeline within a Timeline.

You don't usually change the settings over time for effects such as color corrections even though they can use keyframes. The simple effects (those you add to the entire clip) were covered in the previous session. Now it's time to add some flare.

In the last session, you worked on a series of tutorials using a single clip: adding a transparency key, adding a color matte, and then adding effects. This process mimics a logical workflow. In this session, all the tutorials are arranged in this fashion. You select one clip, you add and modify its effects, and then you move on to the next clip. Also, you work mainly from the beginning to the end of the project, rather than jump all over the Timeline. As you add different effects, you see some of the impacts of using them. For example, certain effects can't be used unless they are the topmost layer (this applies to time effects). You see how to manipulate the Timeline to make it work. This involves some clip splitting and track shifting — nothing you can't handle at this point.

TOOLS YOU'LL USE
Timeline window, Effect Controls palette, opacity rubberbands, Cross Fade tool, Video Effects palette, Effect Controls palette, Enable Keyframing control, Keyframe navigator, Add/Remove keyframe control, Next /Previous keyframe controls, Paste Attributes command, Paste Attributes Again command, Sharpen effect, Directional Blur effect, Posterize effect, Strobe effect, Image Pan effect, Fast Blur effect, Noise effect, Time Echo effect, Brightness & Contrast effect, Radial Blur effect, Levels effect, Levels histogram

CD-ROM FILES NEEDED
Session 13 project file you created or the session13.ppj file from the CD-ROM
Session14a.mpg and Session14b.mpg preview files from the premierecc_samples folder (for reference)
windsurfer.1v1 from the extra_video folder (for reference)

TIME REQUIRED
90 minutes

Tutorial
» Focusing the Traffic Lights

The first clips you work with in this session are the pair of traffic-light video clips in Video 2. The original clip was split in a previous editing session to isolate the parts of the clip where the lights change color. In this tutorial, you apply the same two filters (effects) to the two clips using different values controlled by keyframes. Follow the sequence of steps carefully. When you work with keyframes, you must coordinate the location of the edit line on the Timeline, the selected effect on the Timeline's effect menu, and the sliders and settings in the Effect Controls palette. Arrange the Timeline and Effect Controls windows on the screen.

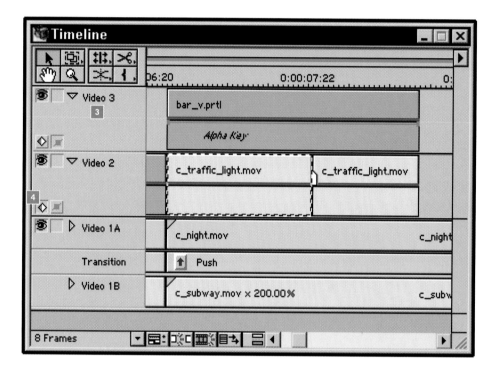

1. **Choose File→Open and navigate to the location where you stored your project files.**
   You can also choose File→Open Recent Project and choose your project file from the list. Open session13.ppj.

   <NOTE>
   If you didn't do the tutorials in Session 13, copy the session13.ppj file from the CD to your hard drive. Open the file and resave it as session14.ppj (or use another filenaming convention).

2. **Resave the project file as** session14.ppj.

3. **Hide all except Video 1, Video 2, and Video 3.**

4. **Open Video 2.**
   Click Display Keyframes, the gray diamond to the left of the Display Opacity Rubberbands icon. When Display Keyframes is active, after you add an effect you see the keyframe line instead of the opacity rubberbands.

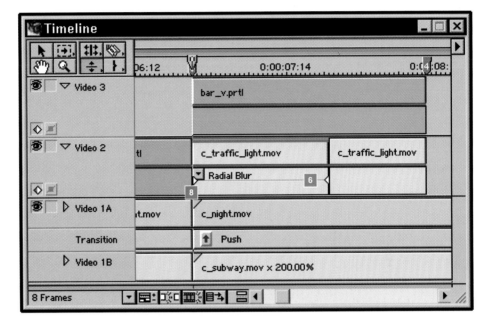

5. Open the Video Effects palette.

Select the Radial Blur effect from the Blur folder. You add a radial blur to the clip to unfocus the edges of the clip, emphasizing the traffic lights.

<NOTE>

The folders in the Video Effects palette have been rearranged to show the effects in the same image.

6. Drag the Radial Blur effect to the first copy of the
`c_traffic_light.mov` **clip in Video 2, starting at 06:24.**
The blue keyframe line is visible on the clip.

7. Open the Sharpen folder in the Video Effects palette.

Select the Sharpen effect. You use this effect to emphasize the traffic lights in the clip.

8. Drag the Sharpen effect to the same copy of the clip in Video 2.
A menu is created when more than one effect is added to a clip, which is the case here.

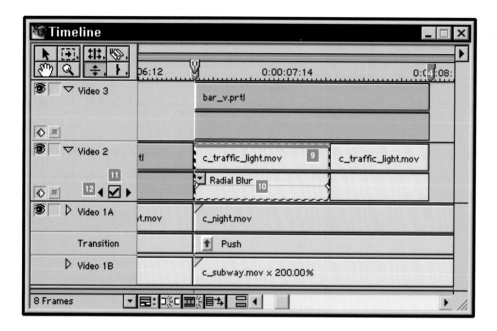

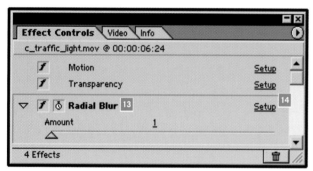

<NOTE>

To remove keyframes you add by accident, click the left or right arrow on the Keyframe navigator to move to the one you want removed. The Keyframe navigator displays a checkmark when the edit line is over a keyframe. When the edit line is over the keyframe you want to remove, click the checkmark. The keyframe is deleted.

<NOTE>

When you activate keyframing for an effect, the shape of the keyframe on the Timeline changes from a square (without keyframes) to a gray/white diamond (with keyframes).

9. **Select the first copy of the** c_traffic_light.mov **clip.**

10. **Select Radial Blur from the effects menu on the clip.**
    An effects menu was created in Step 8. Click the arrow and select Radial Blur from the list.

11. **Click the Keyframe navigator to activate it.**
    The Keyframe navigator becomes visible for any clip using keyframed effects when you select the clip in the Timeline. You use the Keyframe navigator for moving between the keyframes rather than manually positioning the edit line on the Timeline.

12. **Click the left arrow (previous keyframe) of the Keyframe navigator to jump the edit line to the beginning of the clip.**
    If you move the edit line manually and aren't on the correct frame, you are accidentally adding extra keyframes.

13. **On the Effect Controls palette, activate Enable Keyframing for the Radial Blur effect.**
    Click the checkbox to the left of the effect's name. A stopwatch icon appears, indicating the effect is active for keyframing.

14. **Click Setup to open the Radial Blur settings dialog box.**

15. **In the Radial Blur settings dialog box, drag the slider to 4.**

You can see the dashes around the edges of the sample angle. This indicates how much and to what extent the image will be blurred around the center of the image. The higher the number, the greater the blurring around the edges and the smaller the unblurred center of the image.

16. **Set the Quality to Best.**

The higher the quality, the smoother the blur appears. You are using keyframes with this effect, so a high quality blur also means the changes in the blur amount are applied evenly over time.

17. **Click OK.**

The Radial Blur settings dialog box closes.

18. **Click the right arrow (next keyframe) of the Keyframe navigator to jump the edit line to the end of the clip.**

19. **On the Effect Controls palette, increase the Radial Blur setting to 10.**

The higher setting means the amount of blurring increases as the traffic light clip plays. The slider on the Effect Controls palette is the same as the slider you used in Step 15 to set the blur in the Radial Blur settings dialog box.

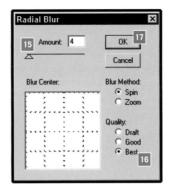

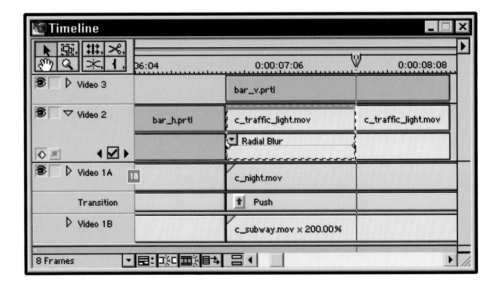

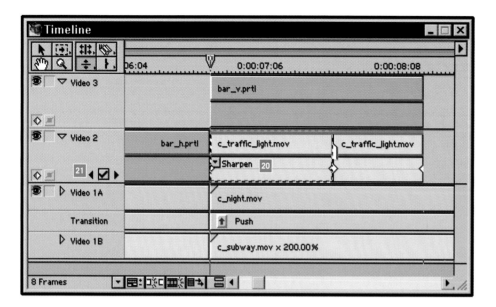

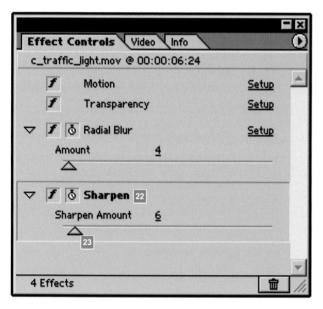

20. **Select the Sharpen effect from the** `c_traffic_light.mov` **clip's effect menu.**

    Click the arrow and select Sharpen from the list. The Sharpen effect name displays above the blue keyframe line.

21. **Click the previous keyframe arrow to move the edit line back to the first frame of the clip.**

    You are going to work with the Sharpen effect and have to start from the first keyframe again.

22. **On the Effect Controls palette, activate Enable Keyframing for the Sharpen effect.**

    Click the checkbox to the left of the effect's name.
    A stopwatch icon appears, indicating the effect is active for keyframing.

23. **Move the Sharpen Amount value slider to 6.**

    The Sharpen effect doesn't have a Setup dialog box, only the slider on the Effect Controls palette.

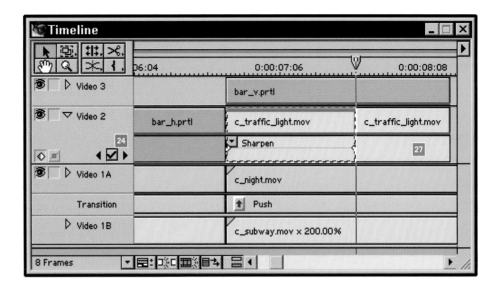

24. **On the Timeline, click the next keyframe arrow to jump the edit line to the last frame of the clip.**

25. **On the Effect Controls palette, move the Sharpen Amount value slider to 13.**
    As the clip plays, the traffic lights in the clip will gradually show sharper edges.

26. **On the Timeline, copy the first copy of the** c_traffic_light. mov **clip you have worked with to this point.**

27. **Select the second copy of the** c_traffic_light.mov **clip in Video 2, starting at 07:23.**

28. **Choose Edit→Paste Attributes.**
    Select only the Filters setting and click Paste.

29. **Click the Keyframe navigator to select it.**
    Click the left arrow to jump the edit line to the start frame of the c_traffic_light.mov clip.

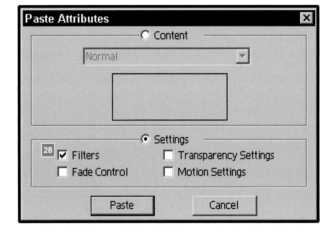

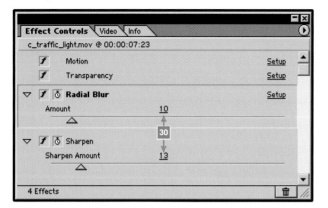

30. **In the Effect Controls panel, set the values for the first frame.**
Move the Radial Blur value slider to 10 and the Sharpen Amount value slider to 13. The second copy of the clip starts with the same settings the first copy ended with. This makes the effects flow from the first to the second clip.

31. **In the Timeline, click the right arrow of the Keyframe navigator to jump the edit line to the end frame of the** c_traffic_light .mov **clip.**

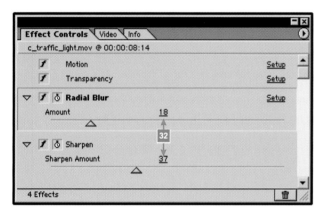

32. **Set the values for the end frame in the Effect Controls panel.**
Move the Radial Blur value slider to 18, and the Sharpen Amount value slider to 37. The second clip ends with more blur and the lights in sharper focus.

33. **Preview the segment.**
Carefully watch the segment where the first copy of the clip ends and the next copy begins. The transition is invisible, and the effects are smoothly applied from the beginning of the first copy to the end of the second copy.

34. **Save the project.**
You worked with keyframes for the first time in this tutorial. You added two effects to each copy of the c_traffic_light. mov clip. When you edited the clips you created two separate clips that together show the traffic lights changing from green to red. Your effect settings were applied to make the two clips appear unified as well. Using the effect settings for the last keyframe of the first clip as the settings for the first keyframe of the second clip, you made one smooth change in effect settings over the time of both clips.

Tutorial
» Posterizing and Blurring Traffic

In this tutorial, you work with the drive through clips in Video 1B. The two drivethrough clips are not very high-quality clips. In this tutorial you purposely decrease their clarity further by posterizing the images. You also add a blur to the second clip. Arrange the Timeline, Video Effects, and Effect Controls palettes on the screen before starting the tutorial.

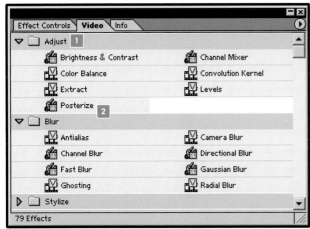

1. **Open the Adjust folder in the Video Effects palette.**

2. **Drag the Posterize effect to the first** c_drivethrough.mov **clip in Video 1B, which starts at 10:11.**

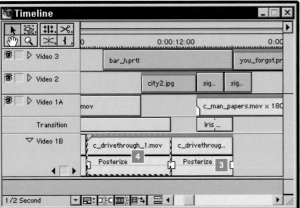

3. **Drag the Posterize effect to the second copy of the** c_drivethrough.mov **clip in Video 1B, which starts at 11:27.**

4. **Select the first copy of the drive-through clip in the Timeline starting at 10:11.**

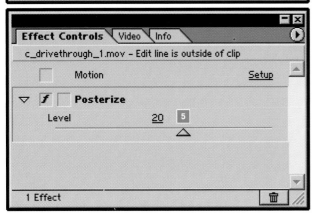

5. **On the Effect Controls palette, drag the Level slider to 20.**
   The Posterize effect specifies the number of brightness levels in an image and maps the pixels to the closest level. Blocks of color in the image become more patchy the lower the value.

6. **On the Timeline, select the second copy of the clip.**
   Set the same value for the Posterize effect in the Effect Controls palette as in Step 5.

< N O T E >
You can also add the effect to the first copy of the clip, copy the clip, and then paste the attributes to the second copy. Because the controls for this effect are so simple and don't require keyframes, the method described here is quicker.

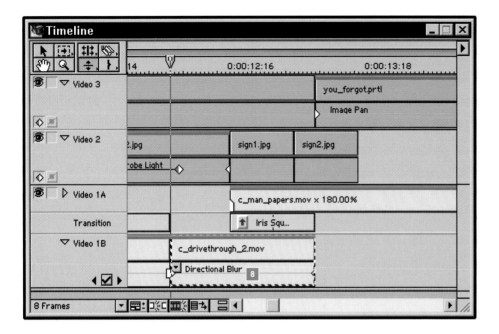

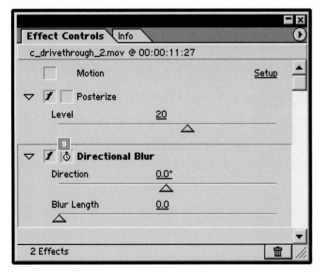

7. **Open the Blur folder in the Video Effects palette.**

8. **Drag the Directional Blur effect to the second copy of the** c_drivethrough.mov **clip starting at 10:11.**

9. **On the Effect Controls palette, click Enable Keyframing for the Directional Blur effect.**

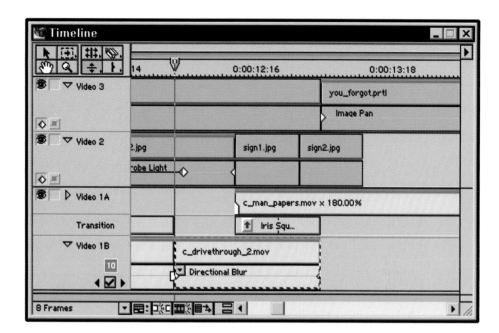

10. **Click the Keyframe navigator to select it.**
Click the right arrow to jump the edit line to the last frame of the clip.

11. **Set the blur Direction slider to 45 degrees.**
At 45 degrees, the blur corresponds with the movement of the vehicles in the clip.

12. **Set the Blur Length slider to 10.**
The long blur length makes the content of the clip indistinct. The blurring enhances the transition you added in Session 5.

13. **Preview the segment.**
The first frame uses no blur. Blur settings are added to the last frame, and the clip gradually blurs as it plays. The images in both clips are broken into blocks of color, giving them a bolder appearance.

14. **Save the project.**
You added effects to another pair of clips. The appearance of the drivethrough clips was altered using the Posterize effect. You also added a blur to the second clip.

Tutorial
» Adjusting Keyframe Positions to Control an Effect

In previous tutorials, you worked with the keyframes in their default positions. The start keyframe is at the first frame of the clip; the end keyframe is at the last frame of the clip. The two default keyframes can be moved from the start and end frames to control when the effect starts and stops. You cannot delete the default keyframes because Premiere needs to know where to place an effect over time. There must always be two keyframes for each effect. Use the Info window for setting precise locations for your keyframes.

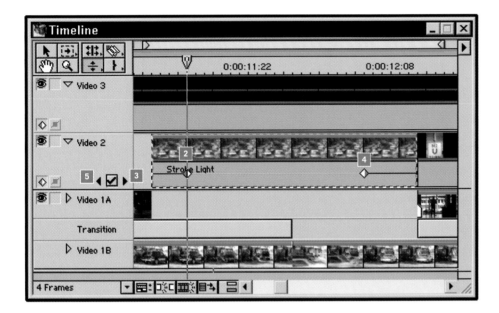

1. **Open the Stylize folder in the Effect Controls palette.**
   Drag the Strobe Light effect to the `city2.jpg` clip in Video 2, starting at 11:11.

2. **Click the keyframe at the start of the clip.**
   Drag it right to 11:15. Slowly drag the keyframe and watch the cursor position in the Info window.

   `<TIP>`
   The start and end keyframes are diamond shapes. In their default locations you see only one-half of the keyframe so it looks like a triangle. When you move the first keyframe from its default position you see the entire diamond shape.

3. **On the Keyframe navigator, click the next arrow to move the edit line to the end keyframe.**

4. **Click the end keyframe and drag it left to 12:05.**
   Again, watch the keyframe's location in the Info window as you position it. You see the full diamond shape when the end keyframe is moved from its default position.

5. **Click the previous arrow on the Keyframe navaigator to move the edit line back to the first keyframe.**
   You start modifying settings for the effect from the first keyframe.

6. **In the Effect Controls palette, click Enable Keyframing for the Strobe Light effect.**

7. **Click the color swatch to open the color picker.**
   Set the color to RGB = 255/255/179. Click OK to close the color picker.

8. **Set the Blend With Original value to 50%.**
   Rather than a bright yellow light, the strobe is partially blended with the original image.

9. **Set the Strobe Duration to 0.15 seconds.**
   This is the length of time for each flash of the light.

10. **Set the Strobe Period to 0.10 seconds.**
    This is duration of time between the light flashes. The short duration of the strobe and the short strobe period (length of time between light flashes) means several light flashes occur throughout the clip duration.

11. **Set Random Stroke Probability to 0%.**
    The clips is short, only 20 frames long, so you need control over the number of light flashes. A 0% setting means the light blinks according to the values set for duration and period.

12. **Choose Operates On Color Only from the dropdown Strobe menu.**

13. **Choose Screen from the dropdown Strobe Operator menu.**
    The Strobe Operators include standard blending options. Screen lightens the image and overlying strobe color when the light is active.

<NOTE>
The Strobe Light effect is a sophisticated effect. Experiment with different setting combinations.

14. **In the Timeline, click the next arrow on the Keyframe navigator to move the edit line to the end keyframe.**

15. **In the Effect Controls palette, use the same settings as the first keyframe with one change.**
    Set the Blend With Original value to 75%. Changing the blend value for the second keyframe means the lights gradually become less bright as they play.

16. **Preview the clip.**
    You see the strobe light flashes as the clips play. You also see the light dims slightly by the end of the second clip.

17. **Save the project.**
    You added effects to another pair of clips. In this instance, you adjusted the start and end keyframes of the clips to control when the effect starts and stops. You added the first complex effect, a Strobe Light.

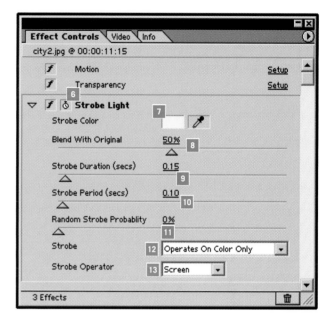

Tutorial
» Ending the First Segment with Flair

Toward the end of the first segment of the movie, you see a man throwing paper into the air. The starkness of the clip adds to the sense of frustration. In this tutorial, you add noise to enhance the emotion conveyed by the clip — as if the poor man didn't already have enough problems! You also learn to use the Image Pan effect. This effect (one of my favorites) can be used to create a sense of motion without using the Motion Settings window.

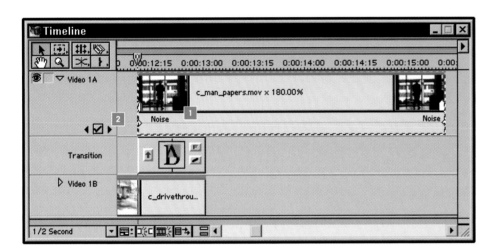

1. **Drag the Noise effect from the Stylize folder in the Video Effects palette to the** c_man_papers.mov **clip in Video 1A, starting at 12:11.**

2. **Click the Keyframe navigator to activate it and click the next arrow to move the edit line to the start keyframe.**

   The edit line jumps according to its previous location in the Timeline. If you are continuing from the last tutorial, the edit line is likely at one of the keyframes in the city2.jpg clip you used in that tutorial. Make sure it is at the start keyframe in the clip you are working with now.

3. **In the Effect Controls panel, click Enable Keyframing.**

4. **Set the Amount of Noise slider to 3.0%.**
   Noise randomly changes pixel values throughout the image causing a speckled appearance. Start the effect with a very low amount.

5. **Deselect the Use Color Noise option.**
   Color noise adds a range of color to the image distorting the central figure. Simple noise adds only black and white pixels.

6. **In the Timeline, click the next keyframe arrow on the Keyframe navigator to move the edit line to the last keyframe.**

7. **Set the Amount of Noise slider to 45.0%.**
   The noise at the start of the clip was set very low at 3%. Increasing to a higher level at the end of the clip gradually makes the image less distinct as the clip plays.

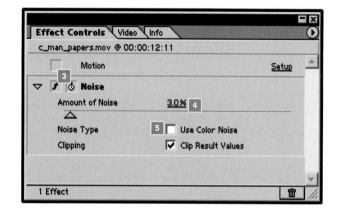

8. **Open Video 2 and Video 3.**
   Click the arrow to the left of the track names to display the lower track content.

9. **Drag the Image Pan effect from the Transform folder in the Video Effects palette to the** `you_forgot.prtl` **clip in Video 3, starting at 13:01.**

10. **Click the Keyframe navigator to activate it.**
    Click a directional arrow to jump the edit line to the last keyframe of the clip. Again, the direction the edit line must move depends on where it is located. If you are continuing from the last effect and haven't moved the edit line, you have to move the edit line forward along the Timeline.

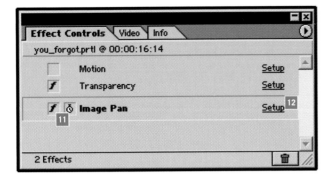

<NOTE>
You don't have to make any changes from the Image Pan effect
default settings for the start keyframe.

11. **In the Effect Controls palette, click Enable Keyframing.**

12. **Click Setup.**
   The Image Pan Settings dialog box opens.

13. **Set the margins for the Image pan.**
   Left — 19
   Top — 21
   Width — 266
   Height — 199
   You can either type the settings or click and drag the handles
   on the Source view. The modifications are shown in the
   Preview view.

14. **Click OK.**
   The Image Pan Settings dialog box closes.

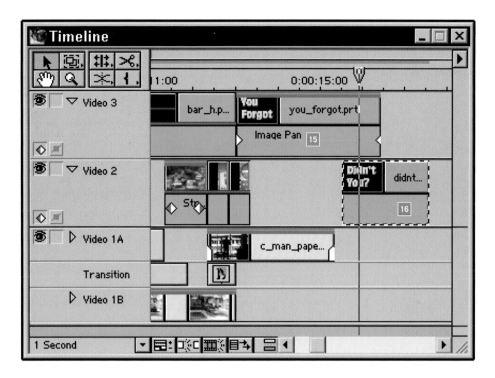

15. **Copy the clip in the Timeline window.**

16. **Select the** didnt_you.prtl **clip in Video 2, starting at 15:16.**

17. **Select Edit→Paste Attributes.**
Choose Settings and deselect all options except Filters. Click Paste. The Image Pan effect settings are pasted to the clip.

18. **Preview the segment.**
The increase in noise added to the c_man_papers.mov adds an edgy look to the clip. As it plays, the image's pixels are progressively disrupted. Each title seems to gradually get larger on the screen as it plays.

19. **Save the project.**
You added noise to a clip and controlled the amount using keyframes. You also used keyframes to control an image pan. The Image Pan effect is very useful for creating a sense of movement without using motion settings. In this case, the titles appear to move toward you over time.

Tutorial
» Using Time Echo Effects

Several clips in the beach segment of the project end with splashing water filling the screen. In this tutorial, you add a time echo effect to three clips (you work on a fourth clip in the next tutorial). The time echo creates a sequence of images over the clip giving an interesting effect. The simplest way to use a complex effect several times is to copy and paste the effect from clip to clip, which is the method you use in this tutorial.

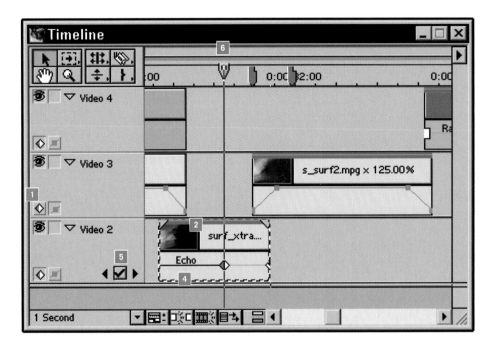

1. **In the Timeline, hide all but tracks Video 2, Video 3, and Video 4.**

2. **Select the** surf_xtra.mpg **clip in Video 2, starting at 28:19.**
   You first add the Time Echo effect to this clip.

3. **Open the Time folder in the Video Effects palette.**

4. **Drag the Echo effect to the** surf_xtra.mpg **clip.**

5. **Activate the Keyframe navigator.**

6. **Drag the start keyframe to 30:08.**

7. **On the Effect Controls palette, set the Echo Time to 0.00.**

   This is the time between echoes. Negative values use previous frames while positive echoes use upcoming frames. This is a start frame, so a time setting of 0 is static.

8. **Set the Number Of Echoes to 6.**

   This is the number of frames combined for the echo effect. A higher number of echoes produces a smoother effect. The effect is based on the image at the current time and the image at the echo time, which is added for each echo.

9. **Set the Starting Intensity to 0.50.**

   This is the brightness of the starting frame in the sequence. A setting of 1.00 is full intensity.

10. **Set the Decay to 1.00.**

    Decay describes the intensity of echoes. A decay of 1.00 means the first echo is the full brightness of the starting intensity, the second echo is one-half as bright, the third one-quarter as bright, and so on.

11. **Select Composite in Back from the Echo Operator dropdown menu.**

    These settings define the type of blending used between echoes. The Add option is the brightest and can produce white streaks. Other settings combine maximum or minimum pixel values. Composites stack echoes either back to front or front to back.

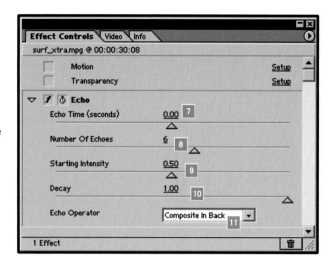

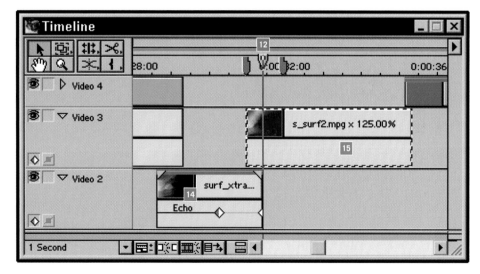

12. **In the Timeline, click the right arrow on the Keyframe navigator to move the edit line to the keyframe at the end of the clip.**

13. **Change the Echo Time to –0.08 seconds in the Effect Controls panel.**

14. **Copy the** surf_xtra.mpg **clip on the Timeline.**

15. **Select the** s_surf2.mpg **clip in Video 3, starting at 30:29.**

16. **Choose Edit→Paste Attributes.**

    Select Settings and deselect all but Filters. Click Paste. The Time Echo effect settings are pasted to the clip.

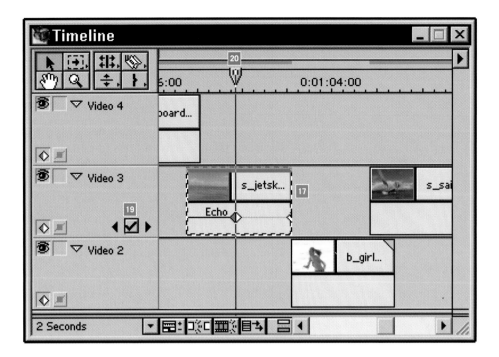

Substituting Effects

You may like the way the Time Echo effect looks but don't care for the amount of tweaking involved. You can look for substitutes. For example, a ready-made filter called Ghosting produces much the same effect as the Time Echo effect. This effect, located in the Blur folder, shows another semi-transparent copy of the clip offset by a few frames. Why not use Ghosting instead? In a word — control. The Ghosting effect is applied to the whole clip; you can't control when it starts or stops or any of its characteristics. Rather than using the Image Pan effect you can use the Cropping effect for similar results. You can also substitute transitions for some effects. For example, various noise and blur effects can be achieved with their transition counterparts.

17. **Select the** s_jetski.mpg **clip in Video 3 starting at 57:13.**

18. **Choose Edit→Paste Attributes Again.**

19. **Activate the Keyframe navigator for Video 3.**

20. **Move the first keyframe to 59:24.**
    Adjusting the start of the echoes smooths the motion of the jetski across the screen before the echoes begin.

21. **Preview the clip segments.**
    You see the frames from the clip combine over time. Frames earlier in time stack behind the current frame, gradually building motion over time.

22. **Save the project.**
    You added a very complex effect. Time Echo is an After Effects effect available in Premiere. It is used to create a visual echo of motion in a clip over time. You use the same effect for a number of clips in the second segment of the project. You constructed the effect in the surfer clip, and then pasted the settings to the jetski clip.

Tutorial
» Combining Time Echoes with Other Effects

The clip you work with in this tutorial uses the same echo effect as in the previous tutorial, but you use different echo settings. You also add other effects to a clip to correct the image.

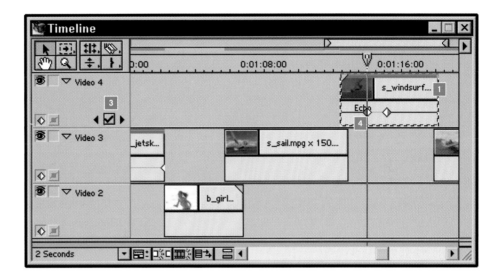

1. **Select the** s_windsurf.mpg **clip in Video 4, starting at 01:12:12.**

2. **Choose Edit→Paste Attributes Again.**
   The settings you used in the last tutorial for the Echo effect are pasted to the s_windsurf.mpg clip.

   <NOTE>
   Use this step if you are continuing from the previous tutorial. Otherwise, select one of the clips from the previous tutorial, copy it, and paste the effect using the Paste Attributes command.

3. **Activate the Keyframe navigator.**

4. **Move the edit line to the first keyframe in** s_windsurf.mpg **and drag the keyframe to the start of the clip.**
   You pasted the attributes from the clip in the last tutorial, which had the start keyframe set away from the start frame of the clip.

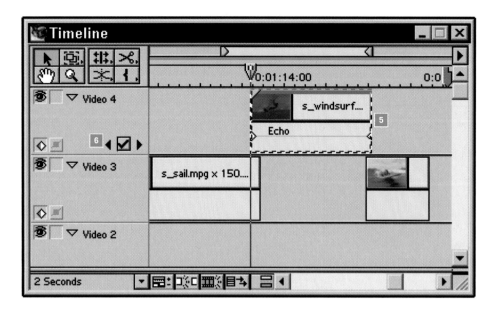

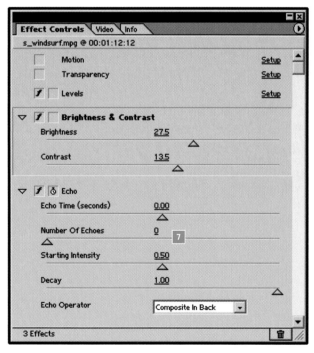

5. **Click the right arrow on the Keyframe navigator to jump the edit line to the last keyframe and drag it to the end of the clip.**

6. **Click the left arrow to move back to the first keyframe.**
   You adjust echo settings for this clip, and it is easier to start at the beginning of the clip.

7. **Set the Echo effect settings in the Effect Controls palette as follows:**
   Echo Time — 0.00
   Number Of Echoes — 0
   Starting Intensity — 0.50
   Decay — 1.00
   Echo Operator — Composite In Back

8. **In the Timeline, click the right arrow to jump the edit line to the last keyframe.**

9. **Change the Echo effect settings in the Effect Controls palette.**
Change the Echo Time to -0.08 seconds, and the Number Of Echoes to 6.

10. **Open the Adjust folder in the Video Effects palette.**
Drag the Brightness & Contrast effect to the s_windsurf.mpg clip.

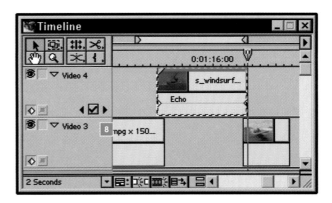

11. **Set the Brightness slider to a value of 27.5.**

12. **Set the Contrast slider to a value of 13.5.**
The brightness and contrast of the clip are adjusted, making the images more distinct.

13. **Open the Adjust folder in the Video Effects palette.**
Drag the Levels effect to the s_windsurf.mpg clip.

14. **Click Setup on the Effect Controls palette.**
The Levels Settings dialog box opens.

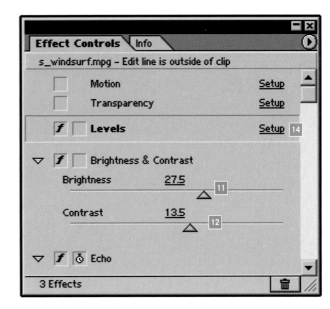

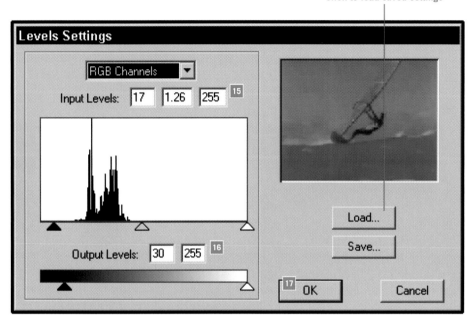

click to load saved settings

15. **Move the Input Levels sliders to values of 17/1.26/255.**
    You can use the sliders under the histogram or type values into the fields above the histogram. The histogram in Premiere is the standard histogram used in image manipulation programs such as Photoshop. The dialog box shows the histogram for a frame of the clip (the first frame). The x-axis of the histogram shows brightness levels from darkest to brightest (values ranging from 0 to 255). The y-axis shows the number of pixels using each value. Dragging the black Input Level slider right increases shadow, dragging the white Input Level slider left increases highlights; the gray triangle controls midtones. In this case, you adjust only the shadow setting.

    < N O T E >
    You can save and load levels settings. The settings for this clip are on the CD in the extra video folder. Instead of manually adjusting the sliders as you did in Steps 15 and 16, click Load, locate the file named windsurfer.lvl, and click Open. The levels you set manually in Steps 15 and 16 are set automatically.

16. **Set the Output Levels to 30/255 by dragging the sliders or typing the values into the fields.**
    Moving the black triangle right decreases some of the dark values in the clip; moving the white triangle left removes some of the bright values from the clip. In this case, you adjust only the dark values.

17. **Click OK.**

    < N O T E >
    You can also adjust the overall lightness of this clip. You can use a combination of the screen operator setting in the Echo settings, and add a brightness/contrast effect with keyframes. The combination of using Levels and echo settings is simpler and more predictable to work with than trying to adjust lightness solely through Echo settings.

18. **Preview the clip.**
    You see the clip is brighter and has less diffuse shadow than before adjusting the levels and brightness/contrast. You also see the time echo running throughout the clip.

19. **Save the project.**
    You have added effects to one more clip. You pasted the Time Echo effect used in the previous tutorial. You made the clip brighter and more clear using the Levels and Brightness/Contrast effects.

Tutorial
» Transitioning Clips Using Effects

This is the last tutorial for this session. You have loose ends to take care of in the middle of the beach segment of your project — you need to add more effects, adjust clip positions, and add crossfades. In this tutorial, you add Image Pan and Blur effects.

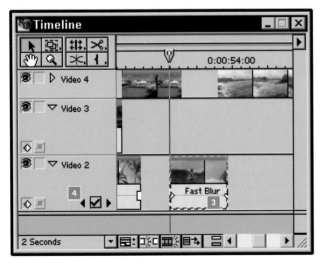

1. **In the Timeline, nudge the** s_surf_girl.mpg **clip in Video 2 to start at 50:14.**

2. **Move the** v_harbor.mpg **clip in Video 4 left to start at 47:24.** Extend its duration to 03:11.

3. **Open the Blur folder in the Video Effects palette.** Drag the Fast Blur effect to the s_surf_girl.mpg clip in Video 2.

4. **Activate the Keyframe navigator.** Move the edit line to the first keyframe.

5. **Click Enable Keyframing in the Effect Controls palette.**

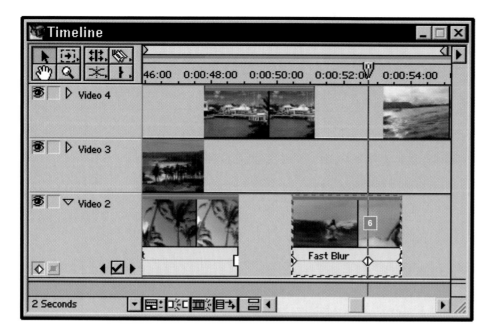

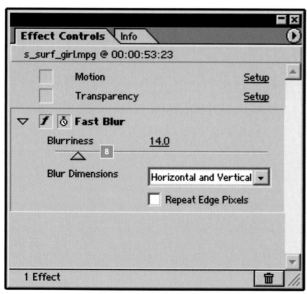

6. **In the Timeline, drag the edit line to 52:21 and click Add/Delete keyframe to add a keyframe.**

   You can manually add a keyframe or move the edit line to the position you want to add the new keyframe and adjust settings in the Effect Controls palette, which automatically adds a keyframe. In this case, you don't change the settings, so the keyframe must be added manually. Alternatively, you can drag the start keyframe to this position on the Timeline.

7. **Click the right arrow to jump the edit line to the final keyframe.**

8. **In the Effect Controls palette drag the Blurriness value slider to 14.0.**

Hints for Experimenting with Effects

Working through these tutorials is an artificial situation. You have been given clips and lists of effects and settings, which doesn't happen in the real world. For testing purposes, make a copy of the clip on the Timeline and paste it to an isolated location, either on an upper track or even after the end of your project. Keep track of the effects you try. Toggle an effect on and off to see its impact. Rearrange the effects list to see if that makes a difference. Experiment until you reach that magical moment when the combination is perfect — it does happen.

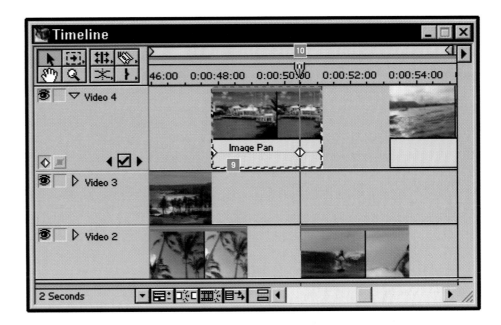

9. **Open the Transform folder in the Video Effects palette.**
   Drag the Image Pan effect to the v_harbor.mpg clip
   in Video 4.

10. **Move the edit line to 50:14.**

11. **Click Enable Keyframing on the Effect Controls panel to add a new keyframe, which is at the same location as the first frame of the** s_surf_girl.mpg **clip.**

12. **Click Add Keyframe on the Keyframe navigator on the Timeline.**
    A new keyframe appears on the Keyframe line at 50:14.

13. **Click Setup on the Effect Controls panel.**
    The Image Pan Settings dialog box opens.

14. **Modify the settings in the Image Pan Settings dialog box as follows:**
Left: 11
Top: 157
Width: 110
Height: 78
You can either type the settings or click and drag the handles on the Source view. In the Preview view you can see the image panned to a section of the water excluding the buildings and pier.

15. **Click OK.**
The Image Pan Settings window closes.

16. **In the Timeline, click the right Keyframe navigator arrow to jump to the final keyframe of the clip on the Timeline.**

17. **Click Setup on the Effect Controls panel.**
Type the same settings you used for the previous keyframe and click OK. Over the course of the clip, the image pans from the full image to the section of green water coinciding with the beginning of the s_surf_girl.mpg clip in Video 2. The pan remains stationary for the remainder of the v_harbor.mpg clip.

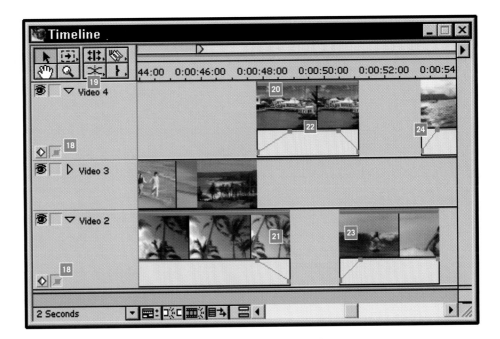

18. **Click Display Opacity Rubberbands on the Video 2 and Video 4 tracks.**
    You have to add crossfades to some clips on these tracks.

19. **Select the Cross Fade tool in the toolbox.**
    If it is not the active fade tool, click the fade tool displayed to open the subpalette, then click and hold the Cross Fade tool to activate it.

20. **Click the** v_harbor.mpg **clip in Video 4 with the Cross Fade tool to set it as the first clip of a crossfade pair.**

21. **Click the** v_palms_rotate.mpg **clip in Video 2 to complete the crossfade.**
    A handle is added to the v_palms_rotate.mpg clip at 47:24, and the clip fades to 0% at its end frame at 48:26. A handle is added to the v_harbor.mpg clip at 48:26; the clip fades in from the start frame to 100% at the new handle.

22. **Click the** v_harbor.mpg **clip in Video 4 with the Cross Fade tool again to set it as the first clip of another crossfade pair.**

23. **Click the** s_surf_girl.mpg **clip in Video 2 to complete the crossfade.**
    A handle is added to the v_harbor.mpg clip at 50:14; the clip fades out from the new frame to 0% at the end frame. A handle is added to the s_surf_girl.mpg clip at 51:05, and the clip fades in from the start frame to 100% at the new handle.

<NOTE>
You can adjust the fades before adding or modifying effects. However, you can't predict exactly how the clip will look after manipulation and often have to adjust the fades.

24. **Add a handle to the opacity rubberband of the** s_boards.mpg **clip at 53:23.**
    Drag the start handle to 0%. The clip fades in from 0% at the start frame to 100% at the new handle.

<NOTE>
You don't need a crossfade between the s_surf_girl.mpg clip in Video 2 and the s_boards.mpg clip in Video 4. At the start of this tutorial you added a blur to the s_boards.mpg clip that creates an interesting effect. Fading the clip detracts from the impact of the blur.

25. **Preview the segment from approximately 47:00 to 59:00.**
    You see the Image Pan effect applied to the harbor scene. From the full harbor view, the clip zooms in to a segment of the water, and fades out as the surfer fades in. The surfer blurs instead of fading at the end of the clip as the next clip fades in.

26. **Save the project.**
    The harbor clip had an Image Pan effect added to provide an interesting background for the following clip to fade in over. You added a blur to a clip that serves as a transition between clips. You also added several fades and crossfades.

» Session Review

This session served two purposes. First, you learned how to work with keyframes and use them for controlling effects. Second, the tutorials were arranged according to the clips involved rather than to a particular sequence for demonstrating the effect categories. This gives you experience in managing different aspects of a clip.

You learned many ways to work with effects and keyframes in different situations. The first tutorial showed you how to add an effect and adjust it over two clips to create a continuous effect. You learned how to use keyframed and nonkeyframed effects in the same clip, and how to work with more than one effect on the same clip. You also learned how to adjust the start and end keyframes on a clip, and how to add new keyframes.

You learned how to use some common effects, and some not-so-common effects. You learned how effects and fades can be used in combination as a type of transition. You also spent a considerable amount of time learning how to use a time echo effect and how to control it over time. The image at the beginning of this session shows the frame of the surfing clip where the Time Echo begins. In addition to learning how the effect works, it was important to show you that effects can be very complex mathematically and take time to learn to use well. The effects, as you can see in the final image in this session, are worth the effort.

Your work with video effects is not finished, however. You still have a few more to add, and you have yet to look at audio effects.

Here are questions to help you review the information in this session. You'll find the answer to each question in the tutorial noted in parentheses.

1. What three parts of the program must you coordinate to work with effects? (See "Tutorial: Focusing the Traffic Lights.")

2. How do you choose the effect to work with when there are many effects added to the same clip? (See "Tutorial: Focusing the Traffic Lights.")

3. How do you remove extra keyframes? (See "Tutorial: Focusing the Traffic Lights.")

4. When is it more practical to add an effect from the Video Effects palette, rather than copy and paste the effect attributes of a clip? (See "Tutorial: Posterizing and Blurring Traffic.")

5. Can you reposition an effect's default keyframes? If so, how? (See "Tutorial: Adjusting Keyframe Positions to Control an Effect.")

6. Can you remove an effect's default keyframes? (See "Tutorial: Adjusting Keyframe Positions to Control an Effect.")

7. Can you use one clip's Keyframe navigator to control the edit line position for another clip? (See "Tutorial: Ending the First Segment with Flair.")

8. In the Image Pan dialog box, can you see the effects of changes as you make them? (See "Tutorial: Ending the First Segment with Flair.")

9. What is the effect of using negative values for the Echo Time setting in the Time Echo effect? (See "Tutorial: Using Time Echo Effects.")

10. Can you modify keyframes on a clip after you paste effects copied from another clip? (See "Tutorial: Using Time Echo Effects.")

11. Can you adjust values for effect settings numerically? If so, how? (See "Tutorial: Combining Time Echoes with Other Effects.")

12. Can you save and reuse settings from effects such as Levels? (See "Tutorial: Combining Time Echoes with Other Effects.")

13. What are the two ways to add an additional keyframe to a clip effect? (See "Tutorial: Transitioning Clips Using Effects.")

14. Do you add crossfades to clips before or after adding effects? Why? (See "Tutorial: Transitioning Clips Using Effects.")

» Other Projects

In this session you worked with the Time Echo effect. Try working with the Posterize Time effect. Use both effects on two copies of the same clip. Compare the output — can you see how the effects are related? Do you prefer the look of one over the other?

Experiment with using a number of keyframes for a single effect. Use default keyframes for one copy of a clip and multiple keyframes for another copy. Are there advantages to using multiple keyframes? Disadvantages? Is it difficult to manage multiple keyframes compared to default keyframes?

Session 15

Adding Visual Sparkle and Audio Effects

Session Introduction

I hope you have made many previews of your movie and watched it numerous times. You should; you have done a lot of work. Your project is very nearly done. In the next and final session, I give you a checklist to go through before ending the construction and starting the export process. However, before you get to that you still need to do some things.

In this session, you find out about different processes and techniques. Some enhance the project; others both enhance the project and provide additional editing techniques. On the video front, you learn how to insert space into the project without destroying the relationships between your clips. Why would you want to jeopardize your carefully orchestrated project? Aside from learning how to manipulate a number of tracks simultaneously, you do it to add space for building virtual clips. Instead of building a sequence of clips and then copying, pasting, and rearranging to reuse them, you can create a separate grouping of elements that together produce a single reusable clip.

You start with a still image. Using four copies of the clip, you create animations showing different segments of the clip in sequence. You construct this animation entirely in the Transparency Settings window. The view in the Transparency Setting window's Sample area is manipulated to create a split screen effect. Resizing the viewable area in the Sample area creates what is known as a garbage matte.

You also return to the audio portion of the project in this session. In Sessions 6 and 7 you worked with audio and audio settings. In this session, you finish audio adjustments and add audio effects. You use one effect for cleaning the sound in a clip, use one effect instead of manually changing the Timeline rubberbands, and use one complex clip with keyframes.

TOOLS YOU'LL USE
Timeline window, Multitrack select tool, Block select tool, garbage matte, Transparency Settings window, Alpha Channel Key, Magnifying Glass tool, Hand tool, opacity rubberband, opacity rubberband handles, Paste Attributes command, Paste Attributes Again command, Zoom control, Block Select tool, Track lock, Fade Adjustment tool, Audio Effects palette, Effect Controls window, Effect Controls sliders, Noise Gate effect, AutoPan effect, Reverb effect, Clip speed setting, Clip duration setting, Shy Tracks commands, Show Black Audio Waveforms preference, Keyframe navigator

CD-ROM FILES NEEDED
Session 14 project file you created or the session14.ppj file from the CD-ROM
layout_grid.gif from the extra_video folder
session15.mpg preview file from the premierecc_samples folder
(for reference)

TIME REQUIRED
90 minutes

Tutorial
» Moving the Project on the Timeline

In this tutorial, you select the content of all the tracks and shift the whole works down the Timeline in preparation for further tutorials. Be careful when you choose the tool to use, as similar options exist. In this tutorial, the idea is to show you how your actions affect other parts of the project, so make sure some tracks are displayed, others are hidden, and others are turned off.

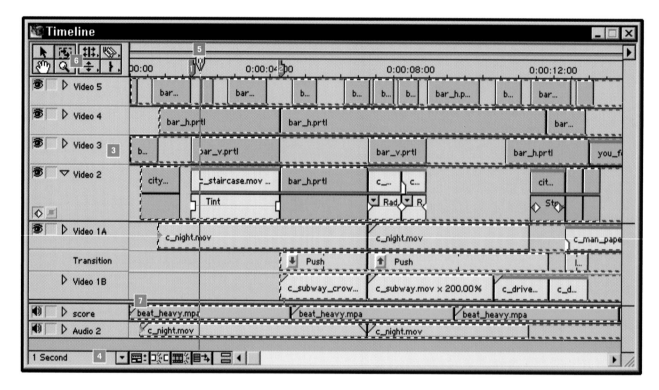

1. **Choose File→Open and navigate to the location where you stored your project files.**
   You can also choose File→Open Recent Project and choose your project file from the list. Open session14.ppj.

   <NOTE>
   If you didn't do the tutorials in Session 14, copy the session14.ppj file from the CD to your hard drive. Open the file and resave it as session15.ppj (or use another filenaming convention).

2. **Resave the project file as** session15.ppj.

3. **Hide all tracks except Video 1, Video 2, Video 3, and the first two audio tracks (score and Audio 2).**
   You need to see some of the tracks, including those that start at 00:00 on the Timeline.

4. **Set the Zoom factor to 1 Second.**
   You need to clearly see the Timeline to set the locations.

5. **Move the edit line to 02:00.**
   You move the contents of the Timeline to the edit line location in Step 9. Use the Info window to help position the edit line.

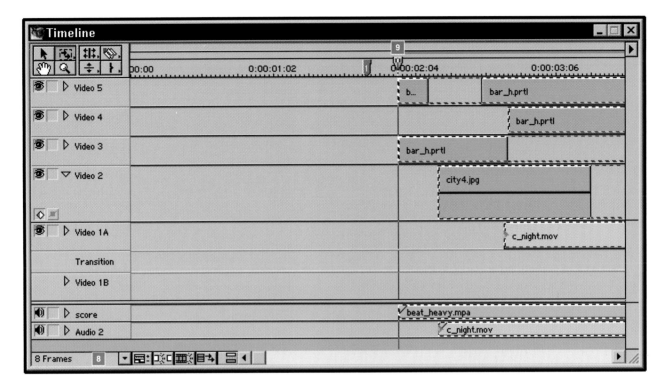

6. **Select the Multitrack Select tool from the toolbox.**

   The Range tools are next to the Select tool in the top row of the toolbox. The Multitrack Select tool shows a pair of heavy arrows inside a box. To select the tool, click and hold the Range tool displayed to open the subpalette. The Multitrack Select tool is the last of four tools in the subpalette. Click to select it.

7. **Move the cursor over the Timeline.**

   The pointer changes to heavy double arrows. Click the tool over a clip that starts at the beginning of the Timeline (for example, score starts at 00:00). The content of all the tracks is selected.

8. **Zoom in to 8 frames in the Timeline.**

   You align the content of your project with the edit line in the next step and need to see the location clearly.

9. **Click and drag over the Timeline.**

   Drag until the clip starting at 00:00 in the score track is at the edit line location at 02:00. The content of all tracks shifts at the same time.

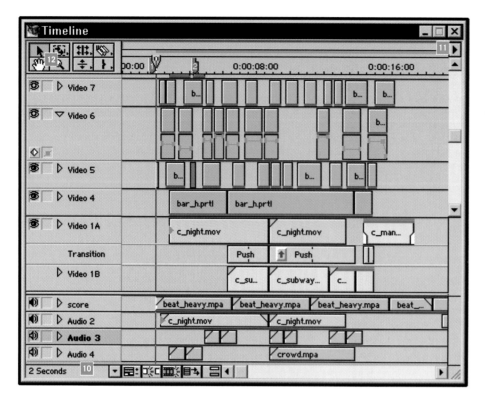

Using Selection Tools

You have a choice of four selection tools. From left to right, the tools are Range Select, Block Select, Track Select, and Multitrack Select (the one you have worked with).

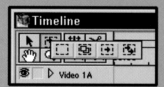

With the Range Select tool, you click and drag to select a number of clips on adjoining tracks. With the Block Select tool, you select the entire content of all tracks for a time you define when you click and drag the tool. The Track Select tool shows one arrow instead of two. The Track Select tool works much as the Multitrack Select, but selects the content of one track rather than the whole project.

10. **Zoom out to 2 Seconds in the Timeline.**
    You look at the overall project in the next steps.

11. **Click the Timeline menu and choose Show Shy Tracks.**
    You can see that all the tracks in the project, whether they are turned on or off, displayed or hidden, move at the same time. You also see that all tracks are selected, whether they were shown or hidden.

12. **Click the Selection tool to deselect the tracks and content.**
    All tracks are deselected.

13. **Save the project.**
    You used the Multitrack Select tool to move the content of your project. The blank space you added at the beginning of the Timeline is used for more clips in a later tutorial.

Tutorial
» Working with a Garbage Matte

Now you have a blank space at the beginning of the project. Putting something in there would be a good idea, don't you think? In this tutorial, you work with four copies of a still image that become a virtual clip in a later tutorial. You work with the image in the Sample area of the Transparency Settings window. The image thumbnail (called a matte) in the Sample area can be cropped. A cropped or reshaped matte is called a garbage matte; only the portion of the image displayed by the matte is shown in the movie. You resize the visible portion of each copy of the clip to show a different quarter of the image. Later, you assemble these clips into a sequence which produces a clockwise display of each segment.

1. **Open the Project window.**

2. **Open the stills bin (within the city bin).**
   Select the `city1.jpg` clip.

3. **Right-click the clip and choose Duration from the shortcut menu.**
   Reset the length to 00:08. The default length of the clip is 05:00. You can also change the duration after you drag the clip to the Project window. Wherever possible, it is better to reset the length of the clip in the Project window. This prevents you from accidentally resetting the content of tracks.

4. **Check the clip settings.**
   You can see the new duration is 00:08.

5. **Import the** `layout_grid.gif` **image to the stills bin.**
   Choose File→Import→File. The file is located in the extra_video folder on your hard drive.

<TIP>
You use this image temporarily for placement of the mattes. No grid or layout guides exist in the Transparency window, but you can use your own image-based grid.

6. **In the Project window, reset the duration of the** `layout_grid.gif` **clip to 00:08 using the same method you used in Step 3.**

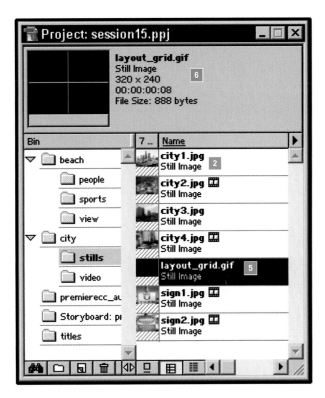

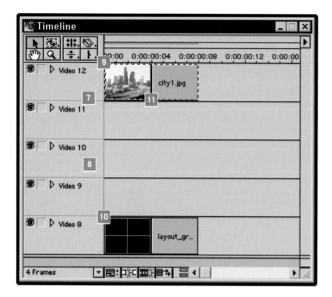

7. **Open the Timeline menu and choose Add Video Track.**
   Add two more tracks, Video 11 and Video 12, for a total of 12 video tracks.

8. **Hide all tracks except Video 8 through Video 12.**

9. **Select** city1.jpg **in the Project window and drag the clip to the Timeline.**
   Drop it in Video 12, starting at 00:00.

10. **Select** layout_grid.gif **in the Project window and drag the clip to the Timeline.**
    Drop it in Video 8, starting at 00:00.

11. **Right click the** city1.gif **clip in Video 12 and choose Video Options→Transparency to open the Transparency Settings window.**

12. **Choose Alpha Channel from the Key type menu.**

13. **Click and drag the corner handles on the Sample window.**
    You see how the content of the thumbnail matte is cropped depending on where you drag the handle. Click and drag the bottom right and left handles up and the upper right handle left to begin to resize the matte to the upper left quadrant.

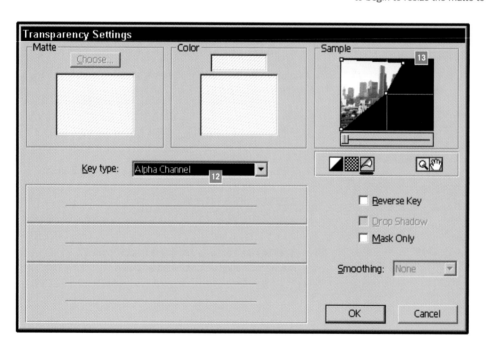

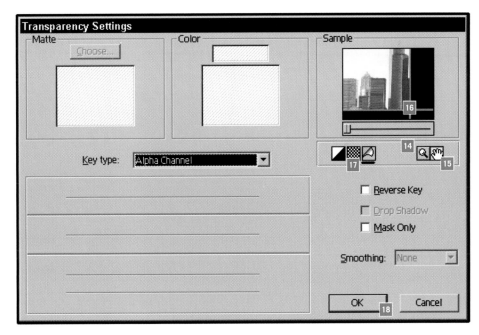

<NOTE>

A partial display of an image using this method is called a garbage matte. In this project you use garbage mattes as a way to animate the image. The clip in Video 12 uses a matte in the upper left quadrant of the image. The clip in Video 11 uses a matte in the upper right quadrant of the image. The clip in Video 10 uses a matte in the lower right quadrant of the image. The clip in Video 9 uses a matte in the lower left quadrant of the image. The layout_grid.gif image in Video 8 shows as the background in the Transparency Settings window.

14. **Zoom in using the Magnifying Glass tool.**

Click the Magnifying Glass tool to select it, and click on the Sample area. You need to zoom in closely to align the edges of the cropped image with the lines on the underlying grid image. You need to view the matte at a high magnification to see edges clearly. The vertical or horizontal edge may appear straight at a low magnification, but when you zoom in you can see uneven edges.

15. **Use the Hand tool to reposition the image in the window as you resize.**

Click the Hand tool to select it. Drag over the image in the Sample area to reposition the segment of the image displayed.

16. **Click and drag the corner handles until the edges of the matte are straight and aligned with the lines on the grid.**

Before you finish resizing, check the upper and left corner of the image. Sometimes when you resize the matte, you can accidentally pull the image away from the edges. You can clearly see blank spaces at the edges of the animation later.

17. **Toggle the background on and off to see the matte without the background grid.**

As you are resizing, toggling the background gives a different contrast and sometimes helps point out misaligned matte handles.

18. **When you have finished defining the matte, click OK.**

The Transparency Settings window closes.

19. **Copy the** `city1.jpg` **clip in Video 12 in the Timeline.**
    Paste copies into Video 11, Video 10, and Video 9 starting
    at 00:00.

<TIP>

When you copy and paste the clip into the other tracks, this
includes the basic transparency settings you already established.

20. **Turn off Video 9 and Video 10.**
    If you turn off the clips below the one you are working with, you
    can see the grid against the background and the matte from
    the other copy of the clip you are matching in the Transparency
    Settings window. The rest of the Sample area is blank, which
    makes it simpler to resize.

21. **Select the clip in Video 11.**
    Right click the clip and choose Video Options→Transparency
    to open the Transparency Settings window.

22. **Resize the matte to cover the upper right quadrant.**
    Be especially careful with the gridline. Decide beforehand
    which copies will cover the gridline and which copies will
    show the gridline. The gridline is two pixels wide; unless the
    mattes cover it, the space shows as a black line in the final
    animation.

23. **Click OK.**
    The Transparency Settings window closes.

24. **Repeat Steps 21 to 23 with the clips in Video 10 and Video 9.**
    Resize the Video 10 matte to the lower right quadrant of the
    image; resize the Video 9 matte to the lower left quadrant of
    the image. Toggle tracks on and off to make viewing simpler.

<TIP>

You have to reopen each clip in the Transparency Settings window
more than once before all mattes are equal in size and aligned precisely. Experiment with the visibility of the other tracks to assist in
matte placement. Before finishing the tutorial, check one last time
to make sure the gridlines are covered, and that the mattes butt
against one another but do not overlap.

25. **Save the project.**
    You added another clip to the project. This clip isn't part of
    the final movie, but instead is used as a placement guide. You
    used four copies of the same clip to create a composite image
    using garbage mattes. Each copy of the clip was cropped to
    display one quarter of the finished image.

Tutorial
» Setting Up the Clip Sequence

You now have a set of four images that together make one complete picture. In this tutorial, you distribute the clips on the Timeline and add fades to them. When the Timeline segment plays, you see the quarters of the image display in a clockwise sequence.

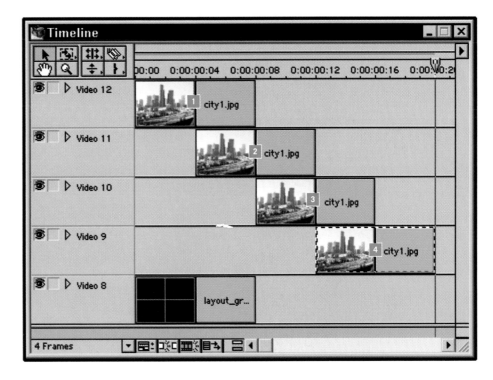

1. **Leave the** `city1.jpg` **clip in its current position in Video 12.**

2. **Move the** `city1.jpg` **clip in Video 11 to start at 00:04.**

3. **Move the** `city1.jpg` **clip in Video 10 to start at 00:08.**

4. **Move the** `city1.jpg` **clip in Video 9 to start at 00:12.**

<NOTE>
You likely have noticed that instructions are listed from higher to lower tracks rather than the reverse. Because the clip in Video 12 starts the sequence, you can keep track of locations more simply by following the animation rather than the track number.

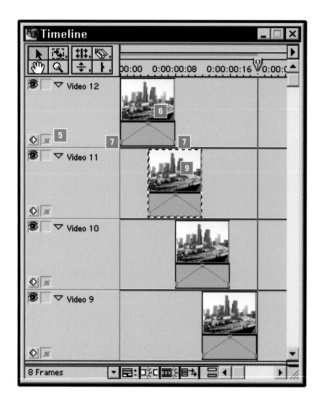

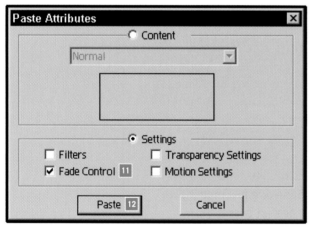

5. **Click the arrow to the left of the Video 12 name to open the Video 12 track.**
   Click the red handle icon to display the opacity rubberband.

6. **Click the Select tool in the toolbox.**
   Add a handle to the city1.jpg clip at 00:04.

7. **Drag the start and end handles to 0%.**
   The clip fades in from 0% to 100% at 00:04 and then fades out again to 0% at 00:08. The clip displays for eight frames. For the first four frames the clip becomes more opaque, for the last four frames it becomes less opaque.

8. **Select and copy the** city1.jpg **clip in Video 12.**

9. **Select the** city1.jpg **clip in Video 11.**

10. **Choose Edit→Paste Attributes.**

11. **In the Paste Attributes window, click Settings.**
    Deselect all options except Fade Control.

12. **Click Paste.**
    The Paste Attributes window closes. The Fade Controls are pasted to the clip.

13. **Select the clip in Video 10.**
    Choose Edit→Paste Attributes Again. The Fade Controls are pasted to the clip.

14. **Select the** city1.jpg **clip in Video 9. Repeat Step 13.**
    The Fade Controls are pasted to the clip.

15. **Preview the segment of the clip.**
    Pay careful attention to the margins of the mattes. Make sure they are straight and that the image segments meet but don't overlap. Because the clips fade in and out, any areas of overlap appear much brighter.

16. **Delete the** layout_grid.gif **clip from Video 8.**
    Preview the segment both with and without the grid. With the grid displayed, any irregular margins or gaps in the alignment of your mattes show the gridline marks. Regardless, make sure the clip is removed from the Timeline before the next tutorial.

17. **Save the project.**
    You distributed the four city1.jpg images evenly on the Timeline, adding a consistent fade to all four clips. As you preview the segment, you see the city image built one quadrant at a time starting at the top left quarter and rotating in a clockwise sequence. This set of four images are used in the next tutorial. Rather than copying and pasting the clips from location to location on the Timeline and adjusting their positions, you make a single clip from the set and reuse that new clip. A single clip created from the contents of a portion of the Timeline is known as a virtual clip.

Discussion
Tips for Working with Virtual Clips

Virtual clips are like secondary timelines. The clips are nested within the larger Timeline. You can nest virtual clips within each other as well — a technique you can use if you want to use more than one transition with a pair of clips at the same time.

Each copy of a virtual clip is called an instance. Each instance is a separate unit, in that you can add different effects or transparency settings to each instance without affecting the other instances or the source clips. If you make changes to the source clips, however, you *will* change the content of each instance of the clip.

Virtual clips work much the same as regular clips, but with important differences, as you discover in the next tutorial. You cannot copy and paste a virtual clip, or paste its attributes to another clip.

Housing the source material for virtual clips is important. It is safer to add blank space to the start of a project and use that space for working on virtual clips. You can also add the content at the end of your project. Whether you use the start or the end depends on the stage of your project. If you are completely finished with the project and there is little or no chance that you will move the content of an entire track, you can safely add the source material for the virtual clip at the end of the project. The project you are working on is an example. Your project is nearly finished at this point, so the clip materials can be added to either the beginning or end of the Timeline.

Speaking of moving — one last point: After you have built a virtual clip, do not move it. An instance of the clip is based on a specific range of time on the Timeline. If you move any of your source material, the virtual clip still points to the original time location. If you add virtual clips to your project, and then see diagonal orange lines where your lovely composition should be, you have moved the source clips. Either move the source materials back to the original Timeline location you defined when starting the virtual clip process or start over.

Tutorial
» Creating a Virtual Clip

Finally, you make a virtual clip. You created a set of four clips which make one complete image in sequence. In this tutorial, you make a virtual clip of the sequence and use it in the Timeline. You use three duplicates, or instances, of the virtual clip in total and add more transparency settings to finish it off.

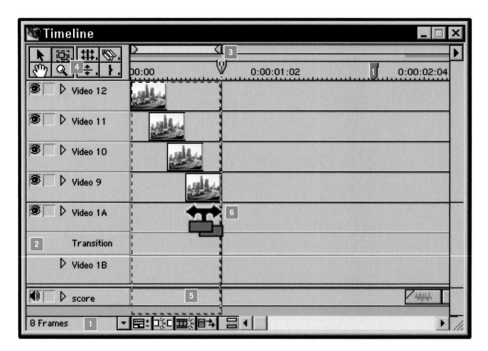

1. **Set the zoom to 8 Frames.**
   You must clearly identify the frames as you work with virtual clips. A zoom factor of 8 frames shows sufficient Timeline detail.

2. **Hide all tracks except Video 9 through 12, Video 1, and the score audio track.**

3. **Move the edit line to 00:20.**
   The frame is the end of the last copy of the city1.jpg clip, and is also the last frame of the sequence.

4. **Select the Block Select tool in the toolbox.**
   To select the tool, click and hold the Range tool displayed to open the subpalette. The Block Select tool is the second of four tools in the subpalette. Click to select it. With the Block Select tool, you select the entire content of all tracks for a time you define when you click and drag the tool.

<NOTE>
The Block Select tool shows two different icons in the Timeline. While you are defining the area for the virtual clip, coming up in Step 5, the cursor shows the usual black arrow and is surrounded by a hatched box. When you have made the selection on the Timeline, the cursor changes to the Block Select (virtual clip) icon.

5. **Move the cursor to 00:00.**
   Click and drag to select the Timeline contents. Slowly drag right to the end of the fourth copy of the city1.jpg clip at 00:20. As you drag, the arrow cursor displays a box around it. Because you have moved the edit line to the correct ending location, the Block Select tool snaps to the edit line for an accurate selection. All the content of all tracks in the Timeline is selected from the time period of 00:00 to 00:20.

6. **Once the Timeline segment has been selected, the Block Select icon displays as you move the cursor over the selected area.**
   The clip can now be duplicated.

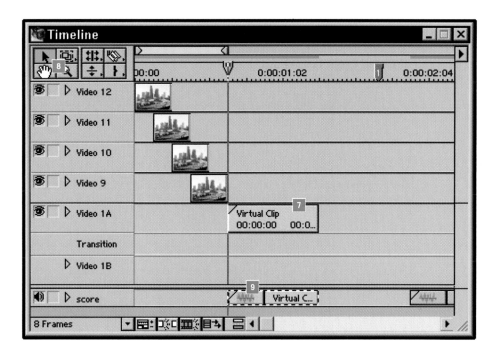

7. **Click and drag anywhere within the selected portion of the Timeline.**

As you drag right you see the outline of a clip appear. Drag right and over Video 1A until the clip outline shows in Video 1A. Continue to drag until the entire clip outline shows on the Timeline after the edit line at 20:00 and release the mouse. The content of the Timeline in the first 20 frames of the Timeline (the selected portion) becomes the first instance of the virtual clip. The virtual clip displays on the Timeline in Video 1A as a pale green clip; the audio portion of the clip displays as a pale green clip in the score audio track.

< N O T E >

You can place the virtual clip in a different video track. If you do, open all the audio tracks and locate the audio portion of the clip. The track location does not change the transparency of the individual clips that are part of the virtual clip.

8. **Click the Selection tool in the toolbox.**

9. **Select the audio portion of the virtual clip in the score audio track.**

Part VII > Session 15: Adding Visual Sparkle and Audio Effects > Tutorial: Creating a Virtual Clip

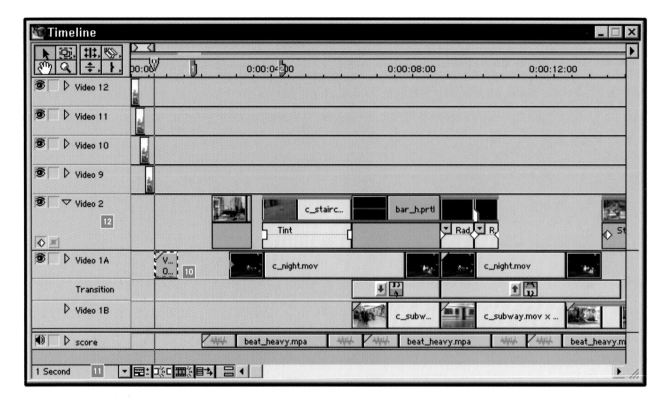

10. Delete the audio portion of the clip.

There is no audio content in the virtual clip; the Block Select tool selects all tracks in the project including audio whether there is content or not. You can see the clip color changes from green to peach. The peach clip color indicates a virtual clip using video content only.

11. Zoom out to 1 Second in the Timeline.

You are going to move the virtual clip to its final location and need to see more of the Timeline.

12. Show the Video 2 track.

The virtual clips you create in this tutorial are placed in a sequence in Video 2.

<NOTE>

Instead of deleting the audio portion of the virtual clip, you can create a clip using only the audio or video components of your project. Once the block is selected, you can press shift and drag from either the audio or video tracks to create a virtual audio or video clip.

394 > **Premiere 6.5 Complete Course**

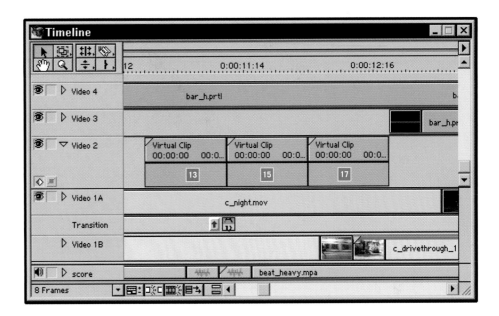

<NOTE>

I zoomed in to the Timeline to show you the final locations of the clips in the image. You have to use a lower zoom to see both the staging area for the clip and its final location.

13. **Drag the virtual clip from Video 1A to Video 2 to start at 10:20.**
Don't move the virtual clip to its permanent location in this project without first following Steps 8 to 10. Unless you use a staging area and delete the audio portion of the virtual clip, you shift clips in video and audio tracks as you move the virtual clip. Using the staging area is a much safer method. For certain projects, you can drop the virtual clip in its final location; this depends on the content and complexity of the project, as well as whether you want to use both audio and video.

14. **Select the Block Select tool again in the Timeline toolbox.**
Reselect the virtual clip source clips with the Block Select tool. Repeat Steps 5 through 10 to create a second instance of the virtual clip.

15. **Drag the second instance of the virtual clip from Video 1A and place it to follow the first instance of the virtual clip in Video 2 starting at 11:10.**

16. **Select the Block Select tool again in the Timeline toolbox.**
Reselect the virtual clip source clips with the Block Select tool. Repeat Steps 5 through 10 to create a third instance of the virtual clip.

17. **Drag the third instance of the virtual clip from Video 1A and place it after the second instance of the virtual clip in Video 2 starting at 12:00.**

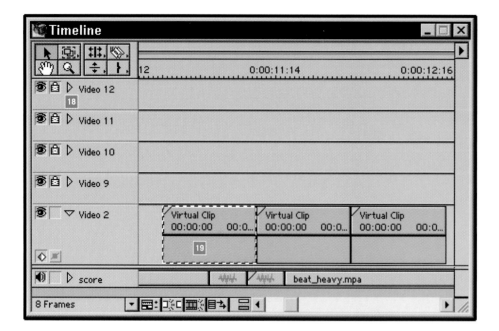

18. **Lock the tracks you used for the virtual clip assembly (Video 9 through Video 12).**

<NOTE>

Don't turn the tracks off, which hides the content of the virtual clip.

19. **Click the Select tool in the Timeline toolbox to select it.**

Select the first instance of the virtual clip in Video 2 starting at 10:20.

20. **Open the Transparency Settings window.**

Right-click the clip and choose Video Options➜Transparency to open the Transparency Settings window.

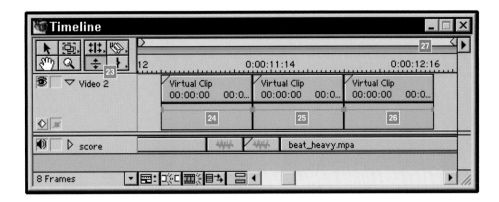

21. **Choose Alpha Channel from the Key type dropdown menu.**
    You previously set transparency for each element of the virtual clip. Now you have to set transparency for the instance of the clip.

22. **Click OK.**
    The Transparency Settings window closes.

23. **Select the Fade Adjustment tool from the toolbox.**

24. **Drag the opacity rubberband for the first instance of the virtual clip to 80%.**

<NOTE>

Virtual clips cannot be copied, which means an instance of the virtual clip cannot be pasted nor can its attributes be pasted. You must set transparency and fades for each instance of the clip individually.

25. **Select the second instance of the virtual clip in Video 2 starting at 11:10.**
    Repeat Steps 20 through 24.

26. **Select the third instance of the virtual clip in Video 3 starting at 12:00.**
    Repeat Steps 20 through 24.

27. **Preview the Timeline segment containing the virtual clips from approximately 10:00 to 13:00.**
    You see the city cycle into view one quadrant at a time starting at the upper left. The quadrants fade in and out of view. The set of three virtual clips create three full clockwise displays of the city.

28. **Save the project.**
    You have accomplished a very sophisticated video editing process. You defined a portion of the Timeline as a source area for a virtual clip and created three instances of the virtual clip on the Timeline. You adjusted transparency and fades for each instance of the clip.

Discussion

Working with Audio Effects

Premiere is not an audio editor, as you learned in previous sessions. You also learned that Premiere still is able to do a substantial amount of editing. This editing includes applying effects.

Premiere 6.5 includes a variety of audio effects. It may be difficult to figure out what to use for what purpose. To help solve the confusion, this discussion goes through the folders in the Audio Effects palette and describes what each does. For each category of effect, you generally find simple effects and a complex effect for more precise control. Like everything else in Premiere, the best way to learn to use audio filters is to experiment.

Bandpass — These three filters enhance the quality of the sound by removing either high or low frequencies, or electronic hum.

Channel — These five filters work on the left and right channels of stereo sound. They control the way sound is heard by shifting sound from one channel to another in varying amounts.

Dynamics — This is a trio of effects that works with the range of the sound. Different filters amplify sound, change the range, or remove background noise.

EQ (Equalize) — These three effects work like the equalizer on a stereo system. You can use the effects to adjust audio tone, or specify frequency ranges.

Sound Effects — These three filters do not correct sound in any way, but are used for enhancing sound. You can add chorus or flange filters (which sound like a multiple of the clip content audio, each effect working on different frequency ranges), or control the effects precisely with the advanced filter.

Reverb and Delay — With these three filters you can add different types of echoes based on time delays.

Other Filters — Several filters don't fall into specific categories. The Direct-X filter is exclusive to Windows, and a group of filters from TC Works is included with Premiere. Use these filters to modify dynamics, equalization, and reverb.

Tutorial
» Cleaning an Audio Clip

You have to do final audio editing before you start the preparation for export. In previous sessions you added and edited the clips, set their fade levels, adjusted gain, and modified their pan/balance settings. In this tutorial, you remove, or clean the background noise from the street clips.

1. **Open the Audio Effects palette.**
   Open the Dynamics folder.

<TIP>
You don't have to organize the Timeline any special way for this type of work. I usually open the track I want to work with and show the first few video tracks for reference.

2. **Select the Noise Gate effect which removes background noise during quiet parts of a clip.**

3. **Drag the effect from the Audio Effects palette to the** c_night.mov **clip in Audio 2 starting at 02:09.**

4. **Open the Effect Controls palette.**
   Choose Window→Effect Controls. The Noise Gate filter is listed in the Effect Controls palette.

5. **Click Enable Effect.**
   Two checkboxes are to the left of the Noise Gate heading. Click the checkbox furthest to the left. You see an "f" appear in the box.

6. **Click Setup to the right of the Noise Gate heading to open the Noise Gate Settings dialog box.**

<TIP>
You can organize and adjust the clips and folders in the Audio Effects palette just as you can with the Video Effects and Transitions palettes. In the image you can see the Audio Effects palette has been combined with the Effect Controls palette and the Info palette.

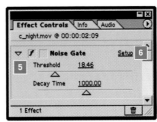

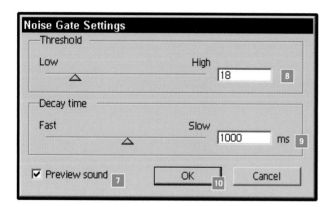

7. Click Preview sound.

If you work in the Setup window rather than the Effect Controls palette, you can preview the sound as you adjust the settings.

8. Drag the Threshold to 18.

The Threshold setting removes some of the lower sounds in the clip.

<TIP>

Experiment with moving the Threshold slider to a high setting. Much of the sound is clipped and you hear very little of the traffic sounds.

9. Drag the Decay to 1000 ms.

A high Decay value creates a fuller sound as the clip progresses.

10. Click OK.

The Noise Gate Settings dialog box closes.

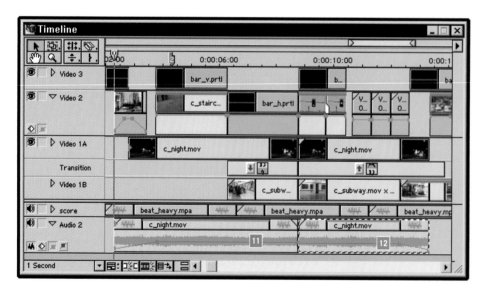

11. Copy the first c_night.mov **clip in the Timeline.**

12. Select the second copy of the clip in Audio 2 starting at 08:24.

13. Choose Edit→Paste Attributes.

Select Settings, deselect all except Filters, and then click Paste. The Noise Gate filter and the settings you created for the first copy of the c_night.mov clip are copied to the second copy.

14. Save the project.

You removed some of the background noise from the audio tracks of the c_night.mov clips using the Noise Gate filter. The street sounds in the clips are more distinct.

Tutorial
» Using an AutoPan Effect

In this tutorial, you use a Channel effect to set panning for two clips. In previous audio sessions you set pan/balance manually. Here's how to do it using an effect. You can see the pan/balance changes you make to the Timeline manually, but they are not shown with the Pan effect.

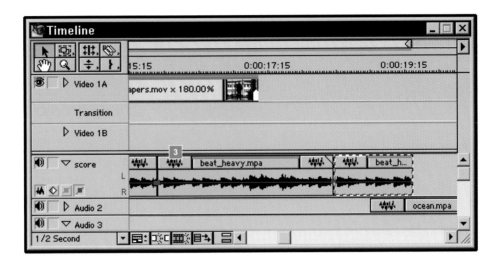

1. **Open the Audio Effects palette.**

2. **Open the Channel folder.**
   Select Auto Pan.

3. **Drag the Auto Pan effect to the** beat_heavy.mpa **clip in the score track starting at 15:27.**
   This is the fourth copy of the beat_heavy.mpa clip.

4. **Open the Effect Controls palette.**
   Choose Window→Effect Controls. The Auto Pan effect is listed.

5. **Select Enable Effect.**
   Click the checkbox furthest to the left of the Auto Pan heading. The "f" displays, indicating the effect is enabled.

6. **Set the Depth slider to 75.00.**
   The Depth determines how much of the sound shifts from channel to channel. A complete movement from channel to channel is a setting of 100.

7. **Set the Rate slider to 0.30.**
   The Rate determines how fast the panning occurs.

<TIP>
If you want to listen to the clip as you adjust the settings, click Setup and make adjustments to the settings in the Auto Pan Settings dialog box.

<NOTE>
You can see the waveform in the Timeline is black. This is an option you can set in the Preferences. Choose Edit→Preferences→General and Still Image. Click Show Black Audio Waveforms and click OK.

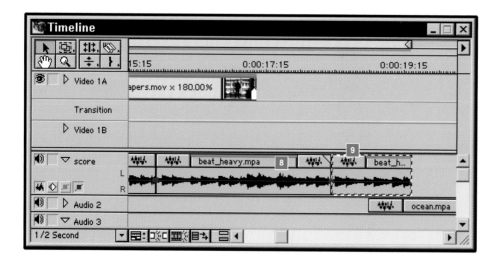

8. **Copy the** `beat_heavy.mpa` **clip starting at 15:27 in the Timeline.**

9. **Select the last copy of the** `beat_heavy.mpa` **clip, starting at 18:14.**

10. **Choose Edit→Paste Attributes.**

    Select Settings, deselect all except Filters, and then click Paste. The Auto Pan filter and the settings you created for the copy of the `beat_heavy.mpa` clip are copied to the last copy of the clip.

11. **Save the project.**

    The score track is modified. You added the Auto Pan filter to the last two copies of the `beat_heavy.mpa` clip that make up the background music for the first segment of the project. The filter pans the sound back and forth from left to right audio channel; you hear the sound cycle between your left and right ears.

Tutorial
» Using Complex Volume Control Effects

In the audio sessions, you added complex volume control to the last two telephone clips in the first segment of the project. In this final tutorial, you make the ring sound even more irritating by adding echoes to it. What an achievement! You add an effect complete with keyframes.

1. **In the Audio Effects palette, open the Reverb & Delay folder.**
   Drag the Reverb effect to the phone.mpa clip in Audio 3, starting at 12:11.

2. **Open the Effect Controls palette.**
   Choose Window→Effect Controls. The Reverb effect is listed.

3. **Click Enable Effect, and then click Enable Keyframing.**
   Click the checkbox furthest to the left of the Reverb heading. The *f* displays, indicating the effect is enabled. Click the checkbox closest to the Reverb heading. The stopwatch icon displays, indicating keyframing is enabled.

4. **Click the arrow to the left of the Audio 3 track's name on the Timeline.**
   This displays the lower part of the track. Click the gray/white diamond to display the keyframes line.

5. **Move the edit line to 12:11, the starting keyframe of the** phone.mpa **clip.**

6. **In the Effect Controls palette, click Setup.**
   The Reverb Settings dialog box opens.

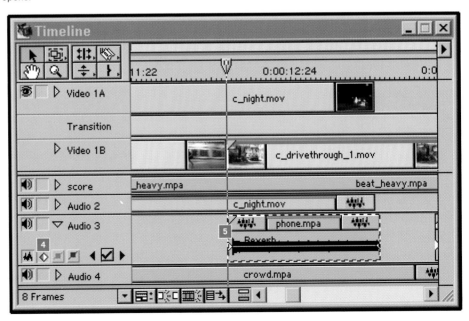

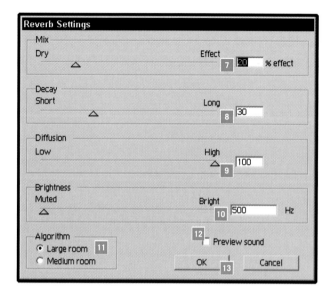

7. **Set the Mix to 20%.**
   The mix is the level of dry (unaltered) sound compared to the amount of sound with the effect applied.

8. **Set the Decay to 30.**
   The Decay is the rate at which the sound dissipates. A higher value simulates large spaces.

9. **Set the Diffusion to 100.**
   Diffusion is the amount the sound is scattered; a higher diffusion makes the sound appear farther away.

10. **Set Brightness to 500 Hz.**
    Brightness does not relate to light — it refers to the detail of the original sound. The clip starts with a low amount of original sound, which increases tremendously over the life of the clip.

11. **Leave the Large room algorithm selected.**
    The Large Room algorithm simulates the sound of a phone ringing in a large room. The Medium room algorithm simulates sound in a smaller room. It is similar but has less depth of sound.

12. **Click Preview sound to listen to the annoying telephone ring.**

13. **Click OK.**
    The Reverb Settings dialog box closes.

14. **On the Timeline, click the right arrow of the Keyframe navigator to jump the edit line to the last keyframe.**

15. **In the Effect Controls window, adjust the settings for the final keyframe:**
    Mix to 40%
    Decay to 100
    Brightness to 15000 Hz

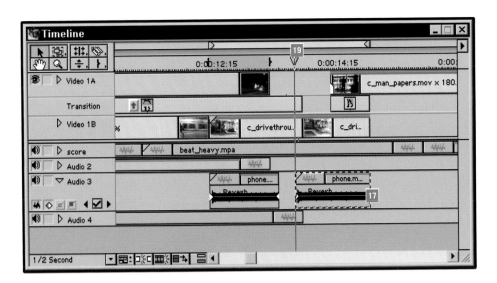

16. **Select and copy the** `phone.mpa` **clip with the added effect, start-**
    ing at 12:11.

17. **Select the second copy of the** `phone.mpa` **clip, starting at**
    13:11.

18. **Choose Edit→Paste Attributes.**
    Select Settings, deselect all except Filters, and then click
    Paste. The Reverb filter and the settings you created for the
    first copy of the `phone.mpa` clip are copied to the second
    copy of the clip.

19. **Nudge the second copy of the clip farther along the Timeline to**
    start at 13:19 from its original location at 13:11.

20. **Right-click the clip to open the shortcut menu.**
    Choose Speed. When the Clip Speed dialog box opens, type
    80% in the New Rate field to decrease the clip's speed. Click
    OK to close the Clip Speed dialog box. The slower rate
    increases the length of the clip to 01:08 and decreases the
    pitch of the telephone ring.

21. **Select the first copy of the clip again.**
    Right-click the clip to open the shortcut menu and choose
    Speed. Type 90% for the New Rate and click OK to close the
    Clip Speed dialog box. The slower rate increases the length of
    the clip to 01:04, and decreases the pitch of the ring.

22. **Save the project.**
    You added a complex audio effect to the telephone clips. You
    used the Reverb filter and keyframes to add and control echo
    in the clips. You reset the speed of the two telephone rings.

<TIP>

A silent duration of 00:08 occurs between the two copies of the
clip. This enhances the effect and its annoyance value.

» Session Review

This session covered some sophisticated clip manipulation. You worked with a sequence of clips on the Timeline to create a cycling animation using virtual clips. You also worked with audio effects and you learned how to use different types of effects, including a complex effect using keyframes.

The first image in this session shows a frame in the first section of the project, which shows the initial split screen with the two clips in separate areas. The final image in this session shows the same frame, but this time with the virtual clip in action. This adds another layer of interest to the movie.

As a review of the information in this session, answer the following questions. The answer to each question is in the tutorial noted in parentheses.

1. What's the difference between the Multitrack Select and Track Select tools? When do you use them? (See "Tutorial: Moving the Project on the Timeline.")

2. When you shift all the content on visible tracks, what happens to tracks that are hidden or turned off? (See "Tutorial: Moving the Project on the Timeline.")

3. How do you resize the matte of a clip in the Transparency Settings window? (See "Tutorial: Working with a Garbage Matte.")

4. What details should you check when modifying the matte of a clip in the Transparency Settings window? (See "Tutorial: Working with a Garbage Matte.")

5. When working with a sequence of images in the Timeline, is it better to work from top down or from bottom up? (See "Tutorial: Setting up the Clip Sequence.")

6. What is a copy of a virtual clip called? Can you change effects on one copy without affecting other copies or change the content of all the instances of a clip at once? If so, how? (See "Discussion: Tips for Working with Virtual Clips.")

7. Can you move the source clips for a virtual clip? (See "Discussion: Tips for Working with Virtual Clips.")

8. What tool is used to define the content for a virtual clip? (See "Tutorial: Creating a Virtual Clip.")

9. What types of audio filters can you use in Premiere, and for what purposes? (See "Discussion: Working with Audio Effects.")

10. Can you preview sound as you are working with the settings of an effect? If so, how? (See "Tutorial: Cleaning an Audio Clip.")

11. Do pan effects display changes on the pan/balance rubberband of a clip? (See "Tutorial: Using an AutoPan Effect.")

12. What is dry sound? (See "Tutorial: Using Complex Volume Control Effects.")

13. What happens to sound when you decrease the clip speed? (See "Tutorial: Using Complex Volume Control Effects.")

» Other Projects

Create another virtual clip. Remember that any clip you build uses content from a selected time frame across all tracks. You may need to construct the clip after the project or move the project content farther down the Timeline. There is an additional still image in your Project window in the stills bin named `city3.jpg`. Try an alternate way to cycle the clip using garbage mattes. For example, rather than use a set of four garbage mattes, use 9 or 16 (16 matches the split screen configuration of the background clips).

Modify the attributes of the source clips for your virtual clip. See how the instances of the clips change.

Exporting the Movie and Archiving the Project

Session Introduction

In this session, you prepare the project for export and for storage. A checklist is included at the end of the session for you to refer to when you prepare this and future projects.

Project cleanup includes several tasks. You remove extra files, trim files for storage, and remove preview files. The point of cleanup is to minimize storage requirements. At this time, your project is over 70 MB, not including sample output files. This may not seem like a large amount of space, but remember this is for a movie of roughly 1½ minutes. Please note that the session16.ppj file does not contain trimmed clip information, which is the task in the final tutorial.

In this session, you create a list of your project's files and print the project Storyboard. Copies of the documents generated from the project are on the CD. A copy of the entire Timeline is also on the CD in PDF format.

You also learn to export a project in this session. You don't find many editing or clip modifications in this session, but you do see how you can handle an "emergency" situation. Here's the scenario: Your project is ready for export; all the files are cleaned. This is when you realize you have used two copies of the same clip when you planned to use one. What to do? You can find another clip, import it, trim it, add effects, and so on. But you don't have to do it that way. You learn a quick way to handle this scenario (which can easily happen!) using the clip that is already in the project.

In this session, you use the Export Settings to define project output settings for certain types of output. You prepare a cross-platform QuickTime version of your movie in this session too.

TOOLS YOU'LL USE
Timeline window, track locks, opacity rubberbands, Fade Adjustment tool, Video Effects palette, Effect Controls window, Horizontal Flip effect, Image Pan effect, Export Movie command, Export Movie Settings dialog boxes, Cinepak codec, Special Processing Export settings, Gamma slider, Clear Timeline Marker commands, Remove Unused Clips command, Export File List command, Project Trimmer

CD-ROM FILES NEEDED
Session 15 project file you created or the session15.ppj file from the CD-ROM
storyboard_project_footage.pdf from the premierecc_samples folder (for reference)
session16.txt from the premierecc_samples folder (for reference)
project_timeline.pdf from the premierecc_samples folder (for reference)
session16.mov file from the premierecc_samples folder (for reference)

TIME REQUIRED
90 minutes

Tutorial
» Making a Final Review of Your Project

Before you delete extra material from your project, it is a good idea to go through the project slowly and carefully. Look for inconsistencies, adjust settings if necessary, and nudge clips as necessary. In this tutorial, you move through your project one last time. No hard and fast rule exists for how to do a final project check, but this is one way.

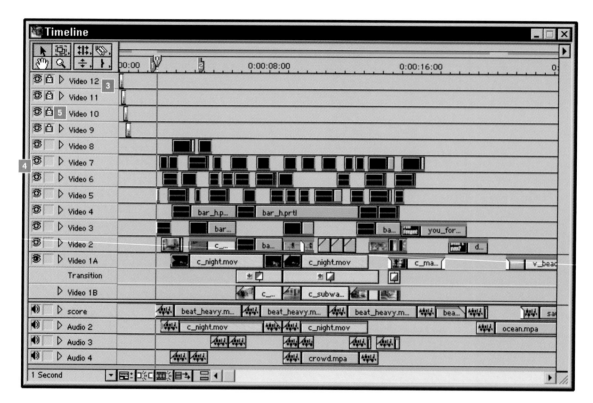

1. **Choose File➔Open and navigate to the location where you stored your project files.**
   You can also choose File➔Open Recent Project and choose your project file from the list. Open session15.ppj.

<NOTE>

If you didn't do the tutorials in Session 15, copy the session15.ppj file from the CD to your hard drive. Open the file and resave it as session16.ppj (or use another filenaming convention).

2. **Resave the project file as** session16.ppj.

3. **Display all the tracks in your project.**
   You need to see the entire Timeline to evaluate its contents.

4. **Turn on all tracks.**
   Shy tracks are visible on export; they are marked as shy only to conserve space in the Timeline.

5. **Lock tracks that you don't want to accidentally move.**
   In the last session, you locked the four tracks you used to assemble the virtual clip. These can remain locked. You don't have to lock tracks before exporting or archiving the project.

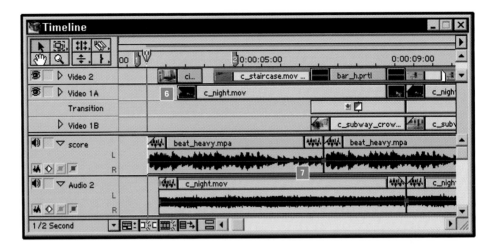

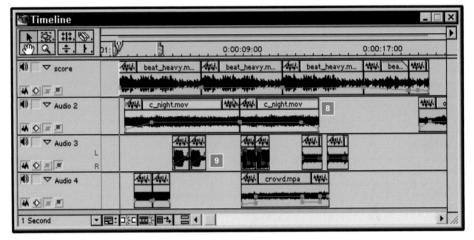

6. **Check the coordination of the audio and video tracks.**

   Look for red triangle markers identifying a clip where the audio and video tracks are not coordinated. There is one instance of an out-of-sync clip in this project. As you may recall, this was done purposely to start the sound of the street before the video starts. The audio portion of the clip is general street noise, so changing the synchronicity doesn't make a difference in the way the movie plays.

7. **Check all audio clips containing effects.**

   Test and adjust effect sequences as necessary. For clips with more than one added effect, make sure the sequence of effects is correct. Effects are rendered in the order they are listed in the Effect Controls window.

8. **Check the fade controls for the audio clips.**

   Check that simple crossfades are present where they should be and that their lengths coordinate with the video. Check complex fades to make sure they work as you intended and that they coordinate with the video.

9. **Check the pan/balance controls for the audio clips.**

   Review the clips you have modified. Adjust pan/balance settings as necessary. Don't forget that some clips may have pan effects added rather than settings modified with the pan rubberband.

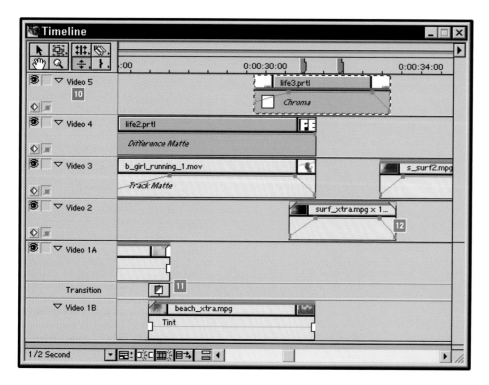

10. **Open the video tracks.**

    Click the arrows to the left of the track names to expand the tracks.

11. **Check the transitions.**

    Make sure the lengths coincide with the start and end frames of the clips in Video 1A and Video 1B. Open the dialog box for each transition and check the settings. Check these settings in particular: the direction of the transitions and the start/end points. If you preview a transition in the Transition Settings dialog box, you can easily forget to return the slider to the correct start/end points.

12. **Check the opacity settings for the superimposed video tracks.**

    Check the opacity level, the fadein and fadeout lengths, and the crossfades for length and coordination.

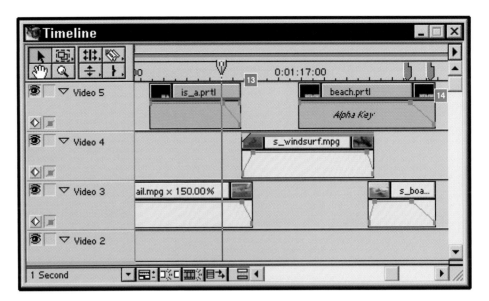

13. **Move along the Timeline to the** is_a.prtl **clip in Video 5,**
    starting at 01:10:12.
    Add a handle at 01:13:16. Drag the end handle to 0%.

14. **Add a handle at 01:21:21 to the** beach.prtl **clip, starting at**
    01:16:27 in Video 5.
    Drag the end handle to 0%.

15. **Check the transparency settings for clips that are superimposed**
    over more than one clip.
    One of the simplest ways to check multiple layers quickly is in the
    Transparency Settings window. Select the clip you want to check
    in the Timeline. Right-click the clip and choose Video Options→
    Transparency to open the Transparency Settings window.

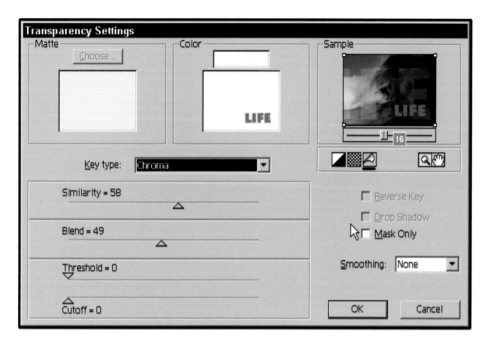

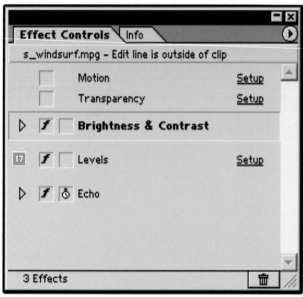

16. **In the Transparency Settings window, use the slider on the Sample window to preview the clip over underlying clips.**

    Click OK to close the window after you have reviewed the clip.

<TIP>

You can quickly check the transparencies in the Transparency Settings window. Create a preview or use the Monitor window if you need to see the effect at a larger size.

17. **Check all clips containing video effects.**

    Test and adjust effect sequences as necessary. For clips with more than one added effect, make sure the sequence of effects is correct. Effects are rendered in the order they are listed in the Effect Controls window.

<NOTE>

The example shown in Step 16 uses the surf_xtra.mpg clip in Video 2 starting at 30:19.

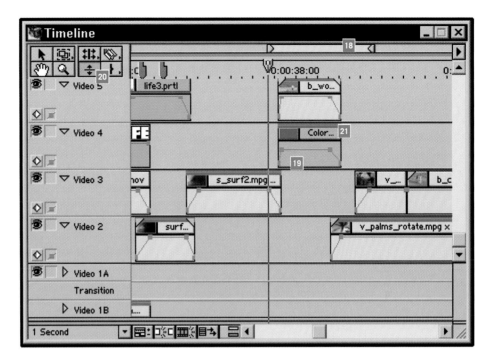

18. **Check color in the project.**
    Preview the section of the Timeline from about 36:20 to 40:05, which includes the b_woman_dog.mov segment as well as the color matte.

19. **Select the color matte in Video 4, starting at 37:05.**
    You adjust the strength of the color in the next steps.

20. **Select the Fade Adjustment tool from the Timeline toolbox.**
    If the Fade Adjustment tool isn't displayed in the toolbox, click and hold the displayed fade tool to open the subpalette and choose the Fade Adjustment tool. When the subpalette closes, the Fade Adjustment tool displays in the toolbox, and is the active tool.

21. **Drag the opacity slider to 70%.**
    At a lower opacity level, the ramp colors are slightly more subdued when blended with the b_woman_dog.mov and still produce the desired effect, which is a clip colored for interest while retaining enough natural color to keep the images recognizable.

<TIP>
Evaluate a strongly colored clip in relation to other clips around it to see how it fits with the overall movie.

<TIP>
You could also change the ramp color in the Effect Controls palette and/or increase the blending between the color matte and the video clip. This is faster.

22. **Preview any segments of the project you changed.**
    Render-scrub through the Timeline or Print to Video.

23. **Save the project.**
    You reviewed the content of the project, opening and displaying tracks looking for inconsistencies that could create errors when you export the project in a later tutorial. You checked the audio tracks one last time for correct audio fades, synchronicity, and pan/balance controls. You checked the video tracks one last time. You checked transitions and fade controls. You learned a simple method to check superimposed layers using the Transparency Settings window. You also made one final color adjustment.

Tutorial

» Handling One Final Clip Problem

What happens if you come to the very end of a project and realize you should have done something a bit different but you have already deleted files? Not to worry. In this tutorial you learn one way you can make a last-minute change using what you have and a couple of effects. You have intentionally used multiple copies of the same clip several times throughout the construction of your project. What if two copies of a clip are used accidentally? There are two copies of the same clip used in different parts of the beach segment. While it isn't necessary to change anything — both copies are edited well and contribute to the movie, it is still noticeable to the careful eye. In this tutorial you change the second copy. Problems like this should be identified earlier in the export planning process; of course, that doesn't always happen.

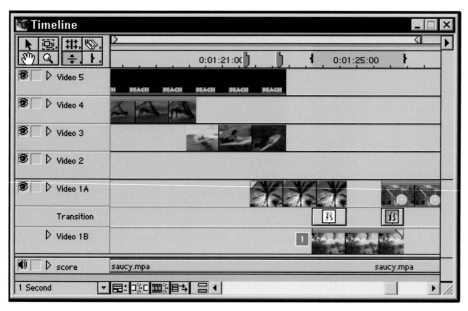

1. **Select** v_garden.mpg **on Video 1B starting at 01:23:21.**
   This clip is the same as the one used for the image matte sequence earlier in the Timeline. The first copy of the clip is in Video 3 starting at 40:23.

2. **Open the Video Effects palette.**
   Open the Transform folder.

3. **Select the Image Pan effect. Drag it to the** `v_garden.mpg` **clip on the Timeline.**

4. **Select the Horizontal Flip effect. Drag it to the** `v_garden.mpg` **clip on the Timeline.**

5. **Open the Effect Controls palette.**
   Choose Window→Show Effect Controls. Click Setup to the right of the Image Pan listing to open the Image Pan Settings dialog box.

6. **Set the Image Pan coordinates as follows:**
   Left: 173
   Top: 116
   Width: 179
   Height: 122
   In the preview window, you can see the bottom right portion of the screen is framed as the image.

7. **Click OK to close the Image Pan dialog box.**

8. **Preview the Timeline segment from approximately 01:23:00 to 01:27:00 and you can see the clip is changed considerably.**

9. **Save the project.**
   Your movie no longer appears to use two copies of the same clip.

<TIP>
You can see the effects of using this quick technique in the book. The images at the start and ending of this session show a frame of the clip on the Timeline. It is difficult to recognize them as the same clip.

<TIP>
This is one instance in which the order you add the filters is very important. Test it for yourself — swap the order of the two effects. If you apply the Image Pan first, the Image Pan effect zooms in on the pink flowers at the bottom right of the screen. If you apply the horizontal flip first, the Image Pan effect zooms in to the same location, but the clip is flipped. You see palm fronds rather than flowers.

Tutorial
» Exporting Your Movie!

In the very first session, you learned how to create project settings. You have used the same multimedia settings throughout the sessions. Now you are preparing for export, and have to change some of the settings. In this tutorial, you learn how to format your movie for export using a basic QuickTime format. You can export a movie using the project settings. In this tutorial, you modify the settings for using the movie in a smaller, compressed version suitable for cross-platform and Web use. By changing the color palette, this format can also be used on a CD. Export settings offer similar choices to project settings. Discussions in Session 1 describe many of the settings in detail.

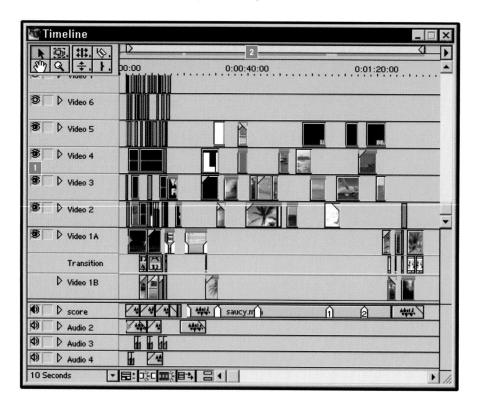

1. **Turn on all video and audio tracks used in the project.**
   The content of any track that is turned off will not be exported.

2. **Extend the work area bar over the entire project, excluding the first two seconds, which were reserved for the virtual clips.**
   The portion of the Timeline identified by the work area bar is exported as a movie.

3. **Choose File→Export Timeline→Movie.**
   The Export Movie dialog box opens.

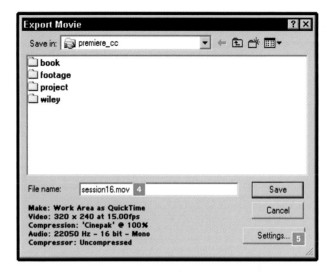

4. **The file is named** Untitled.mov **by default. Name your movie.**

5. **Click Settings to open the Export Movie Settings dialog box.**
   The Export Settings dialog box opens with the General settings panel displayed.

6. **Select QuickTime from the File Type dropdown menu.**
   The menu also includes other export options such as filmstrips and image sequences.

<TIP>

Do not choose AVI movie from the options if you want a cross-platform movie; AVI is a Windows-only format.

7. **Select Work Area from the Range options.**
   Don't choose the Entire Project option, because you have a portion of the Timeline set aside for the virtual clips.

8. **Select both Export Video and Export Audio options.**
   Open when Finished is selected by default.

9. **Click Next to open the Video settings panel.**

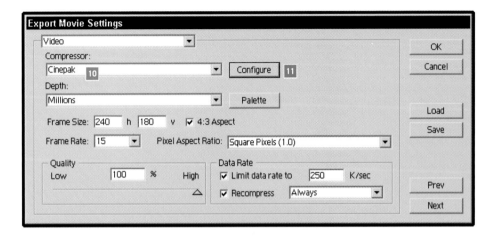

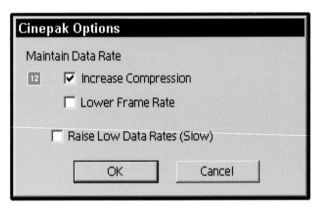

10. **Select Cinepak from the Compressor dropdown menu.**
    A codec compresses the video data for saving, and then decompresses it for playback. The Cinepak codec is a codec option that allows for custom settings you add in this tutorial.

11. **Click Configure.**
    The Cinepak Options dialog box opens.

12. **Select Increase Compression and click OK.**
    The movie you want to export is used for cross-platform and Web use. Increasing compression decreases the file size of the movie. The Cinepak Options dialog box closes.

13. **Set the Frame Size to 240 pixels horizontally (h) and 180 pixels vertically (v) in the Export Movie Settings window.**
    The movie is planned for Web use. The frame size is adequate for clear viewing and saves file space by being smaller than the default frame size.

14. **Choose 15 from the Frame Rate dropdown menu.**
    The original frame rate of 30 fps is too fast for Web display, and contributes to file size.

15. **Type 250 in the Limit data rate to field.**
    Click the checkbox to the left of the Limit data rate to heading to select it. Limiting the amount of data that is processed at one time may produce smoother movie playback.

< T I P >
The Indeo, Cinepak, and Sorenson Video codecs allow you to enter a specific data rate.

16. **Select Recompress and choose Always from the dropdown menu.**
    Each frame of the project is compressed when it is exported.

17. **Click Next to open the Audio settings panel.**

18. **Choose 22050 Hz from the Rate dropdown menu.**
    The project settings used a 44100 Hz rate which works well
    for screen playback, but isn't necessary for Web playback. The
    higher rate adds to file size.

19. **Choose 16 Bit - Stereo from the Format menu.**
    This setting produces the best clarity of sound for music
    playback.

20. **Set the Interleave rate to 1/2 Second.**
    The interleave rate specifies how often audio information is
    inserted into the video frames in the exported movie. For every
    one-half second of video playback, one-half second of audio is
    loaded into RAM and plays. A rate of 1/2 second works well
    with most hard drives.

21. **Select Best from the Enhance Rate Conversion dropdown menu.**
    In Step 18 you set the rate for the movie, which is downsam-
    pled from the project rate of 44100 Hz. The Best rate conver-
    sion setting resamples the audio at the highest quality.

22. **Select Use Logarithmic Audio Fades.**
    The first part of the movie uses a number of sound effects
    with gain and fade changes. Logarithmic audio fades process
    sound that is more like what the human ear hears.

23. **Click Next to open the Keyframe and Rendering settings panel.**

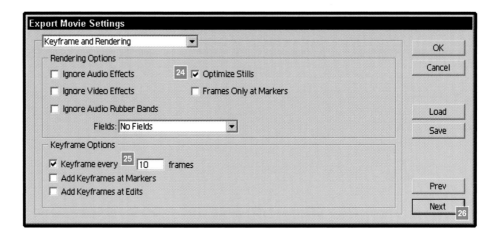

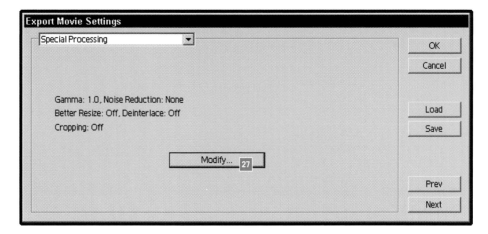

24. **Select Optimize Stills.**

Optimizing stills saves processing time. Rather than rendering a still image many times (once for each frame for the length of time it appears on the screen) the image is rendered only.

25. **Type** 10 **as the Keyframe rate.**

Rendering keyframes refers to producing output. The codec you chose for the export allows setting keyframes, which are an efficient way to process information. Rather than processing all the information in all the frames, each tenth frame is processed and only changes in the frames between keyframes are processed.

26. **Click Next to open the Special Processing window.**

27. **The Special Processing panel lists other export processing settings.**

Click Modify to open the Special Processing panel to change settings.

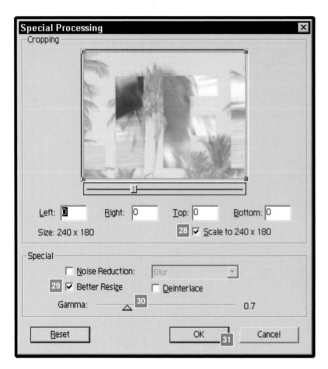

<NOTE>
The project processed in nine minutes on a computer with a 1.8 GHz processor and 1GB RAM. This may be a good time to walk the dog!

<TIP>
Choose Project→Settings Viewer to see the export settings. They are listed in the Settings Viewer along with the Project Settings you created at the start of the project.

28. **Select Scale to 240 x 180.**
There are different frame sizes used in your project. Scaling everything to the same size removes any fringing or distorted lines from the edges of the screen.

29. **Select Better Resize.**
As the movie is scaled, selecting Better Resize uses Premiere's resizing method rather than that of the codec. Premiere's resizing method is of higher quality than most codecs, including Cinepak.

30. **Drag the Gamma slider to 0.7.**
The default Gamma setting is 1.0, which refers to the value of the midtones in an image. A Gamma setting of 0.7 is the recommended level for best color contrast in both Windows and Mac OS.

31. **Click OK to close the Special Processing window and return to the Export Settings dialog box.**

32. **Click OK to close the Export Settings dialog box and return to the Export Movie dialog box.**

33. **Click Save on the Export Movie dialog box, and then be patient as your movie renders.**
The length of time depends on the speed of your processor, memory available, and the impact of any other programs you may have running.

34. **Preview the finished movie.**
You modified Export Settings from the original Project Settings. The Export Settings were changed to produce a cross-platform movie in QT format. The movie is also suitable for Web view.

Tradeoffs

The QuickTime movie you produced in this tutorial is small in dimension, but over 20MB in file size. You must always weigh file size against image quality, sound quality, and smooth motion. File size increases with a larger frame size. If you use a low data rate, the output is pixelated. If you use a codec for the audio or a high interleave setting, you may save file size but have poor sound quality. You can experiment with different settings using a small portion of the movie, such as one to two seconds.

Discussion
Web Movie Formats

You can use a number of different output formats to deliver content over the Web. In addition to the formats provided by Premiere and its plug-ins discussed here, other third-party formatting software is available. The option you choose depends on the material you are working with and the way you want your users to access the movies.

Exporting Clips

You can export single clips from your project. This type of export is the same as for an entire movie, with one exception. Rather than identify the portion of the Timeline you want to export using the work area indicator bar, you select the clip on the Timeline. Choose File→Export Clip, and choose an option from the list. You adjust Export Settings for a single clip as you do with a complete movie project. Instead of choosing between the range identified by the work bar on the Timeline or the entire project (as you learned when exporting your movie) you choose between exporting the selected clip or the In to Out points on the Timeline for exporting a clip. Both audio and video clips can be exported.

Progressive Download — Movies are constructed to allow movie play from a cache after a certain amount has downloaded. You can create progressive download movies with Windows Media or RealVideo plug-ins. Version 3.x and later browsers support this movie format.

Streaming Video — This is a format served over a browser. Streaming video files cannot be downloaded to a hard drive. The limitation of streaming video is bandwidth, of course. Movies you want to use for streaming formats need to be compressed and need a low frame rate and small frame size. Streaming video can be created through the RealVideo and Windows Media plug-ins.

MPEG — These formats can produce output for streaming video and audio. MPEG is a file architecture that produces a range of formats including $*.mpa$, $*.mpg$, $*mpeg$, $*.mpe$, $*.mp3$. The Windows version of Premiere 6.5 includes the Adobe MPEG Encoder, and the Macintosh version of Premiere 6.5 includes the QuickTime File Exporter.

Exporting Your Movie to Other Programs

You may want to use your movie in other programs such as After Effects, Acrobat, or Flash. Plan for this before you export. If the receiving project is intended for cross-platform use, use codecs and formats such as QuickTime. If your movie needs transparency for use in another program, maintain alpha channel transparency on export. If you use a codec, such as Intel's Indeo codec, you can choose transparency. If you have the hard drive space, you can export your Premiere movie without any compression. This preserves the best picture quality. In addition to using your finished movie as part of an After Effects project, you can export an entire Premiere project for use in After Effects.

Discussion

Other Export Formats

You already have experience with certain export types. You used Print to Video as an option for viewing your project. You exported single frames from your project to use for other purposes, such as applying effects. Later in this session, you print a file list.

Exporting the Timeline in any format requires the same general process you used to export the QuickTime movie. Other common export types are discussed below.

Sequence of Still Images — Use the still image sequence format if you want to paint on the individual stills but your computer doesn't have the processing power to work with a filmstrip file or you want a sequence of still images to use in motion graphics programs such as After Effects. In the General panel of the Export Settings dialog box choose a still-image sequence format from the File Type. Name the sequence and save it to a new folder. The sequence is named and numbered sequentially as you can see in the image.

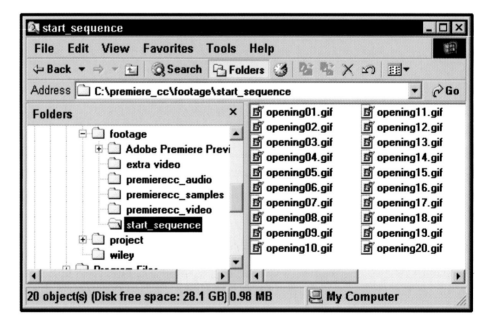

Filmstrip — Filmstrip files are formatted specifically for rotoscoping use in Photoshop. Rotoscoping is a process of painting directly on frames. A filmstrip sequence shows the frames you selected in a numbered sequence surrounded by gray borders. Each frame is identified by number, name, and timecode as you can see in the image. After you finish working with the filmstrip, you can import it into a project, just like any other type of clip.

In the General Settings panel of the Export Settings dialog box, choose Filmstrip from the File Type list. Choose a frame rate from the Video panel of the Export Settings dialog box. The exported movie is stored with a .flm extension.

Audio — A completed sound track from a project can be exported to use in other projects or other programs, or on a CD. Use the Audio export option to export only the audio portion of your project. Adjust Audio settings in the Audio panel of the Export Settings dialog box and export the sound track in several formats, including AIFF, MP3, and WAV (Windows Audio Waveform).

Export to Tape — Your project can be exported directly to videotape. You need external devices, of course, such as a DV camcorder or VCR. For certain boards or cameras, Premiere can control the export process. When you export from the Timeline, you use the original Project Settings you created for your project. With the proper hardware you can use the Export to Video option to actually export your project to videotape, rather than use this option as a viewer.

Edit Decision List (EDL) — An EDL is used when your project is developed offline but requires further editing in a post-production studio. Several EDL formats are available for use with different production systems. An edit decision list includes information about the clip including timecodes, edits, and transitions.

Tutorial
» Deleting Extra Material from the Timeline and Project Windows

The project you built is quite tidy overall. No extra copies of clips are sitting anywhere in the Timeline. Just to be sure, scroll along the Timeline and check to see that you didn't drop anything into a track for safekeeping or future use. In this tutorial, you clean up the Timeline and remove extra clips from the project.

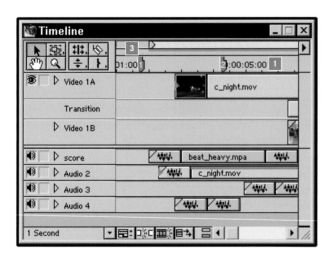

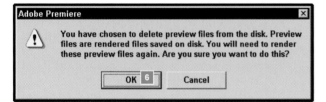

1. **Right-click the time ruler on the Timeline.**
   A shortcut menu opens.

2. **Choose Clear Timeline Marker→All Markers.**
   All markers on the Timeline are removed, including In and Out point markers and numbered markers.

3. **Move the cursor over the preview indicator bar.**

4. **Press Ctrl + Alt + Shift (⌘ + Option + Shift).**
   The cursor changes to a trashcan.

5. **Click the preview indicator bar.**
   A confirmation dialog box opens. The confirmation dialog box explains that preview files are rendered files saved on disk, and deleting the files means you will have to render them again.

6. **Read the confirmation dialog box.**
   Click OK. The dialog box closes.

<NOTE>
You can also delete either the audio or video previews. Use Ctrl + Alt (⌘ + Option) to delete video previews, and Ctrl + Shift (⌘ + Shift) to delete audio previews. Because this is the project cleanup stage, remove all the previews.

7. **Expand the Project window.**

<NOTE>

You don't have to view the Project window to remove extra files;
you do this to compare the before and after file lists. Before
cleanup, your project contains 71 files.

8. **Open the titles bin.**
   There are 13 files in total; matte.prtl and matte2.prtl
   are unused.

9. **Choose Project→Remove Unused Clips.**

10. **Look through the bins in the Project window.**
    Note that all remaining files are used in the project. If you
    count the number of clips in the bins, the total is now 56
    files.

<NOTE>

The titles bin, for instance, contained files that weren't used on
their own in the project. Remember the image matte you used for a
sequence of clips in the beach segment? This image matte is
stored as a title file on your hard drive and accessed from the project file storage for use as an image matte. This doesn't require the
matte to be listed as a project file. Only those clips that are physically added to the Timeline remain.

11. **Save the project.**
    You cleaned up the Timeline deleting Timeline markers and
    preview files. You also removed extra clips and copies of clips
    stored in the project.

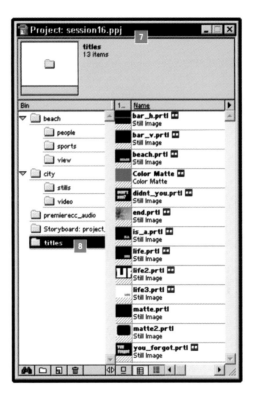

Why Do So Many Extra Files Exist?

An additional still image was added for experimenting in the first
segment of the project, and title versions that you made were used
as an image matte. As you built the storyboard, you created duplicates of a number of files. The storyboard lists itself as a separate
project bin and stores copies of the clips used in the storyboard. As
a result, all clips that are on the storyboard are in both the storyboard bin and the bin you originally used for storage. When you
clean up the project using the Remove Unused Clip command, the
clip copies in the original storage bins are removed, leaving only the
copies attached to the Storyboard and stored in the storyboard's bin.

Tutorial
» Preparing Project Documents

You can create a number of documents for a project. These can be used for a variety of reference purposes. In this tutorial, you generate a list of the files you used in your project. You also learn how to print components of your project, in this case your storyboard.

```
Text: C:\premiere_cc\footage\session16.txt                                    [6]
    view
        C:\premiere_cc\footage\extra video\beach_xtra.mpg      beach_xtra.mpg
        C:\premiere_cc\footage\extra video\v_drink.tif      v_drink.tif
        C:\premiere_cc\footage\premierecc_video\v_garden2.mpg      v_garden2.m
        C:\premiere_cc\footage\premierecc_video\v_harbor.mpg      v_harbor.mpg
        C:\premiere_cc\footage\premierecc_video\v_palms_rotate.mpg      v_palm
        C:\premiere_cc\footage\premierecc_video\v_resort.mpg      v_resort.mpg
city
    stills
        C:\premiere_cc\footage\premierecc_video\city1.jpg      city1.jpg
        C:\premiere_cc\footage\premierecc_video\city2.jpg      city2.jpg
        C:\premiere_cc\footage\premierecc_video\city4.jpg      city4.jpg
        C:\premiere_cc\footage\premierecc_video\sign1.jpg      sign1.jpg      [4]
        C:\premiere_cc\footage\premierecc_video\sign2.jpg      sign2.jpg
    video
        C:\premiere_cc\footage\premierecc_video\c_staircase.mov      c_stairca
        C:\premiere_cc\footage\premierecc_video\c_traffic_light.mov      c_tra
premierecc_audio
    C:\premiere_cc\footage\premierecc_audio\beat_heavy.mpa      beat_heavy.mpa
    C:\premiere_cc\footage\premierecc_audio\car.mpa      car.mpa
    C:\premiere_cc\footage\premierecc_audio\cellphone.mpa      cellphone.mpa
                                                                      [5]
```

1. **Choose File→Export Timeline→File List.**
   The Save File List dialog box opens.

2. **The project file name is used by default.**
   Choose a storage location for the file.

<NOTE>

For Mac users, you can choose whether or not to include the path file names. Select Include Full Path Names on the Save File List dialog box if you want the paths listed.

3. **Click Save.**
   The text file is saved and the Save File List dialog box closes.

4. **The text file opens in Premiere.**
   Scroll through the list vertically. You can see the files are listed according to the bins you established in the project.

5. **Scroll horizontally to view an entire file listing.**
   Each file is listed with its directory structure, followed by the name used in the project. A file with a clip name alias lists the alias in the second column.

6. **Close the text file.**

<NOTE>

A copy of this file, named session16.txt, is on the CD in the premierecc_samples folder.

7. **Choose File→Open.**
   In the Open dialog box, locate your project's storyboard file in the project folders on your hard drive. The file is named project_footage.psq. Click Open to open the file.

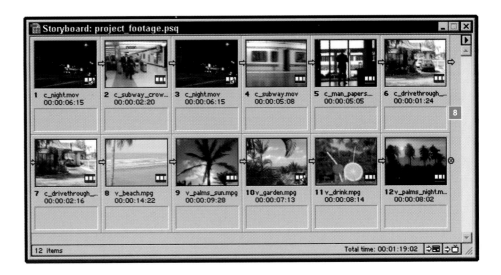

8. **Resize the Storyboard window to a convenient size for printing.**
   Here the storyboard is sized to print on one page with a land-scape orientation.

9. **Choose File→Page Setup to open your printer's setup dialog box.**
   Specify page options if necessary — this example uses a landscape orientation. Click OK to close your printer's setup dialog box.

10. **Choose File→Print.**
    Choose your printer settings and options. Click Print.

11. **When the file is printed, close the Storyboard window.**

< T I P >

Print setups are controlled by your printer, not by Premiere.

< N O T E >

You can also print the Project, Timeline, Clip, File Properties and Data Rate Graph windows. Select the window in Premiere to make it active. Choose File→Print.

< N O T E >

A copy of the storyboard exported from the project is named storyboard_project_footage.pdf. A copy is on the CD in the premierecc_samples folder. The entire Timeline from the project is also on the CD. The file is named project_timeline.pdf. It was exported from Premiere as a number of pages, composited in Photoshop, and converted to Photoshop PDF.

Tutorial
» Trimming the Project Footage

This is the last tutorial of the last session. It's been fun! You have one last task to take care of. Rather than store your final project file and all the source material in different folders, you can combine the whole project into one folder. In this tutorial, you use the project trimmer. It removes extra frames from your source clips, which leaves you with a compact set of project files that are ready for archiving.

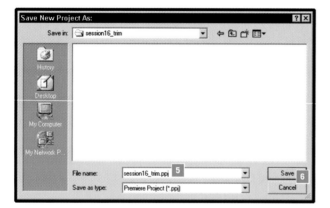

<NOTE>

There is *no* copy of this trimmed project on the CD. The trimmed version is 56MB.

Creating a Trimmed Batch List

Use the Create Trimmed Batch List command on the Project Trimmer dialog box to create a project and batch-list file. Deselect Copy Trimmed Source Files, type a frame handles value, and create a separate project. The list logs In and Out points of clips used in the Timeline. If you used low resolution images for construction, for example, you can use the list to redigitize high resolution footage for final use. This process commonly is used with video footage.

1. **Choose Project→Utilities→Project Trimmer.**
   The Project Trimmer dialog box opens. You must have the Project window displayed for this command to be active.

2. **Select Copy Trimmed Source Files.**
   The Project Trimmer process copies all of your project files. It includes only the clip segments you actually used in the project plus the specified number of handle frames.

3. **Type 2 as the value for Keep frame handles.**
   After trimming, your clips will be the edited length as they appear on the Timeline plus two frames before and after the In and Out points.

4. **Click Create Project.**
   The project is processed. The Save New Project As: dialog box opens.

5. **Specify a name and location for the new trimmed project.**
   Create a separate folder on your hard drive for the project and the trimmed files.

6. **Click Save to close the dialog box and save the project.**

7. **In Premiere, choose File→Close to close the** session16.ppj **project file.**

8. **Choose File→Open.**
   In the Open dialog box, locate the trimmed project. Select the file and click Open. The trimmed version of your project opens in Premiere. Check the relative sizes of the projects to see the effects of the trimming. The project and source files are reduced to 56MB after trimming; the source files you used in the project are approximately 71MB. After you check the trimmed version of the project, you can delete other source material and project files from your hard drive. Wait until after you successfully export and test the project and are pleased with the results.

Discussion
Exporting and Archiving Checklist

At the start of this session, you were told to use a checklist to prepare your project for export and archiving. Table 16.1 lists the items to check before you finish your project. These are a summary of the processes you worked through in this session.

Table 16.1: Exporting and Archiving Checklist

Be sure to ...	Because ...
Turn on tracks	Only visible tracks are exported, including virtual clip tracks.
Take one last, slow look	You may see inconsistencies when you view the entire project in total that you didn't notice when working on different segments.
Delete markers	Markers aren't required for a completed project.
Make a file list	Record the names and locations of the source files used in your project.
Define output requirements	Define the criteria for exporting to make the most efficient and effective file depending on the type of output.
Export and test	What's the point of building a dynamite movie if nobody sees it? Test the output settings and adjust and rebuild until you are pleased with the results.
Delete previews	Previews aren't required and take a lot of room to store.
Remove extra files	Save storage space.
Trim clips	Trim the clips used in the project to save storage room, and combine project materials into one folder for easy archiving.

» Session Review

For those new to Premiere at the start of the book, this session brings your first adventures in video making to a close. In this session, you learned a method for making a final review of the project before exporting. Why review before export? Rendering the project can take a significant amount of time. Reviewing your work carefully before you click that button can save you a great deal of time.

In this session, you also learned how to make a few final adjustments to the project content, including adjusting color in one clip to match the overall project, and manipulating a clip to make it look like a different clip. The images at the start and ending of the session show the same frame, but their appearance is very different. The Final image may bear a resemblance to the earlier copy, but it is difficult to tell it started from the same source clip.

You made a movie in this final session. Along with the excitement of producing a finished product, you learned how to prepare the project for archiving. Some of the other movie export types you can explore using one of several plug-ins were described as well.

Here are questions to help you review this session. You'll find the answer to each question in the tutorial noted in parentheses.

1. Do you have to remove the shy setting from tracks before export? (See "Tutorial: Making a Final Review of Your Project.")
2. Should tracks be locked or unlocked before export? Does it make a difference? (See "Tutorial: Making a Final Review of Your Project.")
3. What is a simple way to modify the appearance of a clip to reuse it in your project? (See "Tutorial: Handling One Final Clip Problem.")
4. What movie formats are compatible across platforms? (See "Tutorial: Exporting Your Movie!")
5. Should you adjust the Gamma setting for your movie? Why or why not? (See "Tutorial: Exporting Your Movie!")
6. How can you view the export settings of a project after they are set? (See "Tutorial: Exporting Your Movie!")
7. How does progressive downloading work? (See "Discussion: Web Movie Formats.")
8. Can streaming video files be downloaded to a hard drive? (See "Discussion: Web Movie Formats.")
9. Can you use an image sequence and a filmstrip for the same purpose? When would you use one method instead of the other? (See "Discussion: Other Export Formats.")
10. Do special requirements exist for exporting a movie to videotape? If so, what are they? (See "Discussion: Other Export Formats.")
11. How do you remove preview files from a project? (See "Tutorial: Deleting Extra Material from the Timeline and Project Windows.")
12. How do you remove extra files from your project? (See "Tutorial: Deleting Extra Material from the Timeline and Project Windows.")
13. Why would you print the content of Premiere windows? (See "Tutorial: Preparing Project Documents.")
14. Is a trimmed project saved as a separate project or saved over your original project? (See "Tutorial: Trimming the Project Footage.")

» Other Projects

Before you started the sessions, you created an animated logo. Revisit that project. Make changes and modifications based on your newly acquired skills. Attach the logo to your book project for a complete presentation.

You are not restricted to the effects you added during the sessions. Please experiment with more effects. The effects used were chosen partially for what they could demonstrate as well as how they impacted the project. Try this one: I used lightning in a preliminary version of the project (this is an After Effects effect, new to Premiere 6.5). Blue lightning bolts appeared to shoot down from the roof and zap the man throwing paper in the air (the c_man_papers.mov clip in Video 1A). I thought he looked miserable enough so I didn't use the effect.

What's on the CD-ROM?

This appendix provides you with information on the contents of the CD that accompanies this book. For the latest and greatest information, please refer to the ReadMe file located at the root of the CD. Here is what you find:

» System Requirements

» Using the CD with Windows and Macintosh

» What's on the CD

» Troubleshooting

System Requirements

Make sure that your computer meets the minimum system requirements listed in this section. If your computer doesn't match up to most of these requirements, you may have a problem using the contents of the CD.

For Windows 98, Windows 2000, Windows NT, Windows Me, or Windows XP

» Intel® Pentium® III 500MHz processor (Pentium 4 or multiprocessor recommended)

» Microsoft® Windows® 98 Second Edition, Windows Millennium Edition, Windows 2000 with Service Pack 2, or Windows XP

» 128MB of RAM minimum required (256MB or more recommended)

» 600MB of available hard-disk space for installation

» 256-color video display adapter

» CD drive

» QuickTime 5.0

For Macintosh

» Mac OS 9.2.2 or Mac OS X v.10.1.3

» 64MB of RAM (128MB or more recommended)

» 600MB of available hard-disk space for installation

» 256-color video display adapter

» CD drive

» QuickTime 5.0.2

Using the CD with Windows

To install the items from the CD to your hard drive, follow these steps:

1. Insert the CD into the CD drive.

2. The interface launches. If you have autorun disabled, click Start→Run. In the dialog box that appears, type D:\setup.exe. Replace *D* with the proper letter if the CD drive uses a different letter. (If you don't know the letter, see how the CD drive is listed under My Computer.) Click OK. A license agreement appears.

3. Read through the license agreement, and then click the Accept button if you want to use the CD. (After you click Accept, the License Agreement window never bothers you again.) The CD interface Welcome screen appears.

4. The interface coordinates installing the programs and running the demos. The interface basically enables you to click a button or two to make things happen.

5. Click anywhere on the Welcome screen to enter the interface. This next screen lists categories for the software on the CD.

6. For more information about a program, click the program's name. Be sure to read the information that appears. Sometimes a program has its own system requirements or requires you to do a few tricks on your computer before you can install or run the program. This screen tells you what you may need to do.

7. If you don't want to install the program, click the Back button to return to the previous screen. You can always return to the previous screen by clicking the Back button. Using this feature, you can browse the different categories and products, and then decide what you want to install.

8. To install a program, click the appropriate Install button. The CD interface drops to the background while the CD installs the program you chose.

9. To install other items, repeat Step 8 for each program.

10. When you finish installing programs, click the Quit button to close the interface. You can eject the CD now. Carefully place it back in the plastic jacket of the book for safekeeping.

NOTE:

Use the interface to install the project files on your hard drive rather than installing them directly from the CD. If you install them directly and are using any version of Windows except Windows XP, you have to change the read-only status of the copied tutorial files. Otherwise, you won't be able to write over the files as you work through the tutorials. To change the status, select all the files in a folder that you copied to your computer. Right-click one of the files and choose Properties. In the Properties dialog box, click Read-only to deselect it.

Also, I suggest that you instruct Windows to display the filename extensions of the copied tutorial files, if it isn't already set up to show them, so that you can see the file formats (e.g., .ppj, .mpg, .mov, and so on). Find your Folder Options dialog box. It's located in a slightly different place in different versions of Windows: In Windows XP, it's in the Appearance and Themes Control Panel; in Windows 2000 and ME, it's in the My Computer→Tools folder; in Windows 98, it's in the My Computer→View folder. Click the View tab. Click Hide File Extensions for Known File Types to deselect it.

Do not work on the project using the files directly from the CD. Premiere doesn't store content in project files, but uses links to file locations. Unless you copy the session project files and the footage files to your hard drive, each time you start working on your project, you have to use the book's CD. You save your project files locally as well.

Each session has its own project file. When you first open a project file, Premiere may ask you for file locations. This is so Premiere can establish links to the files it needs. If you work on a single session more than once, you won't have to identify file locations.

Using the CD with the Macintosh OS

To install the items from the CD to your hard drive, follow these steps:

1. Insert the CD into your CD drive.

2. Double-click the icon for the CD after it appears on the desktop.

3. Double-click the License Agreement icon. This is the license that you agree to when you use the CD. You can close this window after you look over the agreement.

4. Most programs come with installers; for those, simply open the program folder on the CD and double-click the Install or Installer icon. To install certain programs, just drag the program folder from the CD window and drop it on your hard drive icon.

NOTE:

Do not work on the project using the files directly from the CD.

Premiere doesn't store content in project files, but uses links to file locations. Unless you copy the session project files and the footage files to your hard drive, each time you start working on your project, you have to use the book's CD. You save your project files locally as well.

Each session has its own project file. When you first open a project file, Premiere may ask you for file locations. This is so Premiere can establish links to the files it needs. If you work on a single session more than once, you won't have to identify file locations.

What's on the CD

The following sections provide a summary of the software and other materials you find on the CD.

Author-Created Materials

All author-created material from the book, including project files, source material, and samples, are on the CD in the folder named Footage.

Files within the main Footage folder include:

» `session1.ppj` through `session16.ppj` — These are the 16 Premiere project files.

» `project_footage.psq` — This is a Premiere storyboard file.

The subfolders within the main Footage folder contain:

» extra video — This folder contains files to use as you work through the sessions, as well as copies of files you create as you develop your project. This folder includes many still image, title, and settings files; and two additional video clips.

» premierecc_audio — This folder contains the seven audio source files for your project.

» premierecc_samples — This folder contains samples of the output from the project sessions. The final movie exported from the project is a QuickTime movie. Sessions 1 through 3 do not have sample files; the first sample file is for Session 4. The rest of the sessions have at least one sample file. Certain sessions have two sample files to illustrate an aspect of the project development, or how the session affected separate areas of the project. This folder also contains samples of printed output from your project, including three PDF files and one text file.

» premierecc_video — This folder contains the first 36 files you work with in the project. Files include QuickTime movies, video files, and still images.

Applications

The following applications are on the CD:

Acrobat Reader 5.0 from Adobe Systems, Inc.

Freeware version — For Macintosh and Windows. This is the reader required to view PDF files. For more information, check out www.adobe.com/products/acrobat/readermain.html.

Adobe Premiere 6.0 from Adobe Systems, Inc.

Commercial Product — 30-day tryout version for Windows and Macintosh. For working through the book projects, the 6.0 version provides most of the functionality you need, except for the Title Designer window. For more information, visit the Premiere main page at www.adobe.com/motion/main.html.

Awave Studio from FMJ Software

Shareware — For Windows only. This is a multipurpose audio tool for converting audio file formats, audio editing, and audio and MIDI playing. Also use it as a wavetable synthesizer instrument editor and converter. This is an unregistered shareware release. To register the product, visit www.fmjsoft.com.

Bias Peak 3.1 Audio Editor from BIAS, Inc.

Trial Version — Fully functional for 14 days. Macintosh only. A fully OS X native audio editing/processing/mastering application. Visit the Bias website at www.bias-inc.com for more information.

Boris FX v6.1 from Boris FX

Demo — Fully functional but does not render. For Macintosh OS X and Windows XP. Boris FX includes hundreds of customizable effects from snow and rain to fire. Use for compositing and keying as well. Find out more information at www.borisfx.com.

Boris GRAFFITI from Boris FX

Tryout — Fully functional for 30 days. For Mac OS X and Windows XP. Graffiti is a vector title animation program with hundreds of presets for animating text on a path or creating type-on effects. Get more information at www.borisfx.com.

Boris RED from Boris FX

Demo — Fully functional but does not render. For Mac OS X and Windows XP. Over 1000 effects. Rotoscoping and vector paint inside program, time manipulation filters, animate text on a path, and much more. Find out more about RED at www.borisfx.com.

SpiceMaster 2.0 from Pixelan Software

Demo — For Windows. A plug-in that customizes, controls, and manages spice effects, it can also animate/flow Premiere video filters. Find out more information on SpiceMaster at www.pixelan.com.

Troubleshooting

If you have difficulty installing or using anything on the companion CD, try the following solutions:

» **Turn off any antivirus software that you may have running.** Installers sometimes mimic virus activity and can make your computer incorrectly believe that it is being infected by a virus. (Be sure to turn the antivirus software back on later.)

» **Close all running programs.** The more programs you're running, the less memory is available to other programs. Installers also typically update files and programs; if you keep other programs running, the installation may not work properly.

» **Reference the ReadMe:** Please refer to the ReadMe file located at the root of the CD for the latest product information at the time of publication.

If you still have trouble with the CD, please call the Wiley Publishing Customer Care phone number: (800) 762-2974. Outside the United States, call 1(317) 572-3994. You can also contact Wiley Publishing Customer Service by e-mail at techsupdum@wiley.com. Wiley Publishing will provide technical support only for installation and other general quality control items; for technical support on the applications themselves, consult the program vendor.

Index

About Seybold Seminars and Publications

Seybold Seminars and Publications is your complete guide

to the publishing industry. For more than 30 years it

has been the most trusted source for technology events,

news, and insider intelligence.

Workflow V
Media Tec
Creation Di
Managemer
Digital Ass
Fonts and
Digital Me
Content Ma
Managemer
Workflow Va
Media Tec
Creation Di
Managemer
Digital Ass
Fonts and
Digital Me
Content Ma
Managemer
Workflow V
Media Tec
Creation Di
Managemer

Produced by

PUBLICATIONS

Today, Seybold Publications and Consulting continues to guide publishing professionals around the world in their purchasing decisions and business strategies through newsletters, online resources, consulting, and custom corporate services.

○ ***The Seybold Report: Analyzing Publishing Technologies***
The Seybold Report analyzes the cross-media tools, technologies, and trends shaping professional publishing today. Each in-depth newsletter delves into the topics changing the marketplace. *The Seybold Report* covers critical analyses of the business issues and market conditions that determine the success of new products, technologies, and companies. Read about the latest developments in mission-critical topic areas, including content and asset management, color management and proofing, industry standards, and cross-media workflows. A subscription to *The Seybold Report* (24 issues per year) includes our weekly email news service, *The Bulletin,* and full access to the seyboldreports.com archives.

○ ***The Bulletin: Seybold News & Views on Electronic Publishing***
The Bulletin: Seybold News & Views on Electronic Publishing is Seybold Publications' weekly email news service covering all aspects of electronic publishing. Every week *The Bulletin* brings you all the important news in a concise, easy-to-read format.

For more information on **NEWSLETTER SUBSCRIPTIONS,** please visit **seyboldreports.com**.

CUSTOM SERVICES

In addition to newsletters and online information resources, Seybold
Publications and Consulting offers a variety of custom corporate services
designed to meet your organization's specific needs.

○ **Strategic Technology Advisory Research Service (STARS)**
The STARS program includes a group license to *The Seybold Report* and
The Bulletin, phone access to our analysts, access to online archives at
seyboldreports.com, an on-site visit by one of our analysts, and much more.

○ **Personalized Seminars**
Our team of skilled consultants and subject experts work with you to create a
custom presentation that gets your employees up to speed on topics spanning
the full spectrum of prepress and publishing technologies covered in our publications. Full-day and half-day seminars are available.

○ **Site Licenses**
Our electronic licensing program keeps everyone in your organization, sales
force, or marketing department up to date at a fraction of the cost of buying
individual subscriptions. One hard copy of *The Seybold Report* is included with
each electronic license.

For more information on **CUSTOM CORPORATE SERVICES,**
please visit **seyboldreports.com**.

EVENTS

Seybold Seminars facilitates exchange and discussion within the high-tech publishing community several times a year. A hard-hitting lineup of conferences, an opportunity to meet leading media technology vendors, and special events bring innovators and leaders together to share ideas and experiences.

Conferences

Our diverse educational programs are designed to tackle the full range of the latest developments in publishing technology. Topics include:

- Print publishing
- Web publishing
- Design
- Creative tools and standards
- Best practices
- Multimedia
- Content management
- Technology standards
- Security
- Digital rights management

In addition to the conferences, you'll have the opportunity to meet representatives from companies that bring you the newest products and technologies in the publishing marketplace. Test tools, evaluate products, and take free classes from the experts.

For more information on **SEYBOLD SEMINARS EVENTS,**
please visit **seyboldseminars.com**.

Wiley Publishing, Inc.
End-User License Agreement

READ THIS. You should carefully read these terms and conditions before opening the software packet(s) included with this book "Book". This is a license agreement "Agreement" between you and Wiley Publishing, Inc."WPI". By opening the accompanying software packet(s), you acknowledge that you have read and accept the following terms and conditions. If you do not agree and do not want to be bound by such terms and conditions, promptly return the Book and the unopened software packet(s) to the place you obtained them for a full refund.

1. **License Grant.** WPI grants to you (either an individual or entity) a nonexclusive license to use one copy of the enclosed software program(s) (collectively, the "Software" solely for your own personal or business purposes on a single computer (whether a standard computer or a workstation component of a multi-user network). The Software is in use on a computer when it is loaded into temporary memory (RAM) or installed into permanent memory (hard disk, CD-ROM, or other storage device). WPI reserves all rights not expressly granted herein.

2. **Ownership.** WPI is the owner of all right, title, and interest, including copyright, in and to the compilation of the Software recorded on the disk(s) or CD-ROM "Software Media". Copyright to the individual programs recorded on the Software Media is owned by the author or other authorized copyright owner of each program. Ownership of the Software and all proprietary rights relating thereto remain with WPI and its licensers.

3. **Restrictions On Use and Transfer.**

   (a) You may only (i) make one copy of the Software for backup or archival purposes, or (ii) transfer the Software to a single hard disk, provided that you keep the original for backup or archival purposes. You may not (i) rent or lease the Software, (ii) copy or reproduce the Software through a LAN or other network system or through any computer subscriber system or bulletin- board system, or (iii) modify, adapt, or create derivative works based on the Software.

   (b) You may not reverse engineer, decompile, or disassemble the Software. You may transfer the Software and user documentation on a permanent basis, provided that the transferee agrees to accept the terms and conditions of this Agreement and you retain no copies. If the Software is an update or has been updated, any transfer must include the most recent update and all prior versions.

4. **Restrictions on Use of Individual Programs.** You must follow the individual requirements and restrictions detailed for each individual program in the "What's on the CD-ROM?" appendix of this Book. These limitations are also contained in the individual license agreements recorded on the Software Media. These limitations may include a requirement that after using the program for a specified period of time, the user must pay a registration fee or discontinue use. By opening the Software packet(s), you will be agreeing to abide by the licenses and restrictions for these individual programs that are detailed in the "What's on the CD-ROM?" appendix and on the Software Media. None of the material on this Software Media or listed in this Book may ever be redistributed, in original or modified form, for commercial purposes.

5. **Limited Warranty.**

   (a) WPI warrants that the Software and Software Media are free from defects in materials and workmanship under normal use for a period of sixty (60) days from the date of purchase of this Book. If WPI receives notification within the warranty period of defects in materials or workmanship, WPI will replace the defective Software Media.

   (b) WPI AND THE AUTHOR OF THE BOOK DISCLAIM ALL OTHER WARRANTIES, EXPRESS OR IMPLIED, INCLUDING WITHOUT LIMITATION IMPLIED WARRANTIES OF MERCHANTABILITY AND FITNESS FOR A PARTICULAR PURPOSE, WITH RESPECT TO THE SOFTWARE, THE PROGRAMS, THE SOURCE CODE CONTAINED THEREIN, AND/OR THE TECHNIQUES DESCRIBED IN THIS BOOK. WPI DOES NOT WARRANT THAT THE FUNCTIONS CONTAINED IN THE SOFTWARE WILL MEET YOUR REQUIREMENTS OR THAT THE OPERATION OF THE SOFTWARE WILL BE ERROR FREE.

   (c) This limited warranty gives you specific legal rights, and you may have other rights that vary from jurisdiction to jurisdiction.

6. Remedies.

(a) WPI's entire liability and your exclusive remedy for defects in materials and workmanship shall be limited to replacement of the Software Media, which may be returned to WPI with a copy of your receipt at the following address: Software Media Fulfillment Department, Attn.: *Premiere 6.5 Complete Course,* Wiley Publishing, Inc., 10475 Crosspoint Blvd., Indianapolis, IN 46256, or call 1-800-762-2974. Please allow four to six weeks for delivery. This Limited Warranty is void if failure of the Software Media has resulted from accident, abuse, or misapplication. Any replacement Software Media will be warranted for the remainder of the original warranty period or thirty (30) days, whichever is longer.

(b) In no event shall WPI or the author be liable for any damages whatsoever (including without limitation damages for loss of business profits, business interruption, loss of business information, or any other pecuniary loss) arising from the use of or inability to use the Book or the Software, even if WPI has been advised of the possibility of such damages.

(c) Because some jurisdictions do not allow the exclusion or limitation of liability for consequential or incidental damages, the above limitation or exclusion may not apply to you.

7. U.S. Government Restricted Rights.
Use, duplication, or disclosure of the Software for or on behalf of the United States of America, its agencies and/or instrumentalities "U.S. Government" is subject to restrictions as stated in paragraph (c)(1)(ii) of the Rights in Technical Data and Computer Software clause of DFARS 252.227-7013, or subparagraphs (c) (1) and (2) of the Commercial Computer Software - Restricted Rights clause at FAR 52.227-19, and in similar clauses in the NASA FAR supplement, as applicable.

8. General.
This Agreement constitutes the entire understanding of the parties and revokes and supersedes all prior agreements, oral or written, between them and may not be modified or amended except in a writing signed by both parties hereto that specifically refers to this Agreement. This Agreement shall take precedence over any other documents that may be in conflict herewith. If any one or more provisions contained in this Agreement are held by any court or tribunal to be invalid, illegal, or otherwise unenforceable, each and every other provision shall remain in full force and effect.

3 5282 00529 7323

3 5282 00529 7331